THE MULRONEY REPORT CARD

Free Trade

Mulroney has launched one of the oldest and most politically dangerous policies of all—freer trade with the Americans. Historically, Conservative leaders have tended to oppose the initiative. In June 1983, Mulroney was asked about the issue. "This country could not survive with a policy of unfettered free trade," he said.

Social Policies

People could be forgiven for being confused about Mulroney's social policies. For weeks, headlines shouted the message that Mulroney had promised not to touch old-age pensions, and then his government's first budget had proposed partial de-indexing.

Taxation

In the 1984 campaign, he promised to trim deficits, spend billions on new programs and not cut the deficit by increasing personal taxes . . . Under Mulroney, the average Canadian family is now paying about 52 percent more in personal taxes. Corporations are paying 18 percent less.

Patronage

By September 1986, Mulroney had poured $195 million into his Manicouagan riding to build roads, ports, airports, and a prison . . . None of Mulroney's lavish projects has better symbolized his fall from grace than the plan to construct a maximum-security prison at Port Cartier.

Foreign Policy

Mulroney has fared better abroad than at home. Given his penchant for overstatement, he has tended to exaggerate his influence on world affairs, but on balance, his pursuit of a policy of "constructive internationalism" has been an area of relative strength.

CLAIRE HOY

FRIENDS IN HIGH PLACES

Politics and Patronage in the Mulroney Government

SEAL BOOKS
McClelland-Bantam, Inc.
Toronto

FRIENDS IN HIGH PLACES

*A Seal Book / published by arrangement with
Key Porter Books Limited*

PRINTING HISTORY

Key Porter edition published October 1987

Seal edition / August 1988

ISBN 0-7704-2275-6

*Seal Books are published by McClelland-Bantam, Inc. Its trademark, consisting of
the words "Seal Books" and the portrayal of a seal, is the property of McClelland-
Bantam, Inc., 60 St. Clair Avenue East, Suite 601, Toronto, Ontario M4T 1N5,
Canada. This trademark has been duly registered in the Trademarks Office of
Canada. The trademark consisting of the words "Bantam Books" and the portrayal of
a rooster is the property of and is used with the consent of Bantam Books, 666 Fifth
Avenue, New York, New York 10103. This trademark has been duly registered in the
Trademarks Office of Canada and elsewhere.*

PRINTED IN CANADA

COVER PRINTED IN U.S.A.

U   0 9 8 7 6 5 4 3 2 1

For Lydia . . .

*Without whom neither my book nor my
life would be complete.*

CONTENTS

FOREWORD TO THE PAPERBACK EDITION

Since this book was published in hardcover last fall, not much has changed for Brian Mulroney, but things have certainly changed for me. I've attempted to update the first edition, although really to keep up with this government you'd need a three-ring loose-leaf binder where pages could be constantly added.

Thanks to this book, I have experienced both the joy of being on the national best-seller lists—at the top of one for many weeks—and the trauma of becoming a free-lance journalist after almost twenty-five years as an employee for various newspapers. While the public seemed happy with my work, my former publisher, Paul Godfrey of the *Toronto Sun*, didn't. In January, after almost a year of hassles with Godfrey over my tough-minded views of Mulroney, I left the paper and became a free-lance columnist with Southam News.

Ironically, I have much to thank Mulroney for. Had he not been the type of person he is and provided such terrific material for a book, I wouldn't have a best-seller. That would have made it particularly difficult to refuse Godfrey's order to leave my Ottawa political column and return to Toronto. And, while I miss Toronto, thanks to Mulroney and Godfrey and the success of this book, my column now appears in newspapers from coast to coast.

Life is funny that way, eh?

CLAIRE HOY, FEBRUARY 22, 1988

FRIENDS IN HIGH
PLACES

On a blustery day during the first week of January, I was walking off the Hill for an off-the-record lunchtime interview with a longtime acquaintance who works in the PMO. Suddenly he said, "Don't look up," which I hadn't been anyway in my efforts to keep my face protected from the biting Ottawa winter wind. "There's a woman up there on the third floor [of the Langevin Block] who works for Don Mazankowski and she's watching us. Now I'll have to think of a reason why I was going to lunch with you."

At first, I thought he was kidding. But his serious look and the tone of his plea made it obvious he wasn't. "What is this," I asked, "Poland?" He glanced quickly up again at the woman who was still there, watching, and said, "In some ways, I sometimes think it is."

Such is the atmosphere one discovers in trying to write anything, let alone a book, that is perceived to be unfriendly to Brian Mulroney. The fate of the faithful who have dared speak critically of him is not a happy story, some of which is retold in this book. The man I interviewed on this occasion was so nervous he wouldn't even let himself be tape-recorded. "It's an eerie thing," he said. "There's a pall hanging over everything we say and do. It wasn't there at the beginning, but when things turned sour they began looking inward. It's like they're sitting around in a big room full of mirrors, reflecting back on each other."

My written request for PMO interviews for this project was sent early on to Bill Fox, then Mulroney's communications boss. He replied in writing two days later, repeating the list of about a dozen senior officials—including Brian and Mila—I wanted to interview. In a two-paragraph letter, Fox wrote simply that he had discussed it with his colleagues, and "we decline, with thanks." Much later, Tom Van Dusen, Mazankowski's press secretary, told me Fox had argued that somebody should present their case since the book would be written with or without them, "but he lost because The Boss was adamant. Now I suppose you'll put their refusal in the book and make them look like assholes."

Some of those people did talk, privately, and I thank them. Others didn't. But there you have it. Even veteran Tory senator Norman Atkins, who had talked openly when I wrote my book on Bill Davis, was too intimidated this time. On two occasions, face-to-face, Atkins promised an interview, but he then refused to even answer my more than thirty telephone messages and a letter. I found this behaviour both instructive and disappointing from a political heavyweight who had always seemed to be his own man.

As for the sixty-odd people who did take the time to give me interviews, I thank them. Their wisdom, anecdotes, and insights contributed substantially to this project. Those who spoke on the record, of course, will find their names recorded. As for those who wouldn't, or couldn't, they know who they are.

As for Mulroney himself, it was not surprising he refused an interview. It is ironic that a man who is such a mediaphile—how else to describe someone who has thirteen television sets in his home—still doesn't understand that the media, or at least most of it, is not on staff. He doesn't grant interviews to reporters he considers unfriendly. While he could have provided some useful insights, and maybe even explained much which seems inexplicable, his actions and words, already on the public record, offer a complete picture of the man and his administration, and interviews with his associates fill in many blanks.

In addition to thanking my wife, Lydia Huber, for her hours of helping me clip, file, and organize, I should also thank *Toronto Sun* president Doug Creighton for his generosity in allowing me extra free time to write the book, my editor Margaret Woollard, and everybody else at Key Porter for their encouragement and direction in shaping the manuscript into a finished book.

I should also thank the staff at both the *Toronto Sun* library and the Parliamentary Library in Ottawa, particularly those down the narrow, winding iron staircase in the clipping room who went out of their way to be helpful. Thanks also to *Maclean's* Ottawa bureau who gave me free access to their files and past issues.

My personal perceptions of Mulroney have been shaped by watching him up close during both his leadership runs and, of course, the bulk of his term as prime minister.

In his own scripted version of *Out of Africa* in February of this year, two events struck me as indicative of the man's character. I'm reminded of a shot former Nova Scotia Liberal premier and federal cabinet minister Gerry Regan once took at current Tory premier John Buchanan (before Buchanan won). Regan said of his opponent, "Down deep he's really shallow."

On a January 29 visit to the legendary Victoria Falls, one of the natural wonders of the world, Mulroney met with the leaders of three front-line states in Zimbabwe, then was driven across the bridge into Zambia for a meeting with President Kenneth Kaunda. At the time, he was approximately three hundred yards from the magnificent falls, but he did not go down to see them. His only concession to the falls, which make Niagara look like a large lawn sprinkler, was to stop the limousine on the bridge, get out, take a quick look, even though 90 per cent of the falls are blocked by a large, jungle-strewn hill, and rush off to catch his charter airplane back to Harare for yet another hotel meeting. It all prompted a local reporter to quip, "He's probably the only person in history who ever came to Victoria Falls and didn't see them."

Three days later, we spent several hours in army trucks bouncing around the edge of the Sahara Desert off Senegal's Barbary Coast in the Gandiolais region near the mouth of the Senegal River. Mulroney had gone there to see a Canadian aid project, where just $300,000 since 1979 had been spent building a buffer of trees between the roaring ocean and the shifting sand dunes. This remarkably simple but effective device meant that 25,000 Gandiole-Gandiole tribesmen clustered in the little villages that poke here and there out of the sand could now grow their own vegetables because the windscreen stopped the dunes from shifting and covering anything they planted.

With the sun relentlessly beating down on Mulroney and his

entourage, we visited six villages that day. At each stop, the locals would dance, sing, and play their spectacularly rhythmic drums. It is hard to describe the warm feeling we experienced after being tossed around in the back of open trucks, swallowing sand, wearing bandanas to fend off the sun, seeing nothing but sand and the odd desert animal for half an hour or more, to suddenly go over yet another large dune and there before us see a large spread of green vegetation. When you consider that much of our aid money goes to buy a new Mercedes for a local dictator or guns for his private army, it is encouraging to see money actually being spent to allow people to help themselves by growing their own food, centuries away from the nearest supermarket.

Yet, despite the unqualified success of this project, and the obvious pride of the natives in their vegetables, Mulroney did not utter anything personal to them throughout the day to indicate he was moved by it all. At one point, he walked briefly into the woods along the tree line and said, "This reminds me of Edmundston, New Brunswick." His hosts gave each other quizzical looks. At another point, he shouted to CBC's Mike Duffy, who was struggling to get down from the army truck, "You'll get an Order of Canada for this, Duffy."

In one settlement, Leona, a group of tribesmen proudly walked past Mulroney's security and handed him two woven straw baskets stuffed with their homegrown vegetables. "Mila, look," he said in French. "Yes," she replied. "Oh, potatoes," he said, rummaging through the baskets, pulling vegetables out one by one. "Carrots, bigger than ours. Onions, cabbage. It's formidable. A grand success. Bravo!" Several times he was heard asking his aides how many more villages he had to visit. He was clearly uncomfortable and wanted to leave, change his shirt, go back to a hotel, a meeting, where they would have an agenda and he wouldn't have to tip his hand about how he really felt.

He's an odd man, our prime minister. He certainly accomplished far more in business and politics than most people even dream of. And while one must admire these accomplishments, there is a quality about the man which most Canadians find disconcerting, an uneasiness one gets when dealing with the slick-talking proprietor of a cut-rate used-car lot.

This book attempts to chronicle this man, his single-minded drive for power, his failures and successes since becoming prime minister, his Diefenbakeresque dive in popularity. I hope it will both inform and entertain you, and perhaps upset you as well, as it probes not just his business and political accomplishments, but his human strengths and weaknesses.

prime minister, his Dictaphone-esque dirc to our future. I
hope it will both allow and stimulate you, and perhaps enable
you, as well, as it probes not just his jnequities and political
accomplishments, but his personal strengths and weaknesses

CHAPTER ONE

THE IMPOSSIBLE
DREAM

The impossible dream was crumbling. The voters who had
rushed to the polls with a vengeance to boot out the hated
Liberals were waking up to find the Tory regime choking on its
own refuse or—an alternative image—sinking under a volcanic
crush of scandal. And Brian Mulroney, the catalyst of the rise
to power, couldn't bear to watch.

It was February 6, 1987, just twenty-nine months after
Mulroney had led the Conservative party to the largest
mandate in Canadian history, destroying John Turner's Liberals, 211 to 40 (with Ed Broadbent and the NDP winning 30).
Now, incredibly, Mulroney was on the ropes.

Daily question period had just ended in chaos for the Tories.
Mulroney had stayed away, holing up at 24 Sussex Drive,
ostensibly to work on a speech to be delivered that night to his
Quebec caucus—a speech that would also fall flat. The bright
new world he'd promised had turned dark; the tentacles of
mistrust, incompetence, stupidity, arrogance, and yes, sleaze
and corruption that had slithered through the party into his
cabinet room and around the necks of some of his most senior
and trusted soldiers were now menacing the trademark chin of
the man who had sold Canadians on his "sacred trust" of a civil,
humane, and honest government.

The marble-lined foyer outside the Commons was a mad-
house, reporters and opposition members abuzz with so many
scandals, near-scandals, and Tory set-backs it was difficult to
know where to begin the chronicle of doom.

High above the swirling, frenzied horde, one of Mulroney's

most faithful lap-dogs, communications commando Bill Fox, peered mournfully over the railing, his droopy eyes witnessing the enemy closing in for the kill. Still loyal, Fox was unable to do anything but watch. And worry.

It had been some day. Oh God, what a day. Not the first such day in recent times, either. The sort of day opposition parties drool for, and governments dread. To the Tories who did have the courage to face it, it must have seemed that the whole world was crumbling around them. Their hopes and aspirations and the ecstatic memory of September 4, 1984, were sliding irretrievably into the muck, as if it had all been a cruel practical joke orchestrated by political gods determined to prove that the Grits, not the Tories, are Canada's natural governing party after all.

How could this have come to pass? How could both perception and reality have reached the stage where Deputy Prime Minister Don Mazankowski, a bright, honest, decent man, was left alone by Mulroney to make a damn fool of himself for all Canadians to see? Among other things in the headlines that day was a story by Southam journalist Les Whittington that Mulroney had personally intervened in a civil suit involving several close friends on both sides of the dispute. Mazankowski, his defences undermined by Mulroney's absence, his will to fight worn down by months of Tory self-destruction, told the Commons that if Mulroney had intervened—which, alas, he really had—"it was a private matter."

A private matter? When the prime minister of the country tries to influence a civil suit? When the man bringing the suit testifies in court documents that he interpreted that intervention as a threat to future government business? The Tories had reached a sorry state indeed when a man of Mazankowski's stature and integrity was reduced to virtual incoherence in defence of a field commander who was at best foolhardy and who had chosen to hide in the safety of his study, a mile away from the slaughter of some of his most trusted lieutenants.

That particular story involved Mulroney's senior advisor and trusted friend, Fred Doucet. Millionaire jet-setter Walter Wolf, who a few years earlier had helped finance Mulroney's underground guerrila war against the then leader, Joe Clark, was suing Doucet for $300,000. Mulroney had discussed the case during an overseas phone call with Michel Cogger, another old pal, whom he'd named to the Senate the previous year. Cogger had often acted as Wolf's lawyer. Mulroney had been accused of suggesting that if Wolf didn't drop his suit he could expect no more business from the Tories.

And so, on that dreary day, a political storm much worse than the freezing cold and blowing snow outside was hammering at the Tory fortress, undermining what was left of its hard-won victory over the once-mighty Liberal forces.

That day it seemed as if the contrast had never been starker between the noble themes of Mulroney's New Canada and the reality that stood revealed—a ghastly partisan pudding of distrust and animosity. Events had pushed to the breaking point the faith of those who had welcomed his vision of a Canada of "small towns and big dreams," of national reconciliation, constructive internationalism, social justice, economic renewal, and, most appealing of all, an end to the patronage-riddled Liberalism of Pierre Trudeau and a born-again burst of public morality.

Earlier that week Mulroney had returned with mixed reviews from a tour of Africa, where the most memorable part of his performance had been his mechanical evocation of John Diefenbaker's heroic role in booting South Africa out of the Commonwealth more than twenty-five years earlier. Watching Mulroney, one got the feeling, as always, that beneath the plastic exterior of the studied politician there was an impenetrable layer of more plastic; that whatever his real feelings about the issue—and there's no doubt apartheid offends him—he none the less was going through the motions, like an actor playing to an audience, hoping to lance a long-festering boil on the world stage not so much to cleanse the sore, but because he wanted history to recall that Brian Mulroney had done so.

It was also the end of a week in which his early promise to heal the long-standing, Liberal-inflicted wounds of federal-provincial hostilities had exploded in his face. Newfoundland premier Brian Peckford had shed his bad-boy image two years earlier to lead the cheering for the New Canada, in which, he claimed, Ottawa and the provinces would be true partners. Once again, the Tories had achieved the impossible—they had so angered Peckford that he'd spearheaded an extraordinary emergency premiers' meeting in Toronto, a show of defiance and anger unmatched in recent history.

What had Mulroney done? He had allowed his officials to bargain away Newfoundland's most precious commodity, its northern cod, by striking a secret deal with the French.

Newfoundland officials had been included in the negotiations right up until two days before External Affairs sneaked privately off to Paris to offer the French the golden cod. Mulroney's motives in this and in his African safari were similar: he had arranged for Canada to host both the Commonwealth conference and the Francophone summit in 1987. Both meetings would give him the chance to appear on the international stage in the role of a great leader. To pave the way, he had told the African front-line states what they wanted to hear and had used the precious Newfoundland cod as bait for the French.

There was more. There was news of an RCMP criminal investigation into influence peddling in Quebec; Tory advance man Pierre Blouin (recently dead from a heart attack) had been convicted of using his influence with the party to help a friend win a $1 million rental contract for federal offices. That story in hand, NDP critics in the Commons pointed the finger directly at another Mulroney heavyweight, accusing Bernard Roy, the PM's chief of staff, of being involved in the RCMP investigation. Mulroney denied it.

Another story held that cronies had massed their energies and partisan clout to win a lucrative contract to build and operate a third terminal at Lester B. Pearson International Airport in Toronto. On any other day, news that such high-profile Tory operatives as William Neville, Frank Moores, Sam Wakim, Paul Curley, Donald Matthews, and Robert Foster had joined together to seek a federal contract would normally have dominated question period. But in the February 6 deluge of spectacular scandals, it barely rated a mention.

The continuing odour from the Oerlikon affair, a questionable land flip near St. Jean, Quebec, that had already cost junior transport minister André Bissonnette his job, added to the stench of a rotting government. Mulroney's friend Jean Bazin was a senior partner in the Montreal law firm that handled Oerlikon's affairs. Despite this cloud, Bazin had been sworn into the Senate earlier that week and was about to become president of the Canadian Bar Association. The Oerlikon matter had also touched both long-time Mulroney friend Roger Nantel, who had acted as the company's communications adviser, and the obsequious Sam Wakim, who reportedly had tried to set up a meeting between Oerlikon and former industry minister Sinclair Stevens. Stevens, of course, had reluctantly resigned in the wake of conflict-of-interest allegations. That embarrassing public drama was still unfolding in a judicial review in Toronto.

To make matters still worse, U.S. senator Lloyd Bentsen, a key player in the ongoing Canada-U.S. freer-trade talks, had introduced sweeping legislation, endorsed by fifty-four of the one hundred senators, urging President Ronald Reagan to get tough with unfair foreign traders. Earlier, Mulroney had captured his only positive headlines of the week when he lashed out at U.S. trade ambassador Clayton Yeutter for showing a "stunning ignorance of Canada." Yeutter had said, not for the first time, that Canada's cultural industries, such as book publishing and broadcasting, should be part of the trade talks. While Mulroney won applause at home for dismissing the suggestion as "completely insensitive and totally unacceptable" to Canada, the story added to the growing spectre of unease over Canada-U.S. talks. Yeutter's comments came just two weeks after U.S. vice-president George Bush had flown to Ottawa on short notice from Mulroney, supposedly to be given a piece of the prime minister's mind and made to understand that Canadian culture is not part of the talks. It didn't help that, the day after Mulroney's tough rhetoric, the White House issued a carefully worded statement softening Yeutter's words but offering no retreat from his position.

The economic news, usually one of the few bright spots for the Tories, had also taken a turn for the worse. Statistics Canada's latest figures showed that the unemployment ranks had swelled by 41,000 to 1.34 million jobless in December 1986.

For some time, Mulroney had been under intense internal pressure to get rid of a number of error-prone ministers, especially veteran Roch LaSalle, the undisputed elder statesman of Quebec Tories. Mulroney was to have visited LaSalle's home town of Joliette that night, but three days earlier the tour was cancelled in the face of recent revelations that two senior staffers hired by LaSalle had criminal records that had not been reported to security. Neither recruit had filled in the mandatory security-check forms. Also under scrutiny were some of LaSalle's own finances, including a series of personal debts to local residents; Mulroney had himself helped organize a $200-a-plate fund-raiser that netted $20,000 to help clear LaSalle's accumulated debts.

Two weeks later, LaSalle was gone, the seventh cabinet minister—and the fourth from Quebec—to have resigned or been fired under questionable circumstances. The end came for the minister after revelations that businessmen had paid $5,000 to attend a 1985 party at which LaSalle, then in charge of public works, was the star attraction. Though LaSalle pleaded innocence, the businessmen said they believed they had paid the money in return for future government contracts.

At home Mulroney's ten-year-old son, Benedict, hurt in a school-yard accident two weeks earlier, still lay in bed with a cracked bone in his back that required a brace. There was little comfort anywhere for Mulroney, as he buried himself in what was to have been a pep-rally speech to the fifty-seven-member Quebec Tory caucus due to meet in the Montreal suburb of Laval.

The situation among the faithful had deteriorated to the point where the Tories had actually hired Jean-Marc Chaput, a corporate morale booster, to attend the Quebec caucus and give the dispirited troops an injection of good, old-fashioned pep.

As Mulroney said to his Quebec Tories, "I won't hide that it hurts. We have made errors and we will make other ones. Unfortunately we're all human beings.

"Today my government, my party, and myself are feeling the results. Some actions have had a negative impact on our political action, and if it isn't fixed our credibility runs the risk of being seriously undermined."

Tory credibility was already at an all-time low. Both Mulroney and his party were running third in the public-opinion polls, the first time that had happened, ironically, since Diefenbaker had been in the process of marching his handsome majority into political oblivion. A Gallup poll a week later put the Tories at 22 per cent among decided voters, with the Liberals at 44 and the NDP at 32. It was the worst showing by a governing party since Gallup began political polling in 1942.

Pointing to the overwheming evidence of a government out of control, the opposition parties charged that Mulroney had lost the moral right to govern. In Toronto Liberal John Nunziata's words, the RCMP was "so busy investigating Conservatives that they have no time to investigate murderers, rapists, and bank robbers." He suggested a special RCMP unit specializing in investigating and prosecuting Conservatives be formed. NDP leader Ed Broadbent, for his part, asked,

"When is integrity going to become the rule of public business for this government instead of the exception?"

As the drama unfolded that day, a senior cabinet minister leaned for a moment against one of the giant pillars that rise majestically from the foyer to the railing above. An aide, thinking something was wrong, turned back and asked the minister if he was all right. "Oh yes," he said. "I'm fine. It's the government that's sick, and I only wish to hell we knew how to cure it."

A suggested antidote came from backbench Tory MP Louis Plamondon of Richelieu, one of the multitude of Quebeckers swept into office on the 1984 tide of Tory Bleu, and hence among those most vulnerable for a quick exit, stage left, once the tide had settled back to its more traditional level. Plamondon put into words what most Tories were just thinking privately when he told an Ottawa *Citizen* reporter, "Our biggest problem is the credibility of the people at the top."

As if to sear that point into the minds of all Canadians, an Angus Reid Associates survey of 1,005 adults across Canada, conducted Thursday through Sunday of that black week, showed that most Canadians agreed with Plamondon's candid assessment.

The survey gave John Turner and his Liberals a commanding 42 per cent. Ed Broadbent's NDP had reached 33 per cent, ten points ahead of Mulroney's wounded Tories. Even the undecided, at 23 per cent, outnumbered supporters of the governing Conservatives. Six in ten disapproved of Mulroney's performance as prime minister, and 58 per cent of how he was promoting fairness and honesty in government; six in ten wanted a full public inquiry into the Bissonnette-Oerlikon affair, and 54 per cent disapproved of the Canada-France fishing agreement. (In Atlantic Canada, where it really counted, 78 per cent said "non.") The Tories were dead last in every region of the country except Ontario, where, despite a booming economy, they sneaked in just three points ahead of the NDP. After twenty-nine months of Mulroney government, only 41 per cent of those who voted for Mulroney in 1984 said they would do so again.

And what did Mulroney say to all this? Well, first he blamed the media, and then he said that the Liberals under Trudeau had been at 23 per cent in 1983 and had recovered to pass the Tories shortly before the 1984 election.

What Mulroney didn't say, however, was that the Liberal

recovery wasn't won by wishing, it was achieved when the party picked a new leader, John Turner.

For the next two weeks, Mulroney and his Tories lurched from one disaster to another. Things were so bad that at least three secret Tory ginger groups involving about seventy-five backbench MPs were holding clandestine, late-night meetings in their Parliament Hill offices or their apartments to plot strategy to "get the Tories back on track." Only one of these groups, spearheaded by right-wing Ontario Tory Jack Ellis, became public, but there was little doubt that if things didn't improve—and soon—Tory unrest would erupt into an all-out, bloody partisan war with the right wing of the party on one side and Mulroney and the predominantly pink Tory faction on the other.

The bad news just kept coming. Gamelin MP Michel Gravel was facing fifty charges of influence-peddling, bribery, fraud, and abuse of the public trust involving alleged kickbacks worth at least $232,000.

On February 18, two days before the regular break in the Commons, finance minister Michael Wilson attempted to salvage something from the carnage by introducing his stand-pat 1987 budget. There were few strong criticisms of Wilson's continuing focus on lowering the deficit—he promised again to get it below $30 billion, having tried and failed to do so in 1986—but praise for the budget was at best lukewarm. Still, given the disastrous state of affairs in every other area of government responsibility, Wilson's boast of falling inflation, low mortgage rates, job growth, and generally good economic performance finally gave the Tories something to applaud about in the Commons.

The brief respite was quickly ended by LaSalle's resignation and by a CBC story that Senator Norman Atkins, a senior Tory election strategist, had advised Mulroney to dump six of his top aides and advisers. The proposal, which was supposed to be secret, once again underscored the seriousness of Mulroney's unprecedented decline.

And so, as Mulroney packed his family off for a ten-day holiday in Palm Beach, Florida, he was faced with the task of determining the future of his own staff, many of them loyalists who had known him since university and who had once before fought off the take-charge intentions of Atkins and his Ontario Big Blue Machine operatives. Two former premiers, Bill Davis of Ontario and Peter Lougheed of Alberta, had met privately with Mulroney in recent weeks, and both had suggested a thorough house-cleaning. But what was Mulroney to do? After all, he had continually boasted of his loyalty, his male bonding, his belief that "you dance with them what brought ya." Now he was faced with firings or resignations of principal secretary Bernard Roy, deputy principal secretary Ian Anderson, senior adviser Fred Doucet, policy adviser Charles McMillan, communications director Bill Fox, and press secretary Michel Gratton.

Then there was the unwelcome chore of setting by-election dates in three vacant ridings—Hamilton Mountain, Yukon, and St. John's East—where the prospect of dismal electoral results would exacerbate the defeatist mood in the party. As it turned out, Mulroney's hesitation was justified, as the surging NDP won all three seats in the July 20 by-elections.

If there was a bright spot for Mulroney, it hadn't been discovered. The effectiveness of the diversionary tactic of introducing the long-awaited capital-punishment debate had been weakened by publication of an internal document showing that Mulroney and his aides wanted the whole issue kept as far away from them as possible. Tory strategy, the document indicated, was to avoid having the issue come before the appropriate parliamentary committee because the Tories on that committee were predominatly pro-hanging.

With its cup of woe running over, the party scarcely needed the newspaper coverage related to a dismal moment from its past, as lawyers in the Sinclair Stevens conflict-of-interest inquiry made their final arguments to Ontario Supreme Court Justice William Parker.

Five days before he left for Florida, Mulroney told about one hundred party faithful in Sept-Iles, the largest city of his sprawling home riding of Manicouagan, that his Conservatives would overcome their problems and win the next election, just as the National Hockey League all-stars, scoring late in the third period, had beaten the mighty Soviet Red Army hockey team 4 to 3 in the opener of a two-game series in Quebec City.

"You saw that the NHL team managed at the very last moment to get that one goal for victory," Mulroney said. "And that's what we're going to do in the next election. We will be diverted from our goal from time to time by events, but the ultimate result will be the decision of the voters at the appropriate time."

Mulroney did not point out that the Soviets had won the second game 5 to 3.

Mulroney's two-day tour, just a week after a similiar jaunt to Quebec City and Chicoutimi, was heralded by his office as part of a new plan to visit Quebec more often between now and the next election. Tory popularity, while poor everywhere, had plunged to 16 per cent of decided voters in his home province of Quebec, while the Liberals were enjoying a 50 per cent standing in the province. Though people at a local shopping mall greeted him enthusiastically, city officials complained after an hour-long private meeting that Mulroney as an MP had become a "handicap" for them. After the meeting at the local airport (before Mulroney headed off to Sydney, Nova Scotia, to open the Canada Winter Games), Sept-Iles city councillor Raymond Neveau told reporters about the complaints, saying that Mulroney's efforts to help other towns in the riding had led to so many attacks that Mulroney is now afraid to help Sept-Iles. "We were told for months and months that it's an advantage to have a prime minister in the riding," he said. "But the people realize today that it's become a handicap because all eyes are turned to the prime minister's riding and the media and opposition look to give him a hard time when he takes a decision in a particular dossier."

As a parting shot at Mulroney, a Commons committee was about to recommend sweeping expansion of the federal access-to-information law. The act, which has given the public and the media access to previously unavailable information, has been fingered by Mulroney and others as partly responsible for the spate of embarrassing disclosures of excessive government spending and questionable decisions. Perhaps the Tories on the Justice and Solicitor General's Committee were oblivious to the problem, or perhaps they just didn't care. Chairman Blaine Thacker, a Tory, said of the move to strengthen the law, "We've made an attack on the senior bureaucrats. They'll object because it's the information they keep from us that gives them their power."

Which prompted one senior cabinet minister to say, "Who needs enemies when our own guys are out there devouring our young?"

CHAPTER TWO

THE BOY FROM
BAIE-COMEAU

Brian Mulroney was out in Western Canada in early July 1984, waiting, like everybody else, for John Turner to announce that the Queen's visit to Canada for later that month had been cancelled because of an election. During a six-day swing through Alberta and Saskatchewan, Mulroney left no doubt what his message to Canadians would be—that re-electing the Liberals would return the same old gang led by a "ballroom dancer," a reference to Turner's famous first meeting with royalty in 1958.

On a Saturday night at the fairgrounds in Vermilion, Alberta, Mulroney exploited his "humble" origins in his finest Horatio Alger fantasy, when he told 1,500 people, coated and sweatered against the chill that "I started off as a truck driver on the north shore of the St. Lawrence River. When I was driving a truck, John Turner was dancing with Princess Margaret.

"I tell you this—there are more truck drivers in Canada than ballroom dancers," he said, much to the delight of this particular crowd—and of dozens of others like it during the election campaign that began shortly after.

It has always been Mulroney's story that he had to overcome tremendous odds to make it. Like many things Mulroney says, there is some truth to it. Like almost everything he says, it is greatly exaggerated. He was never "a truck driver," in the real sense of the word. He drove part-time in the summer, but never for a living.

Brian Mulroney was born in the north-shore town of Baie-

Comeau, on March 20, 1939, the first of the family born there. He had two older sisters, Olive and Peggy, and was followed by Doreen, Gary, and Barbara. His Irish ancestors had immigrated to Canada in 1841 to escape the great potato famine, settling at Ste. Catherine de Portneuf, just outside Quebec City. In the 1930s, Colonel Robert Rutherford McCormick, who owned the *Chicago Tribune,* bought the *New York Daily News* and needed more newsprint. The Quebec North Shore Paper Company decided to open a paper mill in Baie-Comeau to supply McCormick's newspapers, and in 1936 Mulroney's father, Ben, an electrician by trade, left his wife, Mary Irene O'Shea, and their two daughters and journeyed the 220 miles up the St. Lawrence to the job site that would become the town of Baie-Comeau. He had planned to stay for six months. Instead, he stayed until he died in 1965. "There wasn't a goddamn thing there," Mulroney would say later. "There was no road, everything went by boat, and they lived in a tent."

The following spring, Ben Mulroney used one of those boats to bring his family to live in a tidy company house on Champlain Street, not far from the mill manager's comfortable house on a hill overlooking the town. In a 1980 interview, Mulroney said, "It was very much a company town. The company owned the houses, the company paid the workers, and the company provided the amenities. But there was no resentment."

His father worked hard and tried to teach his kids the value of working hard. He would put in a regular shift at the mill, where he became foreman, then go out at night to work as a part-time contractor installing electricity in new homes. It hardly made them rich, but when your father is the foreman in a company town and has his own business on the side, it isn't bad. Certainly not as rich in "poor-boy pathos" as the way Mulroney sometimes likes to tell it.

He was raised bilingual, going to the Catholic school l'Académie Ste. Emelie, joining one of two English classrooms among the thirty or forty French classrooms. But he walked to and from school with his French friends, took some classes with them, and grew up with the ability to switch comfortably back and forth between the languages—an ability that has been a valuable political asset.

Winters were difficult in Baie-Comeau. And long. "My God almighty, those winters were unending," he would say. "They started in October, and by the time June came along it seemed like the ice was just starting to break up." The first piece of art he ever bought was a Stanley Cosgrove painting of the Rivière St.-Maurice, because "it looked exactly like Baie-Comeau at four in the afternoon in the middle of February. Bleak, dreary, cold, the wind coming off the bay, the snowbanks as high as your house."

Mulroney said he was "one tough little kid. Big mouth too." He says he was ambitious, starting work at the Hudson's Bay store washing vegetables when he was ten, working summers at the mill and Christmas at the post office.

When Mulroney was a little boy, he and his friend Jimmy Green got a terrific belting when they tried to set fire to a neighbour's house by piling some wood against a wall of the house and lighting it. He used to hang around, too, with Jacques "Pom-Pom" Provencher. In the winter they would wear "les pichous," the Indian trappers' winter boots, in which they would slide the mile and a half to school behind the bus, grabbing on to the bumper when it came to their stop. They hit a dry patch of pavement one day and, in the ensuing tumble, Mulroney broke his now-famous jaw. As a kid, Mulroney was shorter than average, but at seventeen he suddenly shot up to his current height of six foot one inch, his thin, gangling appearance earning him the nickname "Bones." Even as a kid, Mulroney began his habit of cultivating tight, lasting friendships. People like Gilles Lachance and Blair Touchie, boyhood pals who chartered two small aircraft and flew to Nova Scotia on August 29, 1983, to help Brian celebrate his by-election victory. And Gérard Guy, a recreation director and one of Mulroney's earliest boyhood friends, who called and congratulated the new Tory leader an hour after his 1983 victory. A year later, Mulroney appointed him to the National Advisory Council on Fitness and Amateur Sport.

Mulroney played sports as a kid, mainly hockey, baseball, swimming, and tennis, but he didn't excel. He did have a definite flair, however, for singing and public speaking, and he often speaks of family and community sing-alongs, of learning the Irish songs and French-Canadian ballads. There was always a piano in his parents' house, and usually Brian or somebody else was playing it. There was no TV and no newspaper; he says he can't remember listening to the radio until he was twelve, and he didn't see a television set until he went to Trois-Rivières at age sixteen or seventeen.

When he was ten, he won the Rotary Club speaking contest with a speech on comic books. His sister Olive, three years older, won the girls' competition with, "Welcome, Newfoundland," a speech on the island's entry that year into Confederation.

Stories abound—some told by Mulroney himself—that as a boy in Baie-Comeau he liked to tell the townsfolk he would be prime minister some day. The story appears in his 1976 leadership-campaign literature and in L. Ian MacDonald's biography. Perhaps he did. But when asked about those stories for a June 20, 1983, cover story in *Maclean's* magazine, Mulroney said, "I have no recollection of any degree of political activity. All of my family were Liberal. That's all I remember." He added that tales of bitterly cold nights at the family's two-storey house were also exaggerated. "There was always enough to eat and a proper place to live, a good education and summer jobs. If we were poor, no one realized it."

Mulroney would say of his father that he was obsessed with educating his children. "There's only one way out of a paper mill town," he would tell Brian, "and that's through a university door." All six Mulroney children went to university, two of them financed by Brian after his father's death. But since there wasn't even a high school to complete in Baie-Comeau, let alone a university, he and his friend Andy Morrow reached Grade 10, then went off to St. Thomas High School in Chatham, New Brunswick, a school run by a group of diocesan priests and lay teachers on the campus of St. Thomas College. The two boys were fourteen when they bade their parents a tearful farewell at the wharf, setting out by boat and train on the six-hundred-mile journey. "I can still see myself arriving there with my cardboard suitcase," Mulroney said. "I felt like Marco Polo."

Years later, when three Montreal writers published *The Boy From Baie-Comeau*, one of the pictures in the book clearly shows Mulroney as he left for school carrying a plaid, cloth suitcase of a type popular at the time. When asked why Mulroney kept claiming to have carried a cardboard suitcase— by the election campaign it had become "an empty cardboard suitcase"—his senior adviser and long-time friend Fred Doucet told a reporter that it was a cardboard suitcase, but that Brian had pasted some plaid paper onto it to achieve the look of cloth.

Mulroney said it only hit him when he arrived in Chatham that he wouldn't be home for a long time. "I can still see Andy and me in this pay phone booth, crying like hell, calling our parents collect. My father said, 'You just have to stay there.'"

From Chatham, Mulroney went to St. Francis Xavier University in Antigonish, where his network of friends who would later become key aides and advisers really expanded. It was there that he met Sam Wakim, a one-time Tory MP, trusted friend and close adviser; Pat MacAdam, still a senior aide in Mulroney's office and a key player in Mulroney's efforts to undermine Joe Clark's leadership; Fred Doucet, another senior aide; Doucet's brother, Gerald, who just missed beating John Buchanan at Nova Scotia's 1971 Conservative leadership convention; Paul Creaghan, former New Brunswick justice minister; Lowell Murray, a senator and Mulroney's minister of federal-provincial relations; and many others who have played important roles in Mulroney's political and personal career through the years.

He quickly became involved in varsity debating, drama, and Conservative politics, introduced to the latter when Lowell Murray took him along to a meeting of the campus Tories. The first person Mulroney remembered seeing was Robert Higgins, a senior assigned to freshman orientation, who later became Liberal leader of New Brunswick before going to the bench. Higgins was wearing a Harris tweed jacket at the time. "I went home that Christmas," Mulroney said in a 1981 interview, "and worked at the Post Office until I earned enough money to buy a Harris tweed jacket." It would signal the beginning of a life-long love affair with fine clothing (that even led to a dog called Gucci), a penchant he would later share with his wife, Mila.

In the 1983 *Maclean's* piece, Murray, now government leader in the Senate, was quoted as saying that Mulroney was "a lot more obviously ambitious personally than the rest of us were. A number of his contemporaries—they weren't his peers, and that was the problem—they held it against him and he felt badly about that for many years." Mulroney himself said, "I was ambitious, and not always in the most pleasant way. I was a bit of a loud-mouth."

St. F.X. at the time was a hotbed of the co-operative and credit-union movement in English Canada, inspired by Father Moses Coady, director of its extension department. The emphasis was on public service and social activism. Mulroney played in *The Caine Mutiny* and *Everyman* and in interclass hockey and football and was undefeated in intercollegiate debates. He became president of the Maritime Progressive Conservative Students' Federation and also served as prime minister of the Maritime University Students' Parliament. He helped canvass for Nova Scotia Tory leader Robert Stanfield and, in 1956, made the thirty-eight-hour train trip to Ottawa as a delegate to the Conservative leadership convention, where he served as national vice-president of the Youth for Diefenbaker movement.

In the winter of 1958, a group of his St. F.X. friends, tired of Mulroney's constant bravado about how well he knew Diefenbaker, challenged him to telephone the Chief. While they all crowded around a pay phone, laughing as Diefenbaker officials tried to brush him off, he suddenly yelled into the phone, "Listen, do you know who this is speaking? This is Brian Mulroney speaking." Moments later, Mulroney said, "Hullo, Chief. How are you t'day, Chief?"

One thing that is genuine about Mulroney is that deep baritone voice of his. Ray McNeil, a long-time public servant for the Ontario government, remembers his first visit to the campus post office. "I was in there to get my key and find my box and another fellow was in there doing the same thing. He was a tall, thin guy with a very short haircut, and we passed back and forth several times, so I stuck out my hand and said, 'Hi, I'm Ray McNeil,' and then this incredible voice comes back, 'Well how are you? I'm Brian Mulroney.' He's seventeen, too, like me, and he scared the shit out of me with that voice. There are still people who say nobody talks like that, but that's the way he sounded as a teenager. It probably got him a lot of attention. I remember going back to my room and telling my roommate I'd just met a guy with a voice like a lumberjack."

As a reporter for the school newspaper, McNeil covered the 1958 Maritime model parliament where Mulroney, as head of the Tories, was prime minister. (The standings reflected the Commons in Ottawa where Diefenbaker was prime minister.) Richard Cashin, former Liberal MP and now Newfoundland fishermen's union chief, was Liberal leader, and Leo Nimsick, who later served in Dave Barrett's NDP cabinet in British Columbia, was CCF leader. Each had an MP seated with him as an adviser. Mulroney had Gordon Churchill, Cashin had Paul Martin, and Nimsick had Douglas Fisher.

"They put on a show there for three days, a hell of a good show," said McNeil. "It was great exposure for those of us who had never seen a parliament in action. I came out of Glace Bay and had no occasion as a teenager ever to see anything like it. It was great theatre. The people who showed promise then delivered on it since. To me, it was no great surprise when Brian Mulroney became prime minister. He'd always had that political bent."

Douglas Fisher, now a strongly pro-Mulroney newspaper columnist, wrote about that model parliament in 1983, saying, "Mulroney and Cashin were boy politicians you had to notice and admire. Beyond the obvious gift of the gab and mask of maturity, one had to remark the sheer charm of the pink-cheeked Mulroney."

Another Mulroney classmate from St. F.X. was Father Jim Conrad. Now a priest in Bracebridge, Ontario, Conrad taught high school and then operated a pub in Toronto before going into the priesthood. There were only about 1,800 students at the university in those days, he recalls, "so we all knew each other." Conrad remembers Mulroney as "a very quick study. In a minimum amount of time he could digest things very quickly." He also noted that, "Even then, Sam Wakim was tremendously loyal to him. I'm always surprised those loyalties have lasted through the years."

Conrad was a Liberal then. "At the time any self-respecting Catholic was, especially in Nova Scotia," although that changed after Stanfield took power in 1956. "Brian was active in that. He knew at eighteen he was going to be prime minister, and he said so. I remember once we were waiting for Lester Pearson to arrive to address us. He had just won the Nobel Peace prize and Diefenbaker came across the campus with his wife looking for the president's office. I'll tell you how much of a Tory I wasn't, I wouldn't tell them where it was. But then Brian came running out of somewhere and he escorted them over to the office."

Conrad expressed the view that Mulroney "has no sense of mission. Where he appears to be dishonest in some of these things, I don't think he's dishonest at all. He's full of a lot of energy, but he doesn't have any sense of direction; and after a while you think he's prepared to go in this direction and then you realize he hasn't got a direction and you feel let down and disappointed. Later on it comes out as dishonesty, but I don't think that's his fundamental motive. I think he wants to govern well and do well, but I think more than anything else he wants to be loved."

According to Conrad, Mulroney "would never have been able to come across as a phony at St. F.X. But as a quick study he was an opportunist, he grabbed things as he went along, he met the right people . . . listen, I voted for him too. I think the Canadian people wanted this man to succeed and he didn't deliver, or hasn't yet, and people feel a tremendous disappointment."

On the broader question of Mulroney's current lack of trust, Conrad said, "I can't answer that. Maybe it's power. He wasn't like that at St. F.X. I get the impression that the politicians who govern this province were good men. Regardless of politics, I get a sense of their goodness. With Brian, that oddly enough doesn't come up. Astute and everything else yes . . . Brian was essentially always a politican who was in business, not the other way around. He's not a businessman who became a politician. Anybody else . . . but some of them who have been attached to him have hurt him. I wish him well, but I'm not optimistic."

After graduating from St. F.X. with his B.A. as a political science major, Mulroney spent a rocky year at Dalhousie University law school in Halifax, a year he's practically managed to eradicate from the public record. In the books written about his career and the long feature articles, the entire year is usually dealt with in a single sentence. Mulroney went to Dalhousie, got homesick for Quebec, and enrolled in Laval the next year. End of story. In a June 1983 interview he said, "I had been in the Maritimes six or seven years and was sort of thinking, 'This is a great place, I might settle down here,' when I suddenly thought, 'Hell, all my roots are in Quebec. I'd better high-tail it back home.'" In the MacDonald biography, Mulroney said he went to Dal on an entrance scholarship, "and then I was ill for part of the year. By Christmas, it was pretty clear I wanted to transfer. I enjoyed it, but I wanted to get back to Quebec."

In fact, he flunked his year at Dalhousie, probably because he was indeed ill for part of the year. Interviews with several Dalhousie classmates from that year (1959) cast a different light on the story that he was drawn back to his roots by homesickness. Several other St. F.X. grads were there at the same time, people like Cashin and Gerald Doucet, many of them living together in off-campus houses. "There was a great clannishness among them," said one Dalhousie alumnus. "Just as there is today among the St. F.X. crowds."

"We were all scared shitless as law students," the same alumnus revealed. "The way they used to put it in those days at Dal is they scared you to death the first year, worked you to death the second year, and bored you to death the third year." At that time, access to law school was pretty well open to anybody who had a degree. There were no admission tests, no line-ups of applicants for each spot, but they would weed people out when the dean opened the year by saying, "Boys, look to your left and look to your right, because one of the three of you isn't going to be here next year."

The consensus is that Mulroney didn't say much in class. He hung around the back of the room trying to avoid eye contact with the professors. Nor was he a diligent student in the sense of spending all his evenings in the library reading cases.

He did continue to be active in Conservative circles, however, and regularly talked to Diefenbaker by phone. Towards the middle of the year, Mulroney and Brian Flemming, now a Halifax lawyer and prominent Liberal (who at one time ran Pierre Trudeau's office) represented Dal at the Canadian debating trials in Montreal. The two students never lost a debate in the Maritimes. Mulroney beat Flemming in a play-off for the Angus L. Macdonald gold medal for debating, his only academic success while at Dalhousie.

During that year Mulroney fell ill, had to spend time in hospital and was forced to miss his classes. Although he appealed to the university president, Dr. Alexander Kerr, to intervene for him with the dean of philosophy for permission to write special exams, even then he didn't pass all those he wrote and he didn't write them all. He and Joe Clark seem to be alike in having failed first year in law school, although Joe failed only one course, and a Dal friend maintains that Joe had a passing mark but was penalized for not attending enough classes. Joe was forced to write a supplementary exam, and got a lot of negative publicity about it later on. Mulroney didn't, because nobody knew about it.

Indeed, in a 1983 story in the Halifax *Chronicle-Herald* on the eve of the Tory leadership convention, Brian Flemming, Mulroney's old debating partner, was quoted as telling the one-hundredth graduating banquet of Dal's law school that the three finalists at the Conservative convention "were all people who had gone to Dalhousie law school." When Flemming named Clark, John Crosbie, and Mulroney, the paper reported, several people in the audience shouted that Mulroney had not gone there, but Flemming said he had and was in his class. Flemming did not want to discuss Mulroney's Dalhousie experience, but the story quotes him as saying, "Quite a few people came up afterwards and said 'You weren't telling the truth.' I said yes, he did, but he so carefully concealed that year, nobody knew about it." Like other things Mulroney had done, somehow it didn't get picked up in the media and his story about being struck by his Quebec roots stuck.

Another Dalhousie classmate, who practised some labour law with Mulroney, says he was good at that because it takes an ability to persuade people and adjust yourself to changing circumstances. "I've always said privately about Mulroney that if there's one Canadian you wanted to go over to Beirut to talk to the Shiites, the Druzes, the Christians and the Israelis and try to bring some semblance of order out of that chaos, Mulroney would be at or near the top of my list. . . . I think that skill has been very valuable to him. Even to this day, I'm told by people inside his caucus, he still is able to carry the caucus with his force of personality, his ability to give them all a story they'll believe in even when they're in revolt.

"That's why the Iron Ore Company was very clever later on hiring him to be the president in Canada. They knew he would take orders from Cleveland on the financial side and they would run the company. But on the P.R. side and labour-relations side and the closing down of Schefferville, Mulroney would be the best man they could find. It was like finding the guy to go into Beirut, and he certainly did it with great panache. For a guy who shut down a major town in Quebec, he's never taken much heat on that."

From Halifax, Mulroney headed to Laval University to earn his law degree, where he gained instant recognition as one of a small group of Anglophones studying in French. About 10 per cent of the class was Anglo, a circumstance Lucien Bouchard would later describe as "the year Westmount invaded Laval." Mulroney's group included Michael Meighen, a grandson of a former prime minister, who later became Tory national president, and Peter White, who owned a small newspaper called the *Eastern Townships Advertiser*, and who later became a close business associate of Conrad Black and national secretary of Mulroney's 1983 campaign. When Mulroney became prime minister, White became patronage chief. (He left two years later, after an unexplained falling out, to return to private business.)

Clearly, Mulroney was continuing his pattern of cementing friendships for the future. Two other bilingual Francophones who became members of his group—Michel Cogger and Jean Bazin—are now both senators and close friends and political intimates.

The five students were the leading organizers of the Laval students' First Canadian Congress on Canadian Affairs, a successful venture that attracted politicans and academics from across the country for a highly publicized week of discussion on separatism and Canadian unity. Among the guests were Quebec Liberal premier Jean Lesage and three other politicans who would become Quebec premiers: the late Daniel Johnson, Jean-Jacques Bertrand, and René Lévesque. According to Lévesque, then a Liberal cabinet minister, Quebec's attitude to the rest of Canada was, "You need us more than we need you." Douglas Fisher, then a CCF MP, responded to Lévesque at the closing session two days later. "René Lévesque said in his speech, 'We don't need you.' Well, I'm tempted to say, 'That goes double.'" For the average voter in his riding (Port Arthur in northern Ontario), said Fisher, French culture meant "Maurice Richard and Lili St. Cyr."

The congress ended dramatically when prominent separatist Marcel Chaput finished his speech and Meighen handed him a telegram saying he'd been fired from his defence-department job because of his public support of Quebec independence.

Veteran *Toronto Star* Quebec correspondent Robert McKenzie, writing of Mulroney's group at Laval, said, "Long before the introduction of Quebec's law to reinforce the position of the French language, the Mulroney-Meighen-White group looked like a new breed of Quebec anglos—a growing bilingual, English elite. Strangely, it never happened. Twenty years later, there are still not many more anglos studying in French, and a similar group would probably cause just as big a stir today on the Laval campus."

As McKenzie wrote, there was a sense of history in the making at Laval then. "How many of those present stopped to reflect that the student organizers might be the next generation to grapple with the problems of Quebec's place in Canada?" Also in the tight-knit Mulroney group at the time were three future Parti Québécois ministers (Jean Garon, Clement Richard, and Denis de Belleval) and two future

federal Liberal ministers (André Ouellet and Pierre De Bané).
Another member was Bernard Roy, a law partner and best man
at Mulroney's wedding. Roy later became Mulroney's principal
secretary in the PMO.

The MacDonald biography quotes Mulroney as saying: "Of
all the times in my life, Laval was the golden years." His
experiences there between 1960 and 1964 paralleled Quebec's
Quiet Revolution, and Mulroney considered himself very
much a part of it. "In 1960, what Quebec had was the
beginning of the process of overturning two hundred years of
history," he told MacDonald.

At Laval, Mulroney was noted as a sharp dresser, showing
up in dark double-breasted suits and a shirt and tie. Using his
legendary persuasive skills, he talked his way onto the local
English television station, hosting a public-affairs show and
attracting the new premier as one of his first guests. He lived
in a small motel room behind an old stone rooming house on
rue Saint-Louis, and spent many evenings prowling the local
bars and restaurants clustered in the shadow of the Quebec
Basilica—places frequented by politicians, students, and local
journalists.

One of those journalists was Peter Cowan, then a cub
reporter with the daily *Quebec Chronicle-Telegraph*. Cowan
and Mulroney used to buy their smokes in the Citadel Cigar
Store and Brian would drink at the Chien d'or (The Golden
Dog), owned by the Noonan brothers. Other favourite water-
ing holes were the Chalet Swiss, known locally as the
Aquarium, a gathering place for late-night drinks and dinners,
and, if you wanted to have a drink after legal closing hours,
there was Aux Delices, a blind pig one street over. "He was
known to reporters and politicians even then," says Cowan.
"He certainly didn't run from journalists. He hung around with
Cogger and Bazin and a lot of rich kids from English families
who went to Laval, like White and Meighen.

"I was told, although I never saw proof of it, that Mulroney
was consulted often by Diefenbaker on Quebec. Certainly
Mulroney used to tell people that. He was well known by what
there was of the Tory party in Quebec, although he never so
much as ran for dog catcher. Daniel Johnson, leader of the
Union Nationale, was one guy who noticed Brian. He
[Johnson] would hold court in the evening, often at the bar at
the Château, and people would drop by and shoot the breeze.
Brian was one of them.

"In those days, we never thought Johnson would become premier," said Cowan. "But you never know. Look what Brian became."

One of the top lecturers who came to Laval in those days was, of course, a Montreal professor named Pierre Trudeau. Another professor who influenced Mulroney and later gave him his big political break was Robert Cliche. Cliche lectured on trial procedure, was leader of Quebec's NDP, and came to chair the inquiry into corruption in Quebec's construction industry. That inquiry made Mulroney a household name in the province; without it he would never have been able to seek the party's leadership in 1976.

In 1961, Mulroney was one of six young political activists invited to participate in a discussion with two editors of *Maclean's* for a special issue called "The Young Canadians." The editors were Peter Gzowski and Peter C. Newman. Newman has since been a consistent supporter of Mulroney in his writing. According to the MacDonald biography, Newman asked Mulroney, at twenty-one the youngest of the group, what attitude the future politician would have towards patronage. Mulroney replied: "I think his attitude is going to be drastically changed from the attitude of those who are in government today. The young people of today are going to strengthen the nation at the cost of partisan politics, and they are going to take a much more idealistic view of things twenty years from now than we do today." It didn't exactly work out that way.

One day at Laval, Mulroney brought Diefenbaker into class to show the doubters that he really did have the contact with the Chief he loved to boast about. Meighen admitted later that "we [had] thought it was bullshit."

In the summer of 1962, Mulroney landed a job as special assistant to federal agriculture minister Alvin Hamilton. He also talked CKRM in Regina into letting him act as an unpaid stringer for the June 18 election, as he campaigned with Hamilton in his Qu'Appelle riding in Saskatchewan and throughout the West. Mulroney called the station twice a day to report on his man's activities. In that election Hamilton was comfortably re-elected, but Diefenbaker's previous huge majority (the largest in history until Mulroney topped it in 1984) was reduced to a bare minority. In 1963, Diefenbaker was defeated by Pearson, Mulroney did little beyond organizing a whistle-stop tour for Diefenbaker through eastern Quebec.

Mulroney idolized John F. Kennedy, an Irish Catholic who had shown he could become president of the United States. "He was unique, absolutely unique," Mulroney would tell his biographer years later. "I don't think there's any way that anyone of my age could have gone through life interested in politics and public life and not have been deeply affected and influenced by President Kennedy." Indeed, in 1983, shortly after winning the Tory leadership on his second try, Mulroney took a portrait of himself, scrolled a Kennedyesque message on it, "The Long Lonely Journey Begins," and gave it to his faithful follower Pat MacAdam, who proudly displayed it on his office wall.

Mulroney and most of his gang clung to their bachelorhood until they were in their thirties. Mulroney had a reputation as a man about town, a heavy drinker and serious carouser. At Laval, he claimed, "I wasn't a big hitter with the girls." But Meighen once told a reporter, "We crammed, organized conferences and chased girls," and Gerald Doucet said, "You can imagine that if he was the kind of guy who would call up the prime minister or go sit in the premier's office, he wasn't afraid to call up girls for dates."

CHAPTER THREE

REACHING FOR THE
GOLDEN RING

Typically, there is more than one version. In the L. Ian MacDonald biography, Bernard Roy was working as an articling student in Montreal when he heard that the city's largest firm, Howard, Cate, Ogilvy, Bishop, Cope, Porteous and Hansard, was looking for another young employee. Roy told Mulroney about it and our young hero, who had an offer to join a firm in Baie-Comeau, jumped at the chance, particularly when one of the senior partners, John Kirkpatrick, inexplicably reached Mulroney—in the law library, of course—and offered to pay his fare from Quebec to Montreal for an interview.

The other version, as told by Mulroney to various reporters and recorded in a masterful full-length feature on June 12, 1983, by *Toronto Star* journalist Robert McKenzie, is that Michel Cogger was studying for his bar exams when a friend received a call from the firm offering him a position as a student lawyer. When Cogger saw that the friend was going to refuse, he asked him to suggest Mulroney's name.

Regardless of how it happened, Mulroney started at the top. With sixty lawyers on staff, the firm was known as "the Factory" and claimed to be the biggest law firm in the Commonwealth. Mulroney began in the general litigation department, as "a gofer," he would explain later, which is customary in these matters.

When Mulroney went home for Christmas that year he discovered that his father had six weeks to live. Ben Mulroney died of cancer on February 16, 1965. In the spring, Mulroney flunked his civil-procedure bar exams, blaming it on amendments to the Code passed by the Quebec National Assembly while he was burying his father and moving his mother, brother Gary (sixteen), and sister Barbara (twelve), to Montreal where he rented an apartment for them. Then he and Jean Bazin, who had also flunked procedure, arranged to spend a month at a country house in St. Sauveur, north of Montreal, studying to retake their exams. Both were called to the bar in 1965.

Mulroney's charm never served him better, as he smiled his way into friendships with senior partners in the firm and, more significantly, with some of the firm's wealthiest clients. Just before Christmas in his early days with the firm he arrived home to find a huge television set in his apartment, compliments of William Bennett, president of Iron Ore Co. A decade later, it was Bennett who offered Mulroney the IOC vice-presidency. Mulroney declined because he was about to take his first crack at the Tory leadership; when he lost, Bennett renewed the offer, hired Mulroney, and started grooming him to take over the presidency when he, Bennett, retired.

Mulroney's big professional break came when a senior member of the firm had a heart attack during a waterfront dispute and Mulroney, who had moved into labour relations, took over the case and proved there was considerable legal skill behind that engaging smile. In those years, Mulroney often appeared on the same cases with his friend Stanley Hartt, fighting the International Longshoremen's Association (ILA), Mulroney on behalf of the Shippers' Federation and Hartt for the Stevedores' Contractors.

Everybody who knew Mulroney then said he did his job well. According to one former colleague, "As a labour lawyer he was really successful. He used to bill his clients in a very creative way, a very high way, but a way that was acceptable to them. . . . While they used to complain about the bills, Brian usually delivered. So if you're successful, then people don't mind as much paying a $50,000 or $55,000 bill. It's when you don't deliver and you try to render those accounts that you get into trouble.

"He also worked very hard. He would work from seven in the morning to one in the morning and get up at five to go at it again, and get into the Scotch the night before. He loved to shoot the bull in the evening if he wasn't working. But he was all work for a period of time in his life, apart from politics and some ladies here and there, and some Scotch. He was a workaholic, no question."

Labour law is like obstetrics in that just as you never know when the baby is going to be born, you never know when a strike or some other labour crisis will flare up. "He was good at that," said another former colleague. "He'd respond quickly any time. I worked with him many times where he'd go in and deal with really hostile union guys and, within a week to ten days, he'd get close to these guys, relate to them somehow, and by the time it was all over they'd like the guy."

In the early 1970s, when a battle over automating the port at Halifax threatened to turn violent, Mulroney went down there to represent the Maritime Employers Association (MEA) as their delegate to a three-man conciliation board. One of the men who got to know him then was Herb Westlake, a member of the negotiating team for Local 269, Halifax Longshoremen's Association. "We were on opposite sides of the fence, but I found him to be very fair and open, the kind of guy who would say, when the day was over, 'Look, we're going in there again tomorrow, there's no use banging our heads against each other, here's what we want, here's what you want, let's try to find some middle road.' Even when the battle was over he was a real nice fellow.

"During negotiations, of course, tempers flare, including his, but when it ended he was friendly and decent about it." The two met again two years later in Saint John, when the port was going through the same thing, and Westlake found him friendly and respectful. "It would have been easy for me not to like him," said Westlake. "He was representing the employers in a bitter dispute, probably the most bitter dispute we've ever had at the Halifax port."

That particular fight was over automation. It meant major technological changes and was a really fierce fight. "A lot of the problems were new to us," said Westlake, and "there were some bogeymen, of course, about fears over job losses. We went from picking up bags of flour and rolling barrels to operating six- and seven-million dollar machinery we had never dreamed possible. I started with containerization in 1969, so I know what he did was beneficial to the port, although it wasn't accepted by the workers at the time. Had we not done it, we wouldn't be the major world port that we are today. He saw that, even then, and while we were naturally nervous, he listened to both sides. If he had to take a hard line at times, as he did, he took it, but he had the wisdom to see it was necessary. . . . It wasn't easy to convince a bunch of people who were worried about losing their jobs to machines. "I don't necessarily agree with his politics," concluded Westlake, "but he did a good job with us. I'll grant him that."

Another Mulroney contact from those days was Arnie Masters, long-time president of the Maritime Employers Association. Masters, a controversial figure, had been campaign manager for Liberal Bryce Mackasey in Verdun, and then Mackasey's assistant when he was labour minister. It was Mackasey who parachuted Masters in as MEA president, a move not universally applauded by everyone in the port business. The MEA, which hired Mulroney as legal counsel, was incorporated in 1969 and represents the ports in Hamilton, Toronto, Montreal, Quebec City, Trois-Rivières, Saint John, and Halifax.

A veteran Halifax company executive, an ardent Tory who dealt with Mulroney and Masters through MEA business, recalls that "you would see him [Mulroney] around at all the parties and receptions and, to say the least, his style of conduct was not prime-ministerial. He had a severe drinking problem then. He had another pattern which would endure, and that is he made a point out of meeting all the senior people in the industry. . . . The stuff he did for the MEA was pretty mundane legal work. Contracts, arbitration, contract negotiations, that sort of thing. But the MEA is a fractious body. There's a lot of acrimony among members. Halifax even tried to get out of it at that time. Some of the key members, particularly Halterm, said they were quitting in ninety days if there weren't changes, and Mulroney was deeply involved in the negotiations settling that thing down, making some concessions to Halterm to keep them in the fold.

"Mulroney made many associations at that time, particularly in Montreal, which have lasted to this day. One of those was Arnie Masters. Mulroney in those days would have been reporting to Masters and the two became good drinking buddies. Masters is a very controversial guy. The Liberals appointed him [Masters] to the board of the Montreal Port Corporation. Companies belong to the MEA out of necessity, in order to employ labour on the docks. The Montreal port is in direct competition, of course, with the Halifax port, offering discount wharfage and other inducements, yet here's the same guy running that port and the MEA."

Though not an earth-shattering issue, the conflict was taken seriously and there were, apparently, hopes that with the change of government Masters would be gone as MEA president.

Officials of various MEA member companies have formally complained both to the association and to Mulroney. In a letter of May 29, 1986, to MEA chairman Norman Wolfe, the president of Halterm Ltd., Brian Doherty, suggested that the board should ask "Masters to resign or refuse to accept re-appointment." There have been similar letters to the MEA and to transport minister John Crosbie from the Halifax Offshore Terminal Services Ltd., the Halifax-Dartmouth Port Development Commission, and the Halifax Board of Trade. And there have been several personal calls to Mulroney's office and to Deputy Prime Minister Don Mazankowski. The issue has even been reported in the Halifax *Chronicle-Herald*. But still Masters, a Liberal appointee, manages to hang on to both jobs.

"Halifax people thought the government turnover would be the end of Masters," said an industry leader. "This guy is in conflict with my own company and the Halifax port. Acting on pressure from us, we had some Halifax MPs go right to Mazankowski to complain about this, and Maz told them there's nothing he could do, he wasn't touching it, it came straight from the PMO. . . . Well, one of these days they're going to have to get the troops up for an election. They're going to have a problem, let me tell you. Party people here are saying, 'We prevailed upon you for help and you wouldn't listen. We're not going to hear you when you call back for help.'"

An interesting sidelight to the Masters saga is that, in early July 1972, when Mulroney was on holiday in the south of France, Masters phoned him in Monte Carlo to tell him of a strike at the Montreal port. It was while Mulroney was back in town working on that strike that Bernard Roy signed him up as a member of the Mount Royal Tennis Club. When the strike quieted down, Mulroney took a couple of days off, went to the club, had his legendary poolside meeting with the eighteen-year-old bikini-clad Mila Pivnicki. Mulroney had always told his friends that he wanted to be wealthy before getting into politics, and he was quite clearly building up both a comfortable nest egg and a fund of political contacts during this period. He wasn't all work, however. One friend remembers that for a time in the early 1970s he had the hots for one of the dancers in the Dean Martin television show, "The Gold-diggers." "On weekends, he used to actually follow them on tour. He was so close to this particular lady we'd often see him on a Friday night at Dorval getting ready to fly to Chicago or Denver or wherever she happened to be that weekend."

As a former colleague who spent time with Mulroney during the 1970 October Crisis in Quebec recalls: "I spent a lot of time in his office in Montreal during that critical lead-up time when Laporte was killed and things were getting very hairy. Brian was the point man for a lot of people, for a lot of passing on of information. He was dealing with Claude Ryan and Bourassa and [Claude] Castonguay, and a whole host of people who seemed to be phoning in and chatting. He was a switchboard of information at that time.

"The interesting thing was news about the proposed provi-sional government. Things were considered that serious for a time. But nobody ever connected him with it. They should have. He was involved in that. He has an uncanny ability to put himself centrally in a lot of things. That was one of them."

Quebec politics in the 1960s was exciting. In her masterful book *Grits*, author Christina McCall-Newman writes, "there was a kind of euphoria. The labour unions' long battles of the 1950s were bringing impressive results in wage settlements and working conditions. The dominance of the church in secular life was being challenged, not just by intellectuals but throughout society. Sweeping reforms were being proposed for the educational system. The civil service was undergoing a reorganization from top to bottom, with many bureaucrats from Ottawa being invited to come home to Quebec to bring about a new era. Patronage practices, notably in the construc-tion industry, were under scrutiny. Duplessis's old habit of paying off newspapermen was discontinued. Marchand was invited to give advice out of his experience as director of the Confédération des Syndicats Nationaux to the government's economic council. . . . Pelletier was hired as editor of *La Presse*, the largest daily. Trudeau was made a professor of law at the university and a member of the Institut de Recherches en Droit Public. It looked like a new dawn."

And Brian Mulroney was dying to be part of it. While the Conservative party in Quebec wasn't exactly part of the mainstream, Mulroney had by the mid-1960s built an impres-sive stable of political heavyweights he could claim as friends.

In the 1965 election, the Tories won eight Quebec seats and (in the MacDonald biography) Mulroney said he had a role "strictly as a worker, raising money, trying to find new candidates. Not a high profile." He also claims to have a curious memory lapse about whether he was a delegate to the November 1966 meeting: "But I'll tell you this. If I was a delegate I would have voted for the idea that Dalton [Camp] was trying to put forward."

Journalist Peter Cowan, who was Quebec City bureau chief for the *Montreal Star* during that period, recalls Mulroney at the meeting of the Quebec wing of the party when the question on the agenda was Diefenbaker's continuing leadership. The meeting, at La Bastogne Motel in Beauport, a Quebec City suburb on the north shore of the river, had attracted both Camp and Diefenbaker. "The old guard was still trying to protect Dief," said Cowan, "but a meeting had been set up with Daniel Johnson. So the old guard went out to the airport to meet Dief and take him to the meeting, and while they were doing that, the young turks of the party were stabbing him in the back. They ran through a motion calling for leadership review, and Brian was very much a part of that. He was one of the leaders of the young turks pushing for review. It was the first sense I had that these guys could play rough."

At the 1967 leadership convention at Toronto's Maple Leaf Gardens, Mulroney supported former justice minister E. Davie Fulton, who ran third. When Fulton went to Stanfield, Mulroney went with him. As prime minister twenty years later, when he unveiled the Diefenbaker statue on the west side of the expanse of the Commons front lawn, Mulroney boasted about how he had worked for Diefenbaker as a young student and how much he had loved and admired the Chief. He did not mention his role during the 1960s, when he had gauged which way the wind was shifting and joined many other former loyalists to plunge the political knife into Diefenbaker's back. On the day of the unveiling, a planned breakfast meeting of old Diefenbaker loyalists, those who had not turned on him, was cancelled under direct pressure from Mulroney. The last thing he wanted was some of his own caucus mates reminding him of his duplicity.

In the 1968 federal election, the Tories dropped to four seats in Quebec, as Trudeaumania captured the hearts of Canadian voters everywhere. Mulroney was named assistant to Jean

Bruneau, one of Daniel Johnson's senior Union Nationale organizers, who was chairing the Conservative campaign. It was the first time Mulroney had had any official organizational duties for the party in Quebec. He would boast later about his influence as the link between the Tories and Johnson's Union Nationale. Among other things he worked to persuade Marcel Faribault, a Montreal financier whom Johnson had brought into his cabinet, to run as the Great White Hope for the Tories in Quebec (the same role he later played getting Claude Wagner to lead the party out of the Quebec wilderness).

Mulroney convinced his good friend Rodrigue Pageau (who would later be a leader in the anti-Clark fight in Quebec on Mulroney's behalf) to run, as a Tory, against Jean Marchand in Quebec City's lower-town riding of Langelier. The Union Nationale threw a lot of money behind Pageau. As Cowan tells it, the Tories made a deal with Réal Caouette's Créditistes. Social Credit would run a low-profile campaign so that the anti-Liberal vote would go to Pageau. But when polls in the riding showed the Socreds ahead, even though they weren't campaigning, they told Pageau all bets were off, and he finished third.

"The feeling I get about Mulroney now is he has learned none of the lessons he should have learned from all this," Cowan summed up. "That it is a long, slugging process. There are no magic solutions [to the Quebec vote]. They know they have to put down roots, but they don't know how."

In 1972, the Tories were still in hot pursuit of that "magic solution" when Peter White, running his newspaper in partnership with Conrad Black, approached Claude Wagner, a popular Quebec judge, to ask if he would be interested in running for the federal Tories (not exactly a plum assignment in those days in Quebec). Wagner, who would have to give up his job on the bench and would be unemployed if he lost the election, asked what arrangements could be made by the party to look after him. White then introduced him to Mulroney, who worked out the details and convinced Stanfield to welcome Wagner on board.

"Stanfield was reluctant," said Finlay MacDonald, the 1972 campaign chairman. "First of all, he didn't know Wagner, and secondly, he didn't want to precipitate any decision that would lay the mantle of Le Chef on anybody without one hell of a lot of thought. But he eventually agreed that if Wagner could be induced to become a candidate, he would have no objection.

"I obviously had a clear interest in recruiting candidates so I quickly became aware of this. . . . I made an appointment for lunch at the Château Champlain in Montreal. We ordered up lunch to my room [lobster salad and a bottle of Pouilly-Fuissé] and I spent two or three hours with this guy I'd never met, just the two of us. Eventually the matter was broached about the sacrifice he'd be making, and he suggested a trust fund for his wife and child. It got down to how much, and the sum of $300,000 was agreed upon. There was absolutely nothing at all in legislation that forbade such arrangements, so I went back and told the party finance committee. They agreed and it was turned over to [Toronto lawyer] Eddie Goodman to discuss the details with Wagner. I have no idea to this day how it was done. I was the one who made the deal, but that's it."

MacDonald said that Mulroney had been instrumental in conducting a poll about Wagner. "The search for a strong man for the Conservatives in Quebec was on, a figure around whom the Bleus could rally. The poll showed a recognition factor of Wagner which was extraordinarily high and very favourable."

Although Finlay MacDonald denies it, another insider from those days says that Mulroney had an even larger role than MacDonald suggested. "There was a meeting at Mulroney's house in Westmount. MacDonald was in on that, Stanfield, maybe even Dalton Camp, although I'm not sure of him. When Stanfield said 'Where am I going to get the money?' it was Mulroney who said 'Why don't you take $10,000 off the central budget from the thirty safest Conservative seats? If they're good Tory seats, they should be able to make it.' And that's what they did. You'll recall that Stanfield lost that election by two seats. They lost enough of those 'safe' seats that some of the people who were organizers of those seats have told me over the years that was partially responsible for it. Mulroney may have actually doomed Stanfield with that one act."

In any event, Wagner didn't exactly lead a Bleu tide to Ottawa. The Tories won just two seats in Quebec, Wagner's own and Heward Grafftey's. In 1974, they won three, when Roch LaSalle returned to the Conservatives after sitting as an independent.

What upset MacDonald, he said, was that Wagner concluded his formal statement announcing his candidacy with the remark that no inducements had been offered to get him to run. "Shortly after, I had a call from Brian. He was appalled, shaken. It was a totally unnecessary thing for [Wagner] to have said. He launched his political career with an untruth, which shocked not only Brian, but everybody who had put such faith in the recruitment of this man."

The lie about the trust fund turned out to be Wagner's Achilles' heel in the 1976 leadership contest, where he lost to Clark but finished ahead of the third-place Mulroney. In the final days of the campaign, Mulroney's people leaked details of the deal to the media, and Wagner posters were stencilled with the figures $300,000. After Mulroney dropped out of the race, LaSalle pleaded with him to go over to Wagner, but Mulroney, who claimed Wagner's people had cut him out of the appointed list of delegates at large, refused. Wagner lost by sixty-five votes. The party would have to wait another seven years to get its first French-speaking leader since Confederation.

It was not Mulroney's active role in the Conservative party that enabled him to be a serious contender for the national leadership. No, what transformed Mulroney from a backroom boy to a public figure was his role in the fall and winter of 1974-75, as one of the three commissioners on the Cliche Commission inquiry into violence and corruption in Quebec's $6 billion construction industry.

By 1973, Mulroney had been appointed the youngest partner in the Howard, Cate, Ogilvy law firm and was a close personal friend of Liberal premier Robert Bourassa. Construction violence had come to a head on March 21, 1974, when Yvon Duhamel jumped into a D-8 bulldozer and smashed electric generators at the James Bay site, the largest construction job in Quebec history. (Duhamel eventually got ten years in jail.) Three days after the James Bay incident, a National Assembly commission studying trade-union legislation was disrupted by thirty men, led by André Desjardins, director of the Quebec wing of the Federation of Labour. The group intimidated politicians and assaulted other trade unionists. No charges were ever laid, but the outcry prompted Bourassa to ask Mulroney's former Laval professor Robert Cliche to head an inquiry. At the same time, Bourassa dispatched labour minister Jean Cournoyer to ask Mulroney to be a commissioner. Mulroney had already earned his spurs in Quebec by settling a bitter strike at La Presse, so he seemed a natural for the job.

The commission did not generate much excitement in the English Canadian media, but in Quebec it was a daily soap opera, involving 80 days of public hearings, 279 witnesses, and almost 1,000 exhibits, an unfolding saga of loan-sharking, pay-offs by companies to keep workers on the job, government corruption, and crime-dominated construction unions. It was an absolute sensation in Quebec, and Mulroney, using his "old buddy" network by playing favourites with the media, became the star.

As Michel Guenard, parliamentary correspondent for TVA (French) Network said in a recent speech to the National Press Club in Ottawa, Mulroney "is a man who came out as a big winner in the art of manipulating the press. . . . [He] didn't play fair ball with the Quebec press covering the Cliche Commission inquiry. He had his own game plan." A big card in his hand was his relationship with Roger Lemelin, editor of *La Presse*. Prior to his appointment as commissioner, he had been a labour-relations consultant for *La Presse* in settling one of their numerous strikes. That gave him constant good head-lines, and Yves Leclerc, the *La Presse* reporter attached to the Cliche inquiry, became his confidant. On the English side, Mulroney picked Irwin Block of the *Gazette*. (Block, inciden-tally, is the reporter L. Ian MacDonald chose to interview about the Cliche Commission for his book.)

According to Guenard, Mulroney established regular close relations with the two reporters, "hotel-suite briefings, off-the-record inside stories, and real scoops, plus the wine-and-dine treatment." That came to be Mulroney's pattern all during the 1970s, early 1980s, and to some extent even today.

In a 1976 interview with the *Toronto Star*'s Robert McKen-zie, Michel Bourdon, head of the Confederation of National Trade Unions' construction unions and the man who brought about the probe by denouncing the rival Quebec Federation of Labour unions for wrecking the James Bay site, repeated the recurring complaint that Mulroney was much tougher on union officials than on companies or government officials at the inquiry.

"Mulroney dominated the Cliche Commission," said Bour-don, according to whom Mulroney was responsible for the recommendation, immediately enacted into law by Bourassa, that created a presumption of guilt for unions and workers involved in illegal work stoppages. Mulroney would say it was necessary to prevent "anarchy" in the construction industry.

Bourdon described an incident at the hearings where a CNTU official broke into tears on the stand as he told how he had received threats against his children from goons from the rival QFL. Bourdon said Mulroney exploded at this man during a recess in the corridor, telling him he "wasn't crying when he helped organize an illegal strike against British-Canadian Aluminum in Sept-Iles."

"I told Mulroney that threats against a man's children were not exactly in the same category as a strike, however illegal, against a company," said Bourdon. When asked about the incident by McKenzie, Mulroney dismissed it as "buffoonery" by Bourdon.

To this day, when the subject at hand involves ordinary working men and women, Mulroney loves to remind us that he was a "labour lawyer," the implication being that he understands the plight of working people. He was a labour lawyer, it is true, but never for labour, always for management. Nothing wrong with that, but it doesn't qualify him for his union card. In a July 1975 interview with *Maclean's*, Mulroney said he still regards himself as a champion of the working class, despite his establishment image. "My father was a unionized man, a member of the QFL, in fact, I spent 11 years as a labourer in Baie-Comeau, so I know a worker when I see one."

Mulroney is proud of his role in producing the 604-page commission report with its 134 recommendations. In a 1981 *Atlantic Insight* interview with Parker Barss Donham he pointed out that every single recommendation "was enacted in law, and there hasn't been a goddamn peep out of those guys since."

One of the more sensational revelations at the commission inquiry was testimony by justice minister Jerome Choquette when he contradicted a statement by Bourassa that both of them had known for only three weeks about an alleged 1970 influence-peddling case. The case involved a civil servant who reportedly paid a cabinet aide $2,000 for an appointment to the Minimum Wage Commission. Choquette testified that he had told Bourassa about the case in September 1970. The MacDonald biography quotes Mulroney's comment that Choquette "was first class in this thing throughout. . . . Jerome is a much-maligned figure, and he ought not to have been." Bourassa was forced to call a news conference and give his side of the story—that he couldn't remember Choquette's having told him—but according to MacDonald, the larger issue was a

dispute on the commission itself about whether to subpoena
the premier. Commission counsel, Lucien Bouchard, wanted
to call Bourassa. Mulroney said no and threatened to quit if
they did because it was "in excess of the jurisdiction of the
commission."

What MacDonald didn't report in his account is that late one
night before Choquette's testimony, Bourassa called Mulroney
over to his house in Maplewood. Cliche was snowed in at his
home in Beauce, and the other commissioner, Guy Chevrette,
was unavailable. According to the notes written at the time by
journalist Gillian Cosgrove, who lived with MacDonald then
and was close to the Mulroneys, "Brian felt he needed a
witness, so he called on Paul Desmarais. The chairman of the
Power Corp. sat at one end of the table, said nothing, and
merely took notes like a dutiful stenographer. Bourassa
convinced them both that Choquette was going around the
bend, was on the verge of crashing, was crazy. The commission
decided to call Choquette anyway—he was actually waiting at
home to testify—and he fingered top officials in Bourassa's
office."

Cosgrove describes Mulroney in those days as "such an
uptight asshole he couldn't even wear jeans. . . . I used to
kid him about that. On my thirtieth birthday, he sent me an
entire case of Scotch and signed it, 'a guy in a three-piece
suit.' . . . I always felt uncomfortable with Brian because I
felt he never could relax."

She said he and MacDonald were both "media junkies, both
JFK junkies, both could recite Ted Sorensen speeches for JFK as
if he'd dropped in. . . . He loves it. He gets enamoured with
his own phrases, all that Kennedyesque stuff."

Two months after the Cliche Commission report came out,
Robert Stanfield resigned as Tory leader. Mulroney decided
his time had come.

CHAPTER FOUR

**

MAKING IT

Nothing bothered Mulroney more in that 1976 leadership
contest than the charge that he was a media mirage—a
candidate from whimsy, one columnist called him—who was
big on panache and nowhere on policy, a man who had never
been elected to anything, yet wanted to start at the top. It was
all true, of course, but he gave it a good run none the less,
thanks to both a large and loyal group of friends and a
considerable stable of oh-so-friendly media people who had
been seduced by his Irish charm and penchant for playing
favourites with those who reported favourably on his activities.

L. Ian MacDonald, of course, was a leader of the fan club,
but other journalists came under his spell too. Incredibly, in
1976 an *Edmonton Journal* columnist said of Mulroney: "His
eyes are Paul Newman blue, his hair has the swoop of the
Robert Redford style, and his voice the resonance of a Lorne
Greene school of broadcasting grad. The jaw is by Gibraltar."
Another notable fan was Bill Fox, then of Southam News, later
of the *Toronto Star*. Even in 1976, years before he left
journalism to work full time for Mulroney, Fox was telling
readers what a terrific leader Mulroney would make. In one
column, a month before the 1976 convention (held February
22), Fox went through the anti-Mulroney arguments one at a
time, knocking each one down, essentially holding Mulroney
up as the right man at the right time.

As it turned out, the delegates disagreed with Fox. They
had concerns about Mulroney's ties with big business, particularly Power Corp. and its chairman Paul Desmarais. Questions
were also raised about Mulroney's role in the Wagner trust
fund and his unelected status. A January 1976 editorial cartoon

by Aislin in the Montreal *Gazette* brilliantly summed up Mulroney's image—he was shown dressed up in wrestler's tights, with frilly neckline and cuffs, fancy boots, the word "Gorgeous," on his chest (for wrestler Gorgeous George), hair pins holding his locks in place and a huge tube of Crest toothpaste in his hand.

As early as 1972 Wagner had created his own weak spot at the news conference in which he said, "I have no need of, I have not asked for, nor have I ever been offered any pension fund or financial compensation." As the guy who helped arrange the deal, Mulroney was in a perfect position to use it against him in 1976—as he did when, as the convention began, his old school chum Peter White started to spread the word. But when asked about the Wagner trust fund in an early February 1976 *Maclean's* interview, Mulroney said, "Don't ask me—ask the guy who got the three hundred grand." The article described Mulroney then as a "soap-salesman type," who had helped dump Dief then worked for Fulton before switching to Stanfield. It quoted a Quebec Tory who had known Mulroney all his adult life as saying, "I couldn't tell you where Brian stands on any issue," and it noted that the Diefenbaker Tories called him "Dalton Camp's candidate."

In a *Montreal Star* article of January 19, 1976, Mulroney flatly denied that he had participated in a meeting at which the Wagner trust fund was established. He also claimed he did not know where his own financial backing was coming from, but added, "There won't be anybody dishonest backing me." Geoffrey Stevens of the *Globe and Mail* wrote of the "Barbie Doll quality . . . a little too collected, serious, intense, programmed, almost calculated. When he is in public, one keeps wishing he would unwind, laugh a bit, let his hair down . . . there is also an air of self-esteem, an assumption of special status. The chilled martini awaits his arrival in Montreal's Beaver Club. The campaign aides rush to perform small services. 'Stephen, a cigarette please.' This to Stephen Leopold who travels with him. Or, 'I need some salt for my dinner, Stephen.'"

Some things don't change. When Mulroney was IOC president, he flew a group of his friends to the company fishing camp in Labrador. There were three planes, one for Mulroney and his friends, one for the booze, and one for the gear. According to Montreal *Gazette* reporter Claude Arpin, on one of those trips Mulroney discovered he'd forgotten his chocolate bars. "He sent the pilot back to Sept-Iles, four hundred miles at night, to get them. He had a love of a special kind of bar, Crispy Crunch, I think, but he'd forgotten to bring them, so he told the guy to go back in the dead of night, take a risk with his life and bring him back the chocolate bars. . . ."

The Mulroney campaign went first class all the way. A sleek, blue and white, seven-seat DH-125 jet, owned by Domtar but leased through Execaire Aviation, was used to get their man around the country. Mulroney, predicting victory, loved to call February 22, voting day, "a day that will last a decade." In early February, a *Toronto Star* poll placed him second among decided delegates, with 14.9 per cent, compared to Wagner at 17.2. Paul Hellyer was next at 10. Joe Clark, at that point, was off the charts.

Again the Wagner trust fund came up, and **again** Mulroney played dumb, promising to take a look at it if he won. "I'm not playing innocent. The guy who is playing innocent is the guy who got the dough. Somebody got $300,000 and it wasn't me. Somebody gave $300,000 and it wasn't me." (Years later, in the MacDonald biography, Mulroney is quoted on his role, which included picking Toronto lawyer Eddie Goodman up at the airport, driving him to Wagner's house, and sitting in the living room when Wagner and Goodman were in the basement working out the specific details. "I knew full well Eddie Goodman didn't go there for the good of his health," Mulroney said.) In Timmins, on January 31, when asked the difference between Liberals and Tories, Mulroney said, "I'll tell you the difference. We're honest . . . that's one important difference. We tell the truth." Asked at the same time about his campaign financing—some were calling him "the Power Candidate"— Mulroney dismissed the question as "frivolous . . . people don't give a damn. What this country needs is more men like Paul Desmarais, more Bud McDougalds [head of Argus Corp.], more businessmen who will build this country."

As the convention drew near, Mulroney took a full-page ad in *What's On in Ottawa*, a magazine distributed free to hotel rooms. His team published a daily newspaper, flooded everyone with glossy, full-colour brochures, and held an endless round of informal meetings and policy sessions. He even held a luncheon press conference for the National Press Gallery, complete with roast beef and red wine (Beaujolais), moving from table to table, charming reporters with his quick wit and mellifluous baritone. Asked at one point how he could expect to be "everything to everybody" in such a heavily ideological party, he said, "Maybe that concern with ideology is why we've been in opposition so long." Such concerns weren't going to stop him.

Mulroney's campaign published separate French and English brochures. The French-language version began: "Curiously, history wills that each generation will see the appearance of a man who brings with him, more than any other, the answers to the problems which beset the country. This man is not really a savior, rarely a predestined being; the sum of his qualities is almost always the result of a coincidence of circumstances, but always he carries within him the potential to bring the society in which he lives to transcend itself." To make the point, the brochure went on to name Winston Churchill, John F. Kennedy, and Daniel Johnson as earlier examples of this lofty ability.

In the English version, delegates were told about his nickname "Bones." Both versions told the story that at twelve he had said he wanted to be prime minister. The English version—but not the French—claimed that in the summer of 1957 he and a friend had put out a monthly newspaper in Baie-Comeau. The paper was called *Politique Neutre*, sold for $1 a copy, and was supposed to be analogous to Pierre Trudeau's *Cité Libre*. Both brochures contained Mulroney's heart-wrenching postscript to the tale of the *Maclean's* article in which he figured as one of the ten young men most likely to succeed. "Dad carried that article in his pocket until the day he died. He showed it to anyone who would give him a minute."

The Ottawa *Citizen* quoted Mulroney on the choice of Wagner in 1972: "[Wagner was] the big blue motor. We were building a pretty nice car, but we needed a motor—and that's why we went after the judge." But a few days later he told another reporter, "I distrust people who never swear, never drink, never smoke. There was always something there, between us."

In mid-February, Power Corp. said it had contributed $10,000 to Mulroney's campaign. Mulroney told reporters on one occasion that his campaign would cost about $150,000. Two days later he said it would cost $175,000. The day after that, he said he didn't know. On the same day, he proudly told a group of delegates he had received contributions from four different trade unions. Then he said things were going so well he had received $7,000 in contributions in a single day. Four days later, an aide told a reporter that the $7,000 had been raised in a week.

There was growing interest in Mulroney's campaign spending for two reasons. First, it was more lavish than that of the other campaigns; and second, early in the campaign Mulroney had criticized other candidates for being "secretive" about their spending and had promised to reveal his own. In the end, however, he was the only candidate who did not reveal that information.

Though the extent of his spending never was known, the name entertainment acts, the expensive silk Mulroney scarfs, the limitless food and booze couldn't have been cheap. Mulroney once put the figure at $319,000, but others estimate it at over $500,000, well beyond what anybody else spent. Joe Clark spent $168,354; Sinc Stevens, $294,107; Paul Hellyer, $287,786; Wagner, $266,538; James Gillies, $192,847; Flora MacDonald, $152,704; John Fraser, $116,107; Heward Grafftey, $83,846; and Richard Quittenton, $9,336. Of the twelve candidates, only Mulroney refused to reveal his total spending and the names of contributors of over $1,000. Michel Cogger, Mulroney's financial agent, claimed that the rules had been changed and that revealing donors "would amount to a breach of trust *vis-à-vis* certain individuals who helped us out." On December 15, when asked if he would disclose his money sources and contributors' names, Mulroney said: "If that's what the party wants, fine. I'll follow the rules, and whatever the rules are, I'll adhere to them strictly." He didn't. But the party president and convention chairman was Mulroney's old schoolmate Michael Meighen. He didn't push it.

Globe and Mail reporter Richard Cleroux interviewed Pierre Gauthier, a Mulroney worker, at the campaign's eleventh-floor hotel headquarters in the presence of two other *Globe* writers and two Mulroney campaign workers. Gauthier was quoted as saying, "I must have paid for four hundred rooms . . . they all wanted to be paid. I'm ashamed to say that most of them were from Quebec. I had delegates demanding $150 to pay for their rooms or they wouldn't stay for the vote."

Mulroney called Gauthier a "seventh-echelon" organizer and said that he had told "an outright lie." After the story appeared, Gauthier said that he had never talked to a *Globe* reporter and didn't even work for Mulroney. "I worked for myself, that's all. I was a delegate." A Mulroney worker who sat in on the interview confirmed that he had heard Gauthier tell the *Globe* reporter Mulroney was paying for delegates. Mulroney said he had never done anything dishonest in his life. "We never bought a vote. I ran an honest campaign." In the fateful Winnipeg convention in 1983 and the subsequent leadership convention, Mulroney loyalists also paid for delegate rooms, registration, and transportation. But then, so did most other camps.

Responding to speculation that journalist Peter C. Newman had written his major campaign speech, Mulroney said that Newman just went to Magog to interview him, as did several other journalists, and that he had no hand in the speech. "I wrote it myself," he said. According to Gillian Cosgrove, however, Ian MacDonald helped write it. "Brian really trusts Peter [Newman], like he trusts Ian, but Brian always operated on a quid pro quo. . . . In fact, there was that big, big thing just before the convention when they all went down to Dave Angus's place in Magog and holed themselves up there to write *the* definitive speech. It was all over the press that Peter C. Newman, guru, was going down there to put his glorious phrases on this speech. If you remember, the speech wasn't that great, and Peter C. Newman was never there. It's all part of the myth and legend. . . . Brian was really on the media bandwagon at the time though. Newman and all those guys thought he was going to win and wanted to write books. Peter has an exclusive now to do a book."

The doctored Mulroney campaign stickers (with the "ULR" folded over to make the sticker read "MONEY" rather than "Mulroney") were the absolute number-one smash hit at the convention. That gimmick was actually the brainchild of Michael Vaughan, then a CBC journalist, who was on leave to work on Flora MacDonald's campaign. "I'll tell you that going into that convention, Mulroney had it won," said Vaughan. "But that party had been in opposition for so long it made them a pretty negative-thinking lot, and they were more used to settling grudges than achieving goals. By the time they got to Ottawa they wanted to stop the Quebecker, Wagner, the Frenchman, and there was a hint of 'Stop Mulroney,' because they always fix on the negative.

"The idea was if you could stop them, somebody could come up the middle. Naturally, we hoped it would be Flora, and with 338 counted, committed votes, we thought, 'Oh boy, it just might be.'" (When the actual vote count placed her well down the track, the "Flora Syndrome" was born into Canadian political life.)

According to Vaughan, "Mulroney had offended a lot of people with a really vulgar display of overspending. The champagne, the lobsters, flights in corporate jets, silk scarves, and the big-name acts, this display of money, money, money. We were thinking about that and then it hit us. Jesus, money. Ding! And these octagonal stickers were everywhere. It just worked out that the spacing of the letters was perfect. Flora knew nothing about this. But you know, he lost it at the convention by being ostentatious."

Mulroney's leadership bid died on the third ballot. He'd finished second to Wagner on the opening ballot, then fell off badly as Clark came up the middle. Despite pleas from the Wagner camp to support a fellow Quebecker, Mulroney refused to endorse anybody for the final ballot, saying, "I'm not going to be king-maker. I'm going to be king." Later, he would blame Diefenbaker for his defeat: "Conventions aren't won or lost on speeches," he told Ian MacDonald. "What really hurt us was Dief." During the Chief's lecture to delegates on the need for ample parliamentary experience, Mulroney leaned over to his wife and whispered, "Mila, honey, we're dead in the water." Shortly after the campaign, however, he told journalist Jonathan Manthorpe that it was Sinclair Stevens who had sunk him. Stevens espoused a hard-line, right-wing view, finished sixth on the first ballot and then went to Clark. "When I saw him walk past on his way to Clark I really had to smile. It was preposterous and so inconsistent with everything he had said and done for four months. But I also knew it was all over for me," Mulroney said. Joe Clark had won.

Manthorpe paints a telling scene of Mulroney at the end of the convention, red-eyed from exhaustion and a hint of tears, trying to leave the Ottawa Civic Centre but surrounded by reporters doing their post-mortems. Bryce Mackasey, a fellow Montreal Irishman, rushed up, told the reporters to leave Mulroney alone, put his arm around Brian's shoulders, and led him away.

As the two men left the building, Mackasey, his arm still around Mulroney's shoulders, said: "The day John Kennedy was shot Patrick Moynihan was interviewed on television. He said, 'If you are Irish you know that at some point the world is going to break your heart.'" And so it did. But not forever.

In May, Mulroney left Howard, Cate, Ogilvy to become executive vice-president, corporate affairs, at Iron Ore Company, effective June 1, a holding pattern until president Bill Bennett's retirement at the end of the year. The two journalists who broke the story were Ian MacDonald and Bill Fox. In any event, it ended speculation that Mulroney would seek a Tory nomination in two October 18 by-elections.

In a July 1977 interview with Hilary McLaughlin of the *Ottawa Journal* at his Westmount home, Mulroney said, "I don't think I have a political future." He promised to be "quietly supportive of the leader," but said that a leader from Quebec would put the party in a better position. "Blood is thicker than water and with the events of November 15 [the Parti Québécois election victory] Trudeau has Joe over a barrel." Responding to a question about Clark's grip on caucus, Mulroney said, "Joe is essentially a conciliatory person. That's one way to lead, by attempting to develop a concensus on all major issues. I think that's consistent with his personality. I and perhaps others would take another tack: they either toe the line or they get out. If anyone bucks the leader on a key issue, he's out. I'm not suggesting one way of leadership is better than another." Six years later, Mulroney would come to Ottawa as the great conciliator, promising to end the years of confrontation under Trudeau by developing a concensus on the major issues.

During this period in his life, Mulroney was successful in business, but his marriage was on shaky ground. He couldn't get over feeling sorry for himself and attempted to drink his way through his drinking problem. While he tried to smile sweetly and say the right things about Clark when asked, sometimes the deep bitterness showed through. The most spectacular manifestation of his true feelings came in a June 1978 feature in the *Financial Post Magazine* written by Halifax journalist Stephen Kimber.

Mulroney told Kimber that Liberal polls showed that with him as leader the Tories could win all west-end Montreal seats but two. He accused the late Tom Cossitt, longtime Leeds Tory MP and Trudeau nemesis, of circulating a petition against him in caucus. "I wasn't a member of their private little club in Ottawa," he said. "I spent my whole life working for the Tory party, working when no one else would. Who the hell are guys like Jim Gillies and Sinc Stevens anyway? What the hell did they ever do for the party before they got elected in 1972?"

Mulroney was thirty-nine, living in a mansion in Westmount—"You know Westmount," he told a reporter who asked where he was living. "Well, right on top of the fucking hill, that's where."—and he was a successful company president. He said he'd never try for the leadership again. "I know you shouldn't say that, but that is my decision. I can't conceive of any circumstances that would change my mind."

Kimber began the interview in Mulroney's limousine in Ottawa then drove with him to Montreal, up the winding, tree-covered slope to his three-storey, stone house on Belvedere Drive. Inside the rambling house, he took Kimber on a tour, showing off his collection of Canadian and Yugoslavian art. "I've become more cultured since I met Mila," he said. Then at dinner, he told Kimber, "If Joe Clark wins the election I'll eat this plate. I mean, let's look at it. Can you see any way that he can win? Any way at all? The PQ wouldn't have won that election if I was the leader. It's true. The Quebec people are looking for an alternative to a profoundly unpopular provincial government. I would have given them that alternative. It's all in my platform. I can show it to you. You know who would have been the provincial leader if I had been elected . . . [a dramatic pause] Claude Ryan, that's who. He would have taken the job. I'm sure of it.

"Look at the Union Nationale and how they came back to life with Biron for Christ's sake. From zero to eleven seats. Imagine what would have happened if there'd been a Tory party in Quebec with a credible leader."

Mulroney then asked Kimber to change the part about his winning, asking, "When is this story going to appear, anyway? It shouldn't go before the election. Seriously, I don't want to sound like sour grapes about Clark, certainly not in the middle of an election campaign. The last thing I want to have happen is that someone will blame me for making things worse for him."

Kimber printed the whole thing, the request not to included. Mulroney denied saying it. He even denied at one point having been interviewed by Kimber, although he'd taken Kimber to the airport and used his own credit card to buy him a plane ticket back to Ottawa at midnight that night. (Kimber later reimbursed him.)

"Before granting me the interview," Kimber said, "Mulroney had me checked out by Peter Newman, which I found kind of strange. Newman called the *Financial Post* for all my stories before Mulroney agreed to see me. I checked out all right, but he held out for a long time. That was a time when everybody thought Trudeau was going to call an election. Everybody thought he would kill Clark. Mulroney knew about magazine deadlines, so if he gave the interview several months would pass and the piece would come out after the election, with Joe gone and him saying 'I told you so.' I didn't push him at all. He spilled his guts.

"After it became obvious there wasn't going to be an election, he phoned me," Kimber continued. "He tracked me down to my mother-in-law's house in New York to try and get the story killed. He said, 'Steve, did I sound bitter?' He offered to give me an exclusive interview later if I'd do the right thing now."

Mulroney later accused Kimber of taking off-the-record stuff and printing it, but Kimber firmly denies the charge: "This is a guy I had never met before. I was taking notes. There was no question it was on the record. He'd had me checked out. He knew I was interviewing him for a magazine piece. I knew Mulroney was saying these things about Joe in private to many journalists, but he felt he was betrayed by me."

Media consultant Tim Ralfe, a former TV journalist, was Clark's communications adviser then. According to Ralfe, Mulroney had tried to convince Clark to give him the go-ahead to talk to the press and tell them what a great guy Joe was, and the Kimber article was an attempt to follow through on that strategy (though Ralfe also says he advised Clark to say no to Mulroney's suggestion).

Ralfe believes it was after Clark lost in 1980 that Mulroney decided to have another shot at the leadership. "Everything he did from that moment on was geared to that end, including giving up drinking and smoking. Joe knew he was running this rear-guard action against him, but he just took that as part of the vagaries of the game. But the Kimber piece was the only place where Mulroney ever really appeared publicly like he was. There were stories around, but nobody ever took that seriously because we all thought we were going to win the election, get a majority, and that would have been the end of Brian anyway."

After the Tory defeat in 1980, Mulroney, who had refused to run or help the party substantially in the 1979 and 1980 elections (he claimed his contract with IOC ruled that out), was touring the country giving a series of public and private speeches, regularly citing the party's poor showing in Quebec, leaving the message that he could do better. At the same time, his loyalists, including Jean-Yves Lortie, Rodrigue Pageau, and Keith Morgan were devising a riding-by-riding organizational campaign to gain control of the Quebec wing of the party. (Still, Mulroney said flatly on CBC television a month before Winnipeg, "I'm going to vote for Clark.") Early in 1982, a group of Mulroney loyalists, intent on replacing Clark with Mulroney, had begun holding secret meetings, mainly in Montreal, to devise strategy. Frank Moores chaired the meetings. At the same time, Mulroney's "inner council" was working hard in Montreal, and Mulroney himself attended those meetings along with such trusty friends as Moores, Sam Wakim, Michael Meighen, Peter White, Michel Cogger, Jean Bazin, Fred Doucet, Fred von Veh, and Ken Waschuk. Mulroney also was in constant touch with Pat MacAdam in Ottawa, whose official job was as aide to various right-wing Tories, but whose real job was to keep stoking the anti-Clark fires on behalf of Mulroney.

Mulroney had also been making some public noises to indicate he was interested. In November 1981, he told Nancy Southam of Southam News, "If you ask me would I be a good leader of the Conservative party, the answer is yes. If you ask me would I be a good prime minister, the answer is yes. If the leadership of the Conservative party comes open in a legitimate and reasonable way, if there are indications of strong interest and support, then yes, I will run. But if I have no support from the Tory caucus, I won't run." Asked to describe himself, Mulroney said he was "a conciliator, a motivator, a catalyst, an ambassador, a street fighter."

His wife, Mila, was saying things like, "nineteen seventy-six was a very difficult year. As Brian says, he realized he wouldn't be pope. I think he should run. It would be a shame if he didn't. I think he'd like to run for MP, but it's his decision. You know, I married Brian Mulroney the lawyer who did labour negotiations late into the night."

In addition to his Westmount mansion and IOC presidency, Mulroney had directorships with the Bank of Commerce, Standard Broadcasting, and the Ritz-Carlton Hotel. He flew to Sept-Iles, Schefferville, Cleveland, Toronto, and Labrador City in a $3 million de Havilland 125 the company had bought from Nelson Skalbania. The boy from Baie-Comeau wasn't doing badly. But he still wasn't king. And he longed for the crown.

As a businessman, he had certainly performed well for his American bosses. In the two years before Mulroney arrived at IOC the company lost $49 million. In the autumn of 1978, after losing $78 million during a four-and-one-half-month strike, Mulroney clamped down on the unions, later claiming that they were filled with "Marxists." In the forty months since then, IOC had not had another strike. What's more, it was finally making a profit. Marius Belanger, a welder who had worked for IOC since the company began twenty-seven years earlier, said at the time that Mulroney "is the first president to really meet us. He comes to the plant and talks to us. The other big bosses—if your hand was on the floor, they'd walk on it."

At the time, Mulroney had given up booze—switching to coffee and soda water ("I don't like Perrier")—but was smoking two packs of du Mauriers a day. He would later give that up too.

In early July 1981, Mulroney held an hour-long meeting with Clark in Ottawa to discuss the possibility of his candidacy in the August 17 by-election in Joliette. Mulroney declined, blaming the Liberals for giving short notice. According to Bill Fox, then with the *Toronto Star*, Mulroney "sources" in Montreal "were quick to set the record straight. They said Mulroney in fact offered to be the Tory candidate during his session with Clark. . . ." Mulroney had renewed his contract with IOC a week earlier for a $250,000 salary. Shortly before that, Mulroney wrote a long letter, which was published in *Le Soleil*, in which he stoutly reaffirmed his undying loyalty to Clark. The candidate-in-waiting also kicked off a national speaking tour in 1982, holding a $100-a-couple dinner at Toronto's downtown Holiday Inn, with 10 MPS among the 325 blue-chip Tories. Again, he pledged allegiance to Clark, but columnist Allan Fotheringham described the event as a "daring and open challenge to Joe Clark's leadership." Mulroney gave similar speeches in Toronto on April 28 and May 5, in Vancouver on May 17, and in Fredericton on May 27.

Clark suffered another setback in May 1982 when Alberta's Don Mazankowski resigned as chairman of the Tory policies and planning committee after disclosure of a secret payment to Clark's friend (and St. F.X. grad) Senator Lowell Murray. Besides his $56,000 as a senator, it was alleged that the party was paying him $60,000 a year as national campaign chairman.

An internal party study later concluded Murray was getting just $24,000 a year extra from the party.

After an Ottawa speech in late April, Mulroney was asked why it took a heckler to force him to endorse Clark's leadership. He replied curtly that he had "endorsed Clark since he became leader six years ago on more occasions than I can count. I don't have to go around wearing a Joe Clark badge, it is well known that I am a supporter of the Conservative party and a supporter of Clark." He denied that his speaking tour was related to the upcoming Winnipeg leadership review, saying, "some people add up two and two and get five. Joe Clark is doing a fine job, and he will continue to receive my full support. I've always said there is no vacancy."

One veteran Tory, who worked for Mulroney during that time, said, "We made a deliberate decision then not to bad-mouth Clark. Everybody saw what happened when Dalton [Camp] criticized Dief. Sure, the campaign worked in that it got rid of Dief, but it made Camp a pariah. We didn't want that to happen to Mulroney. So while the speaking tour was obviously meant to drum up support for him, there was no advantage to saying that."

(Mulroney hadn't always been so discreet. At the annual press-gallery dinner in the spring of 1980, after Clark had lost the election and before Mulroney had quit drinking, New Democrat MP Lorne Nystrom was standing in the corridor, called the "Hall of Honour" at about 2:00 A.M. when Mulroney came lurching up to him. "I wondered what he wanted," said Nystrom. "I said hello to him and he leaned over and said, 'You know how fucking stupid Joe Clark is? He's so stupid even my five-year-old son [Ben] calls him a fucking wimp. That's how stupid he is.' And then he went staggering off down the hall somewhere. I couldn't believe it, talking like that about the leader, especially to a guy from another party. I used to always think about that whenever Brian was publicly declaring his allegiance to Joe," said Nystrom.)

Tim Ralfe, Clark's communications adviser, has his own view of Mulroney's strategy between 1980 and 1983. "He made noises about supporting Joe, but he didn't do anything in seventy-nine or eighty as he had in the past. He just stayed right out of it." But Ralfe was convinced that Pat MacAdam and to a lesser extent Rick Logan were working against Joe, on Mulroney's behalf, to create disarray within the caucus, and to encourage the feeling that caucus members could dissent openly without getting into trouble with the leader. "That had never happened anywhere I know of in any political party . . . and where it got to the point it was almost respectable to be talking about it openly. That was their first step, and they managed it well.

"They just kept stirring things up with the caucus so it just made it very difficult for Joe to function. That's what killed him, the caucus thing. . . . He could have stayed on after Winnipeg, but the problem was the caucus wouldn't let him function. There were enough people in caucus with enough clout, they just would have made life miserable, so his view was he had to clear it up."

Ralfe said that some of the tactics were to make the caucus appear more "democratic," when in fact it gave the anti-Clark forces even more power. Rather than appoint the whips and other positions, Clark agreed to have caucus elect them. He also agreed to the same procedure for choosing the three representatives on the party's national executive, choices the leader had always made in the past. "Joe gave in to the pressure to have these things elected, and guys like Al Lawrence . . . made things difficult for Joe at that level. They raised questions about Lowell Murray's furniture and stuff because the party rented him a furnished apartment. It was just a constant stirring of shit. They descended on Allan Gregg because when Public Affairs International bought Decima [Research Ltd.] and the owner of PAI was an established Liberal . . . Lawrence and those guys said to Joe he was using a Liberal pollster. Well, what the hell. Allan Gregg a Liberal pollster? They just played all these bloody games and it eventually wore Joe down. . . . It was an effort to get the caucus working together instead of spending all their time working on this sort of stuff." Ralfe said about one-third of the caucus was actively against Clark, one-third was in favour, and the other third didn't really have strong feelings on either side.

A group of Mulroney's Quebec backers tried to force Clark to call a leadership contest after the 1981 general meeting, where Clark got only 66.4 per cent, but Clark refused, thinking that having just lost his brief minority government in 1980, much of the vote against him at the 1981 meeting was a result of that. With two years until Winnipeg, he could turn it around in his favour. In their book *Connections*, authors Allan Gregg, Patrick Martin, and George Perlin argue (partly on the strength of party documents first published by the *Globe's* Jeffrey Simpson) that from 1980 until the 1983 Winnipeg meeting, Mulroney worked hand in hand with some of his most trusted friends and advisers to undermine Clark, while at the same time continuing publicy to pledge allegiance to the leader. (The most memorable example is the dramatic show of unity with Clark in Montreal, on December 6, 1982, a little over a month before Winnipeg.)

"That was an incredible display," says *Gazette* reporter Claude Arpin. "He had Joe over at the Ritz. It was unbelievable. They had forty people crammed into a tiny room and Brian actually put his arm around Joe and said 'He's my leader, he always will be.' And a lot of us knew that Mulroney's guys were out there with thousand-dollar bills buying delegates who were going to go to Winnipeg later to vote against Joe. That's really when I turned off him I think."

In March 1982, Clark referred to an "anonymous plotter from Quebec" who was "deliberately trying to cause internal difficulties in party ranks." Asked about this by the media, Mulroney said he was shocked to be suspected by anyone. "He [Clark] clearly is not referring to me, because I have said nothing except extremely positive things about him, his leadership, and the party."

The affair blew up at a weekend convention of the Quebec wing of the Tory party when president Peter Blaikie accused Mulroney supporters of seizing control of the wing as a first step towards forcing a review of Clark's leadership. It gathered steam when Clark warned that the plotters faced "grave consequences."

Journalist Peter Maser covered that Quebec meeting for the Ottawa *Citizen*. It was his first meeting with Mulroney. "Blaikie is out there and he's telling people, there's a war going on. There's a goodamn war going on in there.'" It turned out eventually that Mulroney supporters had captured every post on the Quebec executive.

In May, Clark took some shots at Mulroney on a Montreal radio hotline show, saying that people who don't show loyalty can hardly expect to receive loyalty in return. He said he planned to hang onto his job for fifteen years and that Mulroney could have it then, "if he's still around."

In early November 1982, when 285 employees were getting ready to trudge off for another day of work at IOC's mine in Schefferville, they heard the news on the radio—Mulroney was closing the mine. And with it, the town. Although that wasn't his story at the time.

As IOC president, Mulroney controlled the fate of several company towns in northern Quebec and Labrador, towns very much like the one he had grown up in himself. While Mulroney boasted of his record as chief of the Canadian operations, others weren't as easily convinced. In early 1981, Michel Nadeau, financial writer for Montreal's influential *Le Devoir*, revealed that the company had begun transferring virtually all company profits to its owners (seven U.S. and one Canadian), reversing a previous policy of reinvestment at a time when slumping iron-ore markets were forcing layoffs of about 1,500 of the company's 8,000 workers. The transfers uncovered by Nadeau included a $97 million (U.S.) pay-out in 1979 and dividends of $82 million (U.S.) in 1980, which led Nadeau to the conclusion that under Mulroney's rule, the cash requirements of the U.S. owners were more important than the long-term interest of the company's Canadian workers. Mulroney, absolutely furious, jumped on Nadeau for confusing the 1979 payment for a dividend, an error the journalist corrected in the rest of his series. Mulroney argued that his payments were reasonable because the company had not paid a dividend since 1971, an argument that no doubt made him popular with his corporate bosses but didn't do much for the miners at Schefferville and elsewhere who were sacrificed as a result. Mulroney also resorted to one of his favourite tricks, claiming that Nadeau had not called him to check the facts. Nadeau said he had spoken with Mulroney at least three times before the story appeared, and that Mulroney had even confirmed that the new dividend policy would continue in 1981.

Nadeau's articles on IOC's activities led to a bitter encounter between Mulroney and Alfred Rouleau, revered elder statesman of Quebec social movements and then president of the Confédération des Caisses Populaires. The caisses populaires, the Francophone equivalent of the credit-union league, are far more popular in Quebec than credit unions in English Canada, with four million clients. In a speech in Sept-Iles, Rouleau said it appeared that IOC was guilty of immoral behaviour in siphoning company profits to its American owners. Mulroney accused Rouleau of "insulting meddling" in his company affairs. For all this, however, Mulroney continued to get good media coverage, drawing on his now considerable stable of friendly media contacts to emphasize his side of the story and downplay the other side.

There is no better example of this than Schefferville, a town he doomed, thanks at least partially to the policy of transporting profits out of the country at the worst possible time for the workers. IOC profits in 1979 were $96 million; in 1980, $81 million; and in 1981, $95 million, three of the company's best years. While that provided ammunition for Mulroney's impressive business C.V., it didn't do much for the workers who marched into the mines every day.

On November 3, Mulroney apologized to local business people in Schefferville because they were the last to learn that the company was "mothballing" the mine. He said it was "not a message of joy," and suggested to residents that they should be thinking about "whether the grass is greener somewhere else." Standing below the town's emblem, "A Ferro Vinces" (Latin for "With Iron We Conquer"), he made a two-hour speech, but many refused to applaud him. He promised $10 million in severance and vacation pay to 450 iron-ore workers but added that the company's Quebec, North Shore and Labrador Railway would have to charge them for moving their belongings to Sept-Iles. Most of the town's 1,200 non-natives were talking of leaving, but Mulroney said "Schefferville will not be a ghost town." Mulroney blamed competition from Australian and Brazilian ore and denied that the Cleveland-based Hanna Mining Co. was closing down Schefferville to concentrate on a huge new investment in Brazil.

When an all-party committee of the Quebec National Assembly went to Schefferville on February 18, 1983, the *Gazette's* Claude Arpin met Mulroney at the airport. He arrived in a heavy snow storm. "He'd been in Florida, practising and rehearsing his speech for weeks. I was the only reporter out there, and he let me into his chauffeur-driven car. We went to the lodge the company owned up there [where Maurice Duplessis had died] and he had the chef prepare lunch. He was nervous. Oh Jesus, was he nervous. . . .

"He did put on a good show," Arpin noted. "He had all those charts, the government people on the committee were all sympathetic, after his presentation he went up to all the media guys and asked if he could help them with anything. It was all pretty slick. And now Schefferville is a desolate ghost town.

"He had about ten plans for the town, but nothing ever happened. He had a great delivery, he had a booklet handed out to all the reporters. He came up to the press table and shook hands with the reporters." In his fifty-six-page brief, Mulroney essentially told the history of IOC and blamed the 1973 OPEC decision to control the supply of crude oil, which he said led to an oversupply of iron-ore pellets because of an unexpected drop in world steel demand. He described how much IOC had paid in federal, provincial, and municipal taxes—$640 million since 1955—and pointed out that during the previous fifteen years another $445 million had been paid in income taxes withheld from employees' salaries. Then of course there were the contributions to hospitals, golf clubs, ski hills, sewer systems, and so on, all showing what a tremendous corporate citizen IOC was.

On November 3, 1982, when the closing was announced, IOC employed 4,113 people in Quebec and Labrador, with another 1,436 on lay-off. There were 167 employees working at Schefferville at the time of closure, plus 449 seasonal workers on lay-off. Of these, 254 had been on lay-off since between 1979 and 1981. Separation pay was based on eighty hours or two weeks' wages per year of active employment at the employee's highest rate of pay in his final two years of work. That meant that 150 full-time employees got an average of $16,400 each, while 375 seasonal employees got about $6,000 each. Mulroney also boasted that, since June 1981, employees who had bought their houses through the company had the right to resell them. He did not say who would buy them. In addition, after July 31, 1983, employees who wished to remain in Schefferville could buy company houses in a designated area of the town for $1.

Mulroney also recommended that there might be a future for Schefferville through a number of possible projects, including a military training school for Canadian Armed Forces or NATO troops, a correctional institute, a northern research centre, an institute of mining and metallurgy, increased tourism because of the "unparalleled hunting and fishing opportunities" and ski hills, a Man-power retraining centre, handicraft development for native people, and a national park.

His closing paragraph was: "Let us try to make sure that Schefferville does not fall into oblivion. We have everything to enable us to launch it on a new economic course—somewhat different and perhaps more modest than before—but one that can ensure a serious and solid future for the region. Let us make certain that we succeed in this task. This is our collective responsibility. You may be assured that this Company will co-operate fully with all interested parties in order to bring to the citizens of this region a well deserved opportunity for a new beginning."

While none of it ever happened, it looked good on paper and sounded good, and stories and editorials praised Mulroney and IOC for the generous treatment of workers. Certainly it didn't interfere with Mulroney's plans for a "new beginning" of his own—to go after the Tory leadership.

In July 1984, when Mulroney returned to Schefferville (which is in his riding) as the candidate, there were 275 non-natives left and about 900 Montagnais Indians. The town is on the edge of Knob Lake, twelve hours and 575 barren kilometres north of Sept-Iles. One woman told reporters that her husband had been five months short of being eligble for his pension at forty-five when Mulroney closed the mine, but that IOC wouldn't give it to him. The open-pit mine was half full of water, and hundreds of rail cars stood empty. The recreation centre was closed, as was the Roxy Theatre, and nine out of every ten houses stood empty. The bulletin board at city hall was filled with change-of-address cards. But it didn't matter. The people who were hanging on had only 665 votes in a riding of 49,000.

On November 26, 1982, Mulroney was in Toronto to attend Grey Cup festivities as a trustee of the Schenley Awards, when he had lunch with Finlay MacDonald, then a senior Clark adviser, at Winston's, a famous and exclusive Toronto eatery. In a column about that meeting, L. Ian MacDonald said his man Brian had decided to come out and support Clark and wanted to work out the details with Finlay MacDonald. The two met again a few days later in Toronto's King Edward Hotel, and agreed to the soon-to-be infamous December 2 Ritz-Carlton joint news conference, where Mulroney pledged his undying devotion to Clark. By doing this, in "the interest of the party and the country," Ian MacDonald argued, Mulroney distanced himself from the anti-Clark movement. "Mulroney was clearly concerned about being labelled as a hatchet man who couldn't care less about the unity of his party. . . . And as one who has worked the barren fields of Quebec for his party going back to the time of John Diefenbaker, he took exception to the impression that he was anything less than a loyal Conservative team player. By standing aside from the review battle, and placing himself above it, Mulroney cannot be blamed for anything that might go wrong for Clark in Winnipeg."

Well, just about everything went wrong for Joe Clark in Winnipeg in late January 1983. He got just about the same support the Tories had given him two years earlier. It wasn't enough, and he called a leadership contest. The lowlight of the convention occurred with Mulroney's man Jean-Yves Lortie showed up with $56,000 in two cheques to register two hundred Quebec delegates. That was supposed to be done individually in Ottawa before the convention started. Mulroney said he was "furious" that the delegates were "abused and humiliated by grossly overpaid party bureaucrats." All that happened was that credentials committee chief, MP Scott Fennell, delayed their registration while their individual credentials were checked. Mulroney called this treatment "unforgivable . . . disgusting in the extreme." While it wouldn't affect his pro-Clark vote, he said, it might have swayed some of the two hundred to vote against Clark.

Tim Ralfe's comments on "all the foofaraw about the delegates," offer an interesting sidelight on this issue. "To get a Quebec delegate to Winnipeg was $1,000. They weren't just handed a thousand bucks. But to get them out there, the plane fare, hotel, was a thousand bucks. And none of those Quebec ridings had any money, so you were paying for it. I forget what the hell we spent, $200,000 or something, getting Quebec delegates out there. He probably spent about the same. The Quebec delegates were evenly split."

Two days before the convention opened, the CBC's colourful Mike Duffy did a piece standing in front of a room in Winnipeg's Westin Hotel saying that behind that closed door the top brass of the party were plotting a plan to stab Clark. He said that the meeting had been organized by Frank Moores, who denied it, laughing into the camera saying, "No, no, I wouldn't do that." On the Saturday night of the convention, Duffy and Peter Mansbridge were commenting again that Moores was working on Mulroney's behalf. The show ended at 7:30 P.M. About thirty seconds later, Mulroney phoned the CBC's unlisted, temporary number in their mobile truck demanding to speak to Duffy, swearing at him and accusing him of trying to tie him to Moores's efforts. Moores, of course, had nominated Mulroney in 1976, worked ever since on his behalf, and was in the middle of another controversy involving $25,000 in offshore money from millionaire Walter Wolf to help finance the dump-Clark movement. Mulroney claimed that Moores was supporting Crosbie. He wasn't.

Mulroney told Claude Arpin in mid-February 1983 that he had decided to "take a look" at running for the leadership again. Reached in a hotel room in St. John's, Newfoundland, Mulroney claimed ignorance of a letter calling on Quebec Tories to elect an unnamed "charismatic Quebec businessman" to head the party. More than two thousand copies of the two-page letter were sent to likely delegates, circulated by a group calling itself "The Leadership Committee (Quebec)," and signed by three well-known Mulroney supporters, Jean Bazin, Rodrigue Pageau, and Keith Morgan. It asked Quebeckers to support a "prestigious" Quebec candidate whose decision to run would be announced soon. "I think they're probably talking about Guy Lafleur," Mulroney quipped.

Around the same time, the *Toronto Star*'s Robert McKenzie reported that Mulroney was at his rented ocean-side apartment in the fashionable resort of Delray Beach, Florida, phoning top lawyers and executives in Montreal, calling in his markers, getting them to approach key Quebec Tories who had supported Clark in Winnipeg. (To demonstrate to Tories how concerned he was with reconciliation, Mulroney in Winnipeg had convinced one of his top supporters, Quebec City lawyer Jacques Blanchard, to step aside in the race for national Francophone vice-president, in favour of Jean Riou, another Quebec lawyer who was backing Clark. Later, Riou would become credentials chairman, a key figure in the ensuing battle for Quebec delegates between Clark and Mulroney forces. He had been in the Mulroney camp in 1976.)

In early March, Mulroney invited three CBC reporters— Mike Duffy, Peter Mansbridge, and Jason Moscovitz—to his suite in the Bristol Place Hotel on Toronto's airport strip. Mulroney had been telling people that the CBC was out to get him because he was "not a member of the parliamentary club," and he wanted to make peace. He told them that he would "work his ass off for Clark." He said he had told Clark that, "I've been part of every conspiracy in the PC party since 1967 and if there's one going on now, I'd know about it." He also described how he had "dragged Little Joe up by the neck" to the 66.9 per cent vote in Winnipeg. Without his support, he said, Joe would have been dead. In light of his efforts, he wanted to know how the media can "condemn me for being involved in a plot against Joe."

In the meantime, the Mulroney plotters were meeting in a downstairs room in the same hotel, and TV cameras showed up to catch them, although Michael Meighen scurried out before the cameras got there. But Jean Bazin and Charles McMillan and other Mulroney boosters were there, about fifteen of them around the table discussing the proposition to dump Clark. On several occasions, Mulroney had telephoned CBC anchorman Knowlton Nash to complain whenever the CBC suggested he had anything to do with the anti-Clark stuff, or whenever they tied him in to Frank Moores's efforts in that regard. When the three reporters went to the meeting with Mulroney, they already had notes on at least three recent "telcons"—jargon for telephone conversations—yet Mulroney opened the meeting by saying, "I only phoned Knowlton once."

The next move by the Mulroney troops was to organize a giant, spontaneous "Friends of Brian Mulroney" night in the ballroom of Montreal's posh Queen Elizabeth Hotel. The idea was to convince a "reluctant" Mulroney that the public loved him so much he had no choice but to respond to this vast outpouring of support and affection and declare his candidacy. Mulroney already had a second-floor office above an elevator-service company on De Lormier Avenue in east-end Montreal, with a dozen full-time workers, largely middle-management executives on a three-month leave of absense from their regular jobs.

"Keith Morgan organized the party," said Claude Arpin. "Before it was held I phoned him up and asked how is it going." He said 'Simply fantastic. We're going to have to stop traffic. We sent out eight thousand invitations and there's only room for four thousand people.'

"So I wrote that the next day [March 9, the day of the dinner], and Christ, I got a call from Brian and I taped him. He was angry. He said 'Claude, this is not going to help me.' I said what do you mean? He said, 'Well, you know, you're making it sound like we're duplicists in some way, we're trying to pack a hall and stop traffic. I don't know where you're coming from. I thought that you understood me and you and I were on the same wavelength.' Then he said, 'You know, Claude, a guy like you, close to the action, there's a book in it for you.' I told him I wasn't interested in writing a book. I was doing news, and if Keith Morgan sends out twice the number of invitations that you can hold in there, it's a story. He said, 'That's too bad, you could have followed me right through on this thing and written a book about it, but I can see now this won't work with you.'

"He was luring a lot of reporters in with the book stuff," said Arpin, "promising the inside track. A lot of them bought it too."

Calling reporters to complain seemed to run in the Mulroney family. On the night of the dinner, CBC's Jason Moscovitz, a no-nonsense journalist, was on a tight deadline and had to file a piece for the Maritime CBC news before the dinner really had a chance to get going. The piece was introduced by an announcer saying that a thousand people were there, when actually about four thousand had showed up. (Mulroney claimed six thousand.) "Late that night CBC got a phone call from a guy with a deep voice," said Moscovitz. "We thought it was Brian. He said 'You guys missed the biggest story in Montreal tonight. Three thousand people disappeared according to your report.' Six months later I was covering a speech and saw [Brian's brother] Gary Mulroney, and he started attacking me for getting the figures wrong and told me he [had] phoned the news room to complain. [He] promised to send me a calculator for Christmas, so I could count the crowds. Sure enough, a week before Christmas, I received a calculator in the mail."

Crowds weren't the only things being counted in those days; delegates were. And nowhere in the country was the scrambling for bodies more vicious than it was in Quebec between the Clark and Mulroney forces.

Mulroney was telling people there'd be no razzle-dazzle in his campaign this time. He wasn't going to make the mistake again of turning off Tories with a lavish campaign. He was trading in his Cadillac for a Chevrolet, his lobster-and-champagne hospitality suites for some Tory policy papers.

On March 20, 1983, his forty-fourth birthday, Mulroney climbed into the IOC company jet and headed eight hundred miles northeast of Montreal to Sept-Iles for a farewell meeting with employees of the company he'd headed for seven years. After that, it was strictly Air Canada economy class for the next few months. No private jets this time, not in what he said would be a "frugal campaign."

The next day, he briefly interrupted his unofficial leadership campaign just long enough to make it official—on the same day, John Crosbie also announced he was running. Speaking to the National Press Gallery in Ottawa, Mulroney dodged repeated questions about his views on such major issues as Canadian oil prices, universality of social programs, capital punishment, and cruise missile testing. He did caution against Reaganomics, saying that, "Conservatives must show the Canadian people that we have about us . . . a dimension of tenderness. Of all the challenges of government, none is more noble, no obligation more sacred." By the end of this campaign and the subsequent election campaign, almost everything was to be declared "sacred" by Mulroney.

His main pitch, then and throughout the piece, was that he could, as *London Free Press* reporter Gary May put it, "twist the tail of the yellow dog that has had Conservatives treed almost continuously since the hanging of Louis Riel." "Yellow-dog riding" was the term given to a riding in which, it was said, Liberals could run a yellow dog and win. Mulroney pointed out that 102 of the 282 ridings had Francophone populations of more than 10 per cent and that in 1980 the Tories had won just 2 of those seats. In Quebec, the Tories' 12.6 per cent of the vote had been the lowest in thirty-five years, and they were even beaten by the Rhinoceros party in two seats.

It didn't take long for the dirt to come to the top. Within the week, stories that children were being recruited to vote for delegates in the rival Clark and Mulroney camps were emerging from Quebec City and Montreal. There were charges from both sides that people were telephoning delegates to say meetings had been cancelled, and there seemed to be more university-campus clubs all of a sudden than there were universities.

A *Gazette* story on March 29 described how a new breed of instant voters, some as young as fourteen, had elected a Mulroney slate in Verdun for the June 8–11 convention in Ottawa. Clark supporters failed to stop the Mulroney machine, but an anonymous call to police almost did. The upstairs room at Labelle BBQ Restaurant was overcrowded, and police sergeant Yves Tougas arrived to count heads. He found about 150 Tories in a room limited to 114. While police pondered the problem, people lined up to vote, including a group of twenty-five young people from Dawson Boys and Girls Club on Woodland Avenue who said they had joined the party two weeks earlier, although none had paid a membership fee. Michael Brennan, the club's program director said, "The truth is, the kids don't really know what PC means or who Brian Mulroney is." But they did understand a free dinner. They were each given a white coupon and sent downstairs to the restaurant. Later a Mulroney organizer came along, counted the white coupons collected by the waiter, and picked up the tab. In the meantime, the police decided the best thing to do was leave and report the situation to their superiors."

On the last weekend in March, Jason Moscovitz and a two-man crew showed up outside the Old Brewery Mission on Clark Street across from the convention centre in downtown Montreal in the riding of St. Jacques. "I had heard earlier in the week I had to go there because a Mulroney guy had said, 'It's going to be our drunks against their drunks.' I saw these guys pouring out of the mission and we got on the bus and I asked a guy if they were Clark or Mulroney supporters. 'Are you kidding?' he said. 'They're all Mulroney supporters.' He was pretty proud of it. There were fifteen or twenty drunks on the bus. It pulled up in front of the hall and we decided to interview the last guy off, because we didn't want to interfere with the picture of these guys getting off the bus all in a line lurching into the meeting. This guy didn't know what planet he was on. I asked him who gave him his membership card, who was he voting for, and he had no idea. He just told me he wanted to get rid of Lévesque. He was completely pissed."

A Mulroney official told Moscovitz the candidate was holding a news conference at his headquarters in an hour, but when Moscovitz arrived there were no other reporters there. Keith Morgan, the office manager, invited him in, and, about five minutes later, the phone rang. "I heard Morgan say, 'What a coincidence, he's right here. Do you want to speak to him?' Then he hands me the phone and it's Mulroney. He's very angry, very agitated." Among other things, Mulroney claimed Clark's workers were "beating people over the heads with baseball bats on the south shore of Montreal," and he berated the reporter for missing the story. (There was never any evidence it ever happened.) "I was obviously set up," says Moscovitz.

The drunks must have done the right thing, because Mulroney got all the delegates from that riding. Three days later Mulroney told a group of McGill University students he had asked his organizers to conduct themselves "the way I conduct myself in my public and private life—with intelligence, probity, and honour." He said he was "somewhat dismayed" that news reporters had emphasized certain unsavoury aspects of nomination meetings. When asked about Moscovitz's story, which had had a tremendous impact across the nation, Mulroney said, "They were all Canadian citizens

and many had fought for their country in the Second World
War. . . . [They have] the same democratic rights as any
other citizens." Anyway, he claimed, Clark had also used
transient men to fill other nomination meetings.

In Ottawa, party president Peter Elizinga, stung by the
Moscovitz story, called a weekend meeting of the eleven
leadership candidates to strike a "mutual agreement" to set
ground rules for future delegate-selection meetings. By that
time, of course, the bulk of the Quebec ridings had already
gone through the process.

On April 28, Mulroney told six hundred guests at a
downtown Calgary luncheon sponsored by the local PC wom-
en's caucus that Clark was endangering Canada by promising
Quebec full compensation if it opted out of constitutional
agreements. "To try to curry the favour of the Parti Québécois
organization during a leadership campaign is dangerous to the
candidate who does it, it's dangerous for the future of the party
he seeks to lead, and it's dangerous to the future of the united
country he seeks to govern." The next year, running as leader
in the federal election, Mulroney not only courted PQ support,
he had separatists running as candidates and working at all
levels of his campaign. In the Quebec provincial election a
year after that, Mulroney openly favoured the PQ over the
Liberals. But in Calgary in April 1983 he got a standing ovation
for this bit of partisan Quebec-bashing.

He didn't get quite the same reaction when he joked with a
woman who asked what role there would be for women in the
PC party he was seeking to lead. The woman, upset because he
hadn't mentioned the subject in his twenty-minute speech,
wondered if members of her sex would have a place in a
Mulroney-led party. "Could we get together for a drink later
and talk about that?" he said, to some laughter and some
audible groans.

In early May, when he launched the Quebec portion of a
cross-Canada tour, it suddenly dawned on Mulroney that he
needed a constitutional position. He had been pressed on it by
hostile French-speaking reporters in Montreal, and again by
more gentle but still insistent reporters in Trois-Rivières.

Claude Arpin, who was covering Mulroney at the time, said,
"It was soon apparent that the nationalist-leaning reporters he
would encounter all week weren't going to be silenced with
the usual platitudes." (He had snapped in Montreal days
earlier, that, "Positions that the party should adopt in constitu-

tional matters aren't devised during leadership campaigns on a Saturday night in the back of a truck.") Well, according to Arpin, Mulroney didn't write his constitutional position in a truck. He did, however, write it on the back of a Quebecair barf bag on a flight from Quebec City to Mont Joli. "I had the barf bag," said Arpin. "They couldn't deny it. They only had nine points and they wanted ten. They wanted a nice round number . . . it was thrown together on a plane ride."

It sounded like it. Their first point was, "Canada is a great country of which Quebec is an integral and important part." It went on to speak of bilingualism as "a noble objective," which should be applied, along with Bill 101, "with generosity and flexibility." It spoke of respecting minority rights, and involving everybody in constitutional changes. It concluded: "My past is a guarantee of success for the future in that, in my professional past, I have created harmony and agreement."

During the third week of May, our rotund CBC man Mike Duffy was in Edmonton on business staying at the Macdonald Hotel. That was the week that Alberta's premier Peter Lougheed had decreed that the Tory candidates should present themselves individually to him and his committee. When Mike Wilson refused to comply, the CBC asked Duffy to hang around and see what happened. Duffy was in the bar drinking a beer and eating a beef dip sandwich when one of Mulroney's agents walked over, said hello, and sat down at the table with him. Before long, there were four other candidates' agents at the table with Duffy and they began discussing a deal to beat Clark, the so-called ABC (Anybody But Clark) plan.

During the discussion, Mulroney's man said he wanted to phone them all on the weekend to discuss a deal. He said that in 1976 Clark had been the beneficiary of a deal among left-leaning Tories and Mulroney wanted to be ready this time. They ended the conversation by exchanging phone numbers. Duffy also wrote the numbers down.

Four days later, on the Saturday of the Victoria Day weekend, Duffy was at home when Mulroney's man called and said Brian wanted to call all the agents but he couldn't find the numbers. He asked Duffy for them. In return for the numbers, he promised to call Duffy back later and tell him how the other camps had responded to Mulroney's call.

Later that day, Duffy taped a piece for the Sunday-night show with Peter Mansbridge saying that Mulroney was "trying to set up" a stop-Clark coalition. Without it, said Duffy,

"Mulroney believes that Clark will win the convention." He added that former Toronto mayor David Crombie's campaign was going nowhere and that Mulroney hoped to get Crombie to pull out and endorse him (Mulroney). He thought that would be quickly followed by support on the floor from Michael Wilson, Peter Pocklington, and John Gamble. He added that because Mulroney had been burned in 1976, "that's why he's spending this long weekend on the telephone, putting together an anti-Clark coalition."

At about 11:15 P.M., shortly after the piece was aired, Mulroney phoned Mansbridge in his CBC studio in Toronto. He was furious, cursing and swearing and accusing Duffy of making the whole thing up. Mulroney yelled at Mansbridge non-stop for more than half an hour.

Mansbridge called Duffy who called Mulroney at noon the next day. (Mulroney had given Duffy his home number at the earlier Bristol Place meeting as a sign of his intention to improve their relationship.) Mulroney was still furious, swearing at Duffy. Two hours later, Canadian Press moved a story saying that Mulroney was suing Duffy over the story. Brian and Mila both denied Duffy's story, claiming they had telephoned only delegates to the conventions (which was true but clearly disingenuous, since all the agents and all the candidates except Pocklington were also delegates).

Because it was a holiday Monday, a slow news day, the story got big play. Shortly after the CP story moved across the country on their news wires, Michel Cogger, Mulroney's lawyer, phoned Duffy to say that everything would be fine. The problem had been that nobody was in the house with Mulroney. They had sent someone over there to cool him out and get him off the phone before things escalated even more. In the meantime, the CBC had interviewed Wilson, Crombie, Crosbie, and Pocklington, all of whom they had on tape admitting that Mulroney had tried to make a deal with them to stop Clark. They weren't all buying the proposal, but they agreed it had been made.

Cogger, getting increasingly worried, called the CBC and begged them for a truce, saying that Mulroney had gotten out of hand and the whole thing would be dropped. Despite that, Mulroney complained for months about how the CBC and others had falsely accused him of trying to orchestrate a stop-Clark deal.

A few days later, in front of several journalists, among them

Toronto Sun editor Peter Worthington, Mulroney again yelled at Duffy over the story, saying that it was a "total fabrication, utter falsification, a grotesque concoction." He accused Duffy of having his own nefarious reasons. Then he said to Worthington, "I see no reason why I should accept lies and incompetent journalism."

When he wrote about the incident, Worthington said, "What is it about Mulroney that is disturbing? I've seen all the candidates and in some ways he's far ahead of the rest. In other ways, something rings wrong. I like what he says. I think relations with Quebec might be improved under him. . . . So where is this false note? Well, if not exactly false, it is a bit slick, a bit shiny and polished, a trifle self-serving. He tends to sound a bit like a pre-taped message, using the same phrases, the same clichés programmed."

On May 21, Mulroney's book *Where I Stand*, published by McClelland and Stewart, hit the newsstands. It consisted of eighteen of his speeches in which he promised "a new kind of leadership" and attacked the Liberals for dividing the country while trying "to impose conformity." The eight-page photo section featured pictures of Mulroney with his family and his father, as well as a 1956 picture of him with Diefenbaker, over the caption, "this is a photograph I treasure." Paul Weed, his campaign manager, said that the book's release three weeks before the convention was a coincidence. "This isn't a campaign document, per se," he said.

The same day, in a small Cessna on the way to Lethbridge, Mulroney said to Ian MacDonald: "The big difference between 1976 and 1983 is that I'm not concerned about something like a bad or favourable editorial. It's what's in this damn briefcase that counts." He thumped it and added, "And that's votes."

Just two days later, in the living room of a private house in St. Catharines, Ontario, with a small group of delegates, Mulroney said that the party was doomed to perpetual opposition if it took the "preposterous" step of electing a unilingual leader, an obvious shot at John Crosbie. "How many seats do you think the Conservative party is going to win in Alberta if the leader can't speak English?" he asked. The following day in Ottawa, he told Canadian Press reporter Edison Stewart that he hadn't said that. "You better go back and check your records. I said no such thing." The next day in Arnprior, he went after Stewart again, claiming he had said no such thing, he had been misunderstood. He had, he claimed, said an Alberta delegate was right in saying it would be preposterous to have a unilingual leader. "I was agreeing with his reaction that indeed that was preposterous from his point of view. Nothing beyond that."

"[Mulroney] came up to me before the event in Arnprior," said Stewart, "and his voice went down and he said, 'Ed, your editors must have done something to your story.' At first he denied he'd even said it, but I'd transcribed my tape and told him I'd go back to the bus and get it. I did that and read his words back to him. By this time a small scrum had gathered and he said he was quoting some mythical guy in Calgary. It was quite a display."

As the convention drew nearer, Mulroney continued to promise jobs for loyal Tories, preferring the phrase "talent attraction" over patronage. In a June 2 speech, he defended his practice of offering perks of power to potential delegates. "If you think by telling Conservatives who have been out of office for twenty-five years that when I get into office I'm going to be looking for help, if you think that offends Conservative delegates, you don't know the Conservative party." He said party workers were "saddened" when Clark won in 1979 and didn't act quickly to appoint the party faithful to jobs. "Then there was no time for the foot soldiers of this party that are its heart and soul. We have a competent civil service, but when we come to Ottawa there's going to be a new game in town," he said.

Mulroney had travelled 38,000 miles and visited delegates in 268 ridings. When he finally beat Clark by 1,584 to 1,325 after nine hours and four ballots in the hundred-degree heat of the jam-packed Ottawa Civic Centre, he became the first Tory leader from Quebec since Sir John Abbot in 1891.

It was exactly 9:20 P.M. on a Saturday night, June 11, 1983, and Brian Mulroney had finally made it.

CHAPTER FIVE

STEPPING UP

Not long after he won the leadership and settled a few details at home—including the announcement that veteran Central Nova MP Elmer MacKay would vacate his seat for the new leader to win in a by-election—Mulroney decided to disappear for a few days to the IOC compound in Florida.

Reporters across the country were looking for him, phoning Mulroney's friends and friends of friends, their editors demanding daily updates on the glitzy new leader and his glamorous wife. Nobody could find him.

About three days into this disappearing act, reporter Claude Arpin, standing by the switchboard at the *Gazette*, just happened to glance down at the waste-paper basket and saw a message saying "Call Brian." "It was a message to Ian MacDonald who was still our columnist, and it had a Florida phone number on it. I couldn't believe it. . . . I dialled the number, and I'll be goddamned if Brian didn't answer. He said 'Who is this?' When I told him, he wanted to know how I got the number. I said everybody's got the number, it's lying around the *Gazette*. He said, 'There's only one person who has that number.' Jesus, he was some pissed off."

MacDonald had been communicating with Mulroney, reading him the content of the daily papers, keeping him informed, and keeping that number away from other reporters. "I confronted Ian with it later, and he said it was a private matter, nothing to do with the paper. I said 'You knew we were all looking for him and you were withholding this information. Who do you owe your loyalty to?' Even then, the answer was obvious."

Loyalty, of course, has always counted more with Mulroney than ethics, honesty, or ideology. It wasn't long after the leadership, for example, when Mulroney was meeting with some senior Tories in Toronto, one of a series of transitional meetings, ostensibly to smooth ruffled feathers between the various groups. The debate was about whether Allan Gregg should be kept on as the main party pollster, and the Toronto crowd was defending him when suddenly Mulroney said, "Yeah, you really don't know what he said about me." He then slipped a cassette into the VCR. An aide had taken the convention television coverage and pieced together every negative comment made about him. "It was incredible," one of those present commented; "absolutely Nixonian."

On his first day as opposition leader, Mulroney met with all the defeated candidates, then with his senior aides and advisers. The next day he was at Parliament Hill at 9:00 A.M. for his first meeting with the Tory caucus and the six Conservative premiers, where he made a pitch for party unity. That afternoon he appeared in the members' gallery, enjoying the applause from all sides of the Commons. Then Mulroney announced the members of his transition team: Michel Cogger, Jean Bazin, Charles McMillan, Roger Nantel, Paul Weed, Rodrigue Pageau, and Fred Doucet. Ottawa alderman Michael McSweeney would be appointments secretary and Pat MacAdam the liaison between the leader and the Tory caucus. Senator Lowell Murray was asked to stay on as national campaign chairman and Senator Arthur Tremblay as chairman of the Conservative policy committee. Another Clark loyalist, Erik Nielsen, was asked to stay on as parliamentary leader. Elmer MacKay was later named senior adviser. Mulroney spent hours on the phone from suite 496 in the Château Laurier hotel calling MPs who had supported other candidates, following up many calls with notes. A voracious newspaper reader, he was reading nine a day—*Toronto Star; Toronto Sun; Globe and Mail;* Ottawa *Citizen;* Montreal *Gazette;* three Montreal French dailies, *La Presse, Le Devoir,* and *Le Journal;* and Quebec City's *Le Soleil.*

A week after the convention he went home to Baie-Comeau to a hero's welcome. Mayor Henry Leonard said, "I hate like hell to say it, but Brian used a very effective campaign slogan [referring to "the boy from Baie-Comeau"] and it worked . . . he is not really one of us any more . . . but we're proud just the same."

Veteran *Toronto Star* journalist Val Sears describes a party Mulroney attended at Michel Cogger's house about that time. He arrived in Walter Wolf's helicopter. Somebody had dumped manure in Cogger's pool the night before—"likely Clark's people," said Sears. "Mulroney was asked to speak. He stood up, looked slowly around the group, and began to point his finger. 'Oh, I see the ambassador over there . . . I see senator so and so, I see the head of a Crown corporation, I see the head of such and such a company.' It seemed to some people, especially in hindsight, to be a perfect indication of his approach to power, that power is a function of rewarding people, what he can do for his friends instead of what he can do for his country, and of what power can do for him."

In early July, Mulroney was nominated in Trenton, N.S., for the August 29 by-election that would get him a seat in the Commons. He rented a fifty-six-year-old log cabin on a huge spread nearby called Pictou Lodge, complete with a floor-to-ceiling stone fireplace, three bedrooms, three baths, plus a spectacular front-porch view of Northumberland Strait, within sight of the spot where the rickety old sailing vessel *Hector* had landed on September 15, 1773, carrying 189 Scots who would eventually populate this scenic part of the country. Elmer MacKay, of course, is a direct descendant of those settlers. At $250 a week, the lodge would be home for Mulroney and his family for the next few months.

Meanwhile Mulroney's own home became an object of interest to the press. A July 5 story in the *Gazette* revealed that Mulroney didn't actually own his impressive Westmount house at 68 Belvedere Drive. The house was up for sale—asking price $750,000—because the family was planning to move to Stornoway, the opposition leader's official Ottawa residence. The story noted that the Mulroneys had held a 4 per cent mortgage from IOC when he was president, but that, according to records at the Montreal registration office, they had not owned the house since November 5, 1981. Moreover, a mortgage had never been entered in the records. The record showed that Mila had bought the house in 1976 under her maiden name, for $1 plus "good and valuable consideration," from local dress manufacturer Arthur Sanft. Sanft had owned it for just two months. In 1981 the house was sold to IOC. Company officials refused to discuss the matter.

After a brief holiday in Bermuda, Mulroney began campaigning in Central Nova, drawing huge crowds, attacking the Liberals, promising prosperity in this poverty-plagued region. He was dubbed, by Liberal candidate Alvin Sinclair, "The Casanova Candidate . . . He'll Love Us and Leave Us"— prophetic words, as it turned out. He took a few days in early August to campaign for Tory Gerry St. Germain in the Mission Port Moody by-election, campaigned with former hockey great Bobby Orr, and met the three Maritime premiers at the Peter Pan Motel in New Glasgow. He repeated his theme that medicare was "a sacred trust" and said he would restore the original 50-50 split between federal and provincial governments to pay for it. He never did. A Gallup poll one month after his convention victory showed that 74 per cent of those polled could name the new leader and 62 per cent believed he'd be an asset to the Tories.

For their part, the Liberals kept sending in their big guns, Jean Chrétien, Gerry Regan, Robert Kaplan, Mark MacGuigan, and Allan MacEachen, but it was a Tory riding with an exciting new leader, and they knew it was hopeless. Liberal president Iona Campagnolo described him as "popular. He's new. I think he's cute and he's very funny. And if he's forced into a tight corner he'll tell you what his pollster told him to say." She said he shouldn't complain about Liberals playing rough. "He's the one who smiled on his leader while his team was undermining the leader. . . . I think of Mulroney in terms of the mythical mugwump. He straddles the fence with his mug on one side and his wump on the other."

No matter, Mulroney's glad-handing, no-policy campaign from his shore-side log cabin buried his opponents. He got 60 per cent of the vote, beating the Liberal by 10,000. The victory prompted him to say, "There is no longer such a thing as a safe Liberal seat anywhere in Canada." Sweating under TV lights, he took Mila's hand and joined the crowd in singing "When Irish Eyes Are Smiling."

Having won himself a seat, he turned his attention to the prospect of a national election, naming Senator Finlay MacDonald as head of a transition team to study government procedures and personnel. "If we gain power I am not going to deliver the party to the civil servants and then ask them what to do and how to do it," he said. He named nine other friends to senior posts. Janis Johnson, a close friend of Mila and ex-wife of Frank Moores, became national director; Cogger, who is considered Mulroney's closest friend, became his chief counsel; top fund-raiser David Angus was named chairman of the PC Canada Fund; Gisèle Boivin Morgan, associate national director. Eric Dorion, a Quebec City student, was executive assistant to Johnson. Two long-time Tory fund-raisers, Don Matthews of London and Irving Gerstein of Toronto, were promoted, Matthews to vice-chairman of the PC Canada Fund and Gerstein to association vice-chairman for Ontario. Fred Doucet was named chief of staff, with Lee Richardson, recruited from Lougheed's office, as his deputy.

On August 31, a hectic day of appointments, Angele Dostaler, who had worked as press secretary for Clark and then for Nielsen when he was interim leader, kept assuring reporters she would try to find out when new appointments would be announced. By mid-afternoon she had an unexpected announcement to make. "I've just been fired," she said.

Finlay MacDonald and Marjory LeBreton, special assistant in charge of the leader's travels, were holdovers from the Clark days. MacKay was now a senior adviser. Charles McMillan was special assistant for policy and research; Pat MacAdam, special assistant; Thomas Van Dusen, special asistant; Ian Anderson, director of communications; Claudy Mailly, Anderson's assistant. William Pristanski and Hubert Pichet became executive assistants, and Ginette Pilotte, Mulroney's secretary from his days with the law firm and as IOC president, became his executive secretary. Not long after that, Norm Atkins, chief engineer of Ontario's legendary Big Blue Machine, was named campaign chairman. Now all Mulroney needed was an election. He was ready.

"I was delighted when Brian won the leadership and, like Bill Davis did in 1971, he immediately made moves to bring together as best he could the factions," said Finlay Mac-Donald, who had supported Clark.

MacDonald said that being in the wilderness for so many years, the Tories had lost a whole generation of potential workers, middle-management people who know how government is run and had had experience running it. In midsummer, MacDonald unveiled his working plan to Mulroney in New Glasgow, and then in September to the Tory caucus meeting at Mont Ste. Marie. The Tory strategy was to be ready for an election by March 1984, no later.

MacDonald said the senior civil servants were completely

co-operative, especially Trudeau's chief civil servant Gordon Osbaldeston. They had regular briefings with the privy council office as well. There was apparently great suspicion among the Tories of Michael Pitfield, clerk of the privy council, a feeling "that he was a rotten, dirty Grit, a close friend of the PM, that he wouldn't give anybody any information." The Tories didn't realize, in MacDonald's view, that Pitfield would have been obliged to give·them information if they'd asked for it. "The longer you're in opposition, the more suspicious you become of the public service" he noted.

On Wednesday, February 29, 1984, with Parliament shut down, Brian Mulroney on a beach in Florida, and John Turner in Jamaica, Pierre Trudeau dropped by Parliament Hill to tell the media he'd taken a long walk in a blizzard the night before and decided to retire. "We had a great snow storm last night. The skies were right. I went for a long walk, came back at midnight, took a sauna, got rid of all the accumulated baggage, and just made up my mind. It was clear to me," said Trudeau. "I went to sleep—just in case I changed my mind overnight. I didn't."

There would be only two serious candidates to succeed him, Jean Chrétien and John Turner. The blue-eyed Turner, the *Toronto Star's* leader-in-waiting ever since he had quit Trudeau's cabinet a decade earlier, had little trouble convincing Liberals his time had finally arrived. On June 16, Mulroney sent a hand-written letter to Turner. It said: "Mila and I have just watched your impressive victory. We want to convey to you, Geills and the children our warm good wishes for health and happiness in the future." The letter was signed, "Sincerely, Brian."

After winning the convention and becoming prime minister, Turner announced his twenty-eight member cabinet on June 30. A Sorecom poll earlier that month showed the Liberals leading the Tories 62 to 28 in Quebec, and other polls gave Turner a small, but soft, lead over Mulroney and his Tories. A week later, Turner flew to London to ask the Queen to postpone her visit to Canada. Buoyed by a Gallup poll showing the Liberals at 49 per cent, compared to the Conservatives' 38, Turner called a September 4 federal election. It was not his best-ever move.

Despite his lead in the polls, Turner was not ready for an election. His staff wasn't ready, his party wasn't ready. And as things turned out, Canadians weren't ready for another four years of Liberal rule. Mulroney was confident from the outset, saying, "We're going to eat them for breakfast," reminding supporters that Diefenbaker had come from behind in the polls to win in 1957.

It didn't take long for Mulroney to say good-bye to Central Nova and announce he would run in Manicouagan, a traditional Liberal riding that includes his home town of Baie-Comeau. On July 13, his voice choking with emotion, Mulroney told 150 people in New Glasgow, Nova Scotia, that he'd never forget their support. A year earlier, 3,000 people had attended his nomination meeting. (Ever since, residents of the riding have complained, he totally ignored them. They even sent a petition to Ottawa at one point to register their unhappiness.)

This was no time to worry about minor criticisms, however. He had a world to conquer, especially the Quebec portion of it, and he wasn't about to rest until he'd won. The turning point came with the TV debates in late July, when he demolished Turner, largely on the question of patronage. From then on there was no looking back. A *Globe and Mail* CROP poll of 456 eligible voters in Toronto and Montreal showed that 47 per cent of the Torontonians and 39 per cent of the Montrealers who had watched the French and/or English debate thought Mulroney had won. Only 16 percent in Montreal and 12 per cent in Toronto picked Turner. NDP leader Ed Broadbent won the hearts of 29 per cent in Toronto, but just 4 per cent among Montreal viewers. The only real question now was how large the Tory majority would be. Few believed it would be as massive as it was.

Ontario premier Bill Davis rushed to campaign for Mulroney, after half-hearted efforts on Clark's behalf in the previous two campaigns. (That was partly because Clark hadn't particularly wanted his help.) By mid-August, the Gallup showed that Mulroney had jumped ahead to a 46-32 lead, a stunning turn-around in a month. Even more spectacularly, the poll gave the Tories an 11 per cent lead in Quebec. Weeks before the election itself, journalists began writing features on the most likely cabinet ministers in the new government, a fair indication of what everyone expected to happen on September 4. Even Mulroney had to cool some of his usual bravado late in the campaign and begin telling Tories not to be overconfident. "The battle is not yet won," he told about 150 people at the airport in London, Ontario, on August 31. "It will go on until the fourth."

There was only one near-mishap for Mulroney on election day, when a group of workers began painting the heavy, wooden platform backdrop in the arena at Baie-Comeau's Centre Récréatif. The set was about half finished when a Mulroney aide noticed that the colour was not a deep Tory blue, but a paler *péquiste* blue. There was a scramble to a local hardware store to get more paint and to repaint the part that had already been done. Everything else went well. The Liberal defeat, the worst the party had ever suffered, left them just 40 seats. There were 211 Tories, 30 New Democrats, and 1 Independent. About 76 per cent of eligible voters cast their ballots, half of them for Mulroney's Tories, the third largest percentage vote in Canadian history, behind the 1917 Unionist party's 57 per cent, and Diefenbaker's 53.7 per cent in 1958. In Quebec, which the Liberals had owned for decades (except for the Diefenbaker sweep), Mulroney scored a stunning break-through, winning 58 of 75 seats. In 1980, Joe Clark had captured one.

Mulroney's friend Sam Wakim, caught up in the election night chanting, clapping, shouting, and dancing by the delirious crowd of several thousand well-wishers, turned at one point to *Toronto Star* journalist Richard Gwyn, and, breaking off a "Brian, Brian," chant, said, "You want to know Brian's vision? This is it. It comes from here. It's all around you."

It was there too. The genesis of his "small towns and big dreams" campaign, the "outsider" who made it to the top, and the tight network of friends who helped him get there and would soon reap their reward. It had been a twenty-five-year network that ultimately forged the win, and by God, they were going to enjoy it.

It was several months before the dream began to sour, but even then at the height of their justifiable euphoria, Gwyn perceptively wrote, "Power, of course, almost always changes almost everything. The sheer possession of power, and its pomp and privileges, will osmotically transform many of those around Mulroney, from aides to ministers, from outsiders to insiders. Anyway, the governing establishment is experienced and resilient and adroit: it has, for instance, turned Clark into one of its own."

It didn't take Mulroney long to break his first campaign promise. While wooing voters in Chatham in south-western Ontario in August, Mulroney had announced that he planned to attend Mayor Margaret Archibald's wedding on September 13. "I'm coming back for that wedding and I want to come back as the prime minister of Canada." Obviously, he couldn't make it. It wasn't a big thing—it was to the bride and groom, of course, and it got Mulroney big headlines in the local paper. But it was typical of his habit of overstating the case with little, if any, thought to the consequences.

(Stewart McLeod, Ottawa columnist for Thompson Newspapers, who first came to the National Press Gallery in 1962, says, "Most of his troubles stem from just overspeaking. Just about everything can be traced back in one way or another to him talking too much. Too many promises. Everything comes back to haunt him. He didn't have to comment on everything, including patronage and his lofty ideals. He could have got elected by saying a lot less. But there's so much on the record. We didn't make it up. It was tossed out by the party. It's right there, all these promises he couldn't possibly keep.")

On September 17 Brian Mulroney became Canada's eighteenth prime minister and immediately announced a forty-member cabinet, the largest in Canadian history. He named sixteen former ministers from the Clark regime, including Clark himself, who got External Affairs. By region, Ontario and Quebec had eleven ministers each; the west, thirteen (including Erik Nielsen from the Yukon); and Atlantic Canada, five. Seven of the eleven Quebeckers were rookies, and few were put in influential portfolios, a sharp reversal from the Trudeau era when most senior jobs went to Quebeckers by definition. Yet it wouldn't be just rookies like Suzanne Blais-Grenier, Andrée Champagne, and André Bissonnette who would stumble. Such seasoned veterans as John Fraser, Robert Coates, Elmer MacKay, Sinclair Stevens, and Walter McLean, none of them from Quebec, would also run into varying degrees of difficulty.

The rest of that month was a public-relations dream for Mulroney, beginning with the pomp and circumstance of the swearing-in and the euphoria of a new government (with more than one hundred rookie MPs), and followed in short order by his televised meeting with Pope John Paul II, an hour-long meeting with U.S. president Ronald Reagan, a speech at his old alma mater, St. Francis Xavier, and, finally, bopping about the country-side as prime minister during the Queen's fourteen-day tour of Canada.

Parliament would convene November 5 and, no matter how you cut it, the world was his oyster.

CHAPTER SIX

DRIVING IN THE WEDGE

It began well. Brian Mulroney had barely settled in his prime-ministerial chair when he announced that the premiers would gather at Meech Lake on November 13, 1984, to discuss the agenda for an economic summit early in 1985. Several times during the election campaign, he had pledged to end the bitter federal-provincial feuding that had dominated the Trudeau era. He promised national reconciliation and co-operative federalism.

"We do not have the answers to all of the problems," he had told four hundred cheering people at an election-campaign barbecue in Scarborough on July 29. "But what we do have is a desire to listen, to understand, and to commit ourselves to an honourable effort to improve Canada for all of you." The Liberal tradition of fighting with the provinces had, he said, inflicted too much "pain and genuine sorrow" on ordinary Canadians.

In November, when the premiers trooped out of their meeting to announce a tentative agenda for a two-day first ministers' economic summit in Regina, to start on Valentine's Day 1985, even Quebec's René Lévesque said, "One swallow doesn't make a whole spring but it was a good afternoon. It's an encouraging step towards co-operative federalism." For New Brunswick's Richard Hatfield, comparing the tone of this meeting with those under Trudeau was like comparing "cheese and chalk." Saskatchewan premier Grant Devine said that Valentine's Day had been chosen because, "It's very symbolic of the change in attitude and atmosphere we felt today."

Mulroney had been working on this aspect of his national strategy for some time. Even before he became prime minister he started trying to mollify the East and the West. In a speech in Calgary in November 1983, during which he won three ovations and was interrupted eighteen times by applause, Mulroney promised to wipe out key elements in the Liberals' "punitive" National Energy Program. He characterized what he called the unfair and unexpected taxes on oil companies as "exactly like a hold-up at the corner gas station at 3:00 A.M." Later that month, speaking to 1,600 Vancouver businessmen who had paid $150 each to attend the biggest fund-raiser in B.C. history, he promised that one-third of a Tory cabinet would go to westerners.

On March 22, 1984, he released his "four pillars" of Conservative policy for "a national program of reconstruction and renewal." Speaking to the Montreal Chamber of Commerce, he listed those pillars as: lower interest rates, development of technology, development of job training, and becoming traders to the world.

In June, on the eve of the Liberal leadership convention that saw John Turner succeed Pierre Trudeau, Mulroney announced he had reached agreement-in-principle with Newfoundland premier Brian Peckford on an offshore energy accord. The pact recognized the recent Supreme Court ruling that says coastal resources belong to Ottawa rather than to Newfoundland; however, unlike previous Liberal offers, the accord allowed the province the right to tax the energy producers separately, rather than settle for a share of federal taxes, as the federal Liberals had offered.

During a campaign speech in Moncton, on August 1, Mulroney said to eight hundred cheering Tories at the Beaver Curling Club, "I have no hesitation to inflict prosperity on Atlantic Canada." A week later, speaking in Sept-Iles, Quebec, he promised to set up a permanent advisory body to give provincial premiers a voice in national politics. "Our first task is to breathe a new spirit into federalism. I am convinced that the serious deterioration of federal-provincial relations is not exclusively the result of the constitutional deficiencies. Centralistic and negative attitudes are much more to blame. How many jobs have been lost, how many projects have failed, and how many opportunities for dialogue have been missed because of the distrustful, quarrelsome, and intolerant attitudes of leaders?"

Speaking to two hundred party organizers packed into his committee headquarters, Mulroney said that a Conservative government's job-creation and economic-recovery policies would be "in harmony with provincial policies." He said his federal-provincial committee of the eleven first ministers would "end parallel or incompatible planning once and for all between the two orders of government."

From the 1960s until 1982, federal-provincial meetings had been held virtually on an annual basis. But Trudeau, angered at what he saw as provincial grandstanding at the February 1982 conference, had simply refused provincial requests for another one. The 1979 Task Force on Canadian Unity, co-chaired by former Ontario premier John Robarts and former federal minister Jean-Luc Pepin, had recommended a permanent new chamber of Parliament—to be called the Council of Federation—composed of delegates appointed by the provincial governments. It would replace the Senate, and its job would be to deal with contentious federal-provincial matters.

There was no doubt that after the Trudeau years Mulroney was a breath of fresh air for the provincial premiers, most of whom at the time were Tories anyway. He did get a bit carried away with his national reconciliation theme during a late August speech in Gander, Newfoundland, when he accused the Liberals of having "willfully excluded" Western Canada from the decision-making process for twenty years. "They have made it a joke. The Liberals kid about how smart they are that they've excluded Western Canada. . . ." When he was asked for details about which Liberals had "joked" about their inability to win Western seats, his press aide Michel Gratton said Mulroney had been speaking "rhetorically. . . . That's just his style."

Mulroney's first cabinet, with its record forty members, had twelve westerners, three from each province, close to the one-third he had promised. Ontario and Quebec had eleven each, Nova Scotia had two, and Newfoundland, Prince Edward Island, New Brunswick, and the Yukon had one each. More importantly, of the fifteen-member exclusive inner cabinet, only three were from Ontario and seven were westerners, even though all the Western provinces plus the Yukon and Northwest Territories combined had elected sixty-one Tories, six fewer than Ontario elected.

By late fall, Mulroney had announced a cavalcade of conferences and consultations, signalling his intention to make people forget the autocratic Trudeau. As well as the premiers' conference, there would be a national economic summit, which, he insisted, would have a major part in government policy-making. Finance minister Michael Wilson would be in charge of the March 22-23 summit, and long-time Mulroney friend Stanley Hartt, a former Liberal, was named chairman. (For his efforts, Hartt was later named deputy minister of finance.) In addition, there would be meetings of federal and provincial finance ministers and ministers of economic development.

Everything was so swell that people barely noticed when Michael Wilson left some confidential notes and letters in a Winnipeg hotel lobby after a news conference with Manitoba finance minister Vic Schroeder and the *Winnipeg Free Press* published them. One letter, referring to requests by Manitoba for a reduction in a $72 million cut in federal equalization payments, contained the statement: "no compelling arguments have been advanced thus far which suggest you should encourage Manitoba to believe that such assistance is a possibility." Mulroney awkwardly corrected John Turner by quoting from documents, then denied knowledge of their existence. He made specific reference to the controversial dossier, then suddenly said, "I have no idea what document [Turner] is referring to." Turner accused Wilson of misleading Manitoba by saying he did not know what the cost of reviewing and raising equalization would be, when "he had in his possession a memorandum from the deputy minister of finance which indicated the cost would be $1.3 billion." Mulroney angrily referred to the documents as "pilfered," prompting NDP leader Ed Broadbent to say, "It is a curious world when a cabinet minister is so sloppy and careless to leave behind a document that the prime minister accuses someone else of pilfering." To make matters worse, John Sadler, a Wilson aide, had secretly taped the meeting without Wilson's knowledge. The two finance ministers only discovered it when they heard an electronic "beep, beep" to signal the end of the tape. Wilson immediately apologized to Schroeder and in the Commons, Mulroney condemned the taping as "unworthy and repugnant," while defending Wilson.

On February 12, 1985, Mulroney and Peckford signed an offshore energy agreement that was touted as the key to solving Newfoundland's chronic economic woes. "Most of all, this agreement is about dignity for Newfoundland and Lab-

rador, long a have-not province," said Mulroney. "Today marks
the beginning of a new era, one that will ensure provincial
economic well-being and collective accomplishments." Known
as the Atlantic Accord, it featured a $300 million development
fund to give to the province the infrastructure needed for
petroleum development. Ottawa would pay $225 million, the
province $75 million. The governments would have equal
representation on a seven-member management committee
headed by a neutral chairman. Ottawa would control the pace
of development until Canada achieved energy self-sufficiency,
and Newfoundland would control the mode of development in
an area covering 1.8 million square kilometres. All they
needed was oil.

Mulroney then left Ottawa on February 13 for Regina. (He
also left behind his first serious political problem, the
resignation that day of defence minister Bob Coates, who quit
after an Ottawa *Citizen* report on his visit to a German strip
club.)

Still, Mulroney was in a buoyant mood, looking forward to
getting on with his new Canada. As he told Regina *Leader Post*
columnist Dale Eisler, "one of the problems with Canadian
federalism is that the well had been poisoned because of the
manner in which the federal government treated the provinces
and the regions of Canada. There was a belligerence in the
attitude that sort of precluded any major successful
initiatives."

He expressed his belief in trying to achieve harmony by
going "the extra mile" because "the process of accommodation
ensures major decisions can be made in a spirit that allows for
economic growth and prosperity. . . . This kind of process,
as exemplified by the ministers' conference, is a process of
healing and coming together."

And come together they did at the federal-provincial love-
in, which opened with Premier Grant Devine greeting
Mulroney on the tarmac and talking of the "extremely
symbolic move and historic move of having a first ministers'
conference outside of Ottawa," and ended with even
Manitoba's churlish NDP premier, Howard Pawley, conceding
that he was "pleased" with the new spirit of the conference.
(Still he couldn't resist one shot at the banks, saying, "This new
government is not going to improve investment, jobs, or
remove the regional economic disparities if we don't ensure
that decisions that are made by politicians are reflected in
Bank of Canada policies.")

As for Mulroney, after announcing that the first ministers had agreed to annual meetings, he said it was "just a beginning. There are bound to be mistakes and heartbreak before we get it right. But I'm satisfied we're headed in the right direction."

As Ontario premier Frank Miller commented, "I came away from the Regina conference with an extremely high impression of his skill as chairman and as a person able to bring the premiers to about as close as a unanimous view as I've ever seen them. Even Pawley was hard pressed to say anything unkind about the prime minister following the meeting."

For various reasons, however, the good impression didn't last. "I think we started to see some chinks in the armour shortly after. There were some very much touted programs by Flora MacDonald in which the government claimed to have new money and it became apparent they didn't. . . .

"Nothing slows a provincial politician down faster than money," said Miller. "So when the money didn't seem to match what some of them thought they heard in Regina, there were at first subdued rumblings, and then later, of course, open ones. . . . I think Brian underestimated even when everybody wants to agree with you, how hard it is to get agreement where money is at stake. Even giving it to them can't buy it. You can't buy, no matter what you give away from the store, peace for long in the Canadian federation."

For a while, according to Miller, Mulroney tried to buy that peace, with the National Energy Program, the Atlantic Accord, and so on. "I think he felt by showing good faith at the federal level, and I think he was trying to show good faith, that it would be reciprocated. They would say, 'Well, fine, let's forget about our problems.' Well, they didn't. They would say, 'We got that, we've still got the problems.'

"I would say he's a much more chastened person at this point in terms of trusting the provinces. I would bet he feels he's been taken to the cleaners rather than the reverse in federal-provincial relations. He's discovered the inevitable fact that whether there's a Liberal or Conservative government in Ottawa, a provincial premier of any stripe is not going to agree with him too long. A premier needs one or two ingredients to win an election in Canada, either a fight with the feds or a fight with the Americans. If you have both, you've really got it going for you."

According to Miller, Mulroney had begun to "withdraw" by the time of the aboriginal conference in Ottawa in early April 1985, and in March 1987, Mulroney again failed to fashion an agreement on native self-government when the two-day conference ended bitterly, with accusations of racism from native leaders and open flashes of anger from just about everybody who attended, including Mulroney. In fact, Mulroney banged the conference table with his fist when Peckford cautioned the natives not to consider inclusion in the constitution a cure for their economic and social woes. "I am a premier, yet I must still talk about our fish, about our right to self-determination, just like you are today," Peckford said. "We are a welfare state, just like the aboriginal people are. Yet you look up to me just because I'm a premier. I'm not so sure you're being as smart as you think." In any event, with Quebec premier Robert Bourassa boycotting the meeting to protest the slow pace of constitutional talks with his province, Mulroney couldn't get the required support—seven provinces representing 50 per cent of the population—for a constitutional amendment, and the meeting ended in a shambles, with native leaders threatening court action and civil disobedience.

Meanwhile, back in March 1985 when the sun was still beating down on his government, Mulroney opened his national conference on the economy with a plea for consensus among the country's business, labour, government, and citizen's groups. He told the 136 delegates at the glitzy, public-relations affair that "We must begin somewhere and it is here . . . that we begin. We have to improve our understanding of the kinds of choices to be faced in dealing with major economic issues. The problems are real. Some of the choices will be hard. The process will be difficult.

"Let those who question the need for consultation examine the record of confrontation in this country and the results of conflict and recrimination . . . let everybody understand the need. Consensus is the only way to let Canada adapt, compete, and prosper," said Mulroney.

While the conference received considerable media attention and Mulroney declared it a success, not all the participants agreed. Six months later, in response to the May budget, more than one-third of them published an open letter to Mulroney expressing their "serious reservations about your Government's economic and social priorities," adding that the budget had not been "an accurate reflection of the majority opinion that you sought at the national economic conference. We expected that you would take our views into account. But you have disappointed us."

Some of the tough choices Mulroney had been speaking of were beginning to surface by this point. When, in April 1985, energy minister Pat Carney ended six months of hard federal-provincial bargaining with her counterparts in British Columbia, Alberta, and Saskatchewan, that agreement—called the "Western Accord"—effectively spelled the end of the 1980 NEP, guaranteeing higher gasoline prices and promising an estimated $8,000 million in revenues for the oil companies in 1985. Referring to Peter Lougheed's famous 1980 critique of the NEP as an attempt by Ottawa to walk into Albertans' homes, Alberta's jubilant energy minister, John Zaozirny, said, "They are not only off the porch, but off the property." But just as Alberta had toasted the NEP originally, only to blame it for all their economic ills, the Western Accord would fall on evil days when the bottom fell out of the oil industry months later.

Even some of Mulroney's public optimism started to fade when he emerged from a two-hour meeting with the provincial premiers on April 5 at 24 Sussex Drive to declare the federal deficit a "grotesque" problem that must be tackled. "We have been left a legacy of historic and unprecedented proportions of mismanagement of your money. We have to deal with it. I wish it were otherwise. I wish I could give you better news, but I can't. All I can tell you is that the chickens have come home to roost. The Liberals have left us with that problem and we are going to have to deal with it."

Wilson announced that the deficit would be increased by $220 million to cover extra equalization payments to the six poorest provinces. While Nova Scotia's John Buchanan praised Mulroney as "the nicest prime minister we've had in my lifetime around here, other than John Diefenbaker," Quebec finance minister Yves Duhaime said that the conversation was "quite general. We had breakfast, good eggs and beans. Well, I mean, eleven people around the table. We didn't have a lot of time to talk." He did, however, have time to register Quebec's anger at receiving only an additional $110 million worth of equalization payments, well below the $263 million it was seeking.

Still, things were looking so great for Mulroney in May that his long-time friend, journalist Peter C. Newman, was gushing in his *Maclean's* business column about the wonders of

Mulroney's "secret political agenda"—to forge an alliance between Quebec and the West, much as Mackenzie King had done, an alliance designed to keep him in power "for at least the next dozen years." Already, wrote Newman, "the transformation of Quebec from the safe haven of Canadian Liberalism to a dependable bastion of Toryism—is in the process of being consolidated." He cited a recent Conservative poll, which indicated that nearly two-thirds of Quebeckers "now consider themselves Conservatives federally. The same survey placed the Liberals in the Prairies at an all-time low of nine per cent." Things would change.

While the apopletic Trudeau-bashing had gone, the four western premiers meeting in May at Grande Prairie, Alberta, still had their same old shopping lists of complaints about such things as loan rates for farmers, tax reform, agricultural stabilization plans, and an age-old lament—Ottawa's attempt to pass its economic problems on to the provinces by cutting transfer payments.

A major change in the provincial landscape occurred when fledgling Ontario premier Frank Miller limped out of the May 2 election with fifty-two seats, four ahead of the Liberals. The NDP had twenty-five. After a series of hectic backroom negotiations leading to a two-year accord with the NDP, Liberal David Peterson finally emerged as premier, ending forty-two years of Tory rule in Canada's largest province. Mulroney had campaigned briefly for Miller, but had retreated quickly when polls showed that the Tories were not doing well. Now he said he would work "as closely and as intimately as I can" with the Liberals. "I have always tried, irrespective of the political stripe of the government, the duly elected government of a given province, to co-operate fully and openly with that government, be it anywhere."

Mulroney even boasted that he had known Peterson for years and would have no problem getting along with him. At a summer caucus meeting, he claimed that he and Peterson used to "whore around" together in Montreal, an expression that upset Tory back-bencher Jim Jepson, a devout Baptist from London, Peterson's home town. Peterson's memory was that he had met Mulroney a few times, but that they weren't quite the bosom buddies Mulroney had described. He did remember going to a party with a woman and having Mulroney leave with her, however. Peterson's press secretary George Hutchison, asked about Mulroney's comments at the time, said the two men had been "social acquaintances. They didn't chum around together though." Asked about the descriptive language used by Mulroney, Hutchison said, "I'm not sure that's how it would be characterized from this end." When Jepson complained to Mulroney's long-time aide Pat MacAdam about what he saw as Mulroney's inappropriate description of their long-ago acquaintanceship in Montreal, an angry Mulroney suggested that Jepson could "fuck himself" if he didn't like it.

Peterson, who had criticized Miller both during and after the campaign for being too cosy with the federal Tories, wasted little time in attacking Mulroney. He accused him of having "systematically neglected Ontario's interests" in such things as funding for youth employment, gasoline pricing, the Western Accord, and equalization. Two days later, after a private dinner in Toronto, Peterson dropped his criticism and said, "I think the prime minister is sensitive to the needs of Ontario as the industrial heartland." After the meeting in a fifteenth-floor hotel suite near Toronto's airport, Mulroney said, "Neither of us would do anything that wouldn't be in the best interests of either the people of Ontario or the people of Canada."

In July, another significant change in provincial politics occurred when Alberta's Peter Lougheed announced that he too was leaving, after fourteen years as premier, joining Bill Davis and René Lévesque on the sidelines. Mulroney commented on the "profound changes of attitude, of personnel, of perception," that these departures meant for the political landscape. Privately, Mulroney aides conceded that their man was pleased by these departures, since he would now appear less of a neophyte in federal-provincial matters. The changes certainly lessened the chances of continued hostility, since Davis was no longer around to fight with Lougheed over oil pricing, and Trudeau and Lévesque couldn't go head-to-head over separatism.

With that in mind, in August 1985 Mulroney announced a series of one-on-one meetings with the premiers, beginning with Richard Hatfield on August 25, and leading up to yet another first ministers' confab (on September 17 in Ottawa) on the question of free trade.

In late August, when he was approaching his first anniversary as PM, Mulroney emerged from a cabinet meeting to declare that his opening year had been a success. "When you see inflation is maintained at a record low, when you see four or five vital economic indicators going the right way, that's a major accomplishment.

"And when you say what did they campaign on, what was the second part of their theme . . . the second part of the theme was national reconciliation. The NDP devastated Western Canada for five years. We solved it. Fifteen years ago, Newfoundland asked for a fair shake on offshore, another regional problem. We solved that. Quebec dropped the separatist option in November and December, because of a new attitude significant for Canada. A record number of agreements signed with the Province of Quebec [indicate] we're reaching out to find a formula to make them part of Canada.

"So those were the two main objectives . . . and I think we've done pretty well, and I think an objective observer would find that." He added that, "for the first time in twenty-five years Western Canada is now very much a part of the decision-making process in Ottawa with literally dozens of powerful cabinet ministers sitting around a table from Western Canada. . . . Western power is back in existence." (Thirteen of the forty ministers were from the West. A Gallup poll released a week earlier showed that Tory support had declined in early July to 40 per cent, down from 44 in June and 60 the previous October.)

In October 1985, Mulroney said that he wanted provincial representatives present during any talks on freer trade between Canada and the United States. "What I would want to see is a mechanism where a senior official of the various provinces would be present during the negotiations to make sure that their input and co-operation were there if there were to be negotiations." Mulroney said that Peterson had asked for this and that "I would do this for all provinces. If we were to have negotiations it would be with an almost daily consultation process with the parties involved, otherwise it would lead to absolutely nothing."

Well, the consultations haven't been "almost daily," although Senator Lowell Murray, the minister for federal-provincial relations, says that the promise to consult the provinces on trade has been kept. "There's a first ministers' conference where the prime minister and the premiers get together every three months and get reports from [trade minister Pat] Carney and [chief trade negotiator] Simon Reisman. They renew Reisman's mandate and he goes back. The trade ministers meet every three months and then after every negotiating session our guys, the federal negotiating team, get up from the table and will have a conference call which may go two hours with their provincial counterparts. The provinces find out what's going on before some of us who are on the cabinet committee know, so they're in tight on things like that."

Murray had also said that first ministers' conferences "threaten to become almost an institution of confederation. What they're doing now that never happened before is finding the first ministers giving a work plan to their ministers and officials between meetings. For example, in Halifax in 1985 they gave the once-over-lightly to women's issues and they decided they weren't very satisfied with that so they left instructions for a work plan for the ministers on training, and sure enough they worked on it."

Things took a turn for the worse in October 1985, when Ottawa told the provinces it planned to advance by one year its plan to shave $2 billion from the federal transfers to the provinces, likely by cutting post-secondary education and health spending. The government had already said it wanted to cut its share of these payments beginning in April 1987, when the five-year federal-provincial agreement expired. Ottawa would be capping its share of transfer payments at roughly the same percentage as current gross federal expenditures. Payments would rise slightly over a new five-year period, but would not keep pace with inflation as they had in the past.

At the same time, Nova Scotia's economy, which had grown a year earlier at 7.6 per cent, the fastest in Canada, was collapsing right along with the dream of a booming offshore oil industry. A year earlier, $508 million in federal grants for offshore exploration had helped sweep Tory premier John Buchanan to his third consecutive election victory. Now Buchanan was looking for a replacement for the federal Petroleum Incentives Program (PIP), which Carney was phasing out, and only two drilling rigs, down from seven, were operating offshore, cutting employment in that field alone from 3,300 jobs to about 1,500 in a year.

Buchanan was also annoyed at Michael Wilson's budget decision to close two money-losing heavy-water plants in Cape Breton, another six hundred jobs lost in an area where unemployment was already at 23.4 per cent. Buchanan, the most loyal Mulroney supporter among the premiers, was reported to be perturbed, a condition exacerbated by effective opposition attacks at home, ridiculing him for having no clout with the federal Tories. Liberal leader Vincent MacLean had said that Buchanan "just doesn't have any friends up there [in Ottawa]."

Signs of regional unrest popped up during Mulroney's November visit to Edmonton to turn the sod for Canada Place, a $200 million federal-government building. During the ceremony, Mulroney was constantly heckled by several hundred men and women (from the locally famous Dandelion Political Action Committee), who greeted him with cries of "Go back to Baie-Comeau" and "You don't act like the son of a working man." With public works minister Roch LaSalle and a host of MPs at his side, Mulroney responded to the placard-carrying hecklers in French, saying he would get to them soon enough. Then in English he said that his government had created 304,000 jobs and that projects such as Canada Place were proof that "the time for economic renewal in Alberta has come." Later, after a ninety-minute talk with new premier Don Getty, Mulroney promised a package to help struggling western farmers, which Getty called Alberta's top priority in federal-provincial relations. Getty congratulated Mulroney for the agreement on natural-gas pricing, announced a week earlier in Ottawa. Mulroney said it showed that "energy can be an instrument of national unity, not dissent. For every dollar spent in Alberta, fifty cents will come back to Ontario and Eastern Canada. . . . What is good for Alberta is positive for Canada."

Two days later, he reacted angrily when Peterson said that Ontario had a constitutional right of veto over the removal of trade barriers between Canada and the United States. At a news conference announcing the appointment of Simon Reisman as trade ambassador, Mulroney said, "We speak for the people of Ontario. We hold that mandate democratically . . . judged by the electorate of Ontario and the rest of the country as competent and able to represent and defend their best interests. And we shall do so. When we were sworn in as government, we did not contract out our national responsibilities to the provinces." However, Mulroney had not mentioned free trade during the election campaign. It had been proposed by John Crosbie in 1983 when he was seeking the Conservative leadership, but Mulroney had ridiculed Crosbie at the time for suggesting it.

As Mulroney and the premiers gathered for a first ministers' conference in Halifax late in November 1985, it was clear the love-in at Regina was not about to be repeated. In an attempt to cut off some criticism, especially among Maritime premiers, Mulroney told a news conference before the first session that transfer payments to the provinces would increase by "more than the cost of living."

Despite this placatory gesture, at the opening session Hatfield said, "The quality of trust around this table is being jeopardized." It was reported that at a private meeting away from reporters, Newfoundland's Brian Peckford had told Mulroney to "cut the crap," and Peterson had scoffed that maybe the U.S. Federal Reserve Board had some part in lower interest rates after Mulroney had taken full credit. Manitoba's Howard Pawley told Mulroney that the "new era" he had bragged about wasn't happening. "On cutbacks for medicare and post-secondary education this federal government's approach is indistinguishable from the approach of the former government." Mulroney shot back that he was "a little astonished at the bleak assessment. I think Manitoba has done extremely well."

Mulroney argued that the federal deficit was the villain. In the mid-seventies, Ottawa had spent $1 on servicing the debt for every $8 spent on programs. Now it spent $1 for every $3.50. He asked the premiers to think of a snowball rolling down a mountain threatening "an avalanche that will crush economic renewal." The premiers weren't buying it. Hatfield, whose province depends desperately upon equalization payments, said that they were counting on Mulroney's earlier commitment not to cut back. "You can't have this, not in this area, not at this time," he pleaded, adding that in New Brunswick the difference between promise and delivery would be about $12 million. However, the angriest exchange came between Peterson and Mulroney, when the Ontario premier accused him of a "breach of faith . . . what you are doing is transferring the problem to us. We are at the bone now." Mulroney angrily replied that his government is doing "infinitely more than anybody can reasonably expect," and accused Peterson of "an unbecoming degree of temerity" in questioning Ottawa's commitment to health and education. Peterson replied that it took "temerity" for Mulroney to suggest that his government was not breaking its undertaking to the provinces.

The federal transfer payments being disputed amounted to more than $14 billion a year. Wilson's budget had promised to continue to increase payments each year, but by less than the Tories had earlier promised. Hatfield at one point said, "Prime Minister, you are breaking an agreement." When the conference ended, Mulroney acknowledged that his relations with the premiers had changed. "Some speak with some surprise at the end of the honeymoon. But for me there is no surprise. It is the normal evolution of a federal state in its relationship with its provincial counterparts." Mulroney said that he had listened "very carefully," to the premiers' plea to reconsider the move. "I did act. I said no. I wish I could have said yes, but I couldn't for reasons that I tried to explain and [that] affect your welfare and mine, the welfare of the country, the national interest."

Clearly, the year had not ended as it had begun, and in early March 1986 Mulroney headed out west for a campaign-style blitz to sell his February 26 budget and himself to an increasingly disaffected population. His roadies hustled from town to town, setting up and taking down thousands of kilograms of sound, light, and video equipment, and carefully positioning his presidential-style podium, emblazoned with the Canadian coat of arms. Mulroney travelled by Challenger jet, and a Canadian Forces Hercules aircraft lugged the sound and video equipment to capture his every appearance for posterity. He attended what were called regional news conferences in Regina and Vancouver, a Tory rally in Prince George, B.C., and a party luncheon in Penticton. Just a week after Wilson had raised personal income taxes and the federal sales tax by $1.48 billion over the next year, Mulroney told his audience, "We'd like to stop taking your money because you're better able to spend it than we are." With unemployment at 12.8 per cent in British Columbia—25 per cent in Prince George and Penticton—and people lined up at Vancouver food banks, Mulroney boasted about the 580,000 jobs his government had created, 83 per cent of them full time. He didn't mention that most of them were in Southern Ontario and Quebec.

In May 1986, there was yet another provincial turnover as Prince Edward Islanders booted out Tory James Lee and elected Liberal Joe Ghiz, forty-one, making it the third province (with Ontario and Quebec) to install a Liberal government since Mulroney had swept to power in Ottawa.

Both sides agreed that recent fee increases for federal services had contributed to the anti-Tory tide. Ottawa had increased from $6 to $10 the entry fee to the Island national park and raised the return fare on the ferries that link the province with the mainland, services that Islanders rely heavily upon. According to Conservative campaign chairman John Carr, "the federal government was a factor in the backlash."

Two weeks later, the Alberta NDP increased its seat total provincially from two to sixteen, and even the Liberals won four seats, the party's first wins there since 1967. Getty led his Tories to sixty-one seats, which would have been considered a landslide in any other province. But six cabinet ministers lost their seats, and province-wide the Conservative popular vote fell by about 220,000 votes to 365,000 compared to 1982; the 50 per cent voter turnout was the lowest ever recorded in the province. In July, Mulroney responded by telling a Calgary audience he would help the West weather its oil crisis. "We're trying to work with the provincial governments on a priority basis, using very scarce resources to be as helpful as we can. In Western Canada people are being unfairly hit with a double whammy—energy and agriculture all at once—and we've got to try and be as helpful as we can to Western Canada in this time of considerable difficulty."

In early August 1986, B.C.'s veteran Social Credit premier Bill Bennett stepped down and was replaced by the blunt-speaking maverick Bill Vander Zalm, fifty-two, a millionaire theme-park owner from the Vancouver suburb of Richmond, who easily won a leadership convention at the picturesque Whistler ski resort. Among others, Vander Zalm defeated two leadership candidates who had close ties with the federal Tory party, and his campaign included virulent attacks on the political and business establishment in Eastern Canada, injecting another unsettling factor into federal-provincial relations after a decade of Bennett.

Vander Zalm barely had time to find his new office before he joined his fellow premiers at their annual get-together, this time at Edmonton's sandstone Government House. While not everyone had good things to say about Mulroney's government, the premiers certainly agreed among themselves. "I don't recall a time of less tension between the provinces," said Peterson.

A week later, Mulroney was in Halifax denying that his new energy package for Novia Scotia was a federal "giveaway," even though it called for $225 million in direct grants. The energy agreement, after eighteen months of negotiations, replaced the federal Liberal accord that had been reached with the province in 1982. It gave Nova Scotia sole authority over oil-industry activity on the gas-rich, seventy nautical-mile area of shallow water around Sable Island and on the Nova Scotia half of the Bay of Fundy. As well, the province got a $200 million 1982 loan written off, a $25 million exploration grant for its debt-ridden Crown corporation, Nova Scotia Resources Ltd., equal jurisdiction with the federal government over offshore developments, and the permanent right to set its own oil and gas royalties.

In Newfoundland a day later for a cabinet meeting, Mulroney acknowledged to a partisan crowd of 1,500 at a steamy St. John's curling club that his government had made its share of mistakes and had not yet discovered how to let that province share in Canada's wealth. "We've made mistakes, as we shall— mistakes being made by men and women trying to do good for you. We never promised perfection. . . ." He said that Canada was doing "pretty well" but that "the great problem is that the wealth and opportunity is not being evenly distributed. . . . Your nieces and nephews and the youth of this province must have a better future other than seeking golden exile in Southern Ontario. . . . Canada owes more than that to Newfoundland and . . . we are going to deliver." Again, however, he offered no specifics.

In September 1986, energy minister Marcel Masse announced that the much-hated federal Petroleum and Gas Revenue Tax (PGRT)—a 10 per cent royalty on oil and gas at the wellhead—would be dropped beginning October 1, some twenty-seven months earlier than was required under Ottawa's 1985 energy accord with Alberta. This would mean a saving of several hundred million dollars to Alberta's crippled oil industry. Mulroney then ventured into the province for some politicking on behalf of the Tories in the Pembina riding, where former Conservative national president Peter Elzinga had quit to run successfully at the provincial level. Mulroney was heckled by striking workers from the Gainers Inc. meat-packing plant, owned by former Conservative leadership candidate Peter Pocklington. Claiming later that one of the hecklers had called him a "frog," Mulroney labelled all the striking unionists "separatists," barking, "I fought separatists in Quebec and I'll bloody well fight separatists here."

The next day, on a swing through Shawinigan, where another by-election was being held after the resignation of Liberal Jean Chrétien, Mulroney told reporters, "We just won Pembina last night. When the man who disrupted the meeting identified himself with the NDP, the NDP just kissed Pembina good-bye." The Tories did win the safe Pembina seat, but by a drastically reduced margin over the NDP. They were clobbered in St. Maurice.

In Ottawa, Liberal House leader Herb Gray and NDP leader Ed Broadbent had both called on Mulroney to apologize for his remarks in Alberta. Gray said, "Brian Mulroney talked about creating a new kind of civility in this country and instead he is replacing McCarthyism of the fifties, unfortunately, with what might be a new kind of Mulroneyism."

Mulroney arrived in Moncton on October 16 to say that "throwing money at the problems in the region . . . hasn't worked." But at a news conference the next day he said that trying to solve Atlantic Canada's problems would "require a substantial commitment of resources." Still, he promised to promote "the principle of fairness which is at the heart of Canada's value system" in order to make sure "your kids get as fair a kick at the can as kids from Ontario" and other more prosperous regions.

The keystone of his Atlantic plan, the Atlantic Canada Opportunities Agency (ACOA), which the government promised in the October 1 throne speech, was the latest in a long line of federally inspired agencies set up to bring prosperity to the Atlantic provinces. Meeting at Charlottetown's historic Province House with the four Atlantic area premiers, Mulroney provided few details about the new agency. Neither he nor the premiers could say after their lunch of shrimp sandwiches and chowder how ACOA would function, how much money it would have, or what powers it would be given.

"We're going to put together an agency that's closer to the ground, more responsive to Atlantic Canada's needs and thinking, where the decision-making process is intimately associated with those who suggest solutions," said Mulroney.

Beyond all the talk of new institutions, the reality on the ground was that family incomes in the four provinces trailed the national average of $38,075 by about $8,400. Unemployment ranged from 12.9 per cent in Nova Scotia to 20.6 per cent in Newfoundland, more than double the national rate. And more than three-quarters of all economic activity in the region was (and is) government spending. The much-heralded Enterprise Cape Breton plan, spearheaded by former industry minister Sinclair Stevens to increase investment there, had attracted $7 million in investments and created only thirty-five jobs. The Atlantic Enterprise Program, announced in Wilson's February budget, was to guarantee up to $1 billion in private lending for new ventures but had not brought in a single project. A poll commissioned by *Maclean's* magazine put Tory support at 32 per cent in the region in September, five behind the Liberals, prompting Halifax West Tory MP Howard Crosby to say, "We've fallen into rhetoric. What people want is action."

A news leak of drastic changes recommended by a commission studying Canada's $12 billion unemployment-insurance system also didn't help the Tory fortunes in the region. Chaired by Claude Forget, it proposed abandoning current rules that favour claimants in high-unemployment areas and recommended that benefits be based on annual income, not ten-to fourteen-week periods of work, measures that could cut incomes in the four Atlantic provinces by $1 billion. The Forget Commission report was subsequently released, filed, and, after a brief flurry of controversy in the Commons, sent off for an indefinite study period.

The Atlantic Tories had attempted to get the regional initiatives off to a glitzy beginning early in September 1986 when the region's six federal cabinet ministers spent two days listening to interest groups attack the government's record. That event was almost spoiled before it got off the ground when Mulroney heard about it and was furious that he hadn't been invited, thinking his Atlantic caucus was working behind his back. Nova Scotia senator Finlay MacDonald blames Mulroney's staff for that mix-up. "We had decided we were going to have an Atlantic forum, just get together all the Atlantic MPs, especially the six ministers, and hold a meeting in Moncton to show how much clout the Atlantic caucus had up here. The meeting had been cleared by the prime minister. We didn't know who cleared it, but we were just trying to show the Atlantic provinces can stand on their own feet and show a strong presence in the government."

Two days before the meeting, Mulroney had noticed the ministers were having a conference to which he hadn't been invited. According to MacDonald, "He blew his stack until it was explained to him. Weeks of work went into it, so one was left to wonder just who briefed him in the first instance. [Forestry minister Gerald] Merrithew had to go to him and say, 'This is what we had in mind and you approved it.' He was puzzled. When it was explained to him he totally agreed."

Even worse, all the public-relations value of the exercise was lost when transport minister Joh Crosbie angered even loyal Tories by an ill-timed comment: "Somebody caught Crosbie at the microphone and he said that thing about being better off here than in Bangladesh," said MacDonald, "and of course that wiped us right off the pages for a couple of days. That was regrettable."

In November, British Columbia's Bill Vander Zalm and Saskatchewan's Grant Devine won majority governments. While Vander Zalm didn't seek any Ottawa help for his easy win, Devine did. He actually got fewer votes province-wide than the NDP but won 38 to 25 on the strength of a sweep of rural Saskatchewan, a vote secured by a mid-campaign deal with Mulroney of a $1 billion assitance package for prairie grain farmers. To get it, Devine made a late-night panic phone call to Saskatchewan cabinet heavyweights Bill McKnight and Ray Hnatyshyn. The call was overheard through a thin motel wall by a local newspaper reporter.

In late October, Mulroney suddenly discovered what regional tension really is when he awarded a $1 billion maintenance contract for the CF-18 to Canadair Ltd. of Montreal instead of to Winnipeg's Bristol Aerospace Ltd., even though Bristol's bid was $3.5 million cheaper and a panel of experts evaluating the technological aspect of the proposals had awarded Bristol 926 points out of 1,000 compared to 843 for Canadair. Even Tories were incensed over the obviously political motive for the decision—to bolster Mulroney's sagging political fortunes in Quebec. "It's a purely political decision that they're trying to justify on technical grounds," said Dauphin-Swan River Tory MP Brian White. Manitoba premier Howard Pawley was furious. His province, he said, "got a raw deal [that] flies in the face of all that's fair, equitable and just." Even the Manitoba Conservative party condemned Ottawa for "abandoning the tender process."

At the same time, Canadian Press established data that supported claims of Quebec favouritism in the Mulroney government, reporting that the Department of Regional Industrial Expansion had channelled $421 million to Quebec between September 1984 and March 1986, as compared to

$257 million to Ontario and $10 million to Newfoundland. About 45 per cent of the Canadian total had gone to one province—Quebec.

The initial CF-18 contract was valued at $104 million for the first three and one-half years. But, with renewals, it is expected to run for between twenty and twenty-five years, and to be worth more than $1 billion. Bristol claimed that the arrangement with Canadair would add $30 million to the servicing costs because Canadair would be forced to purchase much of the technology from Bristol's allies in the bidding consortium.

Pawley demanded and got a face-to-face meeting with Mulroney in a Langevin Block office early the next week, a meeting that by all accounts was extremely bitter on both sides. According to one participant at the meeting, Mulroney reeled off a shopping list of things he had done for the West in "You-got-this, Quebec-got-this," fashion, and concluded that therefore everything was fine. "It was apparent," the participant observed, "that he did not understand what people are really pissed off about. To tell Manitobans about the money that went into the Alberta oil industry and into bailing out Alberta banks—those aren't big home runs in Manitoba."

Mulroney clearly underestimated the depth of anger in Manitoba, assuming that it was just the NDP'S Pawley being partisan and hysterical. Yet with Pawley at the meeting were Winnipeg Chamber of Commerce president John Doole and Manitoba Chamber of Commerce president Donald Henderson, and they weren't any happier than Pawley. An Angus Reid Associates poll taken from November 1 to 4, showed that, with the exception of Quebeckers (who liked the decision), 56 per cent of Canadians said it was unfair to award the contract to Canadair when Bristol had a lower and technically superior bid. Only 18 per cent said that the decision was fair. For Quebeckers, 60 per cent believed it was fair, 19 per cent unfair.

After his ninety-minute meeting with Mulroney, Pawley said, "I believe it is not due to any particular power bloc . . . it is a desire to make up for the anti-Mulroney government feeling that exists in the province of Quebec." Asked if he believed that Mulroney himself had tallied the political gains and decided to give the contract and jobs to Quebec, Pawley said, "I believe so." Manitobans could no longer trust Mulroney, he announced. "I'm as angry and disappointed as I have been at any time during the time I have been elected since 1969." At one point, he even threatened to boycott the constitutional talks aimed at getting Quebec into the constitution.

Mulroney emerged from the meeting speaking so low he was barely audible, saying there was a need to "re-establish" relations with Manitoba, but then calling the Bristol firm "foreigners" because they are British-owned, although they've been established in Winnipeg for much of this century.

Pawley did not get much support in the Commons from either Liberal leader John Turner or NDP leader Ed Broadbent. However, neither wanted to upset Quebeckers by aggresively opposing a deal that was seen as a good one in that province, so both left the issue to their Manitoba members.

When Mulroney arrived at the first ministers' conference in Vancouver in November 1986 he was greeted by placard-carrying Bristol workers. Pawley brought the CF-18 matter up at the meeting: "The CF-18 was, and is, a symbol. A graphic symbol of the frustration we have felt over many decades—the traditional frustrations of Western Canada seeing national policies favour the centre seeing our own prospects and priorities put second, or lower, behind those provinces and regions which have greater electoral weight.

"This federal government promised to address them in a way that would be fair and positive," he said.

Mulroney, visibly angry, launched into a tirade, accusing Pawley of spreading a "misconception" that Manitoba is suffering economically, saying that the province's unemployment rate of 6.9 per cent was as low as Ontario's. Mulroney, offering another non sequitur, said that Pawley hadn't accused him of being "unfair" in 1983 when Mulroney had "defended the rights of Franco-Manitobans." At the time, Pawley had also defended them; it was the provincial Tories who were opposed, not the NDP.

Bristol eventually was given a $350 million maintenance contract for the CF-5 training jet, as a consolation prize for losing the big one to Canadair. But as if he was deliberately trying to rub salt in Manitoban wounds, Mulroney told a Tory fund-raising concert in Montreal in December that Montreal has "a new vocation" as a world centre for aerospace and high technology and that his government could take the credit, a clear reference to the CF-18 decision. "There is renewal, there is progress, there is economic health in Montreal, and we in the government in Ottawa—with the Quebec government and the Montreal government—have contributed to this relaunching of the Montreal economy, and we are proud of it." Even so, the latest Sorecom poll in that province put the Tories at 26 per cent in voter intentions, well behind the NDP at 30 per cent, and the Liberals at 43.

According to Nova Scotia Tory MP Howard Crosby, the controversy over the CF-18 shows that "national reconciliation as a love-in of first ministers is an attempt to do the impossible. It's just going to last so long as there isn't an issue to separate them. I mean the CF-18 deal, which got Pawley so exercised, Bourassa would have been just as upset if it had gone to Manitoba. . . . Really, if you were serious about national reconciliation and the relationships to the provincial premiers, what you would be talking about is not your personal ability to get them together but your ability to establish a mechanism to resolve disputes between them and yourself."

In mid-December, a report by the federal government's Petroleum Monitoring Agency said that, compared to a year earlier, the fist six months of 1986 had showed the most dramatic downturn in the oil patch's forty-year history. Net income dropped 56 per cent to $650 million, internal cash flow fell 32 per cent to $3.8 billion, and capital expenditures dropped 14 per cent to $4.4 billion, reflecting a 50 per cent plunge in world oil prices earlier in the year.

New Brunswick finance minister John Baxter then accused his federal counterpart, Michael Wilson, of reneging on a promise to give the poorer provinces an extra $175 million in equalization payments. Wilson had upset New Brunswick provincial officials a week earlier when he told them during a Toronto meeting that they would only get half the additional money in 1987. Wilson denied that he had promised the extra money, saying it had been "merely a proposal."

Early in the new year, Calgary oilman Jim Gray placed an advertisement in the *Alberta Report* that opened with the blocklettered message: "THE CF-18 DISGRACE MUST NEVER HAPPEN AGAIN. AND THERE IS ONE WAY TO MAKE SURE IT DOESN'T." The advertisement was pushing the establishment of what is called a "Triple E" federal Senate—Elected members, with Equal representation from each province, armed with Effective power. Bow River Tory MP Gordon Taylor introduced a private member's bill in December for Senate reform. "There's a growing force in Alberta that feels if we can't get some protection in the Senate there's no future for them in Canada," he said in a recent newspaper interview. Gray says "with 170 seats in Ontario and Quebec . . . the mathematics of Canada stipulates that if you're going to sustain yourself in power you must sustain power in Ontario and Quebec." According to him, the only way to overcome this built-in regional inequity is to opt for equal representation in the Senate.

As a partial response to the need for better representation, the Commons will grow by thirteen seats to 295 for the next election. Alberta will grow by five seats to 26, British Columbia by four to 32, and Ontario by four to 99. All other provinces will remain the same: Quebec, 75; Nova Scotia, 11; New Brunswick, 10; Newfoundland, 7; P.E.I., 4; Manitoba, 14; Saskatchewan, 14; Northwest Territories, 2; and Yukon, 1.

On representation-by-population basis, there will be one MP for every 85,136 Canadians based on the 1986 interim population of 25,116,102. The Yukon will have one MP for its 23,022 people while, at the other end of the scale, Ontario will have one MP for each 91,439 people. Other provinces will be represented as follows: Alberta, one MP for each 90,309; British Columbia, 89,352; Quebec, 86,376; Newfoundland, 80,623; Nova Scotia, 78,767; Manitoba, 75,351; Saskatchewan, 71,445; New Brunswick, 70,347; P.E.I., 31,345; Northwest Territories, 25,692. Until the change, Alberta had the fewest MPS per person, followed by British Columbia, and then Ontario.

Proposals for Senate reform have been around nearly as long as the Senate itself. Indeed, in March 1985, Mulroney said that a proposal to curb the powers of the Senate would be considered the next week by cabinet and that legislation would follow quickly. He had been outraged when the Liberal-dominated Senate (sixty-six seats, compared to thirty-two Tories, five independents, and one independent Liberal) got involved in a five-week battle over a bill authorizing the government to borrow money. The senators had refused to pass the bill until the government tabled its spending estimates for the 1985-86 fiscal year. "The Liberal party feels that, even though it has been dismissed overwhelmingly by the Canadian people, they still have a right to obstruct the wishes of Parliament," said Mulroney, adding that he wanted to "remedy an unacceptable situation where a bunch of Liberal rejects hold up a unanimous agreement by the elected members of the Canadian Parliament."

Mulroney characterized the Senate as "not a particularly useful organization, given the enormous cost involved." However, that was before he too appointed several of his personal friends—among them Jean Bazin, Norm Atkins, and Michel Cogger—to the upper chamber. NDP leader Ed Broadbent wanted the Senate abolished, "considering that this useless body costs Canadians almost a million dollars a week," and Tory John Crosbie said he did not see "that the Senate performs any really useful function." However, that controversy soon blew over and it was basically business as usual.

A Canadian Press survey in January 1987, showed that less than one-third of the 104 senators attended regular sittings during the fall session to earn their $65,000 annual salary and expenses. Senators are supposed to lose $120 a day—$60 in salary and $60 in tax-free allowances—for each day beyond twenty-one days missed in a session. But none of the twenty-two senators who were absent that much was docked any pay. Gord Lovelace, co-ordinator of Senate Information Services, said that senators have many other duties to perform besides sitting in the chamber, among them working on committee, meeting in caucus, working on budgets, and speaking to various groups.

Despite Deputy Prime Minister Don Mazankowski's statement that Senate reform isn't a priority, Alberta's federal and inter-governmental affairs minister Jim Horsman insists that the Triple-E Senate "remains a priority with us. . . . We believe Senate reform is important to Western Canada. I don't think the federal government can ignore the necessity of Senate reform."

P.E.I.'s Joe Ghiz also joined the chorus: "The West and the East feel frustrated . . . impotent . . . alienated . . . cheated . . . set outside the boundaries of federal decision-making," Ghiz told the Canadian Club of Montreal. "Confrontation develops between the provincial and the federal governments simply because there is no other access to influence."

In March, federal-provincial relations minister Lowell Murray, government leader in the Senate, said that reform of the unelected Senate would be on the constitutional front-burner if Ottawa succeeded in getting Quebec to sign the constitution. He added that they hadn't forgotten Mulroney's 1985 pledge to seek a constitutional amendment to weaken the Senate powers. (That proposal, introduced with great fanfare by the Tories, died on the order paper.)

The big federal-provincial item early in 1987 was once again pressure from Alberta for help because of the collapse in the oil patch. Ottawa turned down an Alberta request for a $200 million back-up loan to complete the $750 million Syncrude expansion project, and Athabasca Tory MP Jack Shields, parliamentary secretary to energy minister Marcel Masse, said, "I am the one to blame," for telling Alberta's energy minister in mid-December that the aid package was "in place." The debate heated up when Premier Don Getty said that he'd had Mulroney's personal assurance that federal participation would be forthcoming. "It's as though we went from 1975 to 1986 and nothing happened," said Getty.

An Angus Reid Associates poll commissioned by the *Calgary Herald* in late February 1987 showed that an overwhelming 70 per cent of Albertans disapproved of Mulroney's performance. Broadbent, on the other hand, had a 60 per cent approval rating, while Turner had 36 per cent. Those dissatisfied with what Mulroney had done for the West represented 69 per cent.

Faced with growing pressure from the West, including a threat from Getty that if the Tories didn't pay now they'd pay in the election, Mulroney did what he usually does—he sent money. In late March, Masse went to Edmonton to announce a $350 million package for Canada's ailing energy industry—a package that, he said, could lead to $1 billion in new investment. Oil-industry officials predicted that the cash incentives would create fifteen thousand jobs.

Earlier, Michael Wilson had said that he couldn't do much to mend regional disparities, since Western Canadians are the prisoners of international economic forces. He pointed out that the government had already implemented a wider range of programs, including the $3.5 billion directed at Western agriculture for everything from drought programs to grain stabilization and fuel tax rebates.

A week later, Wilson introduced a bill giving the seven poorest provinces $5.6 billion in equalization payments in the coming fiscal year—$300 million more than last year. Newfoundland was to get $732 million in the 1987-88 fiscal year, plus $785 million the next year; P.E.I., $151 million, plus $162 million; Nova Scotia, $654 million and $696 million; New Brunswick, $669 million and $731 million; Quebec, $2.783 billion and $2.945 billion; Manitoba, $469 million and $489 million; and Saskatchewan, $142 million and $139 million.

Wilson also increased spending for regional development by 2.5 per cent to $1.16 billion for fiscal 1987-88, and announced that more of it would be aimed at the Atlantic provinces. One project was an $8.2 million grant to Hermes Electronics Ltd. of Nova Scotia to set up a manufacturing plant to produce sensors to detect submarines. The plan was expected to generate about $88 million in export sales in the United States in its first three years and create twenty-eight jobs.

At least as bitter as the CF-18 controversy was the fight in late January 1987 sparked by the Mulroney government's interim agreement with France over the disputed waters off southern Newfoundland. "Apparently when France rattles its swords, Canada bends its knees," said Conservative premier Brian Peckford. "It's a terrible situation and they did it behind our backs."

Though quotas for Canadian fishermen had been cut, Ottawa gave France fishing rights in disputed waters plus the right to take fifteen- thousand tonnes of Canadian fish elsewhere off Newfoundland and agreed to refer a maritime boundary dispute to international arbitration. France has claimed a zone about the size of Nova Scotia for St. Pierre-Miquelon, while Canada argues that the tiny French islands off its coast should have a territorial sea with a radius of only twelve nautical miles.

The deal was struck after federal negotiators secretly flew to Paris to reach a settlement without telling the Newfoundland officials, who had, up until then, been involved in the negotiations. Transport minister John Crosbie called on his own government to apologize to Newfoundland for unilaterally signing away some of its precious cod to the French. Mulroney was in Harare, Zimbabwe, in the midst of an African tour when he was asked for his reaction. He simply denied that Crosbie had asked the government to apologize.

Mazankowski did call Peckford to apologize, but Peckford demanded that the deal be scrapped, even if it meant risking a diplomatic rupture to enforce Canadian boundary claims. "My God, we're a country," said Peckford. "We have certain rights of sovereignty." Curiously, Mulroney defended the deal on his return from Africa by claiming his government has not "given away a single cod fish." He blamed a 1972 treaty negotiated by the Liberals for giving the French the right to fish there, ignoring the fact that the Article 3 of the treaty said clearly that the French were to vacate the Gulf of St. Lawrence by May

15, 1986. Both Mulroney and fisheries minister Tom Siddon claimed that the Liberal treaty had given the French "perpetual" fishing rights.

When he was asked how something like this could happen, Tom Van Dusen, Mazankowski's communications chief, said, "It's not hard to do. It's a little short-sighted and a little stupid, but you get into these bureaucratic deliberations, which is what these things are all about . . . and their mandate is not to pay attention to the emotional issues, the political impact of cod in Newfoundland. They're looking up charts and maps like bureaucrats always do. They don't know about reality. I don't blame them for that. It's not their mandate to know about reality. . . .

"But we know about reality, yet sometimes we can't always bring that into play," he said. "I don't think enough people knew. It's simply human failing, something as simple as Maz telling Joe [Clark] to make the phone call to Peckford and Joe forgetting to do it. He had something else on his plate, as we all do. Those kinds of things can happen in government and create great disasters. . . . There wasn't anything complicated about it. It was a very simple situation of not making a call at the right time. It hurts. It couldn't have happened at a worse time."

Peckford was certainly making his calls, contacting all the premiers to organize an emergency premiers' meeting in Toronto, claiming that Ottawa had begun hatching a plot to exclude his province from the deal at least one month before. Peckford said that cabinet had discussed the northern cod issue in Ottawa in December. Cabinet had been divided, but the PMO had stepped in to dictate terms.

Way back when John Fraser was fisheries minister, he had been told by the PMO to accommodate France on the fishing-boundary question as part of the negotiations leading up to the Francophone summit. Fraser sent a short, sharp note back to the PMO telling them to mind their own business, and the matter was temporarily dropped. A current cabinet minister, speaking privately, has said: "There is no question the whole deal was tied in with that [the Francophone summit in Quebec City this fall]. . . . [Mulroney] doesn't want any irritants overshadowing the show. He wants a celebration of French culture and the French language, and wanted to [prevent] something like a fishing dispute from spoiling the celebration.

It's fairly obvious if you think about it. Don't blame Siddon. He had no say in it."

In the wake of the growing controversy, even the French began to wonder about the deal, saying they'd be willing to take another look at it but only if they could get larger quotas. Mulroney made a last-minute appeal on February 8 to the ten premiers not to condemn the agreement, sending a Telex to Getty on the eve of the premiers' emergency meeting in Toronto, contradicting Mazankowski's earlier statement that the treaty might be renegotiated. Mulroney dispatched his senior negotiators to attend the meeting "to provide a full and confidential briefing."

Clearly the dispute had escalated dramatically from a quarrel with one province to a full-blown conflict of federal-provincial relations. Crosbie said openly that the government had "made a bad mistake," but Mulroney continued to ignore demands in the Commons to admit it. He retorted that the government would not surrender its right to "speak for all of Canada."

On February 11, angry residents of St. Pierre-Miquelon, who also object to consistent overfishing by the French, refused to unload a French trawler and asked its captain to leave port. Eventually, Ottawa promised Peckford to put shared jurisdiction for fisheries on the next constitutional agenda, a promise Peckford saw as a major victory. "We've been at this now a long time. If we can now start talking seriously about some joint management and shared jurisdiction over the fishery, it would allay a lot of fears that we have for the future of the resource."

On March 17, Canada closed all its ports to French fishing vessels, an unprecedented action designed to tell France to stop overfishing in disputed waters. Announcing the move, Siddon and Crosbie also threatened arrest for any French vessel caught fishing in the area. While the move sounded tough, in reality there is little Canada can do because the French rarely use Canadian ports and seldom fish in the Burgeo Bank off Newfoundland anyway.

In the words of Nova Scotia Tory MP Howard Crosby: "I subscribe to the Lyndon Johnson school of politics where you don't really have to worry about what your enemies say about you. . . . But what your friends say about you can harm you immensely whether it's true or not . . . What matters is that Brian Mulroney, Progressive Conservative prime minister of

Canada, is being criticized by Brian Peckford, Progressive Conservative premier of Newfoundland, and to a degree by John Buchanan, Progressive Conservative premier of Nova Scotia. It's harmful. The mere criticism is harmful regardless of the content of the criticism."

What had begun so well had deteriorated to the same low point as that reached near the end of the Trudeau era. Even British Columbia was angry with Ottawa—for retroactively closing a twenty-one-year tax exemption on securities issued by SkyTrain, a venture backed by the province. "The government is trying to kill us every chance they get," said Vander Zalm. "I just can't believe what they're doing and I'm absolutely fed up."

Peckford was still fuming over fish; Pawley had not forgotten the CF-18. In Alberta in the early spring Edmonton-Strathcona Tory MP David Kilgour announced publicly that he felt "betrayed" by the government because it wasn't doing enough to help the West and it was bogged down with scandals and moral decay; Mulroney stripped Kilgour of his job as Crosbie's parliamentary secretary and told him to stay away from caucus. And in Toronto, Wilson's announcement of international banking centres for Montreal and Vancouver but not Toronto quickly became a political symbol in the country's largest city.

Federal-provincial minister Lowell Murray still insists that the government has made good on its promise for national reconciliation. "The tensions are reviving anyway," he said. "There's a basic problem in the country now in the fact that we have not one but several economies . . . you only need to look at the unemployment rate in Southern Ontario and, say, Manitoba, and then look at Quebec and the Atlantic provinces and the double whammy in the western provinces on wheat prices and oil prices and see that you've got these two economies and see why the tensions are there."

According to Murray, the West is hypersensitive these days to anything that looks as though it might be favouring Central Canada, whereas if times were better for the Western economies they'd probably overlook some things that they are presently hypersensitive about. Murray believes that the explosions on the CF-18 issue and on fish are exceptions that prove the rule, and that in general there is a pretty good working relationship between the federal government and the provinces.

The federal government has shown that it has the "political

will" to clear up the major conflicts with the West and Atlantic Canada, Brian Peckford's views notwithstanding, Murray feels. "Well, I don't mind him [Peckford] attacking our policy and even the process, especially the process on this fish business. But going right after our motives is something else. He wasn't complaining about our motives when we put a couple hundred million dollars on the table in the Atlantic Accord. He didn't get that by going to Toronto and meeting with Howard Pawley, David Peterson, and Don Getty. He got it because Mulroney and the Tory government was elected and wanted to do the right thing by Newfoundland.

"It just goes to show you what happens when we fail to consult and allow the process to break down," Murray concludes. "I think that agreement is probably quite defensible . . . but the process is bad. We're getting hammered on the process, and with good reason. We consulted them and the industry right up to the last moment, and then bang, we cut them out and go our own way and we're paying a heavy price for that."

Murray still insists that the government's record has been "pretty damn good . . . to the extent that national reconciliation means trying to clean up the relationships between governments, I think it's worked.

"Federal-provincial harmony in a country such as this is almost an end in itself. You can't do anything if the two levels are constantly at loggerheads. You just can't. It's impossible," Murray insists. "What we're trying to do is run a country on the basis of five distinct regions. Our predecessors didn't have to. They had a coalition of two regions, Ontario and Quebec, and that was it. They didn't lie awake nights worrying about the rest. We've got to."

CHAPTER SEVEN

TALKING TORY,
ACTING GRIT

As a leadership candidate, Brian Mulroney talked tough. As Conservative leader running for prime minister, he promised the world. As prime minister, the first thing he did was break the promise. And so it goes. To Tory delegates, Mulroney sold himself as a hard-nosed deficit-slashing businessman. In the 1984 campaign, he still promised to trim deficits, but he also promised to spend billions on new programs and not cut the deficit by increasing personal taxes. When he achieved power, his first real economic decision was already upon him—whether to allow a Liberal one-percentage-point hike in the federal sales tax. He had railed against it in opposition. During the campaign he said that former Liberal finance minister Marc Lalonde had "sneaked in [the tax] in his last budget." In government, alas, Mulroney changed his tune, a decision that cost Canadians $300 million in taxes that fiscal year, plus $900 million more in 1985–86.

It was the first in a series of tax increases from the man who used to say Canadians paid too much tax. On November 29, 1984, the Economic Council of Canada had advocated higher personal taxes on the grounds that spending cuts weren't enough to lower the $34.5 billion deficit. In response, Mulroney said he did not favour higher personal taxes to reduce the deficit because "Canadians are already overtaxed. . . . There are other possibilities available to us, and we will examine them carefully."

How carefully? Well, under Mulroney, the average Canadian family is now paying about 52 per cent more—or

$1,300—in personal taxes than under the Liberals. At the same time, corporations are paying 18 per cent less.

In a March 14, 1982, Tory fund-raising speech, Mulroney said that one of the most objectionable aspects of the budget process "is that budget measures usually take effect the moment they are announced. I believe it should be accepted as a matter of principle that no new budget measure takes effect until it is actually passed by Parliament and given royal assent." Each of his government's budgets has had several instant tax measures without prior parliamentary debate, let alone royal assent.

As opposition leader in 1983, Mulroney consistently attacked the Liberal deficits, accusing them of "disastrous policy errors" and arguing that their $31 billion deficit was preventing interest rates from falling and keeping unemployment high. In a year-end interview on CTV's "Question Period," Mulroney said that the Liberals showed "no respect for the taypayer's dollar, no sense of frugality in the administration of public funds. . . ." The Conservatives, he said, were "going to have one mother of a mess to clean up when we get in there." He had that right.

On March 6, 1984, Michael Wilson said in the Commons, "We would cut spending. We would not raise taxes. Tax levels in Canada are already too high." Now, after Wilson's 1984 economic statement and three successive budgets, tax levels are much higher—except for those on corporations—and so is spending. As for the deficit—the proclaimed object of the exercise—it has barely changed. During the last full year of Liberal administration, the deficit was $32.4 billion. In his November 1984 economic statement, Wilson put it at $34.6 billion. After four years of economic recovery, and despite a $6 billion increase in taxes, the deficit was $32 billion for fiscal 1986–87, with a promise (for the second year in a row) to reduce it to just under $30 billion by next year. What's more, Wilson used some economic flim-flam to crack the $30-billion forecast—making employers send income tax returns twice a month instead of once, allowing Wilson to count an extra $1.2 billion under the current year instead of 1988–89 where it belongs.

On July 9, 1984, Mulroney said that the Liberals "must answer for four years of financial management that has tripled the annual deficit and raised the net government debt to $180 billion, an amount that equals $16,500 owed by every taxpayer." According to Wilson's current estimates, that same debt at the end of fiscal 1987–88 will be close to $300 billion, the equivalent of $26,700 for every taxpayer, an increase of $10,000 or about 67 per cent of additional debt per taxpayer in two and one half years.

Mulroney formally announced his economic policy on March 22, 1984, in a promise-studded speech to the Montreal Chamber of Commerce. He unveiled a strategy based on "four pillars" that were to get the country moving again: lower interest rates, more high-tech research and development, high-tech training for Canadian workers, and increased trade. He promised to reduce the debt through civil-service incentive programs to encourage efficiency, "sunset laws" to kill off costly ineffective programs, detailed parliamentary scrutiny of Crown corporations, elimination of pork-barrel capital spending, rethinking of subsidies and grants to business, targeting housing assistance to those who need it most, and reviewing and simplifying tax laws to reduce cheating and lower taxes by broadening the tax base.

During the election campaign, Mulroney's refrain was that, once the Tories had won, "billions of dollars" worth of private capital would begin to be invested. "You're going to see tens of tens of thousands of jobs being created just as quickly as a new government is sworn in."

In July 1984, an Ottawa *Citizen* reporter spotted a document carried into a Tory planning meeting by finance critic John Crosbie that put a $20 billion price tag over the next five years on Tory campaign pledges. Tory aides denied the newspaper report. Mulroney conceded that there was "a short-term cost" to his promises, but said he would release precise figures later. "You have an economy that's over a barrel and we've got to get it moving again, so there will be a cost." He quickly backed away from his 1983 projection that the deficit could be cut to $3 billion by 1990. A day later, after his initial denial, Mulroney admitted that a paper prepared for Crosbie estimated that Tory campaign promises would cost an additional $20 billion over five years, but said that the real cost would be "absolutely" lower.

In the televised leaders' debate, Mulroney was asked if he supported a minimum income tax to insure that high-income earners can't use tax loopholes to avoid paying any tax. He replied that he did, saying it was "unfair. . . . Yes, I agree. . . . They should pay a handsome tax." Two days later, the Montreal *Gazette* reported that Mulroney had invested in an oil company as a tax shelter. He had sunk about $50,000 in 1981 in tax-sheltered drilling funds sold by Pillar Petroleums Ltd., a Calgary oil company. Mulroney was also a director of the company. The drilling fund he had purchased allowed investors to own a piece of an oil well and write off 69 per cent of their purchase on the first year's tax return, writing off the rest during the next four years. Mulroney flatly refused to answer questions about it, but his press aide Bill Fox described it in patriotic terms as "an investment in a Canadian energy industry."

In August, Mulroney said that Canadians wouldn't know whether a Conservative government would raise taxes until after the election because the Liberals were not levelling with people about the size of the federal deficit and the state of the economy. Campaigning in Halifax, Mulroney said that uncertainty surrounding the state of the economy might make it difficult to follow through on an early campaign pledge to give cost figures for the projects and programs the Tories were promising to implement if they won. Later, he accused John Turner of withholding from the finance department damaging new data that were "substantially at variance with the projections put forward in the February budget, which affect rates, unemployment and growth." Turner said Mulroney had the same economic forecasts that he had.

In a campaign stop-over in Gander, Newfoundland, Mulroney claimed that two million Canadians were unemployed (the acutal figure was 1.3 million) and pegged a Conference Board of Canada deficit prediction at $34 billion, instead of the board's $32.7 billion figure. Later in the same speech, he put the deficit at $36 billion. It didn't matter. The Gallup poll showed Mulroney fourteen points ahead of Turner. When asked by reporters where his contradictory and erroneous figures had come from, Mulroney snapped, "Just read it. It's in the speech. The figure is accurate."

On August 28, Mulroney claimed that his campaign promises would cost $4.3 billion over the next thirty months, but that $2.2 billion of that could be offset by unspecified savings, spending cuts, and tax reform. Two days later, retiring finance minister Marc Lalonde cited fifteen major promises Mulroney had not included in his cost figures and estimated the cost of just four of them at $22.1 billion over four years. Lalonde said that the cost of replacing the petroleum and gas-revenue tax and incremental oil-revenue tax alone wold be $10.4 billion. Proposed homemakers' pensions would cost $4 billion, and more aid to single pensioners, $1.1 billion.

After winning the election and studying the accounts, Mulroney claimed that "The [economic] situation is rather worse than even we had anticipated." Mulroney added that Jean Chrétien had "said ten days ago that they had left the cupboard bare. For once, Mr. Chrétien was given to understatement." Mulroney wasn't. In a telephone interview from his Shawinigan cottage, Chrétien told reporters he had never made such a comment. "You can write that ten days ago he [Chrétien] was looking at the leaves turning from green to red at his summer cottage and didn't give a damn about Mr. Mulroney."

At a meeting in Nanaimo, B.C., shortly after taking office, Mulroney denied ever saying he could reduce the deficit to $3 billion by 1990. "You never heard me say that," he said. In fact, the figure of $3.1 billion was his. It came from estimates prepared by a private firm, Data Resources of Canada, at his request—using his data—and released by his campaign staff with great fanfare just before the 1983 leadership vote.

One promise he moved on quickly was his pledge to his own Manicouagan riding that they would receive "priority" treatment from the government. In October, Mulroney ordered employment minister Flora MacDonald to relocate up to one thousand residents of his riding who were losing jobs through a mine closing. MacDonald noted that she was acting at Mulroney's request and said, "I would like to let you know of . . . my intention to implement the measures to ensure that all possible assistance is provided to these workers," adding that it could cost $1.3 million to give each worker up to $9,000 in relocation aid.

Meeting for the first time with his inner cabinet at a plush lakeside retreat in the Gatineau Hills on October 23, Mulroney vowed that his government would end Ottawa's "orgy of spending." Newly appointed finance minister Michael Wilson conceded that that meant putting some Tory campaign promises on the back burner. "We're not going to be able to move as quickly as we said we would with the promises we made during the election," said Wilson.

Casually dressed in a sweater and open-necked sports shirt, Mulroney said that his aim was to give direction to an economy that was "in bad shape and a fiscal situation that's out of control.

Now the hard realities begin: How do we try as best we can to get it back on track? It's not a pleasant job but it has to be done." He dismissed as "modest" his announced doubling (to $15 million) of the budget for his ministers' personal political staffs. He also released a list of salaries of Crown-corporation heads, making it clear he thought some were too high and promising to review the payments. He singled out a few who received directors'. and management fees from subsidiaries that amounted to more than their salaries. Petro-Canada chairman Wilbert Hopper, for example, received $300,000 in addition to a salary of between $114,000 and $135,000; Petro-Canada president Edward Lakusta also received $300,000 over a salary in the $97,090 to $114,260 range; and Canada Development Investment Corp. president Joel Bell received $100,000 in addition to a salary of between $135,000 and $160,000. "Those are pretty handsome numbers for anyone running a corporation that doesn't have to declare a profit," said Mulroney. For the most part, Crown-corporation heads are enjoying even larger salaries and benefits now.

Early in November, Mulroney began a series of speeches warning Canadians to brace themselves for "hard but fair measures. . . . I didn't mean that there was going to be any mean-spiritedness or careless or vexatious action—there will be none of that. I think what you can expect is a setting out in a clear-cut way of the views and the philosophy of the Progressive Conservative party that we've brought to government, and where we'd like to see Canada be in the next few years, and the kinds of reasons that we see for hope and the causes for concern."

In his first throne speech on November 5, 1984, Mulroney promised to slash the deficit. At the same time he announced a series of costly programs, including "an innovative employment strategy" and "accessible and affordable child care." Canada would again "play its full part in the defence systems of NATO" and there would be more money for war veterans and pensions for widows and widowers. Eight months later, his attempt to renege on the pensions sparked his first real political crisis.

On November 7, 1984, Mulroney made his first speech in the Commons as prime minister, promising "a new era of prosperity. . . . We believe we can—and we shall—bring a new degree of prosperity to Canada and to Canadians."

The next day, Wilson tabled a document called "A New Direction for Canada: An Agenda for Economic Renewal," setting out the ideology of the administration, basically a small "c" fiscally conservative approach concentrating on deficit-cutting, cost-paring, and promising a review of social programs and corporate subsidies. "Our immediate goal is to reduce the deficit through expenditure reductions and not through major tax increases," said Wilson, announcing that more than $4.2 billion in spending cuts and revenue-recovery measures would be implemented in 1985–86. "Economic renewal will not come easily," he said, adding that his spring budget would contain more spending cuts and tax increases. "There are no easy solutions to problems that have built up over a decade."

As an example of restraint, Wilson cut Mulroney's salary by 15 per cent to $123,945, and cut the thirty-nine cabinet ministers' pay by 10 per cent. (On closer examination, reporters discovered that the cuts came only in ministerial salaries, not in the basic MP's pay or in tax-free allowances and other perquisites.) Wilson said that the Tories remained committed "to making steady progress" towards their promised 0.7 per cent of Gross National Product for foreign aid. (They've never come close to that. They later changed their target to 0.5 per cent, and didn't hit that either.) He also promised to devise a minimum tax system as well as a $1 billion job-creation program. He cut $154 million from Defence, despite Mulroney's campaign pledge to increase defence spending, and slashed $93 million from VIA Rail (the Tories in opposition had raised a huge outcry when the Liberals cut back a few under-used routes). Mulroney stoutly told reporters, "You'll find nothing inconsistent . . . in regard to our promises."

On November 22, NDP leader Ed Broadbent rose in the Commons to press Mulroney about his campaign pledge to institute a minimum tax for the rich. "The commitment that I gave that evening was to a mimimum tax and to that sense of fairness that inspires both of us," Mulroney said. "And we shall follow through on that with regard to a minimum tax." Broadbent wanted the tax before Christmas, but Mulroney said, "I give him the assurance that it shall be in the [spring 1985] budget." (It wasn't. Indeed, in Wilson's 1987 budget the promise still hadn't been met, although it was being promised, after a study the previous year, as part of a comprehensive tax-reform system. What's more, by February 1987 the $34.6

billion deficit Wilson had claimed in his November 1984 economic statement had grown mysteriously by $3.5 billion. In the February 18, 1987, budget speech, Wilson said, "When we took office, the deficit was more than $38 billion.")

In 1983, on page 53 of *Where I Stand*, Mulroney had written: "The major support and background papers that provide the detailed rationale and evidence used by the department of finance to advance various policies should be made public. We would then know the principal basis of government policy.

"It would have the salutary effect of enhancing the quality of such papers if their authors knew they would be scrutinized by outsiders. Inasmuch as we are paying for this information, it does not seem unreasonable that we should have access to it. Freedom of information should apply to the finance department as well as to veterans affairs."

On November 26, when Broadbent repeated a long-standing demand for government studies predicting the possible effect of recent budget cuts on employment, Mulroney refused to make them available. It would, he said, prevent civil servants from giving the government "unfettered and unvarnished advice . . . we want to protect the public servants. We want to make sure they are not criticized for being political and we do not want to politicize the public service."

Late in November, Mulroney took credit in the Commons for a drop in both inflation and interest rates and for the fact that 32,000 jobs had been created. "I never at any time suggested there was going to be an economic utopia," he said. "I indicated across the country the new government would be confronted with grave economic problems and that was true. But, in point of fact, since the election and the swearing-in of the new government, 32,000 new jobs have been created. The improvements are modest, but they are there." In November 1984, the jobless rate dropped from 11.3 to 10.8, the lowest level since mid-1982. During the first three post-election months, 96,000 jobs were added on a seasonally adjusted basis. Even then, they were concentrated in Central Canada, with 23,000 in Ontario and 17,000 in Quebec. British Columbia, on the other hand, lost 9,000 during November. As time went on, and the jobs continued to be created at an impressive clip, they were concentrated more and more in Ontario, giving an overall impression of a healthy economy, but masking serious regional economic woes outside of Ontario. From January 1986 to January 1987, for example, although Canada had a net increase of 115,000 new jobs, Ontario alone enjoyed an increase of 127,000 new jobs in that period, so there was in fact a net loss of 12,000 jobs in the rest of Canada.

Still, in January 1985, Mulroney said, "I'm encouraged that the trend is going the right way. I suppose the important thing is that, consistent with what we indicated during the campaign, Statistics Canada revealed this morning that 100,000 new jobs—full-time, permanent jobs—have been created since October."

Early that month, Mulroney started his campaign of preparing Canadians for more budget cuts in April, saying, "The budget, which calls for restraint, as did the statement in November, will have some difficult aspects to it." Mulroney hadn't shown much restraint in spending $24,000 to hand-deliver copies of Wilson's economic statement to the provincial premiers by using government-owned jets. (A private courier company could have guaranteed same-day delivery for $105.)

In a February 2 interview with Hyman Solomon of the *Financial Post*, Mulroney said, "We view the private sector as the principal instrument of economic growth in Canada. The risk takers and the builders know now that we are trying to create a climate of cooperation within which their efforts are going to be rewarded. What we've tried to do is begin the larger process of constructing a lean and durable framework for this."

At his maiden first ministers' conference, Mulroney again pushed his theme of fighting the huge federal deficit as the key to economic prosperity. Job creation should be left primarily to the private sector, he proclaimed and, to make the event even sweeter, announced a $695 million job-training and employment program earmarked especially to help youth, women, the chronically unemployed, and workers needing skills upgrading. All ten premiers welcomed the plan at the time, but soured months later when the promised funding didn't materialize.

At about that time, a series of newspaper stories quoted business-community officials who felt that Mulroney was not serious about deficit reduction and detailed how Wilson had lost a cabinet battle to use some of the money saved on social programs to write down the deficit. The government seemed to be retreating from its commitment to save money on social programs, signalling to the business community a lack of political will to match tough talk with fiscal action. Although Mulroney went out of his way to defend Wilson at a news conference, businessmen were dismayed that he continued to rule out the major elements of a deficit-reduction strategy—cuts in transfers to individuals or provinces, personal income tax increases, and an overhaul of corporate taxation. Mulroney was still saying the things businessmen wanted to hear in public, but in private he was saying he wanted the Tories to stay away from the right-of-centre policies of Ronald Reagan and Margaret Thatcher and remain a centrist party. Big business was becoming confused.

Nor did the business community feel any better after the March 4 edition of the U.S. magazine *Fortune* quoted Mulroney as saying: "We do not have a very good track record. Our products have not been of the highest quality. Our deliveries have been lacking in reliability. Our expertise has been in large measure borrowed. Our technology has been purchased. What the hell makes us so special? If somebody wants to buy some oil, somebody wants to buy some wheat, hell, we're in business. That's what it's all about. Forest products, mining—God, we'd love it if somebody wanted to joint-venture with us in mining development, taking our products at competitive prices. Damn right we would."

When accused of having put Canada up for sale, Mulroney said, "Who wants to buy it? What is there so compellingly attractive about Canada that causes us to think that anybody is going to rush in simply because somebody says, 'I'd like to do business with you'?"

Not surprisingly, this remarkable interview stirred up emotions in the Commons. As John Turner said, "This shows why there is little confidence in this country . . . when the prime minister himself has no confidence in the Canadian business community." Turner accused Mulroney of reinforcing business doubts about the Canadian economy, and thus contributing to the breathtaking freefall of the Canadian dollar, which closed at 71.44 cents (U.S.), 3.2 cents less than a week earlier.

The next event on Mulroney's fiscal agenda was his $1 million, two-day national economic conference (March 26–28, 1985), the centrepiece of his proclaimed new era in public consultation. Nothing was too good for the two hundred invited guests, who included senior business and labour leaders, economists, representatives of women's groups and poverty organizations, and native leaders. The extravagant event opened with a gala dinner in the red, blue, and gold Confederation Room in Parliament's West Block. Delegates aired myriad conflicting views, which Mulroney promised to consider, but the meeting was hardly the new beginning of "pride and inspiration" that Mulroney had predicted. It did, however, prompt an open letter of complaint signed by about thirty-five labour leaders and twenty leaders of social and religious organizations expressing their disappointment at Mulroney's plan to offer "a meaner, leaner future for most Canadians."

In late March, Mulroney laid the groundwork for his controversial prison in Port Cartier, Quebec (in his home riding), when he told the townspeople that half the workforce of 6,700 was jobless, but vowed that this would end "in the near future." Speaking at a civic reception, Mulroney promised to pump government money into the town if no private investors came forward. He reminded them that he'd already dispatched nearly $10 million into the riding since the election. "The local population has suffered enough." (Mulroney felt some personal responsibility for that, since he was instrumental in one of two severe economic blows which had hit the town. A giant rayon plant had shut down in 1979, throwing 1,300 people out of work. And three years later, the mining facilities that had kept the town's deep-sea port operating were shut down by Mulroney as president of the Iron Ore Company.)

By April, Mulroney was telling the provincial premiers in an emergency, two-hour, pre-budget meeting at 24 Sussex Drive, that the debt was "grotesque." Wilson had announced earlier in the week that the deficit would be increased by $220 million for extra equalization payments to the six poorer provinces.

In May 1985, a week before Wilson's first full-fledged budget, Mulroney sent each of his 210 Tory MPS a memo ordering them to "hit the ground running" to sell "the positive message of the [May 23] budget." There was to be a command performance of all MPS the day after the budget as a show of support for Wilson. Senior cabinet ministers were taking to the road to explain budget measures, field complaints, and reinforce Mulroney's tough-but-fair theme. As well, MPS were to have special briefings plus their own budget kits in question-and-answer format (including a text for local radio shows). An information hotline for MPS would be installed the weekend after the budget. Informal instructions were also issued on the use of appropriate buzzwords and phrases, particularly "getting our house in order" and "restraint is a must after the mess we inherited from those confounded Liberals."

In the days leading up to the budget, Mulroney went to Western Canada to talk "tough but fair," promising deficit and program cuts and saying, "If we are to meet the twin challenges of deficit reduction and job creation, we must all be prepared to sacrifice." (A CBC poll showed that 51 per cent of those asked favoured increasing the deficit if that would create jobs.) Meanwhile, Mulroney toured the West promoting deficit-cutting as his top priority and telling a Winnipeg audience that durable jobs can't be created by "simply spending borrowed or printed money."

On budget day, before Wilson had finished his eighty-two-minute presentation, John Turner stormed out of the Commons saying that it was "the most overdue [budget] in Canadian history—and it wasn't worth the wait." Indeed, had it not been for one explosive plan for the partial de-indexing of senior citizens' pensions, the $105-billion document would have been a yawner. For all the talk about deficit-cutting, Wilson expected to trim only $1.1 billion, giving up another $900 million in revenue over two fiscal years by awarding individual investors a lifetime capital-gains tax holiday of up to $500,000. Saying that the budget challenges Canadians "by rewarding success," Wilson promised to eliminate 15,000 of the 258,000 federal-government jobs over six years and trimmed $78 million from the $2.1 billion set aside earlier with great fanfare for job-creation and retraining programs. He also announced $10.1 billion in spending restraints over the next two years and a $2.6 billion increase in personal income taxes—including an eighteen-month surtax of either 5 or 10 per cent on incomes above $40,000 and $60,000 respectively. There were hikes in excise and sales taxes, including two cents a litre on gasoline and—the old standbys—twenty-five cents on a large package of cigarettes and 2 per cent on alcoholic drinks. To "encourage enterprise," Wilson reduced corporate taxes by a net $455 million, although he placed a one-year surtax on large companies. The Tories were also to start selling off Crown corporations that were not fulfilling "a public policy purpose." (Subsequently Canadian Arsenals Ltd. and the federal interest in the Canada Development Corp. were sold. Tele-globe Canada, the federal communications company, was also sold—just before the 1987 budget—to help Wilson claim he was getting the deficit below $30 billion.) Overall, the 1985 budget was not the long-promised new departure but simply a continuation of the process of shifting money around to balance gains and losses.

Mulroney immediately declared that it was "gratifying to see that the budget, which is such an important one, is met with, by and large, widespread favour," and headed off to Montreal and Toronto, selling guide in hand, to trumpet the "tough-but-fair" theme. "Our strategy calls for individual Canadians—not politicians or bureaucrats—to decide what is best for them-selves and for Canada," he told the Canadian-Italian Business and Professional Association in Toronto. That strategy repre-sented, he claimed, "a fundamental change in philoso-phy . . . designed to unleash the full enterprenurial dy-namism of individual Canadians."

Mulroney and Wilson were soon forced to retreat on their pension de-indexation, and by August, Roger Hamel, head of the Canadian Chamber of Commerce was saying publicly that Mulroney had to make some tough choices and prove he could be decisive. Many businessmen were wondering why he hadn't implemented the widespread changes in every depart-ment, aimed at cutting spending, recommended by Erik Nielsen's task force.

In the meantime, several Western Conservative backben-chers were upset with Petro-Canada's $866 million purchase of Gulf Canada Ltd. assets just ten days after Olympia and York Developments Ltd., the Reichmann family's Toronto-based company, had swallowed Gulf's Canadian subsidiary. Energy minister Pat Carney denied that federal politicians "were in the room" when the deals were struck, but added, "it was probably fair to say" that the Reichmanns would not have been able to finance their purchase of Gulf without the backing of Petro-Canada. "We wanted Gulf to be owned if possible by Canadians." Mulroney dismissed the concerns of what he called "only one or two" Alberta MPS, saying, "It is Conserva-tive policy to maintain Petro-Canada. It is Conservative policy to Canadianize the oil industry. That transaction enhanced Canadianization by almost five percentage points. It's a major step forward for Canada. Some people have reservations about it. I can understand that. But it is Conservative policy to proceed exactly as we have."

A few months later Mulroney was forced to defend the

purchase in the Commons against opposition charges that Canadian taxpayers had lost $1 billion in a sweetheart tax ruling by Revenue Canada. At issue was the question of tax expenditures—multi-billion dollar tax breaks designed to promote economic growth but that wealthy Canadians can use to avoid taxes during takeovers.

The sale was completed on August 2 when Olympia and York got 60.2 per cent interest in the Gulf Canada assets held by Chevron, the U.S.-based parent company. Ten days later, Petro-Canada bought Gulf's refining and marketing assets (from a Gulf-Norcen partnership created to hold certain Gulf exploration properties). Had Petro-Canada bought those assets directly from Gulf, Gulf's tax bill would have been high. Companies are allowed a tax break on income when they depreciate the value of their assets, and Gulf would have owed the difference between the sale price and the current depreciated value. According to documents obtained by the *Globe and Mail*, the tax on Gulf's Edmonton refinery alone would have been substantial. The refinery was sold for $275 million, and the depreciated value was about $102 million, meaning that Gulf would have owed taxes on at least $173 million.

However, the assets reached Petro-Canada through an indirect route that was approved by Revenue Canada in advance, so Gulf did not have to pay the tax. Oil-industry analysts estimated the total tax savings at $1.65 billion, and opposition critics in the Commons said that Canadian taxpayers had lost at least $1 billion. The transactions attracted the attention of Auditor General Kenneth Dye, who had already attempted without success to get the finance and energey documents relating to Petro-Canada's 1981 purchase of Petrofina Canada. (During a campaign speech on August 11, 1984, given in the, pouring rain outside Kingston's City Hall, Mulroney had challenged Turner to open the books immediately so that taypayers could judge whether their money was wasted or not in the deal. "Secrecy, stealth, and stonewalling have become trademarks of the present government," he had said. "When [the auditor general] says 'I want to look at those books,' he's got to be able to look at those books for you." No doubt Dye was cheering right along with the Mulroney partisans when he heard that promise. If so, the cheering didn't last. When Mulroney got elected he too refused to let Dye see the documents, ultimately fighting the auditor general in court to keep him from looking at them.)

On his way into a cabinet meeting at Meech Lake on September 6, 1985, shortly after the [Donald] Macdonald royal commission report had recommended cutting the deficit by $10 billion by 1991, Mulroney startled reporters by blurting, "All we've been saying is that the country is broke. We've been trying to tell you for some time this country is bankrupt.

"This government and the previous government for twenty years had been spending more than it was taking in. We are now spending more on interest payments than it costs for our entire social apparatus," he said. "That's a tragedy."

It also wasn't true. For 1985, Ottawa was paying $25 billion in interest on the national debt, but $45 billion on social programs. Moreover, the Macdonald Commission had not said the country was bankrupt. Instead, it had warned against substantial cuts in the deficit until the economic recovery was further advanced, unless the government was willing to lower interest rates enough to offset increases in unemployment. Should that happen, the commission recommended both spending cuts and increased taxes to reduce the deficit.

The fall of 1985 had arrived and Mulroney was planning to turn around his sagging personal popularity through a series of "positive" government announcements, when suddenly the Canadian Commericial Bank collapsed. During a stormy Commons question period, Mulroney said that Canadian bankers would be hauled into court if any unlawful actions of theirs had contributed to the collapse. Wilson confirmed that he had asked executives of Canada's five largest banks in August if they could help save the Edmonton-based CCB. The previous March the banks had put up $60 million of a $255 million federally organized rescue package. In June, Bank of Canada governor Gerald Bouey had told the Commons committee that the central bank needed to put several hundred million dollars into both the CCB and the Calgary-based Northland Bank to replacing fleeing deposits. Now, Turner charged that banking's big five had led the run on deposits that sealed the CCB's fate.

The government's immediate problem was finding $1 billion to cover the depositors in the bank collapse. Mulroney, of course, blamed the Liberals. "There can be no doubt about the genesis of the difficulties. It's the National Energy Program, which devastated the economy of Western Canada." On September 1 Ottawa ordered the liquidation of the bank's assets and decided to fully protect all depositors. Deposits above $60,000 normally aren't insured, but Barbara McDougall, minister of state for finance, promised that Ottawa would protect the $420 million in uninsured deposits at CCB. Turner also revealed in the Commons that just before the Mulroney government had organized the $255 million bail-out package—without even bothering to order an audit of the books—the CCB had transferred $300 million worth of loan assets to its failing California subsidiary, the Westlands Bank of Santa Ana. Turner accused Mulroney of postponing the bank's collapse to avoid being embarrassed while hosting his high-profile national economic conference.

It was the first Canadian bank to go belly up in sixty-two years. The second one took about three weeks, when the Northland Bank also crashed. It had grown with the Alberta oil boom from 1981 assets of $388 million to $1.3 billion in mid-1985 but was hit by a series of business failures in the recession that swept the West after 1982. Ottawa appointed a temporary overseer for the Northland on September 1, the same day it closed the CCB, but frantic attempts to save the Northland finally failed and Mulroney had two bank collapses to his credit.

Mulroney named Supreme Court Justic Willard Estey to probe the bank failures, after convincing Chief Justice Brian Dickson it was an issue of "national importance." (In August, Dickson had told the Canadian Bar Association that judges were jeopardizing their impartiality by heading government-appointed commissions.)

In March 1986, William Kennett, the federal bank regulator who was at the centre of the political storm when the banks failed, asked for early retirement from the public service, saying, "I'm going to take a rest." Kennett, fifty-three, said that his departure had nothing to do with the bank controversy or the testimony critical of himself and his staff during the Estey inquiry. The toughest evidence came from McDougall, Wilson, and Bouey, all of whom testified that they had relied on Kennett for information about the health of the two banks. For his part, Kennett had testified that he and his staff had acted on the best information available but that they did not have the money or the people to keep a constant watch on the approximately seventy chartered banks in Canada. (In the wake of the controversy, the government initiated a review of financial regulations in Canada and increased the staff of the

Office of Inspector General of Banks to seventy from about forty-five.)

By the end of 1985, the Tories were just barely ahead of the Liberals in the Gallup poll—40 to 36—continuing a slide that had been going on for months. Party officials were particularly concerned because this was happening when the economy overall was performing relatively well. The jobless rate had fallen a full percentage point in the past eight months, to 10.2 per cent seasonally adjusted in November. Mulroney was claiming that "this government had created more jobs in fourteen months than the Liberals did in fifty-five months. That is the reality." Housing starts were up 65 per cent over the previous year and starts of multiple-unit dwellings were up 82 per cent. The Gross National Product grew by 4 per cent, the Canadian balance of payments were showing a strong surplus of $353 million in the second quarter and Canada had sold $13.3 billion more in goods than it bought from the rest of the world during the first three quarters of 1985, down from $14.8 billion a year earlier. In late October, the Bank of Canada interest rate hit a seven-year low of 8.77, and the consumer price index was up a modest 4 per cent.

"This is very good news for Canada," said Mulroney, adding that "the doomsters and gloomsters of the NDP do not like good news, but hang on to your hats, because you are going to have nothing but good news from this government."

Despite Mulroney's optimism, Wilson was forced into some high-stakes gambling when the Canadian dollar tumbled below 70 cents (U.S.) early in February 1986. "The general view is that this government has not lived up to expectation," said New York analyst Norm Klath, vice-president of the international economics department at Morgan Guaranty Trust Co. "It seems the government has backed away from confronting significant interest groups in the review of spending programs."

Wilson at first said that speculators betting on the decline of Canada's dollar would lose. Less than twenty-four hours later he launched a series of worldwide manoeuvres to support the currency including the offer of a $1 billion bond issue to attract U.S. dollars in Europe, and an increase in the bank rate from 10.8 to 11.47 to make Canadian dollars even more attractive. By the end of the second week of the month, the dollar had rallied to 71.07 cents (U.S.).

Wilson's March 1986 budget promised to inch the deficit just below the $30 billion mark. Revenue-raising measures included: a 3 per cent surtax on personal income tax beginning July 1, a one percentage point hike of the federal sales tax starting April 1, 4 per cent and 6 per cent increases in alcohol and tobacco taxes respectively, a 3 per cent surtax on corporate income tax, and the phasing out of a variety of tax breaks, such as the inventory allowance and the investment tax credit. The basic corporate tax rate was to fall from 36 to 23 per cent in 1989, but taxes paid by corporations would increase because of the lost tax shelters. Spending proposals included a $700 million farm financial-assistance policy and, for about one million low-income (under $15,000) families, November payment of the child-tax credit of $300 per child, just in time for Christmas shopping.

Wilson based his projections on the assumption that oil prices would rise to $22.50 (U.S.), which they never did, and by September he had to announce a $2.5 billion increase in the deficit to $32 billion because of lower-than-expected oil prices and slow economic growth. The national debt was expected to hit $233.4 billion by the end of March 31 fiscal year, gobbling up $25.6 billion in service charges.

In March, Deputy Prime Minister Erik Nielson finally unveiled his study of waste and inefficiency in government ordered by the Tories in Wilson's 1985 budget. The twenty-one-volume study, which looked at almost one thousand federal programs involving $92 billion in government spending, concluded that federal spending is "out of control" because too many politicians and civil servants don't understand the total impact of the hundreds of programs, tax breaks, and regulations they administer. It said that Canadian firms have become "program junkies" because of an "overly rich and overlapping" network of subsidies and tax breaks for business. However, while Ottawa gives "with both hands," the funding shows dubious economic results.

The study group added that systems for evaluating programs are "generally useless," and that programs are rarely challenged or eliminated because "self-serving" civil servants want to preserve the status quo. It concluded that between $40 billion and $60 billion worth of government real estate, including harbours, airports, and buildings, are "undermanaged and overstaffed," and recommended selling many properties to other governments or the private sector. For all that, Nielsen said that the proposals did "not represent government policy, nor are they decisions of the government." In the end, most of the group's recommendations were ignored.

Though Ontario's economy continued to gallop along, the West was struggling with low oil, grain, and lumber prices, and the East with chronic unemployment and little investment activity. Even within Ontario there were problems. The golden times were restricted to the Golden Horseshoe, a 186-kilometre stretch along Lake Ontario from Oshawa to Niagara Falls. In towns like Sault Ste. Marie in the north, unemployment was 12 per cent, compared to 5 per cent in Toronto. Still, Ontario exports rose 9 per cent in 1985 to $59.4 billion, and the boom wasn't slowing in 1986, as the projected growth rate of 4.5 per cent was a full percentage point above that estimated for the nation as a whole. The lower oil costs that were devastating Alberta's economy saved Ontario businesses and households $2.5 billion in 1986. Much of the boom was due to the auto industry. General Motors announced a $2 billion plant revamping in Oshawa, and Suzuki and GM combined for a $500 million auto plant near the small southwestern Ontario town of Ingersoll. In the past three years, Asian and North American car makers had announced five new car plants for Ontario, and investment of $1.8 billion, providing seven thousand direct jobs. Ontario's Liberal premier David Peterson beamed, "This is a situation where everyone wins."

Well, not quite everyone. From July to September, Canada's overall economy had limped through its weakest three-month period since the end of the recession four years earlier. The gross domestic product grew at an annual rate of 1.2 per cent for the period, down from a revised 3.2 per cent in the second quarter. Inflation rose 4.9 per cent, ending three consecutive quarters during which it was 2 per cent or less.

The prestigious C.D. Howe Institute issued a stern warning to the federal government in its year-end review in December, telling Ottawa to stick to its course or face a rocky ride. "Canada's economy is like a ship sailing in turbulent international waters," the report read. "Though the overall attitude of the ship's crew has improved, its determination to cope with heavier seas is not assured."

According to the institute, the government's economic strategy began well with Wilson's November 1984 economic statement, "but that vision has since been blurred by events." It recommended a $26 billion deficit for 1987 to avoid the "crisis of confidence" that would result if it failed to meet its deficit forecasts "in a relatively favorable economic environment."

In a Gallup poll in late January 1987, 60 per cent of respondents felt that the Mulroney government was mishandling the economy, an increase of 10 per cent in one year. Even in prosperous Ontario, 65 per cent said they believed the federal government was not handling the economy properly. Mulroney's most positive rating was in Quebec, where only 51 per cent accused him of mishandling things (36 per cent said he was doing the right thing), while the worst rating was in British Columbia, where 68 per cent turned thumbs down on his economic management.

Nevertheless, in his February 18, 1987, budget, Wilson said, "If I had to choose just one message for Canadians today, it would be this: our economic-renewal program is working. It is delivering more growth, more jobs and more opportunities now. It is building confidence at home. By changing our image abroad, it is helping to attract the investment that Canada needs."

This time Wilson took another $600 million bite from consumers on gasoline, junk food (potato chips, pretzels, nuts, Popsicles, and granola bars), cigarettes, and a host of other items. The opposition called it a "non-budget," mainly because it seemed to be little more than a holding pattern before the long-promised comprehensive tax-reform package later that year. Mulroney had been promising tax reform since the 1984 election campaign. Two months after taking office, he announced that Wilson was devising a fundamental reform of the tax system. This was to have been included in the 1987 budget, but in early February it was "still being studied." Finally, on June 18, Wilson unveiled his tax-reform package, promising to lower income taxes in four of five Canadian households, increasing corporation taxes slightly, and slapping a 10 per cent tax for homeowners and businesses on long-distance telephone calls. Wilson put the really bad news on hold, at least until after the election, offering three options for some time in the future: a national sales tax that would incorporate provincial retail-sales taxes, a federal value-added tax, or a federal tax on goods or services. In any event, a late March poll for Southern News by Angus Reid Associates suggests he'll have a tough selling job. The poll found that 68 per cent of those surveyed believe that ordinary Canadians pay too much tax, while 43 per cent felt that small businesses are overtaxed. At the same time, 70 per cent think large corporations aren't paying their fair share and 76 per cent that the rich are undertaxed. Wilson proposed to lower the rate of sales taxes but apply a tax across the board to all manufactured goods—a "consumption tax." While widely used in Europe, the tax was opposed by 63 per cent in the survey, and approved by just one in four.

Wilson's budget did nothing to correct the perception that personal tax rates are disproportionately high compared to corporate rates. Personal income tax revenue would rise 14.5 per cent, to $37.8 billion in the fiscal year ending March 31, and another 14.6 per cent to $43.3 billion the following fiscal year. Corporate income taxes during the same period would rise only 2.2 per cent for the 1986–87 years, and 3.9 per cent, up to $9.8 billion, the next year.

The losing battle to get his proposed deficit below $30 billion continued with some fiscal sleight-of-hand. Employers were to send in their tax returns twice a month instead of once, allowing Wilson to "borrow" $1.2 billion from the 1988–89 fiscal year and apply it against the deficit. Otherwise, the deficit would be $30.5 billion.

As well, the government sold Teleglobe Canada, the national overseas communications carrier, to a little-known, and much smaller, Montreal company, Memotec Data Inc., in a deal it claims is worth $608.3 million. Wilson also suggested that Air Canada and Petro-Canada might be sold. "More privatizations are coming," he said. "The sale of interests in Air Canada, Petro-Canada, and other Crown corporations, possibly by public share offerings, is under review." In the previous two years, eleven Crown corporations had been sold, matching sentiments expressed by Mulroney many times both during and after the election campaign. Some, like Canadian Arsenals Ltd., went quietly, while others, like Boeing's $155 million purchase of de Havilland Aircraft, caused a stir. In October 1984, the Tories had produced a list of 57 parent Crown corporations with 134 wholly owned subsidiaries and investments in another 126 companies, for a total value of $77 billion. Many of these companies they wanted to either shut down or sell. The de Havilland dispute wasn't so much over whether they should sell as over whether they gave the firm away at fire-sale rates. In late December 1985, John Turner said: "What we have really given to Boeing is a $1 billion Christmas bonus." (Defence minister Perrin Beatty says that privatization has been good for business and has helped create 1,100 new jobs at the firm's Metro Toronto plant, but in April 1987, Boeing officials complained that the company was in such a sad state when they bought it that Ottawa should now pay them compensation of between $6.7 and $21 million.)

Privatization minister Barbara McDougall announced in March that the process of turning Air Canada and Petro-Canada over to the private sector was well under way. Other agencies, among them CNCP Telecommunications and CN Hotels, are also under review. Transport minister John Crosbie predicted that a decision on whether to sell Air Canada would be made by summer, and on April 9 he said that the federal government was ready to transfer ownership and control of all its seventy-seven airports to local authorities or lease them to private interests. In the meantime, a select group of civil servants and brokerage houses were asked by McDougall to submit a plan by April 1 to privatize Petro-Canada, leaving little doubt that the Tories plan to continue their love affair with privatization.

On CTV's "Question Period" after his last budget, Wilson said that he had probably reached the limit in raising personal income taxes, but warned that many corporations have been ripping off the tax system and that he planned to get tougher with them.

In 1984–85, the last year of Liberal mandate, individuals paid $29.3 billion in income taxes and $14.1 billion in sales and excise taxes. In 1987–88, individuals will pay $43.3 billion in income taxes and $22.8 billion in consumption taxes, an increase of $22.7 billion or 52 per cent. Corporations, on the other hand, paid $9.37 billion in 1984–85, and in 1987–88, will pay $9.78 billion, a tiny increase of $401 million, less than 5 per cent. In 1984–85 the oil and gas industry paid $2.56 billion through the PGRT; now it gets off completely because the PGRT was abolished.

For 1988–89, Wilson forecasts that personal income taxes will go up another 14.6 per cent. Corporate taxes will rise a mere 3.7 per cent, despite a projected 20 per cent increase in profits.

On March 5, Wilson said that 675,000 jobs had been created across the country since the Conservatives took power, 356,000 of them in Ontario. Between July and March, 191,000 jobs were created in Canada, 116,000 in Ontario. At the same time, Statistics Canada reported that economic growth virtually stopped during the final quarter of 1986, when the economy expanded by only 0.1 per cent. The overall growth rate was 3.1 per cent for the year. The trade deficit in goods and services with the rest of the world hit a record $8.8 billion.

A survey of two hundred business, labour, and government leaders by Hay Management Consultants also offered little cheer, as half of the people in the annual survey said they were dissatisfied with the way the country was heading. The pessimism in the survey is a sharp turnaround, Hay's report says. "In previous years, the consensus view was that the Canadian economy and political system was becoming more efficient." Among the major problems perceived were a slippage in Canada's international competitiveness, erosion of the country's natural resources, increased U.S. protectionism, cutbacks in research and development, large government deficits, and industrial overregulation.

According to Tom Trbovich, Wilson's chief of staff, "the deficit cutting of course is an integral part of managing the economy, but most people don't understand or know or care about the deficit. . . . We've managed to knock it down to a manageable level and that's good government. This government has a damn good track record, not just on the economic side either . . . why we don't get credit for that, well, it's partly a lack of communication . . . but it's also because the public gets sidetracked on a lot of the peripheral issues that come up and they lose sight of the good things we've done."

Trbovich concedes that "some of the success of this government is attributable to things the U.S. has done . . . but although we have some significant regional difficulties, we've made significant policy changes. . . ."

Trbovich claims that not everything the government has done to improve the economy is measurable. "Some of it is confidence. How do you measure that? If investors have a feeling that things are going well and going to continue to do well, they do invest. . . . And we've done that. We've created confidence."

Liberal finance critic Raymond Garneau offers a different perspective. Quoting Charles Dickens's famous line, "It was the best of times, it was the worst of times," Garneau says that those words "have a special significance to many Canadians today. The election of this government on September 4, 1984, was to be the dawning of a new golden age. However, it has become in reality a time of shattered dreams and broken promises. It has become a time when the government chose to give to the privileged few and take from the many. History will record that this government turned its back not only on the regions, but also on the most disadvantaged in our land. [It is] . . . the Tory tale of two Canadas, one Canada composed of the haves and one Canada composed of the have-nots."

Bill Neville, a senior Conservative adviser and president of Public Affairs International, notes that "those high expectations in September 1984 were part of the problem. The situation had nowhere to go but down. It was highly unlikely Brian or anybody else was going to meet people's expectations given such a massive mandate.

"It's worth recalling also that it was a style mandate more than a substance mandate," Neville observes. "We didn't come out of that election with a real indication of what the Canadian people wanted us to do as much as how they wanted to do it." In short, although people knew they wanted an end to "the old Liberal way of doing things"—to overspending, for example— their wishes weren't much more specific than that. "It is not surprising then," Neville maintains, "that the main policy thrusts of the government are not really things that came out of that campaign. . . .

"The government came out of the chute with the November 1984 economic statement by Wilson. That was a real attempt to set an agenda in keeping with their mandate, insofar as they had a coherent mandate. Then they proceeded for the next year and a half not to stick to their own mandate. [People] . . . got confused because of the mixed signals. I think that's a big part of the trust issue. People wonder if these guys stand for something."

Neville believes that it is "absolutely essential . . . to be able to look at a leader and say, 'Well, even if I don't agree, at least I know what that leader stands for.' That's what made Reagan and Thatcher so successful, the view they've got a belief structure they didn't just make up in the morning. . . . The most important thing is for people to think, 'Here's a guy you can rely on to act in a certain way because he really believes in that.' Successful leaders have that quality. Mulroney and the government let that slip away."

CHAPTER EIGHT

*

DANCING ON THE WORLD

Less than a month after Brian Mulroney took office as prime minister, former Ontario NDP leader Stephen Lewis, writing in *Maclean's* magazine, was not exactly congratulating Mulroney for his recent trip to Washington to meet President Ronald Reagan.

According to Lewis unnamed observers thought that Mulroney had "acted with indecent haste, grovelling reverentially to the White House. Others are faintly euphoric, arguing that the restoration of continental unity is once again in sight. For my own part, I think that both views are right, and the implications are not pleasing."

A week later, largely as a result of the forceful intervention of former Ontario premier Bill Davis, Lewis was appointed Canada's ambassador to the United Nations, this country's major international representative. Lewis said at the time that he was "flabbergasted" when approached for the job. "I could barely credit it. Not in a million years would I have expected it. In fact, I was physically shaking."

Within a year, Lewis would be transformed from launching fiery ideological attacks on Mulroney and the Tories, to picking lint off the prime minister's suit at the U.N. appearance, patting him encouragingly on the back, and gushing to the media about how wonderful Mulroney was on the international stage.

However, though Lewis has been widely regarded as a force to be reckoned with at the U.N., and is thought to have played a key behind-the-scenes role in the June 1986 agreement for a

five-year African economic-recovery program, Mulroney
hasn't been able to match his ambassador's success. While his
efforts have garnered some rave reviews at home, they have
been practically ignored abroad. "He had to follow Pierre
Trudeau," explained a senior external affairs official. "And that
was no easy task. For whatever Canadians felt about Trudeau
at the end, and there's little doubt what that was, the fact is, he
was respected around the world. The only place Trudeau was
unpopular, outside of Canada, of course, was in the United
States. It's the old story, you know, about the prophet being
more popular away from home. So far, the prime minister
[Mulroney] hasn't been able to achieve that status. It's not that
he's unpopular abroad, it's just that not many people even
know who he is."

Recognizing that, in June 1985, External Affairs released a
glossy, thirty-six-page bilingual booklet about Mulroney, to be
distributed to the media wherever he travelled. Packaged in
Tory blue and entitled "The Right Honorable Brian Mulroney," it contains eighteen large photographs of the prime
minister (each printed twice, in both languages). There are
pictures of Brian with Mila, with Diefenbaker, with the
Queen, with Gorbachev, with Reagan, and with the Pope.
There are also such stirring excerpts from Mulroney speeches
as, "I believe in a Canada that believes in you."

During the government-in-waiting stage, when the Liberals
were just playing out the string and the Tories were counting
the days to an election they were convinced would give them
power, Toronto businessman Sinclair Stevens made no secret
of the fact that he lusted after the external affairs portfolio. It
seemed logical, since he was the opposition's external affairs
critic, but when it came time to choose, Mulroney picked
former prime minister Joe Clark. It has proven to be one of his
best moves. Ideology aside—since many Conservatives still
cringe at the thought of Clark's pink-tinged Toryism—Clark
has emerged as one of the few bright lights in the current
administration, handling himself well both in and out of the
Commons, gaining more respect in most quarters than he had
when he led the fractious Tories from victory to defeat. Mind
you, Clark has suffered some public humiliation, first when
Mulroney nixed plans for a six-city Canadian tour of public
hearings on arms control and disarmament issues because he
was worried that Clark was up to partisan "mischief," and
second at the Bonn economic summit, when Mulroney
publicly contradicted Clark, who was standing right at his side.

In the period leading up to the election, Mulroney displayed little personal interest in international matters. He had planned a European visit to meet Margaret Thatcher, Pope John Paul II, NATO officials, and European business leaders, but it was cancelled when the Liberals decided to bring down their budget on February 15, the week he had planned to be away. At first, Mulroney said he would "absolutely" go on the trip anyway, but reversed himself the next day. He angrily accused the Liberals of chicanery, claiming that Trudeau had promised to keep that week clear for his trip. Finance minister Marc Lalonde, calling Mulroney "rather childish and petulant," said that the Tory leader had told them he planned to be away the previous week. Indeed, Trudeau had been quoted earlier as saying, in a cabinet meeting, "You can't do that," when Lalonde first proposed a February 9 budget.

In late February 1984, Mulroney met secretly with diplomats from Iraq, Saudi Arabia, Jordan, Algeria, Tunisia, Morocco, and Somalia to reassure those Arab states that, under the Tories, friendly relations with Israel would not mean unfriendly relations with the Arabs. The meeting was arranged after a December speech in Toronto in which Mulroney had referred to Israel as an ally and the Arab world as an open wound. Mulroney had not wanted the meeting to be publicized, but Montreal's La Presse reported that he had been apologetic about his Toronto remarks and quoted the comment of one attending diplomat that "We were made to understand quite clearly that the use of the word 'ally' was to be interpreted as nothing more than a statement for domestic political purposes" (translation: it had been used primarily to please Canadian Jews).

However, the next month Mulroney lashed into his caucus after four Tory MPS accepted an unapproved freebie trip to the Middle East as guests of the Arab League. The reproof came after B'nai B'rith spokesman Frank Diamond complained that meeting "with a terrorist . . . is an offence to all Canadians."

In April, Mulroney told an Israel Bonds fund-raising affair in Montreal that Israel must help resolve the "plight of the Palestinians," perhaps by agreeing to a Palestinian homeland on the West Bank and Gaza, but not until the Palestinians "forswear the use of violence and terrorism, recognize the state of Israel, and commit themselves to a political solution," a view that matched Canada's official policy under the Liberals at the time.

That same week, Mulroney protested the appearance of a PLO official at a Senate committee meeting, not mentioning the fact that Tory MPs had been accepting all-expenses-paid trips to meet Arafat for years and that late last year, one (Fundy Royal Tory MP Robert Corbett) had even been photographed dancing with the PLO chieftain.

During the election campaign, Mulroney rarely mentioned international affairs and, apart from seeking improved relations with the United States, which Mulroney calls "the cornerstone of our foreign policy," Conservatives have not made many changes in Canada's traditional role as a middle power trying its best to get along with everybody. There have been some changes. Mulroney did surrender to the romance of a Gallic galaxy of nations, a Commonwealth-like organization of French-speaking countries that Trudeau had long opposed because France had demanded de facto recognition of Quebec as a country in itself. Mulroney also continued Canada's leading role in the Commonwealth, an organization dominated by concerns over South Africa's racist policies. At a Nassau meeting, Mulroney engineered an impressive agreement between opposing factions. He has also tried, with some results, to improve relations with the Soviets, and has managed to gain admittance into the so-called G-7, an economic congregation of the industrial world's most powerful nations. In short, generally speaking he has fared better abroad than at home. Naturally, given his penchant for overstatement, he has tended to exaggerate his influence in world affairs, but on balance, his pursuit of a policy of "constructive internationalism" has been an area of relative strength. When, for example, news of the horrible famine in Ethiopia hit the west in the fall of 1984, underscored by a daily diet of the extent of the tragedy through television, Canada acted quickly. Clark went to Addis Ababa in early November to meet Ethiopian leader Mengistu Haile Mariam, and the government offered to match funds collected from private donations and shipped thousands of tons of food and emergency supplies to the drought-ravaged nation. Clark told Mengistu he wanted observers to monitor the movement of food from port to feeding stations to avoid "horror stories" of food piling up or being stolen. Mengistu gave Clark his "total blessing," and, pointing to the statues of Marx and Lenin that are prominently displayed in the capital, quipped, "If other people are able to help us, we'll recognize them appropriately too."

In the early 1960s, Senegal's poet-president Léopold Senghor, Tunisian president Habib Bourguiba, and King Norodom Sihanouk of Cambodia began to talk about "la Francophonie," a term coined by a French geographer in 1880 and revived by Senghor to describe a French-speaking commonwealth that would serve as a cultural and political equivalent of the English-speaking Commonwealth. This vision appealed to many French-speaking intellectuals, and to romantics hoping to restore the French language and French-speaking peoples to the status they had once enjoyed in the world. The main stumbling block was Trudeau's concern throughout the 1970s about fuelling an "indépendantiste" fervour in Quebec, a fear that prompted him to reject provincial demands for de facto national status at any Francophone meeting. France took the position that no summit could be held without Quebec, and twice during the Trudeau era plans for a summit collapsed on the strength of that disagreement.

With Trudeau gone, however, French prime minister Laurent Fabius visited Ottawa in November 1984, and Mulroney said that he accepted "the legitimacy of privileged, direct relations between Paris and Quebec." Within weeks, both Mulroney and Lévesque had dispatched senior officials to hammer out a formula for Quebec's participation in a Francophone summit.

The federal-provincial deadlock ended with a compromise late in the fall of 1984 between Mulroney and the outgoing Lévesque, when it was agreed that Quebec could participate as an "interested observer" in summit discussions on international politics, and could intervene, or act like a country but with federal permission, on economic issues it felt would affect its interests. Quebec officials would also sit alongside federal representatives in plenary sessions, identifying themselves as "Canada-Quebec," while displaying their provincial flag. In June 1986, Mulroney told four hundred people at a St. Jean Baptiste Day celebration in Ville Marie, Quebec, that the Tories had proved their commitment to the French language by ending the fifteen-year deadlock. "I am proud to say this formula . . . was found by my government, a government headed by a Quebecker from Baie-Comeau." The deal, endorsed by Liberal premier Robert Bourassa, also was extended to include officially bilingual New Brunswick. Manitoba and Ontario sent non-participating observers.

Having two people speaking for Canada led to a tricky problem of just who would speak when. While acknowledging that Quebec would have a "privileged role" in the summit, Mulroney said, "I will represent the whole country . . . at all times and in all circumstances." It didn't take long for the fighting to begin, after Bourassa angered Mulroney by suggesting—without consulting Mulroney first—that European countries give their enormous stockpile of surplus food to hungry Third World states. At a wrap-up press conference, Mulroney warned Bourassa to behave himself at the next summit in Quebec City. "Do it to me once, blindside me once, and you've got a problem the next time we meet," he said. Minutes later, Bourassa appeared to be breaking their agreement when he told reporters he intends to rush ahead to try to win international backing for his proposal.

During the February 1986 Paris summit, Mulroney spoke for Canada at the formal opening session held at the historic palace of Versailles, while Bourassa addressed the closing session. Mulroney's compliance with demands from France won him the right to host the summit in 1987 in Quebec City. Hosting both the Francophone summit and the Commonwealth conference in Vancouver would afford Mulroney a valuable international stage on which to strut his stuff in the months leading up to an election.

Before the summit began, Mulroney announced a $400,000 gift to the Académie Française, a 352-year-old institute of scholars whose forty élite members meet every Thursday in secret to work on a massive dictionary of the French language. The gift is to provide an annual literary prize for authors working in French anywhere around the world. In return, when Mulroney toured the Académie on February 20, he watched the members decide, after a ten-minute discussion, to add a French-Canadian word—"la foresterie"—to the language. Before that, the French had been getting by with the word "la sylviculture."

In an interview published in the French weekly magazine *Le Point* right after the summit, Mulroney portrayed himself as a link between the Francophone and Anglophone worlds, saying, "Canadians are fond of the British and are very close to the Americans. I have a weakness for the French. We [Canadians] have two mother countries, France and Great Britain. I know the French and British don't necessarily always agree, but I have the advantage of getting along well with both."

For his first appearance on a world stage as prime minister, Mulroney chose a sure bet, a meeting with leaders of the seventeen English-speaking Caribbean nations in Kingston, Jamaica, in February 1985. Mulroney's concentration on deficit-cutting at home, particularly Finance's November announcement that CIDA's growth would be curtailed, had Caribbean leaders fidgeting over whether he would honour Trudeau's pledge of $350 million in aid between 1982 and 1987. They needn't have worried. He made the promise after a one-hour private session with Jamaican president Edward Seaga, shortly after arriving in Jamaica from a vacation in Florida. (Ottawa regards the Caribbean as a Canadian "sphere of influence." Since 1966, Canada has poured more than $500 million into the region, second only to the United States.)

For his part, Seaga proposed a one-way free-trade deal for Caribbean products entering Canada. Mulroney promised to look at it, although 93 per cent of imported Caribbean products were already entering Canada duty-free and the rest received preferential tariff treatment. Seaga wanted removal of trade barriers on textiles, footwear, and cigars, and reductions on non-tariff restrictions on Caribbean rum.

In his opening speech (not entirely felicitously) Mulroney compared his relatively comfortable upbringing in Baie-Comeau with the poverty-ridden lives of most Caribbean people, where 65 per cent of youth had no jobs, violence had hit epidemic proportions, and inflation was over 50 per cent. Saying he couldn't discuss aid "without a word of personal history," Mulroney spoke about how he had left Baie-Comeau as a young student to go "to what I thought were pretty faraway places in Eastern Canada. My experience was not unlike that of many young Caribbean students who leave their homes and villages to study at what appears to be a distant technical or university campus."

For all that, however, they loved Mulroney in Jamaica. Seaga said that the other leaders wanted to record their "delight" at his performance with a special mention in the conference's final communiqué, but Mulroney "modestly declined." Seaga said Mulroney was "a big hit. We have found another friend in another leader of another country." Dominica's prime minister Mary Eugenia Charles, who had deliberately not telephoned Trudeau to warn him of the impending 1983 U.S. invasion of Grenada (U.S. and Caribbean officials felt Trudeau was too far left to be trusted), said of Mulroney that she "liked him very much."

In March, Mulroney left Ottawa for Moscow to attend the funeral of Konstantin Chernenko, saying that he hoped to underscore Canada's interest in maintaining a constructive relationship with the Soviet Union. Mulroney couldn't resist suggesting that he might act as an honest broker between the Soviets and the U.S.: "We thought it appropriate that I personally attend." He added that he hoped it would "lay a cornerstone" for the upcoming Soviet tour by Clark. Mulroney met privately with Mikhail Gorbachev, and spoke of him as "a young man, a younger man of vigour and good health and strong views." On his return to Ottawa, he praised Gorbachev as "extremely competent," but played down his role as a go-between leading up to the Geneva arms talks, snapping to reporters, "I was there as the representative of the government of Canada." (After the forty-five-minute meeting with Gorbachev in the great palace of the Kremlin, Mulroney quickly scribbled twenty-five pages of notes, keeping one copy himself and giving another to his literary executor Peter C. Newman.)

In April 1985, British officials were muttering in exasperation over what was to become a pattern with staff people, particularly Bill Fox, who were arranging the prime minister's trips abroad. Mulroney had planned a brief stopover in London on his way to the Bonn economic summit, including an audience with the Queen and a meeting and dinner at 10 Downing Street, the British prime minister's official residence. Fox was looking for every chance to enhance his master's image, but British officials became annoyed at what they considered his aggressive tactics. The usually unflappable British expressed irritation to reporters when Fox pressed for TV coverage of Mulroney's audience with the Queen, something that "just isn't done" in tradition-conscious Britain. Fox also wanted to move furniture in Westminster Abbey to allow for a better camera angle of Mulroney at a wreath-laying ceremony there. According to one British official, Fox "wanted to turn the meeting with the Queen into a rolling cinéma vérité, which, of course, is not our style." Fox in his turn, said that he found the British reaction "outrageous," and that he was merely "reflecting the interest of the media. . . . I told them [British officials] they were telling Canadians they could not see a photograph of their Queen and their prime minister together." Fox, clearly angry at not being allowed to get a photographer inside Buckingham Palace, commented to reporters that, "The president of Egypt can get his picture taken with the Queen and so can King Ooga-Booga . . . but the prime minister of Canada can't." When Mulroney arrived at Heathrow airport, he called the accusations against Fox "false" and "unbecoming. . . . The British expressed no displeasure." Meanwhile members of his staff were mimicking the accents of their hosts and one aide passed out pictures of the Queen and quipped that he would autograph them himself. When Fox jokingly asked reporters to help him storm the palace, it suggested that feathers had indeed been ruffled, despite Mulroney's denials.

A former PMO communications official who used to work for Fox, claims that it wasn't all Fox's fault, that he was under a lot of pressure in the job and that Mulroney counted on him for more than he should. . . ." When he [Fox] is under a fair bit of pressure his neck tends to disappear. I don't think Bill's neck has been seen in probably three years now. . . .

"The problem was that everybody else had to operate under Mulroney's orders, and that was to get the Boss what he wanted. If Fox was trying to get cameras into Buckingham Palace, I can tell you from experience it would be because Mulroney had demanded it."

Before he left London for his first major international appearance, at the Bonn economic summit, Mulroney was again trying to cast himself in a greater role than seemed reasonably justified. Portraying himself as "the new guy on the block," he predicted that he would play "a vigorous role, not a pretentious one" in representing Third World concerns, particularly over repayment of foreign debts burdening the poor countries. "I think it's my responsibility to make sure for those who aren't there that their voices are heard," he said.

Mulroney went even further, offering himself as a potential mediator between France and the United States over reform of the international monetary system. "Obviously, because of our background, we would be disposed, if called upon, to provide any bridging assistance required," he told reporters after what he described as a "terrific" lunch with the Queen. Reagan had just ruled out any immediate move on monetary reform, but the next day French president François Mitterrand said that he could not accept negotiations on trade issues unless the United States dropped its opposition to starting important talks on currency. Britain, West Germany, and Japan all sided with Reagan. So did Michael Wilson in his November

economic statement, leaving reporters to ask Mulroney about
Canada's de facto participation in a common front against
France on the issue. Mulroney replied that Canada would
"never participate in a common front against France . . .
[we] will always look for ways to reconcile French and
Canadian positions," and would vigorously oppose "any attempt to isolate the French." His words would come back to
haunt him months later when his government gave France
everything it wanted in a fishing agreement off the coast of
Newfoundland.

The situation prompted then Liberal external affairs critic
Jean Chrétien to accuse Mulroney of "trying to use the
monarchy to get some publicity. Is it not time that the prime
minister of Canada stops doing show business and starts to do
business?" That prompted Deputy Prime Minister Erik Nielsen to say, "We can be thankful at least . . . [that he] didn't
slide down the bannister at Buckingham Palace and do
pirouettes while he was over there," a reference to Trudeau's
antics. Chrétien added that Mulroney would do better in his
self-proclaimed role as defender of the Third World if he
restored the money cut from Canada's foreign-aid program.

At the summit itself, Mulroney was barely noticed by the six
other world leaders and three thousand journalists, although
that wasn't the story he was telling Canadian journalists. On
opening day, senior Mulroney aides tried hard to undermine
Trudeau's international reputation. "Trudeau's problem was his
credibility," senior policy adviser Charles McMillan (asking
not to be identified) told twenty-five Canadian journalists at a
briefing on the summit. "Mulroney had credibility. He
[Trudeau] was despised by summit leaders, especially Margaret Thatcher and Ronald Reagan." The move was designed
to enhance Mulroney's stature by downplaying Trudeau's role
as an international statesman and Third World spokesman.
(McMillan's statement ignored the fact that Trudeau had
earned praise from dozens of world leaders, including former
West German chancellor Helmut Schmidt, who had once
called Trudeau "a senior statesman" and "a priceless asset.")

Mulroney did manage to humiliate Joe Clark in front of the
cameras and reporters. Clark had followed his instincts and
expressed Canadian displeasure at the U.S. trade embargo of
Nicaragua, particularly at the fact that Canada had not been
notified in advance. Later, answering the same question, with
Clark looking on, Mulroney said he was "not at all displeased"

at the U.S. move. He even ridiculed the suggestion that the United States would want to consult Canada "when they knew our answer in advance."

When Mulroney left the Bonn summit on May 5, he claimed he had acted as a mediator between the United States and France to help set a date for trade negotiations, and that he had made progress on behalf of poor nations. However, senior officials from other participating countries could think of little to say about Mulroney's contribution. A Thatcher aide said that Mulroney was "taking a low profile, as it should be." Mitterrand noted that Mulroney had "looked for conciliation" in the French-U.S. trade fight that dominated the summit.

Mulroney and his officials had seemed obsessed with controlling every event, to the point where Canadian embassy officials complained privately to reporters that their advice was seldom sought, and ignored when it was volunteered. Because Mulroney's staff refused to allow embassy personnel to handle arrangements (as they would normally expect to do), there was a last-minute scramble for accommodations for the Canadian contingent. Mulroney, unable to find a suitable hotel, booted the ambassador out of his residence and took it over himself for the summit's duration.

When *Toronto Star* bureau chief Bob Hepburn returned to Ottawa, he phoned embassy officials in Bonn to find out details of the story. "The person I talked to there said 'I can't talk to you.' This surprised me, because while we were in Bonn this person was quite helpful. The embassy official said, 'They've been looking for us,' 'they' being Fox and other aides, who hadn't liked the press stories quoting embassy officials.

"They knew which embassy officials had been assigned to talk to the media, and they knew which embassy officials were staying at the hotels we were staying in, so they figured they were the ones who were telling negative stories and they were out to find out who talked," said Hepburn. "This person ended up being transferred, pulled out of Bonn, all because of the reporting that was going on. That's not a good way to run a ship."

In late May, Clark tabled a Green Paper on international affairs that was so lacking in substance that opposition members laughed at it and refused to take part in a year-long parliamentary hearing to chart Canada's new course in foreign policy. Featuring a stylized map of the world with Canada poised between the United States and the Soviet Union, the document posed, but does not answer, fifty-two questions on subjects ranging from human rights to defence, foreign aid, and Canada's relations with other countries of the world. The forty-three-page document listed as cornerstones of Canada's foreign policy support of NATO and the defence of North America, and touched on growing pressure for a free trade arrangement with the United States. Ater an opening flurry, the Green Paper quietly disappeared onto a shelf somewhere in External.

In October 1985 Mulroney attended the United Nations' fortieth anniversary celebrations in New York. Before his speech—a hard-hitting attack against South Africa's apartheid—Mulroney met privately with Reagan, and, during a meeting with Japanese prime minister Yasuhiro Nakasone, agreed to stay in Japan an extra week after the next Tokyo summit. In another private meeting, he accepted an invitation to visit Israel from Prime Minister Shimon Peres. Earlier, Mulroney had also agreed in principle to visit the Soviet Union.

On November 21, Mulroney, Clark, and several aides flew overnight to Brussels, then back home the next day, stopping over just long enough to hear Reagan tell the NATO allies about the success of the Geneva summit. Mulroney said later that the allies were "unanimously . . . well pleased . . . there was no euphoria. Nobody was standing up cheering. But there was pleasure that constructive and honest dialogue had begun." It cost about $70,000 to take the Boeing 707 for what amounted to about two hours of actual appearances. Canada already has three ambassadors and their staffs permanently stationed in Brussels—one for the country, one for NATO, and one for European Common Market trade matters. Besides Clark, who brought two senior aides of his own, Mulroney brought six aides plus security personnel.

Nineteen eighty-six got off to a good start on the international front for Mulroney when Japanese prime minister Yasuhiro Nakasone dropped by for a three-day Canadian visit in what was called the "haiku summit," a reference to Nakasone's penchant for writing poetry. Nakasone became the first Japanese prime minister to address a joint session of the Senate and the Commons.

Japan is our most important trading partner after the United States and, for the most part, the two countries' $12 billion annual trading relationship is harmonious, so the two men concentrated on defence, disarmament, foreign aid, and trade protectionism, in preparation for the May 4-6 economic summit in Tokyo. However, the trip followed two major Japanese investment announcements—Honda's $100 million doubling of its car-assembly plant near Alliston, Ontario, and plans for a $400 million Toyota plant near Cambridge, Ontario—which effectively muffled complaints among Canadian business leaders that about 70 per cent of Canadian exports to Japan are raw materials, while most Canadian imports from Japan are manufactured products, a trade relationship that creates many Japanese jobs but few Canadian jobs. In fact, the summit generated no specific initiatives. But with the wheels continuing to fall off on the domestic front, it afforded Mulroney a welcome chance to strut his stuff with a major world leader.

Shortly before he left Canada to return Nakasone's visit, Mulroney invited his old friend Bob Coates to join him on the post-summit part of the trip to South Korea, which was scheduled to follow hot on the heels of a few days in China. Coates, honorary president of the Canada-Korea Parliamentary Friendship Society (which he founded in 1979), has been described by the iron-fisted South Korean president Chun Doop-Hwan as one of that country's closest friends. Coates made at least five trips to South Korea and even received an honorary doctor of law degree from Chungang University after his resignation from cabinet. At the time of the trip Chun had launched a new crackdown on dissidents and human rights advocates, many of whom had been inspired to action by the so-called people's peaceful revolution in the Philippines.

Mulroney's invitation to Coates came shortly after Deputy Prime Minister Erik Nielson had rebuked a delegation of six Conservative MPs for accepting an all-expenses-paid trip there without preregistering the trip, as new Commons rules require for any trips funded by foreign governments or business groups. When news that Coates had been invited to come along at public expense stirred up a mini-controversy, Mulroney simply withdrew his invitation and left Coates at home.

At the Tokyo summit, Mulroney did not swagger into town as the great western honest broker. As a result, he avoided embarrassing himself again and actually made a mark on the event. First, he managed to get Canada a partial membership in what is known as the G-5, the United States, Japan, West

Germany, Great Britain, and France. He also spearheaded a drive to put the costly U.S.-European grain-price war on the agenda for a new round of meetings by the ninety-member General Agreement on Tariffs and Trade (GATT).

These successes gave Mulroney and his loyalists reason for rejoicing. Unfortunately, with the Sinclair Stevens conflict-of-interest allegations erupting on the home front, nobody noticed. For some time, Mulroney steadfastly resisted pressure to answer reporters' questions about Stevens. When he finally gave in he had reporters (who weren't allowed to stay in the same hotel with him) summoned from their digs at the Hilton International to the plush Lotte Hotel. After reading a brief statement on Stevens, he still refused to answer questions. He was stalking out when *Toronto Sun* reporter Derik Hodgson shouted, "Why don't you go back home and face it." Mulroney's face reddened, his jaw tightened, and he turned to Fox. "Who said that?" he snapped.

"It wasn't meant to be a pejorative comment," said Hodgson later. "The House was at a virtual standstill at the time over Stevens. He wouldn't talk about it. Nielsen was stonewalling on his orders. It was a fair question."

Michel Gratton, then Mulroney's press secretary, ordered the journalists back onto the bus to return to their hotel. This time, they wouldn't go. "A bunch of us decided that wasn't good enough," said Hodgson. "We were going to stake him out until he commented on Sinc." The best chance would be at a photo opportunity set up that afternoon with Rick Hansen who, as it turned out, was in Seoul on his way around the world to collect money for spinal-cord research. Mulroney invited Hansen into a hotel room and the disgruntled journalists milled around outside. Finally, after what Hodgson describes as an "interminable time," Mulroney came out the door. "We couldn't believe what he was doing," Hodgson recalls. "He was pushing Hansen's wheelchair, using him as a shield to keep away from us. . . . It was incredible. Instead of answering questions about a senior minister, he hid behind a legitimate Canadian hero."

In August, months after that trip, the Ottawa *Citizen* reported that DND had spent nearly $300,000 on a flight that ferried a video film crew around Asia to record Mulroney's efforts. Obtained under the access-to-information rules, the documents show that a Canadian Forces Hercules flew two video and audio technicians from Tokyo to Peking and then to

Seoul while Mulroney was visiting those cities. Mulroney had been criticized a few months earlier for spending $40,000 to have a Hercules carrying a seven-member technical team and two vanloads of equipment accompany him on a Western Canadian tour. At that point, the government had spent about $360,000 using DND aircraft to record Mulroney's travels, including trips to the Caribbean and Europe, between February 1985 and April 1986. Moreover the latest $300,000 tab did not include the cost of using a DND jet to fly Mulroney and his eighty-three-member entourage from Ottawa to Vancouver for the opening of Expo '86 just before his Asian tour.

In October, the *Citizen* reported that Mulroney's Asian tour had cost the taxpayers $1,116,849, the bill for him, his wife, Mila, and their fifty-two-member entourage. This sum did not cover hotel, meals, and incidental expenses for Mulroney and eighteen members of the delegation that were paid by the host governments. Mulroney took along a butler and a maid, although he denied it. When it came up during a CBC television interview, Mulroney said, "I didn't take a butler. I didn't take anybody. I took the people who help us travel."

The records show that Mulroney took along Ashraf Khan, a butler, and Linda Narcisco, a maid, both employees at 24 Sussex Drive. After Mulroney's denial, Solicitor General James Kelleher, who was saddled with the task of explaining the situation, claimed that both are federal GR2s, general service employees, part of the "internal security" operation for the prime minister. Marc Lortie, a senior Mulroney official, said that the servants' duties included observing meals, pouring tea, and helping both the Mulroneys dress. Mulroney called the story "false," adding, "I can't explain the exaggerations in the press."

In a September speech to the Inter-American Press Association in Vancouver, Mulroney strongly reiterated his government's concern about superpower interference in Central America. While chastising the United States for its interference in Nicaragua, Mulroney delivered an impassioned—and loudly applauded—plea for press freedom: "I invite the Sandinista leadership to recall the spirit in which their revolution was born. In that spirit, a bishop would not have been barred from his pulpit, and a newspaper would not be banned from the streets." Mulroney then slipped out of a press conference and out of British Columbia without answering a single question. He had not held a formal press conference in

Canada in nearly six months, but he would neither meet the media nor answer reporters' questions shouted at him as he came and went from various events.

In March 1987, Mulroney officials announced that the prime minister had decided not to visit the Soviet Union in June, although his aides were working with Soviet officials on plans for a fall visit. At the same time, Governor General Jeanne Sauvé arrived in China for a ten-day visit partly to smooth over a political snub made by Mulroney during his China visit. Sauvé met Vice-Premier Li Peng, whom Mulroney had refused to meet. (This upset both Canadian and Chinese officials; Li, one of five vice-premiers, has emerged as the leading candidate to become China's next premier.) Three times the Chinese had asked Mulroney to meet Li, and had even offered to have Li come to the state guest house where Mulroney was staying. Mulroney officials denied having snubbed Li. "There was no snub by the prime minister whatsoever," said Lortie. "He met with the entire senior leadership." He did not meet with Li.

Also in March, Canada's high commissioner Roy McMurtry told the Canada-United Kingdom Chamber of Commerce in London that historic ties between Canada and Britain have been gradually weakening and that a new relationship should be forged. "The experience of the last fifteen years has shown that the forces of a shared history are no longer sufficient to sustain the future vitality of the relationship or to provide a basis for expansion," he said. "Traditional and sentimental ties with Britain now have to be seen against a backdrop of the U.K.'s increased involvement in the Common Market and Canada's preoccupation with its relations with the United States. A new beginning has to be made. . . ."

The new beginning sounded like a good idea, but given the political climate in the Commonwealth, McMurtry's call seemed unlikely to be heeded. Early on, Mulroney had claimed to have one of his "special relationships" with Margaret Thatcher, but this supposed cordiality was threatened by their conflicting views on the issue that had dominated the Commonwealth for the past two years—what to do about South Africa. Thatcher opposed all-out economic sanctions, arguing that it would hurt the blacks more than it would help them. Mulroney, on the other hand, saw himself as the leader of the movement in the west to give the African front-line states the sanctions they wanted. He had ambitions to emerge from the dispute with the international status John Diefenbaker had attained back in 1961 when he led the fight to have South Africa tossed out of the group. Of course, Mulroney is helped in his stand by the fact that Canada's economic ties with South Africa are so small that cutting them off completely would barely cause a fiscal ripple.

At 11:00 A.M., on January 27, 1987, after an all-night flight aboard a DND Boeing 707 from Rome, Brian Mulroney stepped into the warm sunshine at Harare International Airport to be greeted by native drums, dancers, a cheering throng, a military salute, and the entire Zimbabwean cabinet. Lamp standards on the motorcade route into the city bore huge Mulroney portraits, and the government-controlled *Harare Herald* welcomed him as a conquering hero.

Mulroney was happy to be there, not just to escape Ottawa's biting cold winter, but to gain a reprieve from the pressure of yet another domestic scandal—this one involving the firing of junior transport minister André Bissonnette over the Oerlikon affair.

Mulroney became the first white western leader to visit Zimbabwe and the front-line states since Zimbabwe had achieved independence seven years earlier from the white-minority-ruled Rhodesia. So Mulroney was happy to be in Zimbabwe, and Prime Minister Robert Mugabe and his friends were just as happy to see him.

In his two years as prime minister, Mulroney had earned the adulation of black African leaders for his efforts in the Commonwealth to bridge the ideological and cultural gaps between themselves and Thatcher, and for his tough, anti-apartheid rhetoric at the United Nations and a series of symbolic sanctions imposed against South Africa domestically.

The Africans were happy for a more important reason, which would become obvious even to Mulroney on the third day of his trip when he flew to Victoria Falls to join Mugabe, President Kenneth Kaunda of Zambia, and President Quett Masire of Botswana in what was supposed to be a private discussion of South Africa. The meeting took place in a modern resort on the banks of the Zambezi River near the world-renowned falls.

Mugabe welcomed Mulroney briefly. The media were then supposed to be hustled out of the room before the private session began. In a surprise move, however, Mugabe suddenly announced that the media could stay. Mulroney was stunned.

A television camera happened to be trained on him at that instant, and his look of shock and dismay and the dagger-like glare he sent Mugabe, belied later damage-control claims by his aides that he had known of the change. At first his aides admitted they hadn't expected an open meeting—"This is the first I knew of it," said press secretary Michel Gratton. Later, however, an external affairs official came onto the media bus to "clarify" the situation and claim that Mulroney had been informed by Mugabe ten minutes before the meeting began.

It took about fifteen seconds to see why Mugabe, Kaunda, and Masire wanted an open meeting. One after the other, they launched into a tirade against U.S. policy on South Africa and openly advocated violence as the only way to overthrow the Pretoria regime. Mulroney, clearly uncomfortable, sat through the speeches, periodically writing notes, but more often sitting, tight-lipped while the three African leaders talked over his head through the media to Thatcher and Ronald Reagan.

"Historically, the United States is a child of violence. It was a child of revolution," said Kaunda, chairman of the front-line states organization. "The conditions which led the American people to fight for their independence exist today in South Africa. Reagan can't decide the struggle in South Africa is different from the struggle the Americans waged more than two hundred years ago."

Mugabe, a former guerrilla leader who is busy turning Zimbabwe into a one-party Marxist state, told Mulroney that "Non-violence is not working in South Africa. We in Africa support all forms of struggle, the violent and non-violent. It is hypocritical to say the downtrodden of South Africa are terrorists for taking up arms to free themselves from tyranny."

All three leaders denounced U.S. secretary of state George Shultz, who, they claimed, had called African National Congress leader Oliver Tambo a terrorist. In fact, Shultz had simply said that the ANC should abandon violence and had expressed concern about their Soviet ties.

Mulroney, shaken by the passionate anti-American sentiment, and not wanting to be seen as advocating bloodshed in South Africa, was clearly in a pickle. "He was sandbagged, pure and simple," said one senior Canadian official.

For his part, Mulroney said that it wasn't up to him to speak on behalf of the U.S. government, although he considers them friends and allies. He also said that all Western leaders, including Reagan, oppose apartheid. "Where we disagree is on the course each country should follow. Canada has charted its own course from which we will not deviate. Justice, fairness, and tolerance must ultimately prevail in South Africa. These are the cornerstones of the nonracial society that must emerge." He added that he himself expected to be able to meet with Tambo.

Back in Harare, Mulroney came to a news conference—scheduled for the night before, but suddenly cancelled after the Victoria Falls event—with a prepared answer to a question he knew would be asked: Do you support the violent overthrow of South Africa and if not, why didn't you denounce its advocacy by the three African leaders?

Sure enough, it was the first question asked. Mulroney, shifting into his deepest, most serious voice, said, "As a Canadian, I can speak only from a Canadian perspective. I have not, in my background in Canada, had any cause to use or advocate the use of violence. I was born and raised in a fully democratic egalitarian state. That is my perspective.

"I cannot speak for Robert Mugabe whose life has been entirely different, who was raised in an entirely different society and who has known repression and the lack of freedom and liberty. So we do not advocate the use of violence. Canada seeks to create a climate where differences are resolved. I recognize, however, that the sources of violence in South Africa are unique."

Some time after the event, a senior external affairs official, who spoke only on condition that he wouldn't be identified, said that the Victoria Falls incident underscored "precisely who no other Western leader has gone there. Nobody likes to get used, however noble the purpose may be, and the pre-departure discussions addressed that issue. It was to avoid just such a thing that our side insisted beforehand that the Victoria Falls meeting be private. It's not terribly polite to put a guest in that position, but obviously they [the front-line leaders] have more pressing concerns than worrying about Mulroney's personal comfort level."

Mulroney went on to visit Senegal—where he was treated like a royal potentate and seemed to toughen his stance on economic sanctions. He said flatly in Dakar that "Canada's purpose is clear; we have imposed economic sanctions against South Africa, and we will impose more, because apartheid is evil and shameful." The day before, in Harare, he had listed a series of conditions for imposing more sanctions, among them the need for prior consultations with the affected parties. When asked about this significant change, Mulroney denied that it was a change.

While on the African continent, Mulroney announced more than a dozen programs, involving more than $125 million, for projects including child immunization, grain-price stabilization, training centres for women, fishing and forestry development, and seismic soundings off Senegal's coast.

He also raised the question of human rights briefly with Mugabe in the wake of ongoing Amnesty International charges that the government was implicated in the abduction, unlawful detention, torture, and disappearance of political prisoners. Despite the evidence, Mulroney pooh-poohed the charges, on grounds that Mugabe, who had spent so much time in jail himself unfairly, would not want to subject others to the same treatment.

Back in July 1985, Joe Clark had announced a series of economic sanctions against South Africa, including closer monitoring of Canadian firms operating in that country; restrictions on the exports of sensitive electronic equipment; refusal to import South African arms; abrogation of double-taxation agreements; cutting off market-development assistance to Canadians exporting to South Africa; and spending of an additional $5 million to help train black South African students in Canada and South Africa. Referring to a "rising tide of revulsion," Clark called Canadian ambassador Edward Lee back for "consultations," a diplomatic manoeuvre countries use to signal their displeasure. Canada also decided to limit the sale of South African gold coins, Krugerrands, a move that saw our own gold Maple Leaf coin replace Krugerrands as the top-selling gold coin in the world.

On August 21, 1985, Mulroney had said at a cabinet meeting in Vancouver that he would order more sanctions within the week because he was "dismayed" at South Africa's failure to deal with its racial problems. Commenting on a speech the night before by South African president Pieter Botha, Mulroney said, "I was struck by what I thought was the tenor of the insensitivity to a fundamental moral issue of racial segregation, which is a society built on that, which is unacceptable to Canada in every way." He strongly denied accusations that his government's bark was worse than its bite on this issue.

Less than two weeks later, on a Global television interview marking the end of his first year in power, he said that his earlier support for sanctions had been a quick reaction to an "abhorrent" situation and didn't take into account the possible ramifications for blacks in that country. He said that he had come to support Clark's suggestion that economic sanctions against apartheid might not be best for the blacks who live in South Africa.

"The question arises, how do you dismantle apartheid or persuade people in a vigorous way to dismantle apartheid without crippling economically the blacks and the coloureds and the Indians who very much need our help?" he said, responding to the argument of Global anchorman Peter Trueman that sanctions would hurt the blacks. His own reaction, and that of most Canadians, Mulroney said, was that apartheid was "wrong, it's bad, it's abhorrent . . . but I suppose, yes, we will have to reflect upon other options [besides sanctions] because there are loud voices now coming to us from South Africa that say these policies may very well cripple us, the people you're trying to help."

A month later, however, he was back to talking tough on sanctions, telling reporters on the eve of a Commonwealth meeting in Nassau that it would be "deeply unfortunate for the Commonwealth" if Britain failed to join the other forty-eight countries in actions to oppose apartheid. He said he hoped to persuade Thatcher to agree to some anti-apartheid economic measures that Canada had already adopted. "I don't say that with any aggresivity, and I know the British position traditionally has been strongly different from ours," he said.

It was Mulroney's first Commonwealth meeting, and he got off to a poor start when his opening speech bombed. But he quickly made up for that by engineering a compromise between Thatcher on the one hand, who as one of her aides said, "wants no truck with sanctions," and the front-line-states leaders, who essentially wanted to send in the tanks.

At midnight, on October 18, 1985, still dressed in his dinner clothes from a formal affair earlier, Mulroney left his advisers and walked up two floors to the heavily guarded suite of Indian prime minister Rajiv Gandhi. Besides Gandhi and Mulroney, Bob Hawke of Australia, Kaunda, and Sonny Ramphal, head of the Commonwealth secretariat had gathered to begin the delicate process of convincing Thatcher to compromise on South Africa in order to save the Commonwealth.

Mulroney and the others had been deeply moved that afternoon when Kaunda twice broke into tears at the sessions as he tried to express his frustrations over fighting apartheid. Mulroney had also been affected by his audience with the Queen earlier that day aboard the *Britannia*. She had told him that "her" Commonwealth was in danger and cautioned against any move to gang up on Thatcher and isolate her.

In her opening speech, Thatcher had made it clear she wasn't budging. "We are not in the business of sanctions . . . we are resolutely and fundamentally opposed to sanctions." Hawke, the hard-nosed union leader who had once won a beer-drinking contest at ̦Oxford, said "We want to bring South Africa to its senses, not to its knees," a phrase Mulroney has borrowed without credit dozens of times since.

The meeting went on for two hours, breaking up with the promise of further meetings. Indeed, Mulroney and the other leaders spent the next three days working long into the night trying to forge a package they could take to Thatcher. By this time, the leaders had left their Nassau hotels and holed up for the weekend in private homes in a fashionable millionaires' retreat at Lyford Cay, blocked off from the prying eyes of the media. When it finally came time to present the compromise to Thatcher, the group chose Mulroney to approach her.

The accord, while hardly dramatic in itself, represented an historic agreement on concerted Commonwealth action, promising sanctions if South Africa didn't make "significant progress" within six months and setting up a committee of eminent persons (which ultimately achieved nothing) to go to that country and try to talk sense to them. Mulroney said that he wanted Trudeau in the group, but he let it slip before asking Trudeau. When the formal invitation was made, Trudeau declined. Referring to the agreement, Thatcher insisted that she had moved only "a tiny little bit," holding her fingers up to illustrate the point. Still, she had moved, and Mulroney had been a key player in the compromise.

Fresh from that victory, Mulroney charged off to speak at the fortieth anniversary of the United Nations. During his tough, seventeen-minute attack on South Africa, he threatened to "sever" diplomatic ties completely "if there is no progress in the dismantling of apartheid." When he finished, the crush of leaders wanting to congratulate him was so great that U.N. president Jaime De Pinies had to ask them to go out in the corridors and not disturb the next speaker. Typically, shortly after the speech a Canadian official came running into the press room furiously searching for a tape of the speech and its congratulatory aftermath, explaining that Mulroney was anxious to watch his own performance as soon as possible.

When Mulroney and his twenty-two-member entourage left Newark International Airport for Ottawa on October 25, 1985, the corks were popping and the champagne was flowing just moments after the Boeing 707 left the ground. By any measure, it had been a successful two weeks for him, and Mulroney sounded almost humble when he told reporters, "I think Canada's interests were put forward in a proper perspective and to that extent I'm pleased." He should have been. Even the opposition sang his praises in the Commons, before reverting to business as usual by going after Mulroney over the collapse of the Canadian Commerical Bank.

A mini-summit of seven Commonwealth leaders was slated for London, on August 3–5, 1986, and Mulroney scheduled a ninety-minute meeting with Thatcher as she returned from visiting Expo '86 in early July at Montreal's Mirabel Airport to discuss her pledge in the Nassau Accord "to consider" banning new investments, tourism, air links, and agricultural imports from South Africa if things hadn't improved. Before leaving for Canada, Thatcher pointedly granted interviews to Canadian journalists stationed there to restate her opposition to sanctions. "What is moral about adding to poverty and unemployment in a country that has no social security?" she asked. By this point, Kaunda had threatened to quit the Commonwealth unless sanctions were imposed, and Malaysian president Mahathir bin Mohamad had said that Britain, not the pro-sanctions members, should get out of the organization.

On July 13, after meeting Thatcher in Montreal, Mulroney said he was ready to risk a Commonwealth split and join other countries in tougher sanctions. In a public warning to Thatcher, he said, "Canada will follow through on its obligations." He added, "The Botha regime hasn't the slightest intention of altering what is a fundamentally evil policy." Thatcher said that only negotiations would end apartheid. "We had to do that when it came to turning Rhodesia into Zimbabwe, and I don't think any other way will do it." At the same time, Canada decided not to join a wave of nations who were boycotting the Commonwealth Games in Edinburgh, Scotland, to protest Britain's opposition to sanctions. "It is not one of the elements that we would consider helpful," said Mulroney.

As he boarded his plane on August 1, 1986, for the Commonwealth meeting, a tough-talking Mulroney said that

Thatcher would "have to accommodate herself as well, as I'm sure she will, to certain realities. One of them is Britain's membership in the Commonwealth, where we clearly stated that, in the absence of any progress, we would get together and consider further measures."

Arriving in London for the opening, Mulroney said: "We want something done here. [The Commonwealth] must stand for strong moral principles, which must rise above balance sheets and commercial trading patterns, and deal with a fundamental evil that exists in South Africa."

As British officials argued, it was easy for Mulroney to moralize about "balance sheets," since Canada's two-way trade with South Africa was quite small (about $345 million in 1985, over half of it with Ontario), while Britian has an estimated $12 billion invested in South Africa and $3.5 billion in annual trade. The British Industry Committee for South Africa, an organization of British multinationals campaigning against sanctions, said that full trade sanctions would cost Britian $9.1 billion annually and put 130,000 jobs at risk. Others pointed to Mulroney's expressed intention to remove limited sanctions against the Soviet Union on cultural, scientific, and educational exchanges to protest the Soviets' invasion on Afghanistan. "Where is the high moral tone there?" one British official was quoted as saying. "The [Afghanistan] war is still being fought, people are still being slaughtered, yet Canada is dropping its sanctions. Could it have anything to do with the relative size of trade Canada does with South Africa and the Soviets [$2 billion-plus]?"

In any event, tensions were high when Thatcher, Gandhi, Mulroney, Ramphal, Hawke, Mugabe, Kaunda, and Bahamanian prime minister Sir Lynden Pindling gathered at Marlborough House, the grand eighteenth-century residence that serves as the organization's headquarters. After the meeting, six of the leaders decided to impose a list of eleven economic sanctions, but Thatcher agreed only to two token measures, and even then, she said, "only with reluctance." (She agreed to voluntary bans on new investment and tourism promotion.) Mulroney said he was "less than ecstatic" about the split; but, he added, "there is little solace in this document for Pretoria." Mugabe was "utterly dismayed and dissatisfied" by Thatcher's stand, and Gandhi's comment was: "Britian is not the leader any more, not in the Commonwealth. It is compromising on moral principles for economic need." After the meeting broke up, the six leaders nominated Mulroney and Clark to stay on for an hour-long private talk with Thatcher, hoping to get her agreement on a ban on air links with South Africa. They didn't succeed. In addition to the sanctions agreed to at Nassau, the leaders added three more: an end to new bank loans; a ban on imports of uranium, coal, iron, and steel; and the withdrawal of all consular facilities except those dealing with a country's nationals. The communiqué added that further unspecified sanctions could follow unless South Africa released Nelson Mandela, the imprisoned ANC leader, and dropped its ban on the ANC within "a reasonable time."

Thatcher, who, as high commissioner McMurty had pointed out, was looking more to Europe than to the Commonwealth, had agreed to accept whatever sanctions the European Community imposed. As it turned out, the EC foreign ministers, meeting in Brussels in September 1986, decided to impose a ban on new investment in South Africa, as well as on the import of South African iron, steel, and gold coins. A ban on coal, which had been agreed upon at the EC's June summit at The Hague, was not approved because of strong opposition from West Germany and Portugal.

(However, while politicians jockeyed for position and polished their rhetoric, Canadian companies with investments in South Africa were actually making a move. During 1987, one-third of all Canadian firms with business interests pulled out, and most remaining Canadian companies are reviewing plans to leave. In 1986, eighteen Canadian companies with financial interests valued at $135 million were doing business in South Africa. But late in the year and early in 1987, six of those, employing more than 8,100 people, sold their investments. These were Falconbridge Ltd., [with shares in a South African platinum mine and refining company]; Bata Industries Ltd., [with South African manufacturing and retail operations]; Dominion Textiles Inc.; Alcan Aluminium Ltd.; Jarvis Clark Co. Ltd.; and Moore Corp. Ltd.)

Though private companies were preparing to act, a secret document submitted by Ontario bureaucrats to the Ontario cabinet in September 1986 stated baldly that "no further measures by the Canadian government are expected before the Commonwealth meeting in Vancouver in October 1987 unless there is substantial change in the South African situation or in international positions towards South Africa with an impact on Canada."

In short, Mulroney was seen to be playing a political game with the issue, holding his cards to be unveiled at the Commonwealth conference he would host in Vancouver, no doubt in order to announce his plans to the accompaniment of substantial media ballyhoo. His African trip, of course, had been designed to maintain interest in the subject leading up to the conference, and it would not be surprising, given the history, if Mulroney announced a complete diplomatic break with South Africa at the meeting.

As if to confirm this view, Clark announced in March that he had received cabinet approval in January for further economic measures but that the time was not yet ripe to impose them. Government watchers may be pardoned for predicting that the Tories are likely to find the time ripest at the autumn summits, when they can exploit any new initiatives for maximum media impact.

CHAPTER NINE

SAYING UNCLE TO SAM

It is important to remember that Ronald Reagan did not actually sing "When Irish Eyes Are Smiling" onstage at Quebec City's posh Grand Theatre with Brian Mulroney on March 17, 1985, at the glitzy $550,000 black-tie finale to the Shamrock Summit.

Oh sure, he and Nancy were up there on the stage, even mouthing a few words, but Reagan had said beforehand that he wouldn't sing and didn't want a microphone near him. Mulroney had asked him to go on stage at a wrap-up of the Gala Soirée, so he went as a favour. But he didn't sing.

Brian Mulroney did sing, however. He has a splendid baritone singing voice, the result of a lifetime of singing for assorted American audiences.

He used to delight in telling the story himself. As a boy soprano in Baie-Comeau, he would sing "Dearie" for American newspaper tycoon Colonel Robert McCormick whenever McCormick came to town to check his paper mill. "He'd give me fifty dollars a crack," said Mulroney. "I remember standing on top of the piano singing the song with Jack Dempsey sitting right in front of me. The colonel had brought him in for some fishing. I just about had a heart attack. I was eight, maybe nine."

Mulroney grew up to be a baritone, and after the Tories weren't buying his song and dance at the 1976 leadership convention, Hanna Mining Company of Cleveland, Ohio, asked him to come and sing the praises of their Canadian affiliate, the Iron Ore Company of Canada. In return, they offered to make him a millionaire and gave him a mansion in Westmount, membership in the best clubs, a fishing camp in Labrador, and four box seats directly behind the Montreal Canadiens' bench at the Forum. He did well by them, too. He ended labour strife and turned a profit, and when it came to a choice between sending dividends south of the border or propping up the mine at Schefferville, Mulroney did right by his American masters—he closed the town.

When he became prime minister in 1984, his first major international serenade was delivered to a blue-chip audience of 1,500 Wall Street barons at the prestigious Economic Club of New York's 306th dinner meeting. There he crooned the welcome news that, "Canada is open for business again." Oh my, how they loved it. He wasn't just whistling Dixie, and they knew it. It was music to their ears after all those years of Pierre Trudeau, who had insisted on singing about economic nationalism and refused to follow the hymn book that had made America great. "The government of Canada is there to assist—and not harass—the private sector in creating the new wealth and new jobs that Canada needs," crooned Mulroney. He was interrupted by applause eleven times.

One of the homegrown cheerleaders, business writer Peter C. Newman, the only journalist at the event in a black tie, could barely contain his enthusiasm when he wrote: "Most Canadians don't realize that Mulroney is genuinely at home with the Wall Street barons who turned out for him." From 1980 to 1983 Mulroney was a director of Hanna, which, Newman wrote, "was the centre of a giant spoked wheel, uniting investments from five great family fortunes: the Mellons of Pittsburgh; the Hannas and Humphreys of Cleveland; the Bechtels of San Francisco; and the Graces of New York. While he never became one of them, Mulroney established the connections and the credibility he is now exploiting to attract new investment funds into Canada."

What constitutes an appropriate relationship with the Americans—and how to achieve it—has always been the great Canadian dilemma, perhaps the most enduring issue for Canadian political leaders since this country's birth. Most leaders have successfully maintained friendly ties; a few—notably Trudeau—have been unnecessarily hostile. But none have been as keen as Mulroney to be loved by an American president even at the expense of Canadian interests.

"He doesn't seem to understand that in politics you have no

friends, just interests," says Quebec television journalist Michel Guenard. "Mulroney wants to reinvent the wheel in his relationship with the Americans. He says they should suddenly wake up in the morning and realize how important Canada is.

"Obviously there are many clashes between the two countries, no matter how close we are. On numerous occasions we are fighting over the same markets, our branch-plant economy means Americans will sometimes make decisions in their own interest which will hurt our interest. So the last thing you do is go off to Washington and hug the president in your arms and say how happy we are."

Guenard points to France and Great Britain as an example. "They've lived together six hundred years. No two countries ever hated each other more or fought more battles against each other, yet gradually, through diplomacy, they both ended up in the Common Market. Not because they love each other all of a sudden, but because they have common interests. Nobody woke up in Paris one day and said, 'Oh, I love the English, I think I'll go over to 10 Downing Street and hug Maggie Thatcher.'

"That's not the way it works. It's done through the normal channels of diplomacy. You had a socialist president and a rightwing prime minister and most things went smoothly between them. Obviously, somebody had done the work behind the scenes. . . . That's the difference between professionals and amateurs."

NDP leader Ed Broadbent notes that political leaders of all stripes, going right back to Sir John A. Macdonald, "have known you have to maintain in this country of ours a healthy skepticism about the United States. Not about the American people, but about the United States as a dominant economic power on this continent and the notion that the shrewd Yankee trader didn't develop by accident. It's because they were a shrewd, competent, commercially oriented nation. That's how they grew to greatness in the world."

In Broadbent's view, all the most competent Canadian prime ministers "have had that sense of Canadianhood, that required standing up to the Americans, to use that phrase, much more often than saying they're good guys. Very often when they're good guys, you said it to yourself and would say it to them privately, but to show the Canadians that their government was really there, you had to make it clear that we were there and send that signal out, not only to the Americans, but to the people of Canada as well."

Broadbent believes that Mulroney "really overdid it. It wasn't seen so much at the time, but it's so symbolic in light of what has happened since the Shamrock Shuffle, this collegiality with Ronald Reagan was entirely overdone, the wrong thing for Canada."

Mulroney's childhood in Baie-Comeau may explain part of it. He grew up knowing that if the Americans hadn't built the paper mill, there'd be no town, so he managed to develop the what's-good-for-the-Americans-is-good-for-Baie-Comeau philosophy into a national policy. "I think there's a real danger of that, because I don't think he thinks deeply about the requirements of national policy," said Broadbent. "He relies too much on the Willy Loman approach to politics, a smile and a handshake. He thinks that's what should get you through life, that's what should get you through Canada–U.S. relations."

From the first Canada–U.S. summit to the last, and at every point in between, Mulroney has openly relied on what he claims is a "special" personal relationship with Ronald Reagan.

Toronto Star Washington bureau chief Bob Hepburn says that Reagan obviously likes Mulroney more than he did Trudeau, "but I don't get any sense that there's this great relationship between the two of them." In a recent interview with Michigan's John Dingell, chairman of the energy and commerce committee (which deals with, among other things, acid rain), Hepburn asked about that. "He [Dingell] said, 'Oh well, all the countries say that. The Japanese say they've got a special relationship with Reagan. The French say that, and they're in here this week. Every foreign country tries to portray their leader as having a special relationship. I have never seen that Reagan feels they're buddies.'"

Again it all seems to go back to those days in Baie-Comeau, and his view that the Americans were going to help him. "They gave his daddy a job in the mill," says Hepburn, "and now his view is that Ronnie's going to look after him. Well, Ronnie is not going to look after him. Ronnie is going to look after himself and his country first. If that helps Canada, so be it. But if it doesn't, as in shakes and shingles, then tough luck."

According to Hepburn, Mulroney's "telephone diplomacy" —his claim that he can call Reagan at any time to discuss issues—"just doesn't exist. It's a myth. They talk on the phone maybe once or twice a year, that's all. . . . Mulroney is banking on his friendship to help him out. Reagan doesn't look at it that way.

"The administration was really enthusiastic when he first started," Hepburn also noted. "They thought this guy was a new era, but they soon found him wishy-washy, he had an inability to make decisions, and he flip-flops a lot and that worries them. In a nutshell, they don't trust him. . . . They think he's easily swayed by how the political winds are blowing at home."

Few prime ministers have been criticized as often as Mulroney for failing to have a vision of the kind of Canada he wants and an agenda, however flawed, to help him achieve it. While that is fair comment in general, Mulroney has launched on one of the oldest and most politically dangerous policies of all—freer trade with the Americans.

Historically, Conservative leaders have tended to oppose the initiative, while the Liberals have supported it. In 1878, Sir John A. Macdonald, running on a national policy of self-reliance, defeated Liberal prime minister Alexander Mackenzie, an avowed free trader. Then Wilfrid Laurier picked up the theme, pushing a "commerical union" with the United States in 1891. He too was defeated by Macdonald. Again in 1911, as prime minister this time, Laurier actually negotiated a "reciprocity agreement" with the Americans allowing a free exchange of a wide range of products, but Conservative Robert Borden, fighting the plan, thrashed Laurier in the election and the agreement was never ratified.

In 1925, Conservative Arthur Meighen, running on a policy of high tariffs against the protectionism of the day—which parallels the current U.S. mood—defeated Mackenzie King by fifteen seats, but King, arguing for lower tariffs, clung to power with the help of the twenty-four Progressives.

In the 1960s, Liberal PM Lester Pearson adopted a sectoral approach to the issue, signing the immensely successful Auto Pact in 1965. Even Trudeau, in 1983, initiated talks on removing trade barriers in specialty steel products, mass-transit vehicles, computer services, and agricultural equipment.

For Mulroney, there has been no more important issue since his 1984 landslide victory, but his endorsement of the concept has surprised many observers. During the 1983 Conservative leadership race, Newfoundland's John Crosbie came out strongly in favour of free trade with the Americans, but Mulroney ridiculed him and the idea. It would be, he pointed out, like sleeping next to an elephant: "it's terrific until the elephant twitches, and if it ever rolls over, you're a dead man."

In June 1983, Mulroney was asked about the issue by John Gray of the *Globe and Mail*. "This country could not survive with a policy of unfettered free trade," he said. "I'm all in favour of eliminating unfair protectionism, where it exists. This is a separate country. We'd be swamped. We have in many ways a branch-plant economy, in many ways, in certain important sectors. All that would happen with that kind of concept would be the boys cranking up their plants throughout the United States in bad times and shutting their entire branch plants in Canada. It's bad enough as it is . . ."

A week earlier, he had told Gray he would renegotiate the Auto Pact and a fishing treaty with the United States, but he avoided offering any details. Lowering his voice another octave, as he does when trying to evoke a mood of serious confidence, he told Gray that some matters had to be kept dark. "One way you bargain, the key to bargaining, is that you never give away anything until you sit down at the table."

One of the major criticisms of Mulroney's handling of the current round of free trade talks is that he did give the Americans major concessions before the talks even began, such as killing the National Energy Program, gutting the Foreign Investment Review Agency, and introducing a pharmaceutical bill that the major U.S. drug companies had been lusting after for years. Critics say if Mulroney wanted to do all those things, he could at least have used them as bargaining chips, rather than making the moves and hoping the Americans would be grateful.

Late in his 1983 leadership campaign, Mulroney repeated his opposition to free trade, saying, "It affects Canadian sovereignty and we will have none of it, not during leadership campaigns or at any other time." He did not mention the topic at all during the 1984 election campaign, but two months later, in his November economic statement, finance minister Michael Wilson spoke of "opportunities to pursue trade liberalization on a bilateral basis with the United States. . . . The question is how best to capitalize on this advantage, while managing the adjustment that freer trade would entail."

The reference was buried inside a long policy paper and captured little attention at the time. A former government official, who was active on the issue in its early stages, said that it all began when Reagan "put a bee in his [Mulroney's] bonnet" at their post-election meeting in Washington in late September 1984. Reagan had always advocated free trade—during his first election campaign he spoke of a North American free-trade agreement. A few days before Mulroney arrived in town, the U.S. Senate adopted a bill giving Reagan authority to enter into "trade agreements that provide for the elimination or reduction of any duty imposed by the United States." Only two countries were named as eligible: Israel and Canada.

At the first ministers' conference in Regina in February 1985, Mulroney announced that he would pursue the matter at the upcoming Shamrock Summit with Reagan in Quebec City in March. Alberta premier Peter Lougheed, long an advocate of the idea, pushed hard for a commitment, while Ontario premier Frank Miller cautioned against such a move until Ottawa had studied the potential impact. Mulroney himself called for "prudence," saying that free trade "conjures up all kinds of scarecrows and myths and problems, and what I think we have to do is try to depoliticize some of it. . . . Free trade is all in the eyes of the beholder."

At a private meeting in Quebec City, Reagan told Mulroney he would "go to bat" for Canada in fighting protectionist sentiments in the U.S. Congress. The two men promised to improve bilateral trade by cutting tariffs and other barriers to trade. "Thank God for Canada," Reagan said. "History has sealed a pact of friendship between us," Mulroney said.

On his way home from the Bonn economic summit in May, Mulroney told *Toronto Sun* reporter Derik Hodgson that in the United States calls for a surcharge on imported goods have been growing. With four out of ten Canadian jobs related to exports, and three-quarters of our trade with the United States, Mulroney said that his friendship with Reagan becomes all the more valuable for Canada as a wedge against U.S. protectionism. "There ain't gonna be no surcharge for Canada—if I'm wrong, you can cut me to bits," he said. He was wrong, as it turned out. During the next thirty months, there would be a series of them.

At a news conference in June 1985, at the start of the summer break, Mulroney said that there was no way to please

Canadians on the question of free trade with the United States. "Put an ideal like that and you can count on the country to come down squarely on both sides of the issue . . . to say nothing of the government," he said. "A trade-enhancement program of any kind in Canada would probably meet with an overwhelming degree of ambivalence. You would get six and you would lose half a dozen, in typical Canadian fashion."

In July, he promised quick action to improve trade with the United States and revealed that cabinet had been studying a discussion paper and trying to decide between a free-trade pact, which would wipe out tariffs and trade barriers in a broad range of industries, or a sectoral approach, such as exists in the auto industry. He rejected the term "free trade," choosing instead, "trade enhancement . . . that's what we want."

In August, Mulroney promised to consult new Ontario premier David Peterson before signing any free-trade pact. After his first official meeting with the new premier, Mulroney told reporters that once the parliamentary committee makes its recommendations on the subject he would be "consulting with" Peterson before making a final decision. Peterson expressed concern that free trade could result in a flooding of Ontario markets with cheaper American goods; that would undermine Ontario's manufacturing base and result in heavy job losses.

A month later, former Liberal finance minister Donald Macdonald's royal commission recommended a "leap of faith" to get free trade talks going between the two countries. The thirty-four-month commission spent $20.6 million and produced a three-volume, 2,011-page report on a range of economic issues, openly endorsing a plan to phase out tariffs between the two countries over ten years and establish a bilateral body to rule on non-tariff barriers, such as quotas and government procurement policies.

After his first year in office, Mulroney, the former opponent of free trade, was saying that Canadian products are too costly and unreliable to stay competitive on world markets, and that a trade deal was necessary in order to secure the giant U.S. market. Tory polls at the time showed that 80 per cent of Canadians believed the country should seek closer ties to the United States, up from just 60 per cent three years earlier. Free trade per se was not a major issue for Canadians, but most had a general sense that increasing two-way trade would be helpful.

Trade minister Jim Kelleher, who was dispatched on a fifteen-city cross-Canada tour to test public support for the notion before reporting back to cabinet, said that the Tories carefully avoided the words "free trade" because "to the man on the street free trade conjures up the image of the United States as a blood-sucking Dracula." Anyway, he said, pure free trade is unattainable. The best that could be hoped for was a comprehensive trade arrangement eliminating most barriers.

In the thirty years before the Tories took power in 1984, Canadian exports to the United States grew from 59.8 per cent of the total to 76.3 per cent. On the other hand, exports to the United Kingdom dropped from 16.9 to 2.2 per cent. Trade with Japan doubled, but was still relatively small, from 2.5 to 5 per cent of total exports.

A few noises were beginning to be heard from opponents of free trade. Edmonton publisher Mel Hurtig predicted that unimpeded two-way trade "could spell the end of this country both culturally and politically," and Harrison McCain, chairman of the board of McCain Foods Ltd. of Florenceville, N.B., sent each premier a two-hundred-word Telex saying that much of Canada's agriculture and food-processing industry could not compete with U.S.-based firms. Even the limited studies available supported the turn-of-the-century arguments that free trade would make us even more hewers of wood and drawers of water than we are, predicting trade gains for some of our raw products, such as forestry products, steel, and processed food, but a loss of trade on such finished goods as computers, appliances, furniture, clothing, and textiles.

While the prospect of having access to a market of 250 million Americans was exciting to many, the notion that those same Americans would have free access to our markets with their considerable economic advantages was frightening to many Canadians as well. And while economists and trade officials on both sides of the argument, and both sides of the border, argue over charts, graphs, and economic models, the truth is, nobody really knows the outcome until it happens.

A leaked Tory strategy paper in late September recommended special research into the benefits of free trade in key Liberal- and NDP-held ridings, a development that prompted Liberal leader John Turner to call Mulroney a "shameless hypocrite," and ask for a debate in the Commons on the trade issue. "There must be more than a leap of faith. I want a full account of the costs and benefits for Canada," said Turner.

Two days later, Mulroney telephoned Reagan to ask him to "explore with Congress" a proposal for talks aimed at negotiating "the broadest possible package of mutually beneficial reductions in tariff and non-tariff barriers between our two countries." A White House official said that Reagan had "warmly welcomed" the offer. Not everyone did. According to Ontario premier David Peterson, a provincial study showed that tariff reductions could threaten 280,000 jobs in Ontario. Peterson complained that Mulroney had moved too quickly and Turner said, "We want a blueprint. We want to know what it is the government is trying to accomplish."

NDP leader Ed Broadbent said that Canada must be tough in the talks so that "when the elephant and the beaver sit down to eat this pie together, the elephant doesn't pick up the pie with his trunk and go home with it." He said it would be better to resolve existing disputes that were already hurting Canadian exports in lumber, fish, and pork.

Mulroney countered with high-sounding assurances: "Our political sovereignty, our system of social programs, our commitment to fight regional disparities, our unique cultural identity, our special linguistic character—these are the essence of Canada. They are not at issue in these negotiations." He did not spell out specifically just what was at issue in the talks.

At the first ministers' conference in Halifax in late November, Mulroney and Peterson were drawn into open conflict over the issue after Ontario released studies of its own warning that as many as 280,000 Ontario manufacturing jobs could be at risk under free trade. Two other Queen's Park studies, by university academics, concluded that U.S. and other foreign investors would pull out or avoid Canada altogether under such a deal. When Mulroney dismissed the studies out of hand, Peterson asked when the prime minister intended to produce some studies of his own to support his claims. Asked by reporters whether shoe manufacturing and other sensitive industries in Central Canada would suffer under free trade— an argument he had made himself in 1983—Mulroney bristled, "Now why would you say that? That's false and everybody knows that."

Undeterred, the premier said in his closing speech, "What we said, and I want this on the record, Mr. Prime Minister, is that full participation [in the free-trade consultations] is not just consultation. The bottom line is that the negotiator will receive his instructions from the first ministers." Mulroney did not contest Peterson's conclusions in his wrap-up remarks.

In interviews shortly afterwards, Peterson, Don Getty, Grant Devine, and Bill Bennett all confirmed that they had been given the impression by Mulroney that the provinces would be full partners in the talks. But shortly after the premiers left, Mulroney said that was only "one way of putting it." He specifically rejected Devine's description of the eleven first ministers acting together as a board of directors to set the policy for negotiations. The first ministers did agree on a vague, twenty-one-line approach that essentially gave everybody ninety days to sort out the details of provincial participation in the talks.

In December, Mulroney took his free-trade campaign to the University of Chicago as the guest at the prestigious *Time* magazine Distinguished Speakers Program. There he told about one thousand listeners that he would never sign a pact that would erode Canada's political and cultural sovereignty. "You will have to understand that what we call cultural sovereignty is as vital to our national life as political sovereignty . . . living as we do next to a country ten times our size." While the speech was widely reported in Canada, it was practically ignored in the United States.

Mulroney had named former federal trade negotiator Simon Reisman, an Ottawa consultant, as chief negotiator for the talks. Reisman, a brusque, tough-talking man who had been a key negotiator in the Auto Pact, was offered $1,000 a day to lead a team hammering out Canada's negotiating position.

In its January 6, 1986, edition, *Maclean's* published a poll, commissioned from Allan Gregg's Decima Research Ltd., that showed strong support for the concept. Asked for their view on the plan, 75 per cent said it was either a very good idea or a good idea, while 22 per cent found it bad or very bad. Also, 44 per cent felt it would mean more jobs, 33 per cent said it wouldn't make any difference, and 21 per cent believed it would lead to fewer jobs. But this heavy support for the concept disappeared rapidly when people were asked if they'd still support a deal that was good for most of the country but bad for their own province; 43 per cent said yes, but 55 per cent said no.

While free trade had become Mulroney's most important single policy initiative, another Decima poll, conducted for the University of Calgary, showed that most Canadians didn't attach much importance to the issue. Participants were given a list of five "problems facing Canada today" and asked to rank them in order of importance. Free trade finished last, well behind the environment, deficit reduction, women's rights, and native rights. Sociology professor J. Richard Ponting, who designed the questionnaire, said that the findings were "surprising to me. . . . These data suggest that Canadians think it's a good idea, but it's not all that important."

In the meantime, U.S. officials, such as trade representative Clayton Yeutter, his deputy William Merkin and Reisman's counterpart, red-headed Peter Murphy, were beginning to worry aloud about Canada's growing list of what it wanted excluded from the talks—for example, cultural industries, the Auto Pact, and marketing boards. "When Ottawa says certain items are not negotiable," said Murphy, "it obviously decreases our interest" in reaching an agreement. From the outset, the Americans took the view that everything was negotiable. Each time an American official said that, Mulroney would hotly deny it, but they kept saying it anyway.

Another aspect to the talks was that all the attention being focused on Canada was actually harming our favourable trade relations. The first time Japanese prime minister Yasuhiro Nakasone visited Reagan, he was introduced as the head of America's "largest trading partner." In fact, Ontario alone does more trade with the United States than Japan, but as long as the Americans thought the Pacific Rim countries and the European Community were the major villains in their swelling trade deficit, the easier it was for Canadians quietly to enjoy the delights of a trade balance heavily in our favour.

Speaking in Montreal in February 1986, Merkin noted that Congress had now begun to realize that Canadian imports accounted for about $22 billion of America's 1985 merchandise trade deficit: "There's a nice little chunk of the U.S. deficit coming from Canada."

According to journalist Bob Hepburn, many trade lawyers and trade experts in Washington "just shake their heads at what Canada is doing in view of the protectionist sentiment in Congress. And we've come to Washington saying, 'We want to talk about free trade and we'll open our markets to you guys,' and they've got a Congress that wants to club someone over the head, and here we are coming and saying 'Here I am. Take me.' We're going to get hurt. We're going to get hurt badly on this stuff, and we're not going to see it for a while. The timing couldn't be worse."

In an interview with the *Financial Post* in February 1986, Mulroney predicted that when Reisman sat down to begin negotiating a deal, "you will hear a call to greatness that will stir the soul of this country." In fact, what Canadians have heard is the scream of American politicians and industrialists as they imposed tariffs and fought Canadian imports on a wide range of goods, including lumber products, fish, potash, steel, natural gas, and agriculture products.

In April, on a bitterly contested tie vote, the Senate finance committee agreed to Reagan's request to put the free trade talks on a "fast track." Under that arrangement, created under a congressional trade bill in October 1984, Congress can only accept or reject a negotiated treaty. Without such a provision, a treaty would get tied up and, inevitably, lost forever in political clause-by-clause wrangling. The entire issue nearly became derailed when committee chairman Senator Bob Packwood, an Oregon Republican, opened the session with an angry attack on the "vague promises and unsatisfactory responses from the Canadian government in a variety of areas. If we were voting today, we would turn that authority down." Packwood and others, angry over the growing Canada–U.S. dispute on softwood lumber, wanted that and other irritants resolved before comprehensive talks began. His unexpected opening remarks led to sharp criticism of Canadian ambassador Allan Gotlieb for having underestimated opposition to the move, and promoted a mad flurry of political persuasion on Capitol Hill to get the fast-track motion by the committee.

In order to get the 10-10 vote at the committee, Reagan, who sent notes to every committee member and called most of them as well, had agreed to press separately for settlement of a long-standing dispute with Canada over softwood lumber, a promise that would create a major problem for Mulroney late in the year and into early 1987.

By May 1986, support for free trade had fallen below 60 per cent, and the Tories sent all senators and MPS tidy blue boxes containing free-trade kits, including a thirteen-minute video cassette stating that "every region in the country stands to gain" under a trade agreement. The video displayed a map of Canada that depicted Newfoundland in the same colour as the United States and omitted Prince Edward Island altogether.

On May 21, Reisman and Murphy and their respective teams sat down at the long oval table in the seventeenth-floor boardroom of Reisman's Ottawa offices to begin, formally, the process of removing barriers in the $170 billion two-way trade by the fast-track deadline of January 1988. On the same day, Reagan personally approved a 35 per cent import duty on Canada's $250 million red-cedar shakes and shingles industry, a move Mulroney described as "bizarre . . . unacceptable." Even more damaging, a coalition of U.S. lumber producers formally asked the U.S. International Trade Commission to impose more than $1 billion in trade penalties against Canadian softwood lumber imports. At the same time, the U.S. commerce department took steps to increase existing duties against Canadian hog imports, and the ITC imposed tariffs on cod fish from Atlantic Canada and raspberries from British Columbia, and recommended a five-year global quota on shoe imports that would hurt the $33.5 million worth of Canadian shoe exports to the United States each year.

In his first nationally televised address as prime minister, on June 16, 1986, Mulroney delivered a pep talk on free trade, calling the talks "an important turning point" in Canadian history. "This is not for the faint hearted, but then our country was not built by the faint of heart." He said if a negotiated deal was not good for Canada, "there will be no deal."

In July, a *Globe and Mail* poll showed support for free trade at 52 per cent, but 36 per cent of the supporters disapproved of the way the Tories were handling the talks. Mulroney appointed Pat Carney as minister for international trade, saying, "She's got the ball. You just watch her run, and hang onto your hats."

During a question-and-answer session with students at the University of Brandon, Mulroney's enthusiasm seemed to have waned as he said that the chances of a deal didn't look good. "If you were a betting man right now, you'd have to say there's going to be no deal, the Americans are going to shoot it down, the Americans don't want a deal. That would be the impression that I would get today."

That impression didn't improve any in November when the Democrats, running on a protectionist ticket, wrested control of the Senate from the Republicans and strengthened their hold on the House of Representatives in mid-term elections.

As for Carney, she tried to handle the growing softwood controversy by at first dismissing American chances—the industry had tried the same arguments in 1983 and lost—then by offering a "once only" final-offer deal of about 12 per cent, then another "final offer" of 15 per cent, thereby giving some credence to American arguments that Canadian lumber was unfairly subsidized. The Americans were seeking a 32 per cent countervailing duty. In October, the U.S. commerce department imposed a 15 per cent duty on Canada's $3.8 billion softwood exports, subject to a final review by December 30. "We're going to fight this all the way," said Carney. "Today it's lumber . . . tomorrow it could be any number of issues. This is not the way to conduct business between trade partners." In a diplomatic note of October 31 to the Americans, Carney called their position "fundamentally wrong."

In November, Mulroney said that the boosting of Canadian lumber prices was "the price of [playing] poker" with the United States, but was not a concession. "There have been no concessions made in favour of the Americans," he told the Commons. At a first ministers' conference in Vancouver later that month, Mulroney and Carney emerged from a late-night session with the premiers to announce that a "deal" had been reached with the Americans. Carney had been discussing the issue by telephone with U.S. trade secretary Malcolm Baldrige and had told Mulroney that the issue was resolved. There were banner headlines in Vancouver newspapers the next morning; it was a critical issue there, since the bulk of lumber exports come from that province.

The next afternoon, after learning that American lumber interests were still not pleased, Carney had to call a news conference and say that she still did not have a deal but that, "there is agreement on the approach that Canada had taken." At the meeting, all premiers except Ontario's David Peterson agreed to boost Canadian lumber prices by 15 per cent if the Americans would drop their 15 per cent duty. The Tories argued that such an arrangement would keep the money in Canada and avoid a precedent for American actions on other commodities.

When Mulroney returned to the Commons after the weekend, Broadbent wanted to know why Carney had announced a "deal" that was then denied within hours by the U.S. commerce department. Mulroney said that Carney had not announced a deal, she had "announced agreement among us all on an approach." Broadbent said, "half the country saw the news report and the minister [Carney] announcing that there was agreement. . . . That is the truth, no matter what the government wants to say today."

Senior Tory adviser Bill Neville has said that a major

problem the government has is its inability "to convey a belief structure," and that trade is a good example of this. "Every second week when the government seemed to imply it had a hard mandate to stick to, they would do something that made it appear as if they were soft on the idea. Mulroney attacked the opponents of free trade, then went out to Manitoba and said there wasn't much hope for free trade. Fortunately, they've bitten the bullet now; perhaps they've decided they're stuck with it and are now going to have to sell it.

"But if people have questions about your trustworthiness you have to be especially careful you're not trying to work both sides of the street on a very basic issue. . . .

"On the softwood lumber issue, they talked tough then seemed to back off, although I'm told that the minister [Carney] misled him on the deal in Vancouver."

Senator Lowell Murray, who was in the room with some other officials when Carney was talking to Baldrige, said, "To start with we did think we had a deal at the time. . . . Carney was the one who made the call. She was talking to Baldrige on the phone and she was repeating what he was saying while the rest of us were taking notes. Gotlieb was talking to somebody else involved in the department at the same time and my impression quite strongly was that he [Baldrige] had agreed to a deal to try to sell the industry on this. Mulroney was back at the table with the premiers. In fact, I went out and reported some of this to him.

"But Carney certainly thought she had a deal. . . ."

In any event, the two countries did strike an eleventh-hour deal on December 30 (while Carney was holidaying in Hawaii). The deal allows Canada to collect between $550 million and $600 million on an export tax. Lumber officials' reactions were mixed; some applauded the deal, while others predicted it would cost the industry up to eleven thousand jobs. According to Adam Zimmerman, chairman of MacMillan-Bloedel, one of Canada's largest forestry companies, the deal "at one step creates an industrial paraplegic out of the lumber industry." John Turner's reaction was, "As a Canadian I feel humiliated. Our sovereignty has been infringed upon." The agreement gave the Americans the right to "inspect and monitor" Canada's compliance. "It's like shooting ourselves in the foot," said Turner. The deal also gave the United States control over stumpage fees charged by provincial governments and prohibited Canada from using revenue from the tax to assist the forest industry directly.

In a letter to the premiers, Carney said any suggestion that Canada had given up its sovereignty was "false and completely without foundation." A week later, the CBC reported that Carney was launching a $12 million public relations program to sell the government's message to Canadians during 1987 and 1988. Carney said that the deal was "the best that could be obtained under difficult circumstances and it was negotiated on our terms"; her request for communications money, she said, was to provide information on all issues, not just free trade.

Despite heavy opposition criticism in the Commons, the lumber-export tax bill was approved in late January, but not before the Mulroney government had sent a diplomatic note to the Reagan administration complaining about the U.S. handling of the issue. In early February, however, B.C. industry spokesmen were predicting a boom year despite the tax on exports, the result largely of low mortgage rates in the United States that have meant a strong demand for new housing.

Still, at a news conference in Montreal, Bill Hatch, president of the Canadian Lumbermen's Association, predicted long-term damage that could affect up to fifteen thousand jobs in the industry. Two small Ontario sawmills had already closed since the tax was imposed, throwing six hundred men out of work, but Canada's forestry ministers were searching for an agreement to replace the controversial deal.

In a year-end CBC television interview, Mulroney predicted that a free-trade deal could create half a million jobs. In March 1987, Senator Lowell Murray dismissed Quebec premier Robert Bourassa's proposal for a formula giving every region the right to veto a trade agreement as a "non-starter. . . . It's the government of Canada that approves international treaties."

In a special Commons debate on free trade on March 16, Mulroney took a new tack. But while he argued that a deal would put an end to regional disparity, the Liberals and the NDP pointed out that Mulroney still had provided no data on how many jobs would be created. For the first time, Carney set out a list of ten items that were on the table and might be part of a draft accord by the summer: punitive countervailing duties must be dropped by the Americans and tariffs in all areas would be phased out over a ten-to-fifteen-year period. An impartial, binational tribunal, not the U.S. department of commerce, should deal with disputes such as the softwood lumber issue. Other items on the table were non-tariff barriers, such as "buy America" or "buy Canada" policies; customs formalities that increase red tape; agriculture; subsidies vital to regional development; intellectual property, including copyright laws and patent protection; services, including engineering, financial consulting, computer, and banking; and investment, worth $6.8 billion in new foreign money to Canada last year.

When Reagan arrived in Ottawa in early April 1987 for his annual summit, Mulroney was looking for some good news. He got a little. At the end of a prepared speech to a joint session of the Senate and Commons—during which he was heckled by some irate anti-American NDP MPs—Reagan added that he would also push free trade and consider negotiating a pact to cut acid rain, another long-standing irritant between the two countries.

(Of course, at their first summit in Quebec City, in March 1985, Mulroney had declared it a great victory when Reagan acknowledged that acid rain was a problem. The two leaders then appointed former Ontario premier Bill Davis and former U.S. administration official Drew Lewis as acid-rain envoys. A year later, at the Washington summit, Reagan had accepted a proposal for a $5 billion clean-up program, to be shared equally by government and industry, and then neglected to include the money to meet that commitment in his next budget. A week before the 1987 summit, in an effort to avoid criticism on the matter, Reagan had reannounced his commitment to solving the problem and said he would try to convince Congress to devote $2.5 billion over the next five years for development of new technology to fight acid rain. [Acid rain is a minor environmental issue in the United States, but a major problem in Canada.] He cautioned, however, that "literally thousands of firms and millions of jobs will be affected by whatever steps we take on this problem—so there are no quick and easy answers.")

The two men did not find agreement on a dispute over the use of Arctic waters, which Canada claims and the United States considers international waters. (The issue had flared up in summer 1985 when the U.S. Coast Guard icebreaker *Polar Sea* traversed the frigid strait between Greenland and Alaska without permission from Canadian officials. In response, the Mulroney government stepped up Arctic patrol flights, drew new boundary maps that clearly established Canadian sovereignty, and decided to build an icebreaker of its own to patrol the waterway.) At the summit, Reagan said only, "We're determined to find a solution based on mutual respect for sovereignty and our common security and other interests."

On one level, Mulroney's highly personalized approach to Reagan has had some positive results. Certainly, Reagan would never have agreed to annual summits with Trudeau, and however limited the summit successes have been, they're at least better than nothing at all.

On the other hand, Reagan has never hesitated to hit Canada in what he sees as the American interest, whether Mulroney is happy about it or not. Mulroney's friendship with Reagan has done nothing to counter the effects of the growing protectionist sentiment in the United States, and revelations about the Iran-Contra affair have weakened Reagan's position at home and abroad, making him a less powerful ally than he was when Mulroney was first elected.

"The Americans do not pay as much attention as they should to Canada," says the *Toronto Star*'s Washington man Bob Hepburn. "There's nothing Mulroney can do that's going to change that. . . . I did a media session with some NATO countries a while back . . . their complaint was all the same. How do we get the Americans to pay attention to us?

"The American media only pays attention when there's a war or something. We got more ink when the separatists were blowing up mailboxes in Montreal than when we do anything else," he said. "They only cover bang-bang stories. We're not a bang-bang story. And Mulroney's not going to change that no matter how much of a pal he thinks he is with Reagan."

CHAPTER TEN

SHARING THE
WEALTH

It was High Noon for Brian Mulroney. June 19, 1985. But instead of facing a big, strong hombre like Gary Cooper on a dusty street in the Old West, Mulroney found himself just outside the Centre Block's west entrance staring down into the flashing eyes of tiny, white-haired Solange Denis of Ottawa. Instead of dodging bullets from a Colt .44, he suffered a direct hit to his public-trust factor from a good, old-fashioned tongue lashing.

"You lied to us," the sixty-three-year-old petite woman said. "You made us vote for you, then, good-bye Charlie Brown. . . . If you do anything [to pension indexing] you won't get back in in three years."

"I'm listening, madame," Mulroney said quietly.

"Well, madame is damned angry," she said.

Nine days later, Mulroney admitted that his government had made a mistake and was scrapping its controversial plan to limit old-age pension increases. "If you're asking me whether I, we, made a mistake, the answer is yes," said Mulroney, referring to the contentious clause in Michael Wilson's budget.

But it was too late. The pictures had been drawn. The image carved in the public consciousness. For weeks, headlines shouted the message that Mulroney had promised not to touch old-age pensions, and then his government's first budget had proposed partial de-indexing. Across the nation, enraged senior citizens held marches and protest meetings and called and wrote to their MPs. Grey Power was on a roll. By the time Mulroney backed down, he not only looked weak and subject to pressure by interest groups, he looked mean-spirited and, worse, untrustworthy for having tried it in the first place.

"Mulroney called liar on pension indexing" read a huge headline in the normally staid *Globe and Mail* on June 20. And who could argue? He had lied to senior citizens. When Solange Denis, whose sixty-seven-year-old husband was a pensioner, focused national attention on Mulroney's credibility, the long, steep slide in his political popularity began.

People could be forgiven for being confused about Mulroney's social policies. Although what he termed "social justice" was one of his major campaign building blocks, he had never been consistent in his public statements on the issue.

As early as January 19, 1976, speaking to a partisan meeting at the Beach Grove Golf Club in Windsor during his first crack at the Tory leadership, Mulroney had called for a five-year moratorium on new social spending until the huge social budgets and the philosophy behind them could be re-examined. The principle of universality, he said, should be "given close study." To avoid universality in the past meant "a degrading means test," but that was no longer necessary in a computerized society.

In a January 25 interview that year with Standard Broadcast News, Mulroney said that although universality might have been justified when many social programs were introduced thirty years earlier, it was now only a source of waste and bureaucracy. Social services could be streamlined by using a computer check-off system connected to the revenue department to determine eligibility. At the time, Mulroney was earning a fat six-figure salary and living in Upper Westmount. "I'd put a moratorium for five years on any new social legislation," he said, "unless it was justified by increases in productivity or unless there was an urgent need for it in some sector of the economy."

In March 1983, when he announced his entry into the Conservative leadership race again, he declined to give his personal view on universality, saying only that it would be considered by an all-party Commons committee should he become prime minister. A month later, in Winnipeg, he said he would allow user fees in the health-care system, but only as a last resort. He said "the boondoggle in the medicare system is on the administrative side. I think those are the areas of excess and abuse, not the poor people in society who are knocking on doctors' doors."

In a 1983 interview with John Gray of the *Globe and Mail* shortly before the leadership convention, he said, "Neither does one need to belong to a political party to believe that men and women will stand on their own two feet when given half a chance; that government must show concern—even ten- derness—in dealing with the less fortunate among us; that only free men and women can sever the knots tied by government bureaucrats."

Asked specifically about the universality of social prog- rams—where everybody gets the benefit, regardless of need or income—he said, "The concept is such that what was good for Mackenzie King is not necessarily good for Canada today, to coin a phrase. . . . Maybe we can do a better job for the taxpayer and for the needy people than by issuing an automatic cheque to someone who is making $200,000 a year, and then hire a couple more civil servants to make sure he adds that to his income, which then jumps him into a higher tax bracket. . . ."

In July, after winning the leadership, he suggested that a government led by him might increase health-care funding to counter hospital user fees. Criticizing the "confrontation and vexatious approach" of the Liberals, he said, "the answer is a civilized, thoughtful, and generous approach . . . recogniz- ing this is very much a priority question and cannot be politicized."

He must have been still thinking about it in August 1983, when he said he wouldn't outline his program for a National Health Act until he saw what the Liberal government pro- posed. "When I see what the Liberals say they want in print and how they are going to finance it, then we are going to tell them what should be in it and how it should be financed." In a Vancouver speech earlier, he said his government would definitely give the provinces more money to ensure universal access to medical care. "It's a question of where your priorities are," he said.

Given his conflicting statements, people still weren't abso- lutely sure where his priorities were, and in March 1984 he muddied the waters even more. On March 7, in response to Liberal accusations that the Tories have a hidden agenda on social-program cuts (because John Crosbie, then finance critic, had said that these benefits should not necessarily be paid to everyone), Mulroney declared that the Tory caucus "unani- mously" endorsed a commitment "to the concept of universality in social programs . . . it shall not be touched." That's clear enough. Or was clear until Mulroney was interviewed two weeks later by the *Financial Post*, when he said, "I have no hesitation in reviewing the concept of universality, provided it's done by a tripartite committee of the House. Such a review would take a look at the concept to ensure that the delivery of public dollars is done in the most efficacious way possible.

"But universality is part of our social fabric. And if it is going to be changed, there have to be good reasons to change it, and there has to be a body of opinion supporting that. So in the next Parliament, I would have no objection whatsoever to us looking at it objectively."

Moving ahead to the 1984 election campaign, on August 10, Mulroney told a Tory rally in Kitchener that the plight of the elderly in Canada was "a national disgrace . . . we have betrayed a generation of Canadians who have spent their lives building our country, raising families and contributing to the well-being of their communities." To set things right again, he unveiled an eight-point program for the elderly. His second point was "restoring full indexing of the old-age pension to the actual cost of living, on a quarterly basis." Indexing had been removed under the Liberal six-and-five restraint program but was scheduled to be restored when the program expired later that year.

Mulroney also promised the full spousal allowance to eligible widows and widowers aged sixty to sixty-five, a promise he kept. In a later speech, Mulroney said that the patronage appointments made by John Turner just after he took over from Trudeau would cost taxpayers $84 million, "enough to pay a supplement to the elderly." He also promised pensions worth at least $144 a month to homemakers, a multi-billion-dollar proposal that he has not instituted. In Vancouver during the campaign, Flora MacDonald also said that there would be "absolutely no" social-budget trimming during the first four years in office. After the election, trade minister Jim Kelleher went one better, saying that the Tories were "not only committed to the maintenance of current income security programs, it is our goal to improve them."

In his November 1984 economic statement, finance minister Michael Wilson said, "The state of our finances will not support the costs of many new [social justice] initiatives"; however, he promised some help to "Canadians in need," extending spousal allowances and increasing veterans' pensions. Wilson also announced a massive review of all social programs, including the baby bonus and old-age security. When asked why he was doing so after referring to these programs during the election campaign as "a sacred trust not to be tampered with," Mulroney said that "personally" he still favoured universality. All the government had done, he maintained, was to "open a dialogue" on the issue, because the economy required Canadians and governments to examine "the best use of available resources." The government was merely asking the question, "Are we using public funds wisely . . . when families with $100,000 incomes receive family allowance? . . . The problem has to be looked at frankly. . . . Are we making proper use of taxpayers' money by giving a bank president who makes $500,000 or $600,000 a year a baby bonus? Could that money not be more properly used to assist someone who desperately needs help? I don't know the answer."

The review of Canada's $40 billion social security system was touted as the most fundamental look at it since the first old-age pensions were introduced in 1927. The process began when Wilson met over breakfast with a group of thirty business, labour, and social-agency leaders the day after his economic statement. He also asked all cabinet ministers responsible for the vast network of federal social programs to prepare outlines of possible spending cuts, saying that after further reviews by parliamentary committees and a special task force, they could get into his spring budget. A Goldfarb poll showed 86 per cent support for the idea of eliminating or reducing social benefits for families with annual incomes of more than $40,000. "Refusing change is no longer an option for Canada," said Wilson, "and some of the changes necessary for an economic turnaround are strong medicine." At the time, 3.6 million parents were receiving family allowances under the 1944 Family Allowances Act, and 2.5 million Canadians were getting old-age security thanks to the 1951 Old-Age Security program. In 1984, the baby bonus cost $2.4 billion, of which about $450 million was taxed back. Old-age security cost $8.3 billion, plus another $3 billion in supplementary benefits.

In a November 17 interview with George Radwanski, then editor-in-chief of the *Toronto Star*, Mulroney said that if the government did end universality of some social programs it might tax the benefits away from the rich and give the extra money saved to the needy. But the money would "absolutely not" be used to reduce the deficit. He suggested that benefits might be paid out to everyone in the target group, as the principle of "universality" would require, then retrieved later from those with high incomes, most likely through the tax system.

In December, the Tories found themselves embroiled in a dispute over what they said or didn't say about protecting universality. On December 13, Mulroney repudiated statements made by Wilson in a taped interview with the Canadian Press. Wilson said that during the campaign the Conservatives had purposely hidden their intentions to redirect social spending because they were afraid the Liberals would distort the policy for electoral advantage. "Nothing could be farther from the truth," Mulroney responded, adding that Wilson's statements had been misconstrued and that the Tories had never discussed such a thing.

In an interview with Montreal's *La Presse*, Wilson said: "At issue is the following principle. Does it make sense for persons whose revenue is superior to the average to receive in their entirety social benefits on the same basis as those whose revenue is inferior to the average or below the poverty line? I don't think so." Mulroney himself agreed, again trotting out the "bank president" example.

He accused the Liberals of resorting to the "politics of fear" to attack Wilson, saying that his finance minister was "simply introducing a note of caution into the debate by suggesting that we as Conservatives—knowing how they [Liberals] distort our positions—have had to be prudent in putting out positions."

In the Commons on December 14, Mulroney first suggested that high-income earners might not need family allowances and old-age pensions, then denied that the government planned to alter universal programs and finally insisted that the government had an "open mind" on the issue. He even denied a quote attributed to Wilson in which, according to the Canadian Press transcript, Wilson had said, "there are people who don't need it [social-assistance programs]. Upper- and middle-income social programs cannot be afforded today." "What I'm saying is that the finance minister never said that," Mulroney said. The opposition was outraged, but the Tories applauded Mulroney.

After the weekend break, NDP leader Ed Broadbent came back to the Commons on Monday and accused Mulroney of "deliberately misleading" MPs, asking him twice to concede he had been wrong on the Friday when he denied Wilson's statement to CP. "I heard it [Wilson's comment] on the radio," said Broadbent, "and I subsequently checked three newspapers. All attributed these precise words to the minister." Broadbent refused to withdraw his accusation that Mulroney was deliberately misleading the House and became the first party leader ever expelled from the Commons. Outside the House, Broadbent called Mulroney's statements "clearly untrue."

In a 1987 interview, Broadbent said: "We had to look at this [universality]. Everyone in the country knew Wilson said it. . . . When we came back on the Monday, I raised it again because by then we had all heard the clips and it had blown up as an issue. So I gave him [Mulroney] a chance . . . to change his argument, because we all make mistakes. I deliberately put it that way. I said the prime minister had time to check the record now will he acknowledge he misinformed the House on Friday and correct the record. I was frankly surprised when he didn't.

"He didn't back down an inch. So in my own view, I said enough is enough of this, he's got to tell the truth. We can't let him get by with this as prime minister."

The day after Broadbent was expelled, the Commons ground to a halt when the Liberals refused to answer the division bells for a recorded vote on their own adjournment motion after Speaker John Bosley rejected Turner's call for an emergency debate on social spending. The Liberals agreed to end the episode only when the Conservatives promised a debate on the issue of universality.

To compound the confusion, Mulroney had said, in response to a Turner question, that a universal program is one that discriminates in favour of the poor. The government's intention was, he said, "to enhance the well-being of Canadians by a proper universal system which benefits Canadians who need it most of all." Moments later, in another reply to Turner, he broadened the definition to mean that every Canadian who contributed to social programs should receive a benefit and said that his government would "respect the principle of universality for all Canadians who have contributed to those programs. . . ."

The next day in the Commons, Mulroney seemed to reverse himself again, saying he would not rule out taxing back benefits to upper- and middle-income people—having categorically denied it a day earlier. By then the government position was so convoluted that even two Tory backbenchers, Alan Redway and Stan Darling, asked for clarification during the daily question period.

In his year-end interview with CTV on December 23, Mulroney again took both sides of the argument, saying that social benefits would continue to be paid across the board but that higher-income earners would be taxed back to make the system more fair. Unless, of course, people didn't like the idea: "then I wouldn't do it." He said that if a consensus was reached by April, details of the new taxation system would come down in the spring budget.

During a thirty-minute CBC TV telecast on December 26, Mulroney accused the opposition of "hijacking" Parliament to create attention for themselves. Although he was committed to maintaining social programs for everyone, he admitted to sending out confusing signals on the issue, muddying it again by adding, "I've always said, we're in favour of universality, we are opposed to a means test. But we ask the question, given the scarce resources of the country: Is there not a better way of delivering to those in our society who need it most, more resources?"

In a New Year's Eve interview on "Le Point" on the CBC's French-language network, Mulroney said that though he believed in the universality of social benefits, he also believed that the rich deserve less assistance from the government than do Canadians in need. He went on to explain this contradiction with his by now well-worn example of the $500,000 bank president. "We are in favour of a formula that allows us to withdraw or give less money to a bank president . . . and to give that money to the less-well-off members of society." The position is reasonable enough, but it does not fit the definition of universality. He then accused the Liberals of "taking up the defence of the bank president against us, who are only asking if we can reach an understanding on a formula that will allow us to give more to those who need it."

In the same interview he dismissed reports that Wilson had called deficit reduction the main object of fiscal reform saying that Wilson's remarks had been misinterpreted. In his November economic statement about the government's fiscal priorities, Wilson had listed as the "first" of a series of challenges, "to put our own fiscal house in order so that we can limit, and ultimately reverse, the massive build-up in public debt and the damaging impact this has on confidence and growth." Officials in the social-service field had been expressing concerns that this emphasis on the deficit meant less money for social programs, particularly since both Wilson and Mulroney had argued that their strategy was not to increase taxes (although they certainly did that) but to cut back on spending.

Mulroney and his ministers had pushed Wilson's upcoming May 23 budget as a "tough but fair document," but when it arrived, *Time* magazine had labelled it "Semitough and Less than Fair," the latter a reference to significant personal tax increases and the partial de-indexing of family allowances and pensions. Child tax credits, which help lower-income families, were increased, while child tax exemptions, which help the more affluent, were to be gradually decreased over three years.

The impact of de-indexing on the baby bonus did not strike a chord with the public, but cutting the old-age pensions certainly did. Seniors' groups began organizing with a vengeance across the country, and the opposition parties kept up a steady attack. The issue dominated the Commons question period for the next month. Wilson's budget had attempted to limit old-age pensions to Canada's 2.6 million elderly beginning on January 1, 1986, when pensions would increase only by as much as inflation exceeded 3 per cent. If inflation was 4 per cent, the pension would increase by only 1 per cent. The Tories had hoped to soften the blow by keeping full inflation protection on the guaranteed income supplement paid to the neediest seniors, and on veterans' allowances.

During a raucous exchange in the Commons on June 6, Mulroney taunted Liberal Sheila Copps, a former Ontario MPP, who had blossomed as an effective critic of the government, by saying that what had upset her was her departure from Queen's Park just when "something good happens." The Tory benches roared with laughter, until it dawned on everybody that the "something good" Mulroney was referring to was the imminent demise of the forty-two-year-old Conservative regime and a takeover by the Ontario Liberals. At that point, it was the Liberals' turn to laugh.

Still, there wasn't much humour in the Commons for weeks,

as opposition critics accused the Tories of being "reverse Robin Hoods" and "purse-snatchers" and the Tories responded that they had no choice because of the legacy of debt left them by the previous Liberal regime. The Tories argued that they couldn't meet all their election promises because the financial situation was worse than they had been led to believe. Critics countered that well after the election, when all financial data was available, the government had pledged not to take money from social programs, including old-age pensions.

On June 7, despite mounting public protest, Mulroney flatly told the Commons, "There will be no change." By then, the Manitoba legislature, including the opposition Conservatives, had approved a resolution urging Ottawa to drop the proposal. On June 10, Mulroney showed the first signs of cracking under the strain when he hinted that the de-indexation might be temporary. He promised "at the earliest possible moment, as soon as resources permit, to be helpful to all those affected. I take no joy whatsoever in cutting back benefits to anyone, least of all to those elderly citizens."

At the same time, Mulroney accused the Liberals of trying to incite "class warfare" by suggesting that Canada's poor would be paying for budget measures to help the rich, and attacked the NDP for fomenting "social discord" by suggesting that the budget gave fresh tax breaks to the rich while forcing the elderly to tighten their belts. He did not deny the substance of their arguments, however, Turner said that the budget measures would force an extra 750,000 Canadians—including 230,000 seniors—to fall below the poverty line in 1986. "One does not control the deficit on the backs of the weak and those who cannot protect themselves."

On June 11, even the country's three major business lobby groups came rushing to the aid of the elderly. The Canadian Chamber of Commerce, the Business Council on National Issues, and the Canadian Organization of Small Business all said pensions for the elderly poor should be fully protected from inflation and that the government could find the money to reduce its deficit elsewhere. The next day in the Commons, Mulroney backed off even more, saying that the budget measure was just a "proposal" and speaking of his government's "apprehension" about it. "You're a disgrace! You're a sham," screamed New Democrat Ian Deans, while Liberal John Nunziata yelled, "You've got no integrity, Mulroney!" The prime minister pretended not to hear a question from Liberal

Brian Tobin asking him to meet representatives of senior citizens' groups. After considerable taunting and baiting, Wilson said he would meet them. The subject sparked a full debate in the Commons as an opposition non-confidence motion. In Montreal, groups representing 200,000 Quebec pensioners demanded that the Tories abandon the proposal. "I don't care if the rich get richer, I just don't want to get poorer than I am," said Joseph Zeldman, eighty-four, representing the six-thousand-member Golden Age Association at a meeting with NDP leader Ed Broadbent.

At a June 13 news conference, Mulroney gave another broad hint that he was looking for a way out of the mess. He was asked about his earlier commitment—broken in the May 23 budget—to apply any savings in social-program costs to other such programs rather than to deficit reduction. "There is no inconsistency in the statements we have made," he said. "You seem to assume there will not be another budget between here and 1990. Life changes, requirements change, and budgets must deal with those."

On June 14, Mulroney admitted that he had the "beginnings of an uproar" on his hands over the issue." He said that the "perception" was that the elderly would face immediate hardship as a result of the move. "It is an erroneous conclusion," he said, pointing out that the provision was not scheduled to take effect until the new year, but adding, "perception sometimes becomes reality and we have to deal with that as well."

At a special closed-door, five-hour meeting with his caucus the next day to defuse hostility from his own members on the issue, Mulroney suggested that he might be able to back off because the rest of the budget was so popular. To support his argument, he brought in Tory pollster Allan Gregg to unveil the results of a nationwide survey, which, Mulroney said later, "conveyed a very high acceptance of the budget in all regions . . . from all walks of life." He told reporters later he wouldn't rule out changing the budget before the June 28 summer recess. "I never rule out anything in politics."

On June 17, Mulroney flew to Sept-Iles to tell about 125 elderly people in the Le Pionnier low-rent housing project that the pension proposal "deserves to be reviewed. . . . I said that I would listen to all reasonable proposals. If I have something to announce, I'll do it at the appropriate time." Mulroney's advisers had deliberately chosen the eighty-five-unit complex, where residents had voted overwhelmingly Tory in the election, as a "safe" forum for him on the subject. He later told reporters he was pleased with the generally friendly reception. "You see what is happening outside Ottawa. There is no panic. On the contrary, there's a degree of serenity and comprehension there."

There wasn't much serenity when he returned to Ottawa and faced a crowd of protesters, including Solange Denis, in the now-famous confrontation outside the Parliament buildings. During the subsequent turmoil in the Commons, Newfoundland Liberal Brian Tobin got tossed out for calling Mulroney a liar and Toronto Liberal John Nunziata avoided being ordered out when he withdrew his shouted cry of "liar," a word forbidden by parliamentary rules. Even the normally placid Wilson seemed to lose his cool. Wilson, the architect of the measure, said that the Liberals "should be embarrassed" by their tactics. "I think the citizens expect more of politicians."

That same day, the Gallup poll showed the Tories down nine points, to 45 per cent, the first time they had dropped below 50 per cent since their election last September. Moreover, the poll had been taken a week before the Wilson budget. Mulroney dismissed it as "part of the ebb and flow of democracy."

Finally, on June 27, Mulroney ordered Wilson to announce a full retreat from the measure, instead opting for extending by six months a surtax of 5 per cent payable on corporations and adding another one cent a litre in excise taxes on gasoline (on top of the two-cent hike already contained in the budget). The two measures were expected to bring in $650 million in revenue. The pension measure would have saved $15 million in the current fiscal year and $254 million the next year.

Mulroney admitted he had made a "mistake" and said that his government deserved "praise" because it had "acknowledged our error and we corrected it. The easier course would have been to persevere and to do nothing."

But Mulroney, even though forced into a public mea culpa, had problems doing it gracefully, suggesting at a news conference that pensioners had been too greedy to help the government fight the deficit. "We believed that the budgetary problem and the built-in debt . . . was so horrendous that we thought that everyone in the country would be ready to pay a small amount as a national commitment to getting it under control. We were wrong and I think in retrospect it was unfair of us to consider that."

In September, at a cabinet meeting at Meech Lake, Mulroney claimed "the country is broke . . . bankrupt," and repeated his false claim that Ottawa was spending more on interest payments "than it costs for our entire social apparatus." The Macdonald royal commission had recommended a $10-billion deficit reduction by 1991 and, among other things, a guaranteed annual income. Health and welfare minister Jake Epp said that he would not rule out the possibility, but was prepared at least to study it. The commission had recommended replacing most federal social-assistance programs with a federal-provincial minimum income package that would guarantee a family of four an income of $13,000 a year but eliminate all government support for a similar family earning more than $35,000.

Speaking to the National Voluntary Organizations in Ottawa in early November, Mulroney defended his government's record on social policy. "I didn't dream up interest rates. We have to lower them and we have. I didn't dream up unemployment. We have to lower that and we have. I didn't dream up reckless government spending and we've got to bring that under control and we have, simply to make sure that we can deliver more money to organizations that legitimately deal with serious social problems without inflation. . . . We want to give you real dollars to deal with real problems, and you can't do that when the economy is ill. You can only do that when the economy is building on new prosperity. . . ."

In February 1987, the National Council of Welfare, an advisory group to Epp, looking back at the 1985 budget, said that poverty-level wage earners had been hardest hit by it, though that hadn't been immediately apparent because many of the tax increases didn't take effect until 1986.

"Many [Canadians] with low incomes find they owe federal income tax for the first time," the council reported, saying that the most important change affecting the working poor was the elimination of the federal tax reduction of $100 a person or $200 a couple for the 1986 tax year. In 1985, for example, people didn't have to pay federal tax until their taxable incomes topped $1,440 a year (which translates into an earned income of $6,296 for a single person). In 1986, however, with the tax reduction gone, people became liable for federal tax as soon as their taxable incomes hit $10 a year (the equivalent of $4,846 in earned income).

Wilson, responding to complaints in the Commons, said that creating jobs was the best way to ease the welfare burden and rejected a call from Turner to introduce a guaranteed annual income. Claiming that the Tories had created 677,000 jobs since 1984, he said, "That . . . is the best way that I know of getting people out of poverty." Turner pointed out that 300,000 Canadians had been forced to rely on volunteer food banks in 1986.

Another issue that would disrupt the Commons in the spring of 1987 first arose in early May 1985, when Michel Côté, then consumer and corporate affairs minister, convened a series of closed-door meetings between manufacturers of name-brand and generic drugs. Côté argued that the existing law, which allowed generic manufacturers to make low-cost replicas of drugs developed at great cost by the bigger drug firms, was unfair. The 1969 law withheld the normal seventeen-year patent protection from the medicines, allowing firms to copy new drugs on payment of a modest royalty. The system didn't please the big drug companies, most of them U.S.-based firms, but it saved Canadian consumers millions of dollars in lower prices for generic drugs.

Côté promised that the legislation would be drafted and passed by the Commons in June 1985, but at the end of May, a report by a royal commission created by the previous Liberal government to examine that very question recommended that generics could continue to copy name-brand drugs but should pay more than the token 4 per cent royalty. Naturally, the debate heated up, and Côté had to go back to the drawing-board and scrap his plans to have legislation before the Commons before the 1985 summer break.

In the fall, Côté repeatedly promised to have the legislation ready, despite the clamour by opponents that the Tories were caving in to American pressure on the drug bill. Critics argued that even if the government did plan to change the Patent Act as the Americans wanted, why not wait and use it as a bargaining chip in the ongoing Canada–U.S. freer trade talks? As for the Tories, they denied that American pressure had anything to do with it. They also consistently denied that it would mean higher drug prices for Canadians, even though in the bill they eventually introduced they included extra money to provinces to compensate for the higher costs to provincially sponsored drug plans.

Despite the government denials, there was solid evidence to suggest that Mulroney was indeed buckling under to American demands. At the annual summit with U.S. president Ronald Reagan in March 1986, Mulroney flatly promised Reagan to introduce drug-patent legislation in the Commons before Easter, the next month.

Bob Hepburn, the *Toronto Star*'s Washington bureau chief, commented that "the one that really hurt him [in the U.S.] was on the pharmaceuticals. The Canadians had been promising the Americans they were going to do something on the issue. Mulroney was meeting with Reagan and a small group of officials in the oval office and he told him directly, he promised him, that the decision was going to be made and announced publicly by Easter. Well, Easter comes and still no decision. May comes, no decision. And finally, on the last day of Parliament in June they scrambled to get something out. "What pisses Reagan off and his people off was that Mulroney told him it was coming and it didn't."

In mid-June 1986, officials in Mulroney's office said that the bill would not be introduced before the summer recess later that month. Then, after American complaints and a change of heart at the last minute, there was a series of foul-ups that would have given the Keystone Cops a run for their money.

Côté took the draft legislation to Governor General Jeanne Sauvé on June 26 for the obligatory vice-regal signature before introduction of a bill in the Commons. But Sauvé wouldn't sign it because the draft contained a typographical error. The bill was quickly reprinted. The next day, the last before the summer break, it was again taken to Sauvé, who signed it. But the courier bringing it back to the Commons was delayed, first by an Ottawa traffic jam and then by an overzealous Commons security guard who refused to let the courier bring the bill into the building. By the time it was all straightened out, the deadline for presenting the bill had passed. Côté made the legislation public anyway, saying that it would be formally introduced when the House returned in the fall.

In the meantime, a cabinet shuffle gave Harvie Andre the job of consumer and corporate affairs minister and he said he wanted to make some minor changes in Côté's bill. He tried to introduce the revised version on November 6, 1986, but was foiled by a series of opposition procedural ploys. He finally got it introduced the next day and it received a second reading on December 8 after the government had invoked a time limit, or limited closure, on debate.

Andre also insisted that the bill would not increase drug prices to consumers, an absurd claim, and denied in the Commons that American pressure had anything to do with it. He said that the move would increase jobs in the Canadian medical-research field by encouraging Canadian firms to develop drugs of their own.

On CBC's "Sunday Morning" radio program in early December 1986, Andre said, "There has been pressure on Canada since 1969 to change that law and it cost us a lot. Because when you go down there [to the United States] to talk about anything, acid rain, you know, lumber, talk about anything and this [drug bill] has been going on a long time, this is raised."

The next day, Turner asked Mulroney why he would make drug prices and the pharmaceutical industry "part of the bargain with the United States. Why would he knuckle under to American interests and inflict higher prices on our pensions, our older people and our sick?" Mulroney said, "There is no knuckling under. There is no inflicting of higher prices on anyone. I think my honourable friend knows that."

Committee hearings on the bill began in January 1987 and ended March 3, when the clause-by-clause study of the legislation by a Commons committee ended. On April 7, one day after Mulroney and Reagan had met for another annual summit, Andre said he was introducing a motion to limit debate on the bill and force a final Commons vote within three days. A total of thirty-three amendments were before the Commons, and it seemed likely the debate would drag on for weeks. Under Andre's bill, makers of brand-name drugs would get ten years of exclusive marketing rights to their products. The legislation would not affect current generic drugs, but copies of new drugs would be delayed a decade. Critics point out that, without competition from generic drugs, drug prices will rise in Canada but Andre claims that his proposed drug-prices review board would take action if it judged price increases excessive.

At Reagan's wrap-up speech to a joint session of the Commons and the Senate, he surprised observers by adding a few lines to his prepared text promising to push free trade and work towards the clean-up of acid rain. It wasn't anything he hadn't said before, but it was enough to allow Mulroney to claim that the summit had not been a total bust for him. A senior government official said, "I wouldn't say that a deal was made. Let's just say the president [Reagan] asked how the drug bill was going and when he was assured it would go quickly, he suggested he could say a little something more about acid rain and trade. I would characterize it more as an exchange of assurances than anything else. But I would say Andre's announcement wasn't a coincidence."

The multinationals had promised to spend $1.4 billion on research and development in Canada and create three thousand new jobs over the next ten years, but there was precious little the government could do to force them to live up to the promises. Opposition amendments, opposed by the Tories, would have given the drug-prices review board more power to monitor prices and roll back excessive ones and would have more clearly defined research and development so that a Canadian plant doesn't simply form a drug made elsewhere into a pill or a capsule.

Once again, opposition MPs launched a series of filibusters and walkouts; even the Senate was making noises about delaying the bill, and Andre warned that their future would be dim if they did. However, on April 15, the last day of sittings before a two-week Easter break, Speaker John Fraser, despite attacks on both Liberals and New Democrats for a partisan ruling, ended a week-long procedural dance and allowed a government guillotine motion to limit debate to three full days in late April. This move virtually guaranteed a speedy passage (barring some extraordinary flexing of legislative muscle from the Senate).

During 1986 and 1987, the Tories' ability to upset their own supporters was much in evidence in a fight with REAL Women, a group of small "c" conservative women that claims a membership of about 45,000. Twice, Secretary of State David Crombie told the group he would not approve their request for public funding, although 650 groups, many of which espouse radical, left-wing views, received $10.8 million from the Women's Program in Crombie's department during 1986. But REAL Women, which has considerable support among many sitting Tory MPs, couldn't even get an acknowledgement of its request for application forms until it posed as the National Association of Lesbian Mothers and received forms, plus a warm and encouraging letter, within a week.

REAL Women promotes a family-oriented society and opposes easy divorce, abortion, and equal pay for work of equal value. Crombie says it does not qualify for funding because it doesn't meet the criteria to "promote understanding and action on status of women's issues" and "carry out projects toward the achievement of equal opportunity for women in Canadian society."

The National Action Committee on the Status of Women was given about $400,000 by Crombie's department last year. It is, of course, fashionably feminist, promoting equal pay for work of equal value, easier divorce and abortion. While Crombie's stubbornness has pleased them, it has angered many people who would be expected to support a Conservative government.

The self-contradictions inherent in the department's radical bias were shown in two unrelated events early in 1987, one an $8,000 grant to the Alberta Federation of Women United for Families, another a $15,000 grant to the promoters of International Women's Week in Ottawa. In February, Crombie stopped payment on the cheque to the pro-family Alberta women's group, ostensibly because they were promoting an anti-abortion position, while at the same time he was preparing to approve the women's week grant for a female-only feminist forum that openly promoted lesbianism and abortion. Despite this, Françoise Guenette, a Crombie official, said, "We don't fund either side of the abortion issue." In fact, they do. Besides such groups as Lesbian Fury and Lesbian Amazons at the IWW event, another active participant was the stridently pro-abortion Canadian Abortion Rights Action League.

The government says it was not actually funding the conference, just giving the group money for advertising. More than half of the events at the IWW seminar (called "Celebrating Women's Diversity") were designated in the program as "W— Women only," and several were coded "L—Lesbian only." London East Tory MP Jim Jepson, one of several backbench Tories to complain about the leftist bias of Crombie's department, said, "I do not believe the taxpayer wants to see money spent on events with this type of focus." An IWW organizer, Joan Riggs, replied, "We feel strongly that lesbians are women and they should certainly participate." REAL Women are women too.

In January 1984, as opposition leader, Mulroney had appointed a former treasury board analyst as adviser on social and economic issues, especially those affecting women, and set up a six-member council composed of Michael Wilson; John Crosbie; Pat Carney; Robert de Cotret (who would later run successfully and become a cabinet minister); Carl Beigie, vice-president and chief economist of Dominion Securities Pitfield Ltd.; and John McCallum, a University of Manitoba professor and *Financial Post* columnist.

In early March 1984, he told 250 delegates to the first national PC women's caucus meeting that homemakers should get pensions, calling it an "honourable" thing to do. Maureen McTeer rankled Mulroney at the same conference when she referred to a "nervousness" among women that Mulroney would go to the right and backslide on women's issues. "She's speaking for people, is she?" snapped Mulroney, when asked about her comments. "I did not hear a single negative comment. I don't know what she is talking about." Mulroney, who has traditionally not fared well among women in public-opinion polls, also promised to force companies seeking lucrative federal contracts to hire more women to perform the work. He said that 30 per cent of about 1,248 jobs on federal boards and commissions would be held by women at the end of his first term. Women held 15 per cent of those jobs in 1980.

Again during his period of opposition, at a Lunches With Leaders event in May 1984, there were audible groans from some of the two thousand women who paid $25 a ticket for the event when Mulroney said that the abortion law would stay untouched if he became prime minister. He said he knows "how sensitive an issue this is," and promised action to improve facilities at hospitals with therapeutic-abortion committees, but added that he does not favour abortion as a form of birth control. "Then you are not in favour of a woman having freedom of choice?" a woman asked him. "I think I have answered the best I can," said Mulroney. "The answer is no." Later, Mulroney was applauded when he repeated his promise to double women's representation on boards and commissions, to reform divorce laws, and to ensure enforcement of maintenance awards. CBC's Barbara Frum hosted the session, the first of three with the federal leaders. The menu included "Positive Power Salad . . . a garden-fresh mix of crunchy vegetables, toasted sunflower seeds, slivered almonds, raisins and a trio of exotic cheeses slathered with Canuons Special Dijon vinaigrette dressing with fresh herbs."

On August 15, Mulroney appeared along with Turner and Broadbent on national television in a debate on so-called women's issues sponsored by NAC. The bureaucratic rules of the debate didn't allow for much give-and-take, and most of the time was used by the three leaders to spout statistics and promise to make life better for women. When asked about his performance after the event, Mulroney quoted a French general who, when asked what he did in the Second World War, said: "I survived."

On September 4, the Tories elected 19 women among their 211 seats, and Mulroney's first cabinet included 6 women—Pat Carney, Flora MacDonald, Suzanne Blais-Grenier, Barbara McDougall, Monique Vézina, and Andrée Champagne.

In July 1985, federal officials said that a scheme to be implemented in the fall would require employers with one hundred or more employees seeking federal contracts worth $200,000 or more to agree to become equal-opportunity employers some time in the future. In March 1984, Mulroney had said that a Conservative government would "ensure that all companies seeking to provide services to the government of Canada hire an increasing number of women to perform those services as a condition of getting the job. We will ask these firms to show us, as part of their tendering responsibilities, how many women will be hired to fulfill those contracts."

Mulroney was well received by five hundred women at the National PC Women's Caucus meeting in October 1985, and was interrupted several times by applause during a speech in which he said that more than half the 284,000 jobs in the first eleven months of his government had gone to women and promised "more direct action" to close the 36 per cent wage gap between men and women. "In the past twelve months, 25.1 per cent of the government's discretionary appointments have been women, an increase of 67 per cent" over the Liberals, he said.

A year earlier, he had told this same group that he would bring in housewives' pensions, a central registry to ensure continuance of court-ordered maintenance payments, and equal pay for work of equal value. He had not kept any of those promises.

In the November 1986 issue of *Chatelaine*, journalist Charlotte Gray published a report card of Mulroney's record on promises to women on ten key issues. The marks ranged from highs of B-plus on jobs, women entrepreneurs, and native women, to lows of D on part-time work and child care. By June 1986, 297,000 more women were working than in September 1984 and the unemployment rate for women had fallen by 2.2 percentage points. The proportion of women on boards and commissions had risen to 25 per cent, and the proportion of women in the senior-management and executive levels of the federal public service had risen slightly from 7 to 7.8 per cent. On child care, Gray wrote: "This is the area in which many women feel their suitor jilted them." In 1984 he had promised to find "rapid, realistic and effective solutions to the urgent problems of child care. . . ."

Indeed, child care was rapidly emerging in 1987 as the issue most likely to dominate much of the fall and spill over into 1988 and possibly even the next election. Everybody agrees that children are important and should be looked after safely. The question is, who should do it and at what cost? Mulroney has flatly rejected universal child care schemes, which it is estimated would cost up to $12 billion a year. In March 1987, he promised to deliver "an effective national child care system," but was not specific about what that meant. About 2.5 million Canadian children aged twelve and under need care, many for most of the day. They are now being cared for in a hodgepodge of systems, ranging from private non-profit and government-run daycare centres in schools, churches, and other institutions to paid nannies, neighbours, other family members, and periodic babysitters. Many "latch-key kids" are left on their own after school until their parents or older siblings get home.

A special parliamentary committee on child care chaired by Tory MP Shirley Martin released a report in late March that recommended spending about $600 million federally on the first stage of a national daycare plan, but rejected free, universal daycare. Fewer than 8 per cent of working mothers can get their children into existing institutionalized daycare facilities. The committee, which heard 975 submissions in 31 communities found strong support for non-profit daycare to be paid by a mix of parental and public money, but the Tory plan emphasizes private-sector care.

This debate, like most others, gets silly at times. In January, for example, health minister Jake Epp said it was poppycock to say youngsters are better stimulated in daycare centres than by their parents. He also said that, given the option, parents are usually the best people to raise their own children, although he freely acknowledged that not everyone has that choice. This was seen by the opposition and the daycare fraternity as an attack on daycare, and both the Liberals and the NDP demanded that Epp resign for saying it. The NDP critic even said at a news conference that Mulroney "should replace the inept Mr. Epp with a woman minister who has an understanding of what today's families are facing."

Unlike earlier polls, in which Mulroney fared poorly among women, a February 1987 survey by Angus Reid Associates showed that more women than men liked his government, although neither figure suggested overwhelming endorsement (28 per cent for women and 19 for men, 23 per cent of decided voters overall).

Barbara McDougall, the minister responsible for women's issues, says that "one of the major changes I see is that, now, there are a lot of men who are allies [with women]. And I think that a lot of women, a lot of women's advocates groups, haven't learned how to use that yet." McDougall, one of the most widely respected ministers Mulroney has, none the less seems underutilized in this role, and in her other capacity as privatization minister, since Mulroney or some other minister tends to make whatever major announcements there are.

Nobody can know for sure what the future holds, but if the Tories ever do decide to match their deficit-cutting rhetoric with action, then the social field cannot escape. Social-development spending accounts for about 60 per cent of the government's total program expenditures. According to Wilson's budget of February 18, 1987, actual spending on social development was $50.54 billion in 1984–85. That increased by 2.5 per cent the next year to $51.81 billion, and by 5.7 per cent to an estimated $54.8 billion for 1986–87. His 1987–88 forecast was for social-development spending of $57.2 billion, a 4.4 per cent increase. In three of the four years, increases in social spending fell below the average of total program spending, but with the daycare fight looming, and an election a year or so away, that could change.

CHAPTER ELEVEN

IMELDA II

Don MacDonald was tired and hungry. Like other journalists covering Brian and Mila Mulroney's exhausting twelve-day trip to Asia's Pacific Rim, MacDonald, the Halifax *Chronicle-Herald*'s jovial man in Ottawa welcomed a day off in Seoul, South Korea. It was May 14, 1986, and our weary traveller was munching on a hamburger and fries at a Wendy's just down the street from It'aewon, the enormous downtown shopping centre near the U.S. armed-forces headquarters, a frantic plethora of small shops and street vendors, where American dollars are accepted and haggling over price is expected.

MacDonald saw a fleet of tow trucks descend on the street out front and begin hauling away several legally parked cars. An American in the next booth said, "They're towing cars away. There must be somebody important in town." MacDonald joked, "Our prime minister is in town. They're probably towing the cars away so his wife can go shopping." The two men laughed.

Moments later, a stretch Mercedes limo, surrounded front and back by a phalanx of police cars and motorcycles, lights flashing and sirens blaring, pulled up to the now-cleared curb. A South Korean in a dark suit jumped out before the car came to a complete stop, dashed to the back door, opened it, and stood at attention while Mila Mulroney and her trusty aide, Bonnie Brownlee, stepped out, took a quick look around, then waltzed off to the shopping district with a group of local officials.

While MacDonald's joking reference to Mila seemed prophetic, the truth is, her propensity for shopping has become such a trademark that even Tories have been heard whispering privately that her nickname is "Imelda Two," after the infamous wife of deposed Philippine dictator Ferdinand Marcos.

A long-time family friend, speaking on condition he not be named—a common request for those not completely enamoured of Mila—said she is "a wonderful woman, very friendly and the key to Brian's equilibrium. . . . But I wouldn't want her for my wife. I couldn't afford her. She spends incredible amounts on clothes for her, for him, and for the kids.

"She spends thousands a month. I've been there and seen her buy four or five Gucci purses at Holt Renfrew in one trip or spent $800 on a designer outfit for one of the kids. It's incredible. I don't know where she gets the money."

For the most part, Mila has received adulation in Ottawa, from the media as well as her husband's political friends and enemies. "She is everything that he [Brian] isn't," says Southam News journalist Peter Maser. "I think she's genuine, she's warm, she's interested. I have to confess I'm quite a suck for her."

He's not the only one. In a controversial article on Mila in the October 1985 issue of *This Magazine*, Ottawa *Citizen* reporter Susan Riley, a tough-minded feminist, wrote, "The prime minister's wife has powerful defenders. At the least whisper of criticism, senior member of the press gallery leap to her defence, convinced she is a helpless victim of feminist vindictiveness. Mila's staff also carefully restricts access to friendly reporters, and bristles at the slightest jibe. She has also let it be known around town that Brian is very protective of her, an unmistakable warning in a hyperpolitical city."

In the fall of 1985, Montreal *Gazette* journalist Linda Diebel wrote a long positive feature about Mila. She wound it up with a quote from aide Bonnie Brownlee saying that when Mila was in labour with Nicolas, her main concern was for the poor reporters staked out in the hospital lobby waiting for news. "Mila may be all kinds of wonderful things," wrote Diebel. "But a saint, too?" That little shot was enough to spark an angry call from Brownlee complaining about the "nasty" article and putting Diebel on the "out" list. Word spreads rapidly in this company town, and reporters who want to interview Mila, not to mention Brian, take note.

Mila's basic biography is well known. She was born July 13, 1953, in Sarajevo, Yugoslavia, to Dimitrije Pivnicki and his wife, Bogdanka (nicknamed Boba), daughter of a European bourgeois family that had prospered in the legal and medical professions of Yugoslavia's pre-Second World War monarchy. When the Communists took over, Pivnicki was a medical intern and Boba a nurse at a local hospital. But Pivnicki was not allowed to practise because he refused to embrace the new truth. In 1957 he spotted an ad in a German newspaper for psychiatrists at the Allan Memorial Institute of the Royal Victoria Hospital in Montreal. After receiving official permission to study in Canada, he emigrated to Montreal that same year in search of freedom. "Canada was the brave new world," Mila would say years later. "You named it and you can do it. There was terrific optimism."

A year later, Pivnicki sent for his wife, Boba, and children, Mila, then five, and John, just an infant. They arrived in New York and started for Montreal the same day, after a horrendous fifty-day voyage stuffed into an old cargo ship. Mila was horribly seasick for most of the trip. When they arrived in Montreal, she remembers, "It was the first time I'd seen snow."

At first, the family lived in a furnished apartment in the McGill University student ghetto. But they were destined for better things, and it wasn't long before the family, which now included baby Ivana, moved to a house bordering Montreal's élite Westmount district. At age six, Mila was skipping off in a green pleated tunic to an exclusive private girls' school called Miss Edgar's and Miss Cramp's, where her father enrolled her after noticing, to his annoyance, that Mila was learning Czech, rather than English, from other immigrant children at the local public school. She was raised in a trilingual environment, speaking French, English, and her native Serbo-Croatian. She also speaks Italian. Of her experience of being raised as an immigrant she says, "You're never like the rest of the children. It just makes you stronger. But I had lots of friends and an open home. My mom was always baking for us."

Even as a child, Mila, an olive-skinned beauty, had a highly charged love of consumerism. She once said that when she was growing up she would always go to her father when she wanted something, such as a new skirt. "My mother would say 'What do you need it for?' and I'd say, 'I don't need it, but I want it.'" The pattern stuck.

She skipped two elementary grades, studied ballet and

piano, and breezed through Westmount High School, where the 1970 yearbook, *Vox Docum* (Voice of the People) lists her favourite saying as, "We were all born originals, let us not die copies." She then enrolled in general arts at Montreal's Sir George Williams University (Concordia since 1974) but after getting a B average in her first term took an aptitude test and switched to civil engineering and "really loved it—I had visions of becoming an architect, originally." She also became involved in politics, working for Tory Michael Meighen in the spring of 1972 in his hopeless attempt to unseat Liberal fixture C.M. Drury in Westmount. Manning telephones and canvassing the riding, she later explained "I am not a camp follower—and I wanted to see change." (Drury beat Meighen by 14,000 votes.)

In this period, Mila, eighteen, also had her now-fabled meeting with a thirty-three-year-old lawyer named Brian Mulroney beside the pool at the posh Mount Royal Tennis Club. She says she didn't like the swaggering Mulroney at first—"He was too brash." But when he persisted, she succumbed to his charms. The story goes that Mulroney, a rising young legal star with a reputation for prowess with women, was reading the *New York Times* when Mila waltzed by in a bikini and he said, "That's for me."

Meighen, who remains one of Mulroney's closest friends, said that "very few women who were young and pretty escaped" the efforts of the eager bachelor. Mila said, "At first, I wasn't really interested. I thought he was too old. But I did think he would be an interesting person to know." She said she was at Meighen's headquarters one day when the phone rang. "I picked it up, and this guy asked for Michael. After I put the phone down, it struck me that I recognized the voice." She said they'd been dating for weeks, but hadn't discussed politics. "We talked about life, our ambitions, our families, but not politics. Brian's like that," she says. "He never tells you about his accomplishments or who he knows. He's not a braggart." Five months later, they were engaged. They were married May 6, 1973.

At first, Mila continued to study engineering, but in January 1976, a month before Mulroney lost his first bid for the Tory leadership, when she was seven months pregnant with her second child, she quit school. She was three courses short of her degree. In a 1983 interview, she said, "Children are worth all the degrees that you can get. I would much rather watch my children grow up for now, enjoy our life and politics. I never do anything that I don't want to do, and I really do not like to make commitments unless I know I can keep them. So while I'll eventually do something, I really do not know what it is now."

A close friend from that early period is CTV journalist Gillian Cosgrove. As a reporter at the Montreal *Gazette*, Cosgrove lived with columnist (and later Mulroney biographer and speech writer) L. Ian MacDonald between 1972 and Christmas 1976. MacDonald introduced Cosgrove to the Mulroney's, and the two couples frequently double dated. Although Cosgrove says her own love of independence makes Mila's acceptance of a more traditional role hard for her to understand, the two became quite good friends. Cosgrove, who also loves shopping, used to prowl Montreal's clothing and antique stores with Mila. "We both liked shopping. She used to take me to the music school there where all the kids were going in to be taught by the nuns . . . there's a little basement shop she had discovered where all the designers came in and you could get $300, $400, or $500 dresses for about 20 per cent of the price. Mila discovered it and would only let her best friends in on it."

Cosgrove credits Mila with an "impish sense of humour," which one day led them to Notre Dame Street where the antique shops are. "She bought this mirror which she knew was just the right size to go over their bed, which she knew would drive them crazy. So she had that. She was the redeeming factor of the two. Him, he was ambitious, driven to meet the right people and stroke the right way, the expensive dinners, the expensive gifts . . . But she brought him down and I guess made him human. I think perhaps she still [does that] politically. When you see her work a room, I mean people warm to Mila. You can see them lighten up when she reaches out and touches them."

On February 6, 1976, two weeks before the leadership convention, Cosgrove sat with Mila at an east-end Montreal delegate meeting at the Richelieu Hotel. Afterwards, the four of them went to Ruby Foo's for dinner. Because MacDonald was planning to write the biography if Mulroney won, Cosgrove noted down for him some of her own impressions of Mila during the speech.

"Mila is glowing, eight months pregnant, black silk Chinese dress, little-girl black patent-leather shoes," she recorded.

"'Does he have notes?' Mila asks somewhat anxiously as Brian steps to the podium. She talks to herself: 'No, stop that about Trudeau. Oh, the flower-power kid has failed. That's a new one. Why does he mention Rocky Mountain, that's Joe Clark's riding? Yea, I like this part.' ['I may make errors but I promise to be honest and true to you,' said Brian.] I wish he'd stop talking about getting Trudeau out of his swimming pool with a crowbar. I don't want the pool filled in with concrete.' [A giggle.]"

On the subject of Margaret Trudeau, Mila told Cosgrove that "Margaret said she didn't realize she was marrying the prime minister when she married Pierre. Whereas I knew what I was getting into when I married Brian—the lawyer, the political ambitions. . . ."

According to Cosgrove, Mila was hurt by a profile of Brian written by Montreal *Gazette* columnist Don MacPherson. The story quoted her comment about how often she had to iron Brian's shirts (he changes shirts several times a day). MacPherson's lead to his story had a very irascible Mulroney saying "Darling, get me my shirts right now." "I guess I learned my lesson," Mila said. She had felt, flying back from Baie-Comeau with Don, Bill (Fox) and Ian, that they were all like Ian and could be trusted. "I know the off-the-record rules," she said in response to a question about whether she was being naive. "But I'm too open a person, I don't think I could ever clam up." Brian and Mila had talked with MacPherson and other journalists on the flight, but Mila said that Mulroney had always expected these personal insights to remain private.

"It surprised me that they were so naive," said Cosgrove. "But Brian always operated on a quid pro quo. He fed you stuff, so you'd always go light on him in any critical vein because he'd feed you great stuff—[though] for his own purposes obviously."

Also in Cosgrove's February 1976 notes are several family-related comments. Speaking of daughter Caroline, then twenty months, Mila said, "She's old enough to know that when Dada puts on his coat in the morning he will be gone for a few days. She sits in Brian's chair when he's gone and says 'Da-da' over and over again. When Brian comes home she runs around excitedly pointing to all the pictures of him in the paper and picking up things that are his."

Asked what she misses when Brian is on the road, Mila said,

"When he calls me at night, he's always tired and he says something like 'It went well.' But I always want to know more. Another thing is we haven't had a really good fight for ages. I told Brian, I am a pregnant woman and deserve to be pampered and I'm going to reserve a night for a rip-roaring fight. . . . You've got to remember that Brian loves a good fight. He's a scrapper at heart."

During that period in their lives, Cosgrove was as close to the Mulroney's as anyone. She said that Brian was "always a master of the grand gesture." Their birthdays were just two days apart, Brian's, March 20, Gillian's, March 18. "I mean, he wouldn't send me one bottle of Scotch for my birthday, he would send me a whole case of Scotch. And on my twentieth birthday, he didn't send me a dozen roses, he sent me twenty dozen roses."

Everyone who knows this country's most famous couple agrees that it was Mila's strength, not Brian's, that really shone in the dark aftermath of Mulroney's defeat at the 1976 leadership campaign. Long a heavy drinker, Mulroney, as one friend put it, "disappeared into the vat of martinis," staying out late at night. It was Mila, after years of putting up with it, who finally told him in 1980 he'd better clean up his act if he ever wanted to be prime minister, and more importantly, if he wanted her and the kids to be there with him. Typically, Mulroney himself has offered several explanations about why he quit drinking (and, later, smoking as well) and Mila has denied any role in it. "I never thought that was my business. I don't think it's a wife business," she said in a 1984 *Globe* interview. "We don't tread on each other's turf."

Family friends tell a different story, albeit not for attribution. "She went through hell because he was feeling so sorry for himself," said one. "I don't know many women who could have stood it, but she did, his boozing and late-night carousing. And if she hadn't, I don't know what he would be today, but it sure wouldn't be prime minister."

This aspect of Mila, the fact that Mulroney leans on her as his crutch, makes her far more powerful in political terms than wives of Canadian prime ministers have tended to be. "He still calls her every night when he's on the road," said one insider. "He consults her about everything, about policy, about cabinet changes. He's always had a reputation for being a good listener, a great conciliator. But you get the feeling he never really listens to anybody except Mila. He listens to her."

During a March 1986 tour of the West, in which she combined partisan events with her volunteer work on behalf of cystic fibrosis, Mila told *Toronto Star* reporter Joe O'Donnell, "I'm a political animal. I love it." The previous year, she had told a French-language television broadcaster that she had used her influence to get higher government grants for medical research. (A check of the supplementary-spending estimates from the treasury board did show that $30.9 million had been added to the $130.3 million in previous estimates for Health and Welfare's Medical Research Council.)

While she appears to revel in the up side of playing politics, Mila clearly doesn't like the flip side. She complained when journalists speculated about her pregnancy with Nicolas (born September 4, 1985, on the first anniversary of their election win), saying "It's up to me to make the announcement to my children. I find this [pregnancy] so personal that I did not appreciate the interest of the media, and I telephoned the entire family to announce what they [had] already learned on television and in the media." It was not too personal, however, to alert the media for every possible photo opportunity at the hospital, or to have her booked into the Ottawa General Hospital three weeks in advance for September 3, so that Nicolas could be induced (as he was, although they deny it) to enter the world just in time for the anniversary celebration of their 1984 electoral success.

Most Ottawa journalists remain too timid to ask why the public should pay for an office and staff for Mila (she is the first prime minister's wife to receive such aid) and, indeed, just how much the public is paying. Mila is not impressed by the zeal of the bolder souls who wonder aloud about it. Unofficial estimates list renovations to her second-floor Langevin Block office at about $100,000, for spiffing up an office and adding a washroom. She has three full-time staffers, plus periodic help from other public servants employed by the Prime Minister's Office. In September 1986, Mila told a reporter, "There are no public expenses of taxpayers' dollars in my office. None, none; that's why they are not on public record." Since the PMO is exempt from access-to-information rules, just what the bill is for Mila's office is not available. Her faithful assistant Bonnie Brownlee claims the Tory party pays for all Mila's stationery and mailing costs, and that travel and other costs incurred during Mila's charity work do not cost taxpayers anything. "You can't let hundreds of letters each month from Canadians go unanswered," she adds. "These are letters directly to the wife of the prime minister." (Even when Brian was opposition leader, however, Mila was given an office in Parliament's South Block and two full-time staffers.)

Mila is not, of course, the first prime minister's wife to receive hundreds of letters each month from Canadians. She's just the first who has a political staff and an office paid for by taxpayers in which to answer the letters. This is one reason for the frequent accusations that she is playing the role of an American-style First Lady. "There's a need to have an office," she once snapped at a reporter. "If there wasn't a need, I wouldn't be here."

When Mila Mulroney arrived in Ottawa after Brian won the Tory leadership in 1983, the local social set was certainly ready to be taken by storm. Prime Minister Pierre Trudeau and his wife, Margaret, had long since parted. Joe Clark's wife, Maureen McTeer, although respected by many for her deep convictions, was none the less prickly and not given to glittering social affairs. And Governor General Jeanne Sauvé continued to become more reclusive, eventually reaching the point where she ordered the public to be kept off the magnificent grounds surrounding Government House, where Ottawa residents had cavorted freely for decades. What Ottawa didn't have, and hadn't for some time, was some good, old-fashioned glamour. Mila supplied it. Indeed, the London *Daily Express* proclaimed her "the most glamorous political star since the early Jackie Kennedy." You couldn't pick up a woman's magazine anywhere without Mila's beautiful face staring back at you, her nose scrunched up in that cutesey-pie style of hers.

Journalist Stevie Cameron, who was Ottawa *Citizen* lifestyle editor at the time, says, "Mila was in great demand when she came in as the leader's wife in 1983. Suddenly every charity in town invited her, and she went. She was terrific. She went to all those things. She cut ribbons, she opened the Ronald McDonald house, she did all this stuff because the PM [Trudeau] didn't have a wife. There wasn't anybody else to do this, and for some reason there still is this myth they need somebody to do it."

In an October 1983 interview with Ottawa *Citizen* reporter Janice Middleton, Mila said, "One of the things people are going to have to permit me to do is find my niche in Ottawa. Going from the private life to the public life all of a sudden . . . it's been a fast transition. I want to do right by women in Canada, but I have to find out what that means for me."

One thing it meant, and still does, is her insistence that hubby comes first, even before the children. This view has been lauded by traditionalists and attacked by such feminists as Doris Anderson, who said Mila was a "a throwback to my mother's day, like the beauty pageants and other things that are still around—just quaint." In a June 1984 Montreal speech, Mila said, "To be honest, I live by one single overriding principle—my partnership with Brian comes first. I see myself as the maintainer of the status quo."

When the family first moved to Ottawa, they stayed at Kingsmere, the Speaker's house, while Stornoway, the seventy-three-year-old house of the official opposition leader was being renovated to Mila's exacting specifications. Indeed, in early summer, before a date was even set for the Central Nova by-election, the couple ignored public works department rules and hired themselves an outside interior decorator, Giovanni Mowinckel, who in 1987 would be at the centre of a controversy involving their lavish lifestyle. The bill was set at $79,000 for those renovations, and the Mulroneys and their three children moved into Stornoway officially on December 5, 1983. The couple revamped the front entrance and walkway, added a wall to the third floor to make three bedrooms, and installed new plumbing in the bathroom. They chose a French blue, red, white, and green colour scheme for the children's quarters, with bunk beds in each room, "for friends to sleep over," and a playroom with "lots of padding" on the floor. The breakfast room was painted bright yellow, the kitchen beige and white. Kitchen appliances were shifted and a second stove and large refrigerator-freezer unit added. Mila, who enjoys cooking, said the new appliances would be used to entertain Conservatives from across the country.

In that first month, they had about two thousand people in for about a dozen parties. Mila even organized a media tour of the house, complete with three printed pages breaking down the cost of the renovations, Christmas cookies (baked by Donna Thacker, whose husband Blaine is an MP) with "Brian Loves Mila" on them, and footmen pouring coffee for the journalists. Nobody had ever done that for the media before, and Mila's graciousness and charm immediately won the hearts of the Ottawa press gallery. She promised a similar tour of 24

Sussex Drive, once she and Brian won the election, but by that time such public-relations stunts weren't necessary and the tour has never been held.

Even then, although most of the media were still overwhelmed by the glitz, there were hints of a petty side to Mila. In the March 1984 issue of *Saturday Night* magazine, freelance journalist Charlotte Gray, writing about the media tour of Stornoway, reported a minor incident in which Mila had boasted to a woman reporter that constituents in Central Nova had sent her some holly. When the perplexed reporter said "What holly?" Mila pointed to some orange berries in an oriental vase. "That's not holly," said the journalist. "That's bittersweet." When this appeared, Mila was furious. She has never been friendly to Gray since.

More than one journalist has reported another odd habit, which has happened in several interviews. As one commentator notes, "She is a charming person to interview. She asks you about yourself, about your kids, and I feel it's sincere. But she is intent on the interview and, about half-way through, while she is still looking straight at you, she will hold out her hand and say, 'Bonnie, a Kleenex,' and Bonnie, or whatever aide is there, will run forward with a Kleenex, put it in her hand, and she blows her nose. It's just like Marie Antoinette. I've never seen anything like it. . . . she doesn't even acknowledge it. It's a gesture which says so much about her."

Mila wears exquisite designer dresses (size 10), and favours cultured pearls and large diamonds. She also dashes off to Montreal every three weeks to have her bangs trimmed by her favourite stylist, Charles of Westmount Square. She shops frequently at Brana, a small boutique owned by a Montreal friend, where she gets a discount on expensive clothes. She also loves to shop at Montreal's Holt Renfrew by staying in her suite next door at the Ritz-Carlton and having clothes brought to her there so she doesn't have to search through the racks on her own. Brian is no slouch himself in the fashion department. He buys his tailor-made suits from Bijan in New York, a Persian tailor who caters to the rich and famous. Bijan's first store is on Rodeo Drive in Beverly Hills, and his suits start at $2,500 (U.S.) apiece.

In the period leading up to the 1984 election, Mila certainly kept busy. In December she was telling Americans on ABC's "Good Morning America" that because it is "important to have your own style," she wouldn't compare herself with Margaret

Trudeau. In January, she raised $15,000 for the Victoria Symphony Orchestra with a fifteen-minute reading from Prokofiev's *Peter and the Wolf* at the Royal Theatre. In February, five hundred women paid $20 each (dozens had to be turned away) to attend a Conservative dinner in Montreal where Mila told them that women are playing more important roles in party politics. Throughout the winter and spring, Mila criss-crossed the country, mixing partisan politics and charity work. In a July interview with Standard Broadcast News, she announced that she would be deeply involved in the election. "My plans are that I'm going to campaign one hundred per cent of the time. The minority issues, women's issues, those are important to me, so I'll be vocal on those. . . . We have to make sure as a party that we speak loud and clear for women in this country." Two weeks later, she had harsh words for John Turner's infamous bum-patting escapade, saying, "I don't think it is a gesture that is appropriate. I would be most offended if he did it to me." (Mila was not the only person offended during that campaign. "We would arrive in a place at eleven o'clock or midnight," said one senior Tory who worked on the campaign tour, "and Mila would decide she wanted something to munch on, usually a Popsicle or licorice, and somebody would have to go out and scour the stores to find it for her. Even people like Pat Kinsella were sent out on these errands, treated like little schoolboys so that Mila could have her wish."

Commenting on what became known as the "Mila Factor," in the campaign, outgoing Ontario premier Bill Davis said to Mulroney at a Toronto rally, "Mila will get more votes for you than you will for yourself." Many reporters who covered that election wrote and broadcast similiar remarks. Many think it's even more true now.

While the local socialites had every reason to be thrilled that Mila was moving into 24 Sussex Drive, it wasn't long before visions of a Kennedy-style White House North were dashed. Just days after the family moved into the thirty-room house in November 1984, she told a gathering of Tories in Stellarton, N.S., that guests at 24 Sussex would get smaller dinner portions in line with federal austerity measures. She also planned to exercise less protocol at dinners and do more mingling with guests. The children would be encouraged to join them at official dinners, so "they will learn to listen as well as talk."

When Mila moved from Stornoway, she took almost all the furniture with her. At the time, Geills Turner, never as popular with the media as Mila, received some bitchy press because she complained about it. "The reason the Turners were so upset when they moved into Stornoway," says one friend of both families, "is there was nothing left there. That house is supposed to come with a basic quantity of sofas, chairs, tables, and stuff like that, but it didn't have anything in it. Mila moved all the furniture which Giovanni [Mowinckel] had covered up to Harrington Lake [the prime minister's official summer home at Meech Lake, Quebec, about twenty miles north of Ottawa] . . . so the Turners had to buy a lot of stuff, and poor old John had that fuss made about the stuff that had to be bought. Mila didn't even leave any curtain rods. . . . Everything was just gone, except the dining-room set, which goes with the house.

"When Geills objected, Mila said, 'There's lots of furniture, you're welcome to look at it, it's in the warehouse.' It was all the rejects from Harrington Lake, the big oval rugs you can buy at K-Mart, old maple furniture, recreation-room-type stuff. It all looks like the stuff you'd buy from Good Will. I don't blame Mila for wanting to get rid of it, but it tells you things about her character that she would tell Geills to go to the basement warehouse and be happy with her rejects."

Mila got herself embroiled in a silly controversy sparked by Brian's hopeless penchant for overstating things. On May 7, 1984, Mulroney told CHCH-TV talk show host Tom Cherington that unlike Trudeau, he would not expect the public to pay for a nanny to watch his kids. When it was learned that Elizabeth MacDonald, a $17,000-a-year nanny, was on staff at 24 Sussex Drive, Mulroney denied she was a nanny. So did Mila. "I will never admit to having a nanny," she said, claiming that MacDonald was a maid who often acted as a "mother's helper." The issue had a short lifespan as "nannygate," the first of a series of stories that only became stories because the Mulroney's chose to deny the obvious rather than admit it.

MacDonald had worked as a nanny for the Mulroneys in Montreal before they got into politics. They took her with them when they moved into Stornoway, and again when they moved up to 24 Sussex Drive. She had been on the federal payroll since October 7, 1983, and indeed was being paid by the public to watch the Mulroney kids at the very time Mulroney was telling Cherington it would never happen. When officials in the Privy Council Office confirmed for

reporters that yes, MacDonald was on staff, Fox told personne
director Sam Morel to stop talking to the press. A reporter
asked then press aide Lisa Van Dusen (she was gone shortly
after) who MacDonald was, and Van Dusen said, "Oh, that'
the nanny . . . she's been their nanny for a couple of years.'

Not according to the officially revised version she wasn't.
Fox said that the Mulroneys had "always said they will raise
their own children, and when one of the children wakes up at
four in the morning, they come to see the parents." Anyway
he said, Mulroney's TV pledge "wasn't a campaign promise,'
because the election campaign had not officially begun at the
time. Enter Fred Doucet, Mulroney's senior adviser. His
explanation was that MacDonald wasn't a nanny—even though
the children called her "nanny"—but was simply an employee
who "interfaced with the children on a habitual basis." (Shortly
after Christmas, MacDonald quit her job to return to school.)

On November 30, 1984, Joe O'Donnell of the *Toronto Star*
ran a story that, in 1987, would explode into a major scandal.
He reported that Mulroney had ordered more than $100,000
worth of taxpayer-funded improvements at his two official
residences—including a satellite dish at Harrington Lake, and
a whirlpool bath and a $5,000 shoe rack for Mila at 24 Sussex
Drive. The design work was being done by Giovanni Mowinckel, head of Colvin Design Canada Ltd., and it involved
mainly redecorating, electrical work, plumbing, and flooring.

Contacted by the *Star*, a public-works official refused to
supply any details on the "extras"—the satellite and whirlpool—or on who was paying, telling O'Donnell he'd have to
call Fred Doucet for the information. A spokesman said
Doucet was not available. Bill Fox was unable or unwilling to
respond to the questions, so O'Donnell wrote the story.

At 8:30 the next morning, Fox called the *Star's* Ottawa
bureau looking for O'Donnell—"Just goes to show how far out
of touch he'd become," laughed O'Donnell, a cherubic, party
type who rarely emerges before noon. Fox, who used to work
with O'Donnell at the *Star*, told office manager Darlene
Newman to leave the following message for O'Donnell: "Tell
him for me I'm going to rip his fucking lungs out." Fox later
apologized in writing to Newman, but never to O'Donnell.

Two years later, on CBC radio's "Media File" show, Fox said it
was one incident where he "presumed on past friendships,"
and "let personal anger get the best of me." Fox claimed he

was angry because O'Donnell had called him late in the day and had agreed to wait for a return call the next day.

Not true, says O'Donnell, whose version, given the competitive demands of the media, is much more plausible. O'Donnell was working on the story when he learned that Liberal MP Don Boudria was going to put questions on the order paper about it the next day. That would mean all journalists would have access to the story, so O'Donnell called Fox well before noon, told him what he had, waited all day for a call, then called him back between 6:00 and 7:00 P.M., only to be told Fox hadn't spoken to Mulroney and wouldn't be able to that night.

"It was a lifestyle thing, not a lot of money involved, but one of those stories which sets a tone, tells people something about the way this guy operates. He's claiming I made an agreement with him to hold off, that's not true. He knew it was on the order paper for the next day, I told him that.

"It struck me as an easy question, did Mulroney pay for this stuff himself or didn't he? That would take about thirty seconds to ask. You'd also expect your press secretary to have good enough antennae to realize a story like that could be damaging, and he'd make damn sure he'd get an answer."

A few days later, Mulroney said he was personally paying for the satellite dish and the hot tub (O'Donnell's only mistake had been in reporting it was a Jacuzzi, which is actually cheaper than a hot tub). Mulroney also claimed he'd saved taxpayers $500,000 by rejecting a consultant's report calling for $600,000 worth of repairs to the official residence and opting to spend only about $100,000 of public money.

On April 8, 1987, the Ottawa *Citizen* reported that decorator Mowinckel had suddenly departed for Italy, leaving creditors unpaid and his business associates stunned. Mowinckel had closed his firm, put his Orléans house up for sale, and left without explanation.

The mystery surrounding his sudden exit lifted somewhat on April 16, when reporters Stevie Cameron and Graham Fraser broke a blockbuster story in the *Globe and Mail* about the PC Canada Fund's payments of about $308,000 over the past two and one-half years to renovate, redecorate, and furnish Mulroney's official residences. These sums were in addition to the $97,500 worth of government-funded renovations to 24 Sussex in the fall of 1984 and $25,000 worth to Harrington Lake.

"Now I can see why they got so upset about that hot-tub story in 1984," says O'Donnell.

The *Globe* story, which immediately had opposition MP comparing the Mulroneys to the Marcos family, told of a clothes closet designed for thirty of Mulroney's suits and eighty-four pairs of shoes, including at least fifty pairs of Gucci loafers. One worker actually counted sixty-seven pairs of Brian's Gucci loafers, all black. The only difference was some had tassles and some had buckles. Mila's special third-floor storage closet (always kept locked), was designed with nine metres of hanging space for blouses and suits, three and one-half metres of hanging storage for evening dresses, and storage for one hundred pairs of shoes.

In addition, the couple had twenty-four malachite placemats custom made at $200 each, and some of these Mila gave away, to Paul Desmarais's wife. Two antique crystal vases with silver mounts cost $3,400, and the walls were covered with almost sixty rolls of Coles from England wallpaper at $100 a roll. There were custom-made bumper pads for Nicolas's crib. There were thousands of dollars worth of antiques, including a $4,800 baker's rack. Mila changed the luxurious, custom-made carpet in the house four times.

PC Canada Fund Chairman David Angus, a Montreal lawyer and long-time Mulroney friend, said that Mulroney had paid back part of the costs under a 1983 agreement the two men had made. However Angus refused to say when Mulroney had paid the money back, or whether there were any cancelled cheques from him for the payments.

Opposition critics agreed that even if no laws had actually been broken, the federal fund-raising laws were intended to help parties finance political activities, not home decoration. Even some backbench Tories were angry, including Calgary MP Alex Kindy who demanded to know "by what authority" Angus had issued the cheques to Mowinckel, and whether the money was intended as a loan. "You have to ask these questions," he said.

The issue was quickly dubbed "Guccigate" by the Ottawa *Citizen* and an "orgy of opulence" and a "scam" by opposition critics, who argued that the law should be changed. NDP leader Ed Broadbent said, "At the very least, people who make donations to political parties should be told how that money will be used," and Liberal House leader Herb Gray said it indicated a need for a review of the current law "because there may be a need for rules on disclosure."

In effect, the system of tax credits for political donations means that much of the money involved *is* public money. Under the law, any donation under $100 earns a 75 per cent tax credit; donations up to $550 earn a 50 per cent credit; and anything above that gets a 33⅓ per cent tax credit.

As well, on September 3, 1986, Angus personally paid an outstanding bill from Mowinckel for $5,494.26. The designer had continued to work on the house through 1985 and 1986 but became increasingly concerned when the bills were not paid. Finally, on July 7, he wrote to Doucet to say that, if he were not paid $38,000 by the National Capital Commission plus another $10,920.62 that had been billed to Doucet on behalf of the Mulroneys, he would take legal action. Doucet replied the next day that an agreement had been reached on the one invoice for $5,494.26 and that he would send it within thirty days. In September, Mowinckel received a personal cheque for that amount written by Angus on September 3 and sent by Doucet.

Speaker John Bosley had hired Mowinckel for a $400,000 job at Kingsmere, the Speaker's official residence. Ironically, it was Mulroney's officials who leaked information to the media about Bosley's extravagance, stories that hurt Bosley and made it easier for Mulroney (who wanted him out as Speaker), to get rid of him.

Mowinckel worked for several senior Mulroney staffers, including chief of staff Bernard Roy, former Mulroney executive assistant Hubert Pichet, and Bonnie Brownlee. He also did work for senior Tories Dalton Camp and Bill Neville and for Mulroney's close friend, Montreal businessman Paul Desmarais.

Mowinckel sent two letters on July 7, 1986, the one to Doucet and another to Bonnie Brownlee, also threatening legal action if the bills were not paid. (The bills had been outstanding for more than eight months.) His bookkeeper, Marie Dorion, sent the letter by courier at about 11:00 A.M. with copies to Hamilton Southam, chairman of the Official Residences Council, Jean Pigott, chairman of the National Capital Commission, and Agney Jaouich, director of official houses for the NCC.

An hour later, Dorion and Brownlee discussed the matter by telephone. When the conversation ended, Dorion immediately wrote down what she remembered from it. Her memo, also obtained by the *Globe*, said that Brownlee was upset that a copy had gone to Southam and asked whether it could be recalled. It was too late. Brownlee also said that Mowinckel would lose his position as designer with the Desmarais family in Montreal if he did not withdraw his demands. "You just can't threaten the prime minister," Dorion quoted Brownlee as saying. "You would lose the Desmarais account."

(Mowinckel did, in fact, lose that account. Among other things, he had been helping plan a new 35,000-square-foot French-style château, Manoir Desmarais, in the Saguenay region of Quebec. A spokesman for the family denied that Mowinckel had lost the account or that there was any pressure from the Mulroneys. "He finished the job," said Françoise Patry. "He had some work to do and it's done. He was not the only decorator working for Desmarais and we never said he would have the contract.")

Meanwhile, according to Dorion, Brownlee said she had been "under the impression that there was an agreement between Mrs. Mulroney and yourself that you would do the work for the publicity you would get from it." Brownlee also did not want to pay one bill for $5,426.36, and there is no record it was ever paid.

In June 1986, Liberal MP Don Boudria had submitted written questions to public works minister Stewart McInnes asking if the government had employed Mowinckel or his company to do any of the work at either 24 Sussex Drive or Harrington Lake and what the cost was. He also asked whether all the work was paid for from government funds. If not, "who paid such costs and what was the amount involved in each case?" In November, McInnes responded that the government had not hired Mowinckel for the work. "I wasn't told the truth and nothing but the truth," said Boudria.

A *Toronto Star* editorial, titled "Imelda Mulroney" printed a fund-raising letter dated September 4, 1986, to "our most loyal and generous donors" asking for contributions "to help us fund the next election campaign. Every penny of your contribution will be held in reserve by the party and will be available only to use in our relection campaign," wrote Mulroney. The *Star* added, "Little did these 'loyal and generous donors' know that Mulroney's definition of a re-election campaign extended to a closet at 24 Sussex Drive for 84 pairs of shoes. Perhaps he intends to walk, rather than fly, across Canada in the next campaign."

About the only one to defend Mulroney at the time was transport minister John Crosbie, himself a millionaire, who said that the prime minister shouldn't be criticized for wanting to maintain his lifestyle after getting elected. He said it was "a noble gesture on the part of the PC party. . . . It certainly hasn't been done by any other government." Asked how many pairs of shoes he had, Crosbie said about eight pairs, but, "some of them are pretty scruffy." During the late fall and early winter of 1984-85 Mila avoided anything too controversial and busied herself with her expanding charity work, especially as honorary president of the Canadian Cystic Fibrosis Foundation.

Periodically, though, something would pop up again about the propriety of Mila's office expenses. In April 1985, Mulroney's then press secretary, Bill Fox (who, incidentally, lives with Mila's aide, Bonnie Brownlee), explained to reporters that there really was no budget because there was really no office. He said that Mila's office was part of the PMO anyway, and would be there whether Mila and her staff used it or not. Later, when the author raised the issue again, Fox angrily telephoned to say that the budget he and Mila had earlier said didn't exist was "all there on the public record." It wasn't.

Mila didn't help the situation any when in April she travelled on a government jet to attend Nancy Reagan's First Ladies' White House conference, although cabinet guidelines say VIP aircraft are for the use of cabinet ministers only. Fox said "We take the view that Mrs. Mulroney's attendance . . . was government business." She was accompanied by Brownlee and Fred Doucet. (In a question-and-answer session with *Maclean's* magazine at the time, she was asked if she has as much influence on Brian as Nancy Reagan has with Ronald in determining senior appointments. "Most of the appointments, yes," she said. "When I was asked I gave my opinion. I think the final decision is certainly his.")

Back home, her husband's political fortunes were beginning to slip, and criticism from feminists was heating up.

In a December 1984 CTV interview Mila had said that she did not favour abortion on demand and had rejected criticism from feminists, saying she did not consider herself "old-fashioned," although she has never been a woman who "made waves. I feel there are other ways of doing things and achieving your goals. I think I'm probably as much a feminist as anyone else, but I have different ways of going about it."

In Halifax in June 1985, she said: "Feminist groups want me to move in other directions, but for the moment I have made my choices." In a feature in the August issue of *Chatelaine*, Hamilton East Liberal MP Sheila Copps (who in March 1987 became the first sitting MP to have a baby), criticized Mila as a poor role model for Canadian women because she derives her identity from her husband's career. Copps, the same age as Mila, said that Mila "has returned us to the days of political wife as ornament. She's taken the notion of liberation back two decades." Mila replied, "I'm a working mother. I don't see anything traditional in what I'm doing. I think I'm very much a woman of the eighties. I've made a lot of choices and a lot of decisions."

One of those choices got her into hot water again in September when she announced she wanted to get back to her "job" and take baby Nicolas with her in a playpen to the office. "I think many working mothers do that and I'm going to enjoy every bit of time I can spend with him." Editorialists joined a chorus of women's organizations in wondering just how many mothers are in a position to bring baby to work in a playpen and how long Mila will go on pretending she's a working mother just like all other working mothers in the country. Mila said she used to take Caroline, then a baby, to university with her when she was studying engineering in Montreal.

In September, the author reported private complaints from the RCMP that security personnel at 24 Sussex Drive had been asked to salute Mila when she arrived in her limo, the same courtesy given to the American First Lady by security. Both Mulroneys were outraged when news of the request became public and flatly denied it. Indeed, speaking on a local interview show with *Toronto Sun* columnist Douglas Fisher, the prime minister dismissed the story as "just one of those vexatious stories that you don't know why anybody—anybody except someone with a streak of cruelty—would write something like that." He said it was a "fabrication." Nevertheless the RCMP launched an extensive internal investigation into the "leak" and ended up moving two officers (one was fired, then rehired and reassigned the same day; the other was allowed to take early retirement.) Even RCMP commissioner Robert Simmonds got in on the act, writing a letter of complaint to the *Sun,* a most unusual action for a man in his position. In denying the story, in fact, Mulroney dug himself in deeper by making a comment insulting to immigrants. Anybody who knows Mila, he said, knows she wouldn't ask Mounties to salute her. "In fact, as I told my caucus, Mila still has the immigrant syndrome. When she sees somebody in a uniform she salutes him." This provoked demands for an apology from various immigrant groups.

In January 1986, Mila refused to appear as a guest at a fundraising event for an Ottawa Tory riding association after learning that comedian David Broadfoot would also be there. The organizers were told that Mila prefers to be the main attraction. The same attitude prevailed during a visit that month to Toronto's Hospital for Sick Children with the wife of the Japanese prime minister. Mila's office told hospital officials before the visit that she wouldn't come unless the media were forbidden to talk to the patients she had just spoken to—a rule that comes into effect when the Queen visits. When a *Toronto Star* reporter tried to ask a child how it felt to meet the prime minister's wife, the journalist was ordered out of the hospital by a Mulroney aide and threatened with arrest if he resisted.

By this time, the defence department was listing Mila on its flight manifest as "The Rt. Hon. M. Mulroney, wife of the prime minister." At about the same time, Canadian officials in Tokyo were ordered to arrange, as a photo opportunity for Mila when she attended the April economic summit with Brian, a visit to cystic fibrosis patients in a local hospital. The officials were unsuccessful because the disease is practically unheard of in Japan. (When the Canadian contingent did arrive in Tokyo, Mila was the object of some polite tittering from the diplomatic corps for insisting on bringing parkas as gifts for their hosts in a city which has had one snowfall in the past twenty years).

In March, during an extensive western tour where Mila mixed partisan and charitable activities liberally, the *Calgary Herald* ran the headline, "Canada's first lady praises Tory budget." *Toronto Star* journalist Joe O'Donnell, who covered most of the trip, saw it as a deliberate strategy to create an even more political Mila. "The new Mila has emerged not as some accident but by deliberate planning," he wrote. "She had thought about it and discussed it with Tory strategists, one of whom warned her against going political and peddling the cause of the party and husband Prime Minister Brian Mulroney's government." In an interview, Mila herself said she had gone "political" in response to many requests, that she is aware her unelected position places restrictions on her, but that she has taken to interceding directly with cabinet ministers on behalf of people who write to her.

While her hubby had received some criticism for adopting his presidential style—one of the more obvious examples was his use of a podium with the prime-ministerial seal on it—Mila had her matching podium dragged around the country for her convenience. In addition, she also hired Quebec artist Joseph Stephanka, well known for his work under the pseudonym J.S. Trencin, to produce a limited-edition, numbered, copyrighted set of three hundred porcelain jewellery boxes, tiny replicas of 24 Sussex Drive, an idea she got from Nancy Reagan's miniature White Houses, which are given to distinguished visitors. The handcrafted boxes, worth several hundred dollars each on the open market, were billed to the secretry of state, and Mila's office refused to discuss the cost. The works are so delicate, Stephanka had to use dentists' tools and a magnifying glass in making them.

On September 19, 1986, the Edmonton Oilers and Montreal Canadiens played an exhibition hockey game in Ottawa, and Dinah Shore thrilled an audience at the National Arts Centre. All this, including cocktails at 24 Sussex Drive, was available for a mere $5,000 per couple, a gala evening organized by Edmonton financier Peter Pocklington (whose 1983 convention support had helped Brian win the leadership contest) and, of course, by Mila, for the benefit of the Cystic Fibrosis Foundation. About nine thousand tickets to the hockey game only were available to the general public at $20 and $30 a seat. The game raised more than $1.5 million. (Incidentally, the Oilers won 8-3.)

Before the event, *Globe* columnist Stevie Cameron wrote a piece suggesting, among other things, that many loyal Tories were upset because of the heavy arm-twisting that had gone on to get them to spring for the $5,000 tickets. A week before the game, about half of the seven hundred "special patron" tickets remained unsold.

"They had a bit of panic near the end trying to sell the tickets," Cameron said later. "The reason we got the story is they were starting to strong-arm people in Toronto into buying tickets and even the most loyal Conservatives were getting upset about it.

"Mila was very angry with me," said Cameron. "It was one of those very strange stories. On the surface, it didn't look as if there was anything wrong. I mean, cystic fibrosis is very lucky to have her as a patron. She works very hard for them, she really does. She talks to the kids, she phones the kids who have this disease. A lot of the kids have her personal phone number at home. She works very, very hard for them.

"The problem was it looked like if you had enough money you could buy access to the prime minister and his wife, and there's only one charity in Canada that has that kind of situation. There are many other deserving charities."

When Cameron's article appeared, Brownlee phoned her and said Mila wanted to speak with her. "What they didn't like, of course, is that I named those people who were organizing the game for Mila, and they included people like Nelson Skalbania, Peter Pocklington, Frank Moores, and Sam Wakim."

Even if hubby Brian were high in the polls instead of languishing in the low 20s, Mila would probably still be by far the more popular of the two. She radiates a charm and warmth he never could, although there have been occasions when her sex appeal has been openly exploited for partisan purposes. *Toronto Sun* reporter Derik Hodgson tells the story of being in London, Ontario, early in the 1984 election campaign, a time when Mulroney was enjoying almost universal positive media coverage. Hodgson, who had never met Mila, had written a piece in that day's newspaper dubbing Mulroney's campaign "Brian Slick and the Monotones," a criticism of the all-style-no-substance Mulroney that later became widespread.

"I was standing outside the Holiday Inn milling around in that crush of reporters and other bystanders," said Hodgson. "They were just about to begin mainstreeting the three blocks to the London Life office, when Mila, still standing on the steps of the Holiday Inn, pointed to me and shouted, 'Oh, hi, Derik. Good to see you.' Now I've always had an eye for the well-turned ankle, and Mila is a beautiful woman. But I had never met her, so obviously somebody pointed me out to her and said there he is, turn on the charm. Not that I didn't like her, but this was a deliberate ploy to get me onside. I thought, boy, what a way to use your wife. I wouldn't use my wife like that."

Despite problems, Mila has been popular—at times wildly popular—for most of her husband's mandate. In its December 1985 issue, *Chatelaine* magazine chose Mila as its woman of the year for 1986, saying, "Mila is a woman who knows her own mind and has the courage to speak it. In the current social climate, many women are often defensive about their choice to be wives and mothers first. Mila says so with conviction and panache."

Mila still generates mixed reviews. She's certainly a major political asset for her husband. Her warm smile, ability to work a room, her youthful exuberance and, yes, her habit of twitching her nose, all contribute to the image that despite some excesses, she's basically a nice person. Indeed, she is.

Still, public distaste was generated by the "Mowinckel revelations" on the renovations to 24 Sussex Drive, and feminists still reject what they see as her old-fashioned value structure. She did at one point create considerable controversy by announcing, somewhat naively, that she planned to take baby Nicolas to work in a playpen, "like many working mothers do."

But even her critics recognize that she has broad popular appeal among Canadians. In her October 1985 article in *This Magazine*, Susan Riley lamented that Mila embodies ideas about marriage that are fashionable but still essential to male privilege. She wrote, "For many Canadians, Brian and Mila and their nuclear family are an ideal, not an aberration. It may be a lifestyle option available only to the wealthy; it may depend on women cheerfully taking a back seat, but it lives on in popular sentiment."

CHAPTER TWELVE

PLAYING FOOTSIE

Brian Mulroney certainly needed a victory. His party was languishing in the mid-20s in public-opinion polls. Two Tory backbenchers, David Kilgour (Edmonton-Strathcona) and Tom Suluk (Nunsatsiaq, N.W.T.) had complained publicly about their own government's record of scandals and neglect of regional issues. Even the most partisan Tory supporters were hard-pressed to find good things to say, and the whole country was talking about the stories detailing his extravagant lifestyle, typified by his sixty-seven pairs of Gucci loafers and Mila's one hundred pairs of shoes and cavernous clothes closets at 24 Sussex Drive.

When Mulroney and the ten premiers arrived just before noon at his Gatineau Hills retreat at Meech Lake on a cool, windy day, April 30, 1987, to discuss Quebec's entry into the 1982 constitutional accord, the chances of a victory seemed about as remote for Mulroney as a sudden turnaround in unfavourable public opinion.

Yet, ten hours later, just after ten o'clock that night, Mulroney, surrounded by the smiling, applauding premiers, was able to say he had a deal. "This has been a good day for Canada and Canadians . . . what you have now is a whole country."

Without exception, the premiers were effusive in their praise of Mulroney's efforts. "We got spectacular gains concerning immigration, concerning recognition of Quebec as a distinct society," said Quebec's Robert Bourassa. "I'm extremely pleased," said Alberta's Don Getty, who had gone into the meeting as a hard-liner. "We have Senate reform entrenched in the constitution." Ontario's David Peterson was no less ecstatic. "I feel good about my country," he said. Even Newfoundland's Brain Peckford chirped, "Not only Quebec, but all the provinces gained."

Next day in the Commons, both John Turner and Ed Broadbent added their voices and congratulatory handshakes to the chorus of praise for Mulroney's efforts. Turner said that the accord made it "a happy day for Canada and Quebec." And Broadbent added, "The coming together of the Canadian family is desired by us all in this House and by all parties and regions in our country."

Mulroney had managed to do what Pierre Trudeau and others had failed to do—get Quebec and the other provinces to agree on a formula—and nobody wanted to rain on his parade. Not right away, anyway.

Yet, despite the words of praise, and the genuine appreciation most Canadians felt for Mulroney's achievement, the question was already being asked: Is the price of making ten premiers happy worth the prize of Quebec's signature on the constitution? It's a question only time can answer, but once the initial jubilation waned and the sounds of clapping became a pleasant memory, many opposition critics, journalists, academics, and constitutional authorities expressed concern that Mulroney might have paid too steep a price for the return he can expect on his political investment.

Even after their initial words of praise acknowledging the significance of the accord, both Turner and Broadbent raised questions about what kind of Canada we will have when all ten provinces have effective veto powers over many traditionally federal decisions. Critics wondered aloud if the new Canada under Mulroney would turn into what Trudeau used to describe as a "consortium of shopping centres," a weak national government surrounded by ten powerful feifdoms, putting a virtual hammerlock on any meaningful constitutional change for future generations.

"I hope it will be seen in the final analysis as something all of Canada can cherish," said Broadbent. "I deeply hope that such study will warrant wholehearted endorsation."

Turner pointed out that the provisions for the provinces to opt out and other sections of the agreement-in-principle raise serious questions about Ottawa's future ability to impose "national" programs. "Does this mean in future a national child-care program is impossible?" he asked. "And what about a guaranteed annual income?"

And former Liberal constitutional negotiator Jean Chrétien said, "I am very happy to see that Quebec has finally signed the Constitution. But I have not seen in that agreement who speaks for Canada."

The very thing that made some people uneasy is precisely what made the premiers so happy—Ottawa's loss of power was their gain. While this is understandably cause for provincial rejoicing, it was just as understandably cause for federal fidgeting.

Bourassa, of course, had agreed to a constitutional accord once before, in Victoria in 1971, only to balk under pressure from his own cabinet. In 1981–82, it was René Lévesque's turn to be the odd man out of the constitutional talks, and by 1987, given a second chance, Bourassa made the most of it. Quebec went into the meeting with five basic demands: recognition as a distinct society; a veto on constitutional change; participation in Supreme Court judicial appointments; increased powers over immigration; and limits on federal spending powers. Bourassa came out of the meeting with everything he asked for. So did everybody else.

To get around the problem of a Quebec veto, which was hotly opposed by several premiers, Mulroney simply gave everybody an effective veto over changes to the Senate, the House of Commons, and the creation of new provinces out of the territories or expansion of existing provinces into them.

The demand for recognition as a "distinct society" had caused fears among other premiers that Quebec could use the definition in court to argue for more powers beyond those Ottawa and the other apparently non-distinct provinces were willing to give. No problem. The solution was to recognize that "the existence of French-speaking Canada, centred in but not limited to Quebec, and English-speaking Canada, concentrated outside Quebec but also present in Quebec, constitutes a fundamental characteristic of Canada." The next sentence commits governments to preserve "the fundamental characteristic of Canada" as defined above.

On spending powers, Quebec wanted to opt out of any federal shared-cost programs in such areas of provincial jurisdiction as daycare or a guaranteed annual income. The accord gives all the provinces the right to drop out of any new programs in this area (they're stuck with the old ones, medicare for example) and to receive full compensation for doing it. This provision sparked the most fears about a checkerboard Canada in which requirements for a "national" program, such as daycare, could vary drastically among provinces.

Agreement on the Supreme Court provisions was relatively easy. After all, tradition had it that Quebec received three of the nine judges, the same as Ontario, while two came from the West and one from Atlantic Canada. Before naming Supreme Court judges, the federal government had long held informal discussions with the provincial attorneys-general involved, so the Meech Lake accord simply formalized what had already been the practice, where provinces will be invited to submit lists of candidates and the federal cabinet holds the final say. Everyone acknowledged it could lead to future deadlocks—if, for example, Ottawa rejects a provincial list and calls for another, and the new list is still not acceptable. They left the detail to work out at some future point.

On immigration, again Mulroney used his favourite technique—hand out the candy to everybody and they'll all be happy. Essentially, Quebec wanted the right to screen out immigrants it didn't want (translation: that normally means non-French-speaking immigrants) and Ottawa agreed. It also offered Quebec up to 5 per cent more people in its quota to compensate for the "leakage" of the 40 per cent of newcomers who leave Quebec each year headed for another part of Canada.

The accord dealt with growing pressure, from the West in particular, for Senate reform—defined by the proponents as less Senate representation for Ontario and Quebec, and more for their regions—by entrenching a series of meetings on, you guessed it, Senate reform. That made Alberta's Getty particularly happy, although it is difficult to see what sort of Senate reform can ever be achieved, since a change now requires unanimous agreement (rather than the support of seven provinces representing at least 50 per cent of the country's population as provided in the old constitutional formula).

From the outset, the deal created problems for John Turner. The Liberals, who had always seen themselves as champions of Francophone rights, did not want to appear to be opposed to bringing Quebec into the constitution, but former cabinet minister Donald Johnston moved the backroom party bickering into the living rooms of the nation by announcing he was stepping down as Liberal external affairs critic so he could work against the accord. He was soon joined by another

Montreal Liberal MP, David Berger, which prompted veteran André Ouellet to accuse them of acting like "Westmount Rhodesians." On the Tory side, only Nova Scotian Pat Nowlan publicly opposed the deal, offering to resign from caucus unless it was fixed up.

While there was considerable opposition, it had not co-alesced around any one issue or person. Then, on May 27, just five days before the eleven leaders were scheduled to finalize the deal by agreeing on the legal wording, Pierre Trudeau charged into the fray by publishing a scathing personal and ideological attack on the deal in both the *Toronto Star* and *La Presse*. Trudeau called Mulroney a "weakling" for giving away so much federal power to the provinces, saying it would result in a Canada "eventually governed by eunuchs."

Suddenly, the debate heated up. Talk shows, newspapers, the Commons, legislatures, everywhere you looked, people had actually begun to argue the question of a strong central government versus strong provincial governments. The eleven Meech Lake authors—unanimously rejecting Trudeau's oppo-sition—rolled into Ottawa on June 2, gathered around an oval table in a fourth-floor, flag-draped Langevin Block conference room, and began what became a monumental hard day's night, a nineteen-and-one-half hour bargaining session that bogged down several times, but ended in success just before sunrise the next morning.

The born-again constitutional deal was essentially the same as the Meech Lake accord, although some of the provisions had been tightened in hopes of allaying concerns of emascula-tion of the national government. At Meech Lake, for example, it had been agreed that a province choosing to drop out of future national shared-cost programs simply needed "its own initiatives or programs compatible with national objectives" to receive compensation. That was changed to "a national shared-cost program that is established by the government of Canada," leaving a better sense that it is Ottawa, not the provinces, that defines what is a suitable program for financial compensation.

Responding to Trudeau's fears that the original wording promotes the divisive notion of "two Canadas," the new phrasing still recognizes Quebec as a "distinct society," but also recognizes "the existence of French-speaking Canadians . . . and English-speaking Canadians," thus defining groups of people rather than naming geographic regions for those people. The first ministers also added a paragraph affirming aboriginal and multicultural heritage rights. On veto powers, Supreme Court appointments, immigration, and Senate reform, the Meech Lake agreement was left virtually intact. It also included provision for public hearings, formal approval by the Commons and the ten legislatures, and a three-year timetable to complete the work and officially adopt it as the country's new constitution.

In a nationally televised address June 4, Mulroney said the deal means "Canada is whole again, the Canadian family is together again and the nation is one again." Turner, speaking after Mulroney, acknowledged the split in his caucus—where ten MPs publicly oppose the deal and were urging Trudeau to act as their "spiritual leader" in the battle—but said despite flaws in the agreement, they "are not serious enough to convince me that they override the necessity of having Quebec sign the constitution." In his turn, Broadbent said that he too would press for changes, but that he supports the deal overall because "reconciliation of the people of Quebec with the Constitution is essential." As for Trudeau, he hinted that Canadians hadn't heard the last of him on the issue. Asked by reporters after the deal was signed if ratification may be just a formality, Trudeau said, "Oh no, I would suspect there would be a great deal of debate. I hope so."

While the concerns over the impact of the accord were real, and legitimate, still because Mulroney had achieved agreement long odds, even the most doubtful observers tempered their stated criticism of the deal.

Mulroney had, however, given Quebec several things he had stated in the past that he wouldn't—most significantly, financial compensation for opting out and a veto on constitutional change. In April 1983, in the midst of the Tory leadership battle, Joe Clark said that, in return for Quebec's signature on the accord, he would offer the province full compensation should it wish to opt out of constitutional amendments. Mulroney refused to match Clark's offer. Mulroney made much of his own Quebec roots in that campaign, claiming that only a native son would be able to overcome Quebec's historical antipathy towards the Conservative party (which was seen largely through Quebec eyes as pro-Anglo and anti-French—a perception neither completely right nor completely wrong). And while Mulroney's Quebec vote at the convention was strong, it turned out to be about the same as Clark's—although both sides claimed they had won Quebec. Clark may have appealed to as many Tory delegates as Mulroney, but as Conservative leader he had won just two Quebec seats in 1979 and one in 1980. Mulroney won a record fifty-eight seats in 1984, beating Diefenbaker's previous Tory high of fifty in 1958.

On May 3, 1983, Mulroney flew into Rimouski on Quebecair and, on the way there, scribbled his nine-point constitutional position paper on the back of a corporate barf bag. He told the Tory delegates that with him as prime minister, he'd "get rid of the PQ and . . . negotiate a constitutional peace with the people of Quebec just like that. . . . I'll have absolutely no problem finding the right constitutional formula if I sit down to a negotiating table with people who represent the true feelings of Quebeckers." Public-opinion polls at the time showed that only 23 per cent of Quebeckers supported Lévesque's "sovereignty-association" stance. Mulroney's instant constitutional package was larded with high-sounding hyperbole— "Canada is a great country of which Quebec is an integral and important part"; bilingualism is a "noble objective"—but it was short on specifics.

The issue of Quebec and its relationship with the rest of Canada has always been a time bomb for Tory leaders, and in September 1983, after Mulroney had won his Central Nova seat and been ensconced in Parliament for less than twenty-four hours, the cagey Trudeau appeared to have baited a trap for the rookie MP by drawning him into the bitter bilingualism dispute in Manitoba where most Conservatives did not share Mulroney's view that the province should become officially bilingual. The federal Liberals and New Democrats and the Manitoba NDP government actively supported the concept, but the provincial Tories and a good many of Mulroney's own caucus were vigorously opposed.

Manitoba Liberal Robert Bockstael asked whether the federal government was going to support the Manitoba NDP government's position. Trudeau said that was "a very difficult and important question" and proposed a meeting with party leaders to seek an all-party resolution, perhaps sponsored jointly by himself and Mulroney, to ask the Manitoba Conservatives to endorse bilingualism. Mulroney, put on the spot, jumped up and asked how soon they could hold a meeting, as several Liberal MPS laughed aloud, feeling they had the new Tory leader in a political trap.

As it turned out, the issue led to one of Mulroney's career high points. The next day, after a twenty-five-minute meeting with Trudeau, neither man was saying much. Two weeks later, Mulroney refused to become involved in a similar dispute between Trudeau and Ontario premier Bill Davis, saying that the Manitoba situation had to be resolved first. Finally, after another meeting, this time with Ed Broadbent present, the three leaders agreed to the all-party resolution. That prompted Dr. William Shaw, vice-president of Quebec's Freedom of Choice Movement, to call the resolution "meaningless when you look at Bill 101 in Quebec, which takes away the right to work in English or to send your children to English schools or to put up an English sign over your store or business."

On October 30, 1983, Mulroney appealed to an overflow crowd of about one thousand in a $150-a-plate fund-raiser in Quebec City to vote Conservative because the party had finally exorcised the ghost of Louis Riel. The party had "paid its historical debt towards all the Francophones of the country. I'm here to tell you that we've finally paid it and now we're going on to new challenges for Canada. . . . I am here before you as a Quebecker and a Canadian."

On December 3 a capacity crowd of 3,200 people at a $200-a-plate dinner at Montreal's Queen Elizabeth Hotel heard Mulroney say that the Tories wanted to support the rights of Anglophone Quebeckers. "If this party has made a commitment to defend the historic rights of the Francophone minority in Manitoba and the rights of French Canadians to obtain economic equality, and it has, I can assure you we shall do no less for the English-speaking minority," he said. He got a standing ovation. Later, however, he refused to specify what he would do to ensure the rights of Anglophone Quebeckers.

In February 1984, Mulroney told renegade Tory MP Dan McKenzie that "all would-be members" of his caucus must support his position on French rights in Manitoba. Many Conservatives agreed with former Tory premier Sterling Lyon that the issue should be resolved in the courts, especially after a provincial referendum showed little support for official bilingualism, even among Franco-Manitobans. Besides McKenzie, four other Manitoba Tories skipped the vote on the all-party resolution—Jack Murta, Lee Clark, Charlie Mayer, and Jake Epp.

McKenzie said that the word "language" should be inserted in the federal Human Rights Act. "English-speaking Canadians are becoming second-class citizens. They can't get a job in government because they can't pass certain proficiency levels of French." Many other Tories privately agreed with McKenzie. In fact it was becoming increasingly difficult for Anglophones to get federal jobs, but the sensitivity to Quebec in Ottawa makes such comments verboten, and the person saying them is usually branded a bigot. The same comments made by Quebeckers about English Canadians, however, are labelled "nationalist."

Howard Pawley's NDP government, recognizing the unpopularity of imposing official bilingualism, let the language package die on the order paper as the legislative session closed.

In March 1984, Mulroney said he was willing to tolerate "a modest divergence of view" among his caucus members on the subject now that the all-party resolution had been approved. "We're in a free country," he said. Three days later, Mulroney said that any Tory MP who did not support the fundamental principle of bilingualism should quit the party. "You're either for it or agin' it," he said. "There can be disagreements with regard to the manner in which a program is implemented, but there is no disagreement with regard to the fundamental principle of the program."

A week later, Mulroney cancelled out as guest of honour at the Winnipeg ethnic community's annual Springtime Ball, claiming "conflicting and pressing commitments in Toronto." But party officials in Toronto said that Mulroney had no Toronto functions scheduled, and Bill Pristanski, Mulroney's executive assistant, said that the Tory leader had some private meetings scheduled, "but we're not exactly sure what they are."

Two weeks earlier, Mulroney had cancelled another planned Manitoba meeting, that one at the Fort Garry Conservative nomination meeting, where provincial deputy leader Bud Sherman, an outspoken opponent of official bilingualism, was seeking the nomination. Instead, Mulroney had appeared as a last-minute guest at an east-end Toronto riding meeting. He dismissed reporters' questions about Manitoba with the comment, "I'm not ducking anything. I'm here, aren't I?"

On March 16, Mulroney called Sherman in an attempt to patch up their differences and invited him to Ottawa for a meeting at Stornoway three days later. After the ninety-minute meeting, the two men still did not agree. Sherman said it was a question of provincial rights. "It is absolutely essential that the position I represent here be understood and accommodated by the national party and the national leader's office," said Sherman.

On March 29, 1984, Mulroney finally went to Winnipeg, where, at the downtown Holiday Inn, he was booed, interrupted by shouts of "Go home to frog country" and "Get out of here!" and called "Brian Trudeau" by a hostile crowd of more than one thousand Tories. Mulroney commented that the Parti Québécois "would love to diminish the rights to the English-speaking minority in Quebec," and that he had "no such right" to tell Manitobans what to do. But, he said, he was asking them "to reflect carefully on the consequences of their decisions . . . the goal of language guarantees is not to make all Canadians bilingual or force people to become something they're not . . . the purpose . . . is to ensure that English- and French-speaking Canadians can be themselves, that they can live their lives, communicate with their governments and with each other in one or the other of Canada's two official languages. That is why these rights must be guaranteed by the most solemn undertakings."

Mulroney was so nervous that at one point he lost his place in his twenty-page speech, fumbling through his papers and saying nervously, in English, "It's coming. I'm getting there."

The dispute essentially revolved around the Manitoba Act of 1870—which was eventually supported by the Supreme Court—by which the new Canadian province had been formed. The act guaranteed those who spoke French the same rights as those who spoke English in Quebec. But twenty years later, in the wake of the Riel Rebellion, Manitoba Liberal premier Thomas Greenway repudiated the guarantees and made English the only language of the legislature, the laws, and the courts of Manitoba. In 1979, the Supreme Court ruled that the 1890 act was unconstitutional and fears were expressed that the 4,500 laws passed since then in English only would be ruled illegal. Pawley then worked out an agreement to amend the constitution and reaffirm original language rights for Franco-Manitobans. (In 1870, half the province's population had been French, but by 1980, it had dwindled to 6 per cent of the population.)

In April, Manitoba Liberal Lloyd Axworthy said that Mulroney would be seen as a "big phoney" if he allowed

Sherman to contest the Winnipeg Fort Garry seat (which Axworthy represents). Axworthy asked Mulroney to do the "honourable" thing, as Robert Stanfield had done when refusing to allow Moncton mayor and opponent of bilingualism Leonard Jones to run as a Tory in 1974. In that election, Jones ran as an independent and won handily.

Mulroney said that the two situations were not comparable, because Sherman had "always supported the Official Languages Act and minority rights" but didn't like the way French-language services were offered in the provinces. In July, speaking at Sherman's nomination meeting, Mulroney received polite applause when he said that Sherman would play "a major role" in a Tory government. "Bud and I have disagreed in the past," he told three hundred Tories, "but in the spirit of Isaiah we have reasoned together." As it turned out, Sherman was one of the few Tories who did lose in the September election.

In an interview with Radio-Canada reporter Jean Pelletier in the August 1984 issue of *Saturday Night* magazine, Mulroney said that some Tory MPS were confused over the issue. "Hell, what are these guys thinking about? That's what being an opposition party for too long does to you. You tend to confuse policies with prejudice. Bilingualism is the goddamn law of the land."

In the same interview, he said of Trudeau, "Let's face it, Trudeau is one of the most impressive political figures in the world." He also said, "I don't see the history of Canada in the same way as someone from the north of Manitoba. So I can understand some of the reactions I witness in Western Canada. I understand—but I cannot share them because I witness them with a totally different perception."

In late March, two days after John Turner entered the Liberal leadership contest, Mulroney tried to deflect the internal Tory squabbling over the Manitoba language dispute by accusing Turner of deserting Liberal principles for "political greed." Turned had refused to commit himself on the issue, saying only that it was a provincial issue and should be settled in Manitoba rather than in the courts.

On March 24, 1984, Mulroney agreed to appear as a guest on Montreal radio station CJAD's open-line show, but only on the condition that no one be allowed to phone in. According to Bill Fox, then his press secretary, phone-in shows are too volatile and can be manipulated by political rivals. Mulroney used the forum to attack Turner for "disavowing positions in regard to protection of minority rights." He predicted that Turner would "sell one million Anglo-Quebeckers and 34,000 Franco-Manitobans down the river." Earlier, Turner had amended his position to say that Ottawa must intervene "at times" to protect minority rights, but Mulroney did not acknowledge the change. Eventually, after dozens of listeners called the station to accuse Mulroney of ducking the issues, he agreed to answer calls, most of which attacked his stance.

(The Manitoba dispute was finally resolved more than a year later, on June 13, 1985, when Supreme Court of Canada ruled that all provincial laws passed since 1890 were invalid, since they were in English only. However, to avoid chaos, the court said that they could remain temporarily in effect while the province translated the laws into French and re-enacted them into law.)

In July 1984, Mulroney announced that he would seek nomination in the Quebec riding of Manicouagan, which included Baie-Comeau, and abandon his Central Nova riding in an attempt to carry out his pledge to break the Liberal stranglehold on Quebec.

Later that month, the media declared Mulroney the clear winner in the French-language TV debate against Turner and Broadbent and, the next night, in English. Two days later he told a Sherbrooke auidence that he was willing to re-open consitutional talks with the PQ government. Turner had said he wouldn't negotiate with separatists and in 1983, as a leadership candidate, Mulroney too had said, "I'm not prepared to sit down with René Lévesque and offer him one plugged nickel until he tells me what he will offer Canada." Now, however, Mulroney said, "It's not up to me to dictate to Quebeckers who they should have as a premier."

In August, Mulroney told a Halifax rally that he would press Ontario's Bill Davis to make that province officially bilingual. "I think it's abnormal for a situation to exist where 450,000 or thereabouts Franco-Ontarians do not have exactly the same rights as everyone else." Davis, while resisting official bilingualism, had quietly extended French services in schools, courts, and the health and social services during his thirteen years as premier.

A week later, campaigning with Davis for three days in southwestern Ontario, Mulroney said he wouldn't urge the Ontario premier to adopt official bilingualism for his province. When asked if he had carried out the pledge he made in

Halifax, Mulroney said, "No, not at all. We've been talking about the issues of the campaign. The issues in this campaign are jobs, job creation, and getting our youth back to work. That's what it's all about." He insisted that there were "no differences" between Davis and himself over biligualism. Davis said that he had no intention of making Ontario officially bilingual.

By early August, public-opinion polls showed that the Tories had almost caught the Liberals in Quebec, where only 12.5 per cent of voters had supported the PCs four years earlier. Speaking at his own nomination meeting in Sept-Iles on August 6, Mulroney promised to try to persuade the Quebec National Assembly to sign the new Canadian constitution "with honour and enthusiasm . . . In Quebec—and it is very obvious—there are wounds to be healed, worries to be calmed, enthusiasms to be rekindled, and bonds of trust to be established." Referring to the Quebec referendum, he spoke of the "collective trauma" undergone by Quebeckers. The speech was seen by most observers as a direct appeal to PQ supporters. Mulroney said that "very few of those who said 'Yes' to Quebec said 'No' to Canada."

The next day, Turner accused Mulroney of courting the separatist vote in Quebec, provoking an angry counterattack on the Liberal prime minister. "I'll tell you this, in 1980 when the battle was on, when it was time for trench warfare on behalf of Canada, I was there in the trenches fighting for Canada and I didn't see John Turner around."

A day earlier, in Wakeham, Quebec, Turner had challenged Mulroney "to explain to the rest of Canada why he has chosen" several former separatist sympathizers as candidates. He named Pierre Menard in Hull, Monique Vézina in Rimouski (who campaigned in favour of the separatist option and became a Mulroney cabinet minister), and Suzanne Duplessis in Louis-Hébert. (As a candidate for the Tory leadership in 1983, Mulroney had accused Joe Clark of flirting with separatists by agreeing to an amending formula favoured by the PQ. "You don't get to be leader of the Progressive Conservative party of Canada by playing footsie with the Parti Québécois," he had told a cheering Calgary audience in April 1983.) In Sarnia, on August 8, 1984, he said he welcomed three former members of the Quebec separatist movement as PC candidates because, "It's time for unity. It's time for reconciliation. It's time for change."

Late in August, Mulroney was heckled by seventy-five sign-waving, chanting protesters in Colwood, a Victoria suburb. The hecklers were demanding an end to official bilingualism. Noting a sign that read "Separate or surrender to the French," Mulroney said, "I want to tell you that for Canada, our dear Canada, we want unity, harmony, and prosperity for everyone. This party stands for the protection of minority rights that we will always honour."

Late in the campaign, *Globe and Mail* columnist Jeffrey Simpson described Mulroney's Quebec strategy: "But now he is engaged in a vast flanking movement, battering the Liberal fortress by sweeping up the nationalists and, with their support, convincing other Quebeckers to join an irreversible Conservative wave. And the soft words of harmony and reconciliation and change, words sent aloft on the air of vapid rhetoric, resonate among a people searching for new heroes and tranquility after their recent battles.

"He is one of them, cracking jokes, telling tales, recalling collective memories, beating the Liberals at their own game of identifying his party with their interests, a politician who learned, changed and may soon conquer."

Five days later, Mulroney not only swept the nation, but won fifty-eight Quebec seats. According to Quebec television journalist Michel Guenard, his colleagues in the French-speaking media "used to joke during the campaign about the English, thinking Mulroney was one of them. He isn't. He was one of us. But the English thought they were buying a Coke, and now they've discovered they bought a Pepsi instead." Guenard, who works out of the Ottawa press gallery for the TVA (French) network, describes Mulroney as "a nationalist like Duplessis, only without the skills of Duplessis. The old chief was there for twenty years. He put Commies behind bars, Jehovah's Witnesses, Italian shopkeepers suspected of being leftists. He was an incredible politican, which formed Trudeau, because Trudeau got into politics by fighting against Duplessis.

"I see Mulroney emotionally as French, but he is English educated. Lots of times I listen to his English and I listen to his French, and he's more at ease in French."

In November, Mulroney rolled out the red carpet for French prime minister Laurent Fabius, the first major foreign leader to visit Canada's newly elected prime minister. Referring to the "confusion" caused by former French president

Charles de Gaulle's 1967 "vive le Québec libre" speech and the
tension that had marred Franco-Canadian relations since then,
Mulroney said it was natural that Franco-Canadian relations
encompassed "parallel relations" between Paris and Quebec.
He told a state dinner that his government "considers it
completely normal and desirable that the Quebeck government maintain with France those relations justified by the
cultural identity of the province of Quebec. Thus we recognize
the legitimacy of privileged, direct relations between Paris and
Quebec, as long as these relations respect federal institutions
and involve subjects that do not conflict with federal
jurisdiction."

As the PQ itself became embroiled in a bitter internal battle
over whether to drop its independence goal from the party
platform in the next Quebec election, Mulroney pointedly
steered clear of the dispute. "It's a question of internal affairs,"
he said. "As a Quebecker, I will wait for events to unfold."
After the PQ did defer the separatist option, however, Mulroney consistently took personal credit for the action.

On December 6, 1984, Mulroney and René Lévesque
discussed the constitutional impasse over a two-hour lunch in
Quebec City. During the meeting Mulroney softened his
previous opposition to a Quebec demand for compensation for
opting out of future constitutional amendments. The two men
agreed to meet again in the spring, and Lévesque said that he
would present specific proposals at that time.

On December 12, Montreal Liberal MP Warren Allmand
accused the Tories of not fighting as hard for Anglophone rights
in Quebec as they did for Francophone rights in Manitoba.
Justice minister John Crosbie had intervened in the Supreme
Court of Canada to uphold Montreal's right to issue parking
tickets in French only, a move Allmand saw as breaking
Mulroney's election promise to uphold minority language
rights. "We believe in the defence of minority rights,"
Mulroney shot back, without explaining Crosbie's action.

In January 1985, Mulroney said he wasn't in favour of
immediately forming a Quebec provincial wing of the party,
much to the delight of born-again Quebec Liberal leader
Robert Bourassa who had just had lunch with the prime
minister when news stories of a Quebec PC party appeared in
Montreal newspapers. "There will not be a Progressive
Conservative party in Quebec without the approval of the
directors of the party," Mulroney told reporters. Asked

whether he wanted one in Quebec, Mulroney said, "No. I do not."

Groundwork for a provincial party had been laid by lawyer André Asselin, president of the Quebec union of regional municipalities and former federal Tory candidate, after polls showed there could be room for a third party to compete with the PQ and the Liberals for provincial support. In Bourassa's opinion, a provincial Tory party with Mulroney's support would "split the federalist vote" and helpt the PQ. There was already considerable media speculation in Quebec (which would later grow to a crescendo) that Mulroney favoured a PQ win over the Liberals.

On March 8, 1985, Lévesque ended an hour-long Quebec City meeting with Mulroney saying, "I can't say I feel like dancing in the streets." He was disappointed over Mulroney's reaction to Quebec's objections to reductions in federal transfer payments and to Ottawa's refusal to give a $117 million grant to Domtar to modernize its fine-paper mill in Windsor, Quebec.

Practically ignored by the English media, the Domtar issue quickly became a cause célèbre in Quebec. Domtar had tied a $1.2 billion modernization of its plant, which employed seven hundred workers, to Ottawa's decision on its request for a grant. "Domtar's financial situation is better than that of the federal government and better than that of the provincial government," Mulroney said. "I'd like to write a cheque for $100 million, but I can't. There is no question of the federal government writing a cheque for $100 million for anybody, particularly not a company which makes $100 million in profits a year."

Just before the 1984 federal election, the Liberals had conditionally approved the grant, but Tory industry minister Sinclair Stevens had said no to Domtar just before leaving on a European trip. Stevens's refusal contributed to the popular Quebec perception that he was anti-French.

On April 6, after taking heat from Quebec MPs, trade unions, the province, and business groups, Ottawa caved in and announced a joint federal-provincial plan for a $150 million, ten-year, interest-free loan to Domtar, repayable beginning in 1995 in current dollars. Under the deal, Ottawa and Quebec would split the interest costs—a sweetener that is expected to cost the federal government $46 million. In addition, the province awarded Domtar a $21 million cash grant.

In May, Lévesque released his demands for constitutional change, which included the recognition of Quebec as a "distinct" society; the exclusive right to determine the province's official language and to legislate on language matters; the right to make exceptions to provisions in the Charter of Rights; veto power over constitutional amendments; and opting-out with full compensation. In Winnipeg a few days later, Mulroney said that Quebec is "of course distinct" and that his government could bring about a "precious dimension of the Canadian dream" by responding with "trust, understanding, and fairness" to Quebec demands.

As he often does, Mulroney decided to make a major constitutional speech on the spur of the moment—Bill Fox told reporters who sought specifics that none were available because Mulroney had only decided on the speech while taking a shower that morning. Mulroney was not applauded by about two hundred Tories at the official opening of new federal party headquarters in Winnipeg when he tried to compare the plight of Quebeckers to the alienation Western Canadians had faced under Trudeau.

On September 4, he claimed, Quebeckers had indicated "that they want to be proud Quebeckers and strong Canadians . . . they were cheering not for Brian Mulroney but for a new kind of Canada. And that's what we've committed ourself to, bringing the West and East together, bringing English and French together . . . [the] Baie-Comeaus of Quebec and Winnipeg . . . said yes to Canada, yes to a new kind of inclusionary Canada, where we are all part of the decision-making process."

By this time, critics were calling Lévesque a lame-duck premier who was just playing out the string anyway. Indeed, Lévesque admitted to reporters that in recent months he had thought about quitting "so many times, you can't imagine." On June 3, the PQ was soundly defeated in four provincial by-elections, including the suburban Montreal riding of Bertrand, where recycled Liberal leader Robert Bourassa took the seat formerly held by the PQ. All four ridings had been easily won by PQ ministers four years earlier and, in the Montreal-area riding of L'Assomption, which was won by Liberal Jean-Guy Gervais, the unofficial Quebec Conservative leader André Asselin finished second, three thousand votes ahead of the third-place *péquistes*.

Three weeks later, on June 20, 1985, just a few hours after Lévesque had said he was not ready to retire, the enfant terrible of Canadian politics and PQ founder closed a colourful controversial twenty-five-year chapter by releasing a one-page letter announcing his resignation. The decision came just two days before what would have been a stormy PQ council meeting.

In June, Mulroney said he would get involved in building a Quebec PC party as soon as the provincial election was over. At the same time, he rejected any preconditions from Quebec for a constitutional accord and, after the Supreme Court decision on the Manitoba question, urged Manitobans "to accept with generosity . . . and pursue with renewed vigour their efforts to build a strong and united society."

On June 28, the final day before the summer break, the opposition parties were attacking Michael Wilson's budget. Suddenly, just an hour after he had criticized the Liberals at a news conference for their lack of decorum in the House, Mulroney lost his temper and accused the Liberals of being "hypocrites" and "against Francophone minorities in Canada." The unexpected outburst came after Ottawa Liberal MP Jean-Robert Gauthier had asked if Mulroney favoured a constitutional settlement to Manitoba's translation problem.

In November, following a blizzard of federal announcements involving aid to Quebec—including support for a $300 million Hyundai auto plant in Bromont, announced during the provincial election campaign—New Democrat Ian Waddell shouted, "All you care about is Quebec." Outside the Commons, John Turner accused Mulroney of openly favouring Pierre-Marc Johnson's PQ over Bourassa's Liberals in the campaign. "He said he was not going to intervene in Quebec . . . but the acts of his government belie that statement," said Turner. He pointed to the visit to Quebec City, by train, of two federal ministers who trumpeted the return of rail service to the city core, the announcement that Quebec would be allowed to join in the upcoming Francophone summit, and the $40 million federal involvement in the Hyundai deal.

Ten days before the December 2 Quebec election (which the Liberals won easily) Mulroney made an open pitch for the PQ during a fun-raiser attended by more than two thousand people at Toronto's Harbour Castle Hilton. The rest of Canada had nothing to fear from the election of a PQ government, he said, because the province "has dropped separatism as a fundamental option . . . in response to the election of a

Progressive Conservative government. I say that's good for Ontario, it's good for Canadian unity and it's good for all Canadians."

When *Toronto Star* reporter Joe O'Donnel reported Mulroney's comments, several Quebec journalists in Ottawa who had not covered the Toronto speech demanded a transcript from Mulroney's office. "It was the only time I'm aware of," said O'Donnell, "where a transcript suddenly wasn't available. They claimed they had some technical problem." A few days later, moments after Mulroney returned from a western trip, Bill Pristanski, then his executive assistant, phoned O'Donnell from the Ottawa airport and said, "The boss wasn't happy with your story." O'Donnell, who had taped the speech, told Pristanski to thank Mulroney for the call and offered to play the tape back to him if he was interested. He wasn't. On election day, Mulroney told five thousand Tories at a mammoth fund-raising dinner that certain "obtuse minds" had accused him of favouring the PQ over the Liberals when in fact, he said, he had maintained "the strictest neutrality" during the campaign.

In a year-end interview on Radio-Canada's "Le Point," Mulroney said he could not promise Quebec a veto constitutional change. "I can't return Quebec's right of veto, because that power has gone to the provinces," he said.

In January 1986, three Tory MPs publicly attacked Mulroney for allowing the closure of a Gulf refinery in east-end Montreal as part of a sale by Gulf Canada Ltd. to Ultramar Canada Inc. The closure had been approved by cabinet and announced in Montreal by Sinclair Stevens. Vincent Della Noce, Suzanne Blais-Grenier, and Robert Toupin openly criticized the deal. "I want my MPs to speak out on issues," said Mulroney, even though he repeatedly told reporters that not a single MP had "expressed his discontent" with the deal.

Public opinion poll now had the Liberals comfortably ahead of Mulroney's Tories in Quebec, 44 to 33 per cent. Blais-Grenier resigned from cabinet to add to his problems there, while Quebec Tory MPs derisively referred to Stevens—still recovering from heart-bypass surgery—as "the minister of Ontario." At the party convention in Montreal that March, Mulroney acknowledged publicly for the first time that the Tories were in trouble in Quebec. "We're going to rebuild what was a pretty impressive organization which we had to dismantle of course because we moved quickly into govern-

ment," he said. "We're not under any illusions as to the
challenges we face. We know that public trust and confidence
has to be constantly earned."

In July, Mulroney sent a secret letter to the premiers asking
them to set aside their demands for constitutional reform until
a formula could be worked out to bring Quebec into the
accord. "The only realistic way to proceed is first to bring
Quebec back into the fold, and to undertake a more extensive
revision of the Constitution at a later stage." Mulroney
appointed Senator Lowell Murray to oversee informal talks
with the provinces, particularly with Quebec's international
and intergovernmental relations minister Gil Rémillard. In
August, Rémillard unveiled his province's five minimum
demands—which he took unaltered to the Meech Lake
meeting. And, at the annual premiers' conference, host Don
Getty announced the so-called Edmonton Declaration, whereby the premiers agreed to set aside their own demands to
begin exploratory talks based on Quebec's proposals.

By the end of August, Mulroney was predicting a Quebec
pact by 1988, after he had begun a series of one-on-one
meetings with the premiers to discuss Quebec's demands. A
week after that boast, he emerged from a meeting with
Bourassa to advocate proceeding "prudently" with the talks. "I
don't think Canadians and Quebeckers want to fail one more
time." Ten days later he told the editorial board of the
Vancouver Sun, "I don't want to take up anybody's time or
anybody's priorities if it's not felt [by the other premiers] that
this is an important national matter. I've got other fish to fry."

To complicate the political situation more, a new language
debate was heating up after a decision of Bourassa's new
Liberal government to suspend prosecutions of merchants for
posting bilingual signs, rather than French-only commercial
signs, pending the Quebec Court of Appeals ruling on the
validity of the 1977 PQ law requiring French-only signs. (The
Quebec Superior Court had overturned the law in December
1984, saying that it contravened the Quebec Charter of
Human Rights and Freedoms.)

Mulroney didn't help matters any when he used the old
separatists' slogan "French Power" twice during a speech to
450 supporters at a dinner in St. Georges de Beauce in late
August. Just a few hours before, energy minister Marcel
Masse—who insisted all departmental briefings be in French
only, and flagrantly ignored English-speaking journalists—had

outlined a plan whereby Quebec ministers would act as surrogates for English ministers, speaking on behalf of Quebec on subjects not related to their portfolios. Tory support in Quebec had fallen to 33 per cent in the polls, well behind the Liberals. Some polls even had them third, behind the fast-charging NDP.

The next day in Fredericton, hundreds of angry protesters confronted Mulroney, accusing him of boosting Quebec's economic health at the expense of New Brunswick's jobless. The protesters were angry because their jobs with Canadian National Railways in Moncton were being transferred to British Columbia.

In September, Mulroney ended a stormy Alberta visit by lashing out at what he called, "separatists, racists, and anti-Semites," at a rowdy by-election rally. More than one hundred striking workers from Gainer's meat packers showed up at the rally. Mulroney said later on an open-line show that one of them had called him a "frog." While some journalists reported that the racist epithet had been used, most who were there say they didn't hear it. (On a tape recorded directly from Mulroney's sound system, a heckler shouting "go home" is audible, as is Mulroney's reply: "I'll bloody well fight separatists like you anywhere.")

In October 1986, Bourassa said he would amend Bill 101 to allow bilingual signs again. "It is not normal for a civilized society to ban languages in such an uncivilized fashion," he said. The next month, Liberal House leader Michel Gratton, who is considered a moderate on Quebec language issues, said that merchants who put up English-only signs were "adding fuel to the fire. . . . English unilingual signs can't be condoned. I think it's mere courtesy, it's mere savoir vivre to respect the majority of Quebeckers who are French-speaking and to give them at least a minimum of service." Canadians from other provinces with small Francophone minorities were puzzled by this attitude and the double standard it represented, given that various courts outside Quebec had declared such things as English-only parking tickets illegal.

In December, on the province-wide Télémedia radio network, Mulroney said, "It is indispensable that Quebec conserve its French face and that the French language suffer no setback." He said there has been "marked progress in the use of French . . . we must not go backward now." A day later, Deputy Premier Lise Bacon warned Mulroney to stay out of

Quebec's language fight, adding that he had "enough problems of his own. He should mind his own business and let us mind ours."

Later, Mulroney reacted indignantly, saying, "I am a Quebecker and a Canadian and the prime minister of Canada and I am minding my own business when I am speaking about the rights of Canadian citizens."

Just before Christmas, the Quebec justice department charged twenty-seven Quebec business with contravening the French-only sign laws. Asked at a December 19 news conference if he would provide the same kind of moral leadership he had shown in the 1983 Manitoba language battle (when he defended the French-speaking minority) by intervening now on behalf of Quebec's English-speaking minority, Mulroney testily said, "There is no comparison whatsoever" between the two situations.

One of those charged by the language police was Maison Earle House, a restaurant specializing in French cuisine located in predominantly English-speaking Wakefield, Quebec. Co-owner Diana Ross said that 90 per cent of their clientele was from Ottawa and the United States. "Most of these people don't understand French." Earlier, inspectors from the Office de la langue française had objected to an English sign over the back door that read: "Deliveries," and had photographed the illegal bilingual signs, sending Ross prints and advising her to replace them by French-only signs. She had removed the offending "Deliveries" sign, but not the others.

On December 22, the appeal court ruled that it was illegal to require French-only signs, but legal to require that French be on signs. That legalized French-only or bilingual signs, but ruled out English-only signs.

Bourassa, however, said that the French-only law would remain in force while the government decided whether to take the case to the Supreme Court of Canada. The five judges unanimously struck down the sections forbidding firms to display bilingual signs or use English company names, but split 3 to 2 in upholding Quebec's power to forbid unilingual English signs.

The next day, two Zellers stores were evacuated following anonymous bomb threats. The chain had become a target of Quebec language zealots because it had posted signs in both French and English and had been charged a week earlier with posting bilingual signs at two of its Montreal-area stores. A group calling itself the Z Cell of the Front de libération du Québec (FLQ) claimed responsibility for firebombing a Zellers store. The company quickly removed the bilingual signs. Rocks were thrown through the windows of a florist shop owned by Kenneth McKenna, one of the businessmen who had successfully appealed the sign law.

In February 1987, Bourassa said that the province would go to the Supreme Court to block a court ruling that would permit English alongside French on public signs. Bourassa's ninety-eight-member Liberal caucus was badly split on the issue, with cabinet ministers and prominent English-speaking backbenchers publicly contradicting each other. After a tumultuous caucus meeting, Bourassa said that the government would honour its 1985 election pledge to ease the French-only rule, adding that a committee of cabinet ministers and backbenchers would decide how far to go in removing "certain irritants" from Bill 101, but that further action was not expected before the fall and possibly not until 1988.

Bourassa was attacked by both sides in the debate for stalling. PQ leader Pierre-Marc Johnson said it was the latest example of Bourassa's inability to deal with the issue. "It's like a game of snakes and ladders. They come to a snake and return back to zero." Michael Goldbloom, executive director of Alliance Quebec, an English-language rights group, called it "a sad spectacle of a government losing the courage of its convictions." Several Anglophone Liberal MNAS were reported ready to leave the caucus over Bourassa's delay in softening the sign law.

Emotional levels on the language issue were also rising among Ottawa MPS. At a December committee meeting, several MPS attacked RCMP commissioner Robert Simmonds for supposedly failing to satisfy quota requirements for Francophone members of the force. Simmonds pointed out that the bulk of RCMP work is in non-French-speaking areas—Quebec, of course, has its own provincial police force—but that didn't cut any ice with the all-party committee, most of whom hurled personal invective at Simmonds. The joint chairman of the committee, Quebec Tory MP Charles Hamelin, said that if the force had responded to the Criminal Code requirements the same way it had to the Official Languages Act, "you would be here in handcuffs." Others argued that the ability to speak

French should outweigh all other qualifications when the RCMP are choosing recruits.

In late January, Kitchener Tory MP John Reimer gave his opinion that political mores and values in Quebec were different from those in the rest of the country, and that that partially explained why the government was having so many problems. As an MP, he said, he had encountered only one flagrant "attempt to bribe me. But it's not so rare in Quebec— it's a different society. They take some of these things as sort of a given." Although the rest of Canada was "not pure," he said, "what we really need is some soul-searching there [in Quebec]."

The next day, under considerable pressure from Mulroney, Reimer made "a full and complete apology" in the Commons "for any direct or indirect inference that reflects negatively upon my colleagues in this House and to the people of Quebec and to all of Canada."

In April, the federal government announced that it would give General Motors, the world's largest corporation, a $110 million, thirty-year, interest-free loan in return for seven years of job protection for the 3,500 assembly-line workers at the firm's St. Thérèse assembly plant, a saving to GM of about $1 billion in compound interest. Quebec kicked in a matching $110 million. Canada was still running a deficit of over $30 billion, while GM was showing a tidy $3 billion profit. The Tories had at first balked at helping GM but, true to form, eventually buckled under pressure.

Leo Piquette, an Alberta provincial NDP member of the legislature, became an unlikely Francophone hero in Quebec in April when he was prevented by the Alberta Speaker from asking a question in French in the Alberta legislature. At a time when his own government was balking at protecting English-language rights in Quebec, that province's communications minister Richard French, an Anglophone, said, "It seems inconceivable. . . . It goes against everything this country is supposed to be about." Though English is allowed in the Quebec National Assembly, it is rarely heard.

Globe and Mail reporter Graham Fraser, author of *PQ: René Lévesque and the Parti Québécois in Power*, points out that Mulroney is "much more comfortable as a politician in French in Quebec than he is in English in certain parts of English Canada. This creates its own vicious circle for him, because when he returns to Quebec, it further reinforces the impression in the rest of the country that he is preoccupied with Quebec. That makes it harder for him to break the unhappiness that's felt about him in the West, which puts even more pressure on him and makes him less eager to go out to English Canada. And it continues the whole process."

In Fraser's view, the problem is partly a function of Mulroney's "coming from a small town in rural Quebec and of having felt slighted, particularly by that part of the Tory party that comes from Toronto and belongs to the Albany Club and went to private schools . . . he has always been very conscious of the kind of social slights, either real or imagined, that he has either suffered or felt he would suffer from the social and economic élite in Toronto which has tended to support the Conservative Party." (Most of that élite, Fraser points out, backed Joe Clark, not Mulroney at the 1983 leadership convention.)

In English Canada, Fraser says, Mulroney is often "clearly uncomfortable," but in Quebec, he is relaxed and often uses self-deprecating humour. "One is much less likely to see him in French, particularly in front of a Quebec City or small-town audience using that inflated vocabulary that so often makes people cringe in English . . . that just drives his advisers crazy. They keep telling him to turn the volume down, to stop using those big words, to which his reaction is, 'If I don't get enthusiastic nobody else will. There's got to be some enthusiasm. Somebody's got to pump up the troops.'

"But the way he does it in English, particularly if he's under attack or if things are going badly and he's feeling defensive, undermines his own credibility," says Fraser, "just because he can't resist the superlatives."

But, given Mulroney's emphasis on his Quebec roots, his better performance at home and his government's penchant for lavishing federal money on the province, why is he faring so poorly in the polls in Quebec? The "intangible thing," says Fraser, is that "Quebeckers want their leaders to have class. Quebeckers wanted to elect a Jean Béliveau and, instead, they elected a Claude Lemieux."

CHAPTER THIRTEEN

THE DISLOYAL OPPOSITION

"No party grows just because of what it's doing. It requires two things. One, others to be doing something wrong, and two, you are doing something right."
ED BROADBENT

"Undoubtedly, as we move towards an election, there's got to be more consistency, more harmony, more purpose, more sharpness. That's true. And it will happen."
JOHN TURNER

In 1975, when Canada's U.N. ambassador Stephen Lewis was Ontario's NDP leader and led his party into second place ahead of the Liberals, he said to his jubilant partisans on election night that, after all those years in the wilderness, it was "great to have a real victory to celebrate for a change, instead of just another moral victory."

Except for some provincial successes in the West, that has been the history of the NDP and its forerunner, the CCF, in this country—they have had to settle for moral victories, as the conscience of politics, and little else.

At the federal level, the closest to real power they could even dream of coming was to hold the balance of power in a minority government.

The current leader Ed Broadbent, who took over the NDP in July, 1975, has fought three national campaigns. He has been as popular personally as any of the leaders he has opposed, usually more popular, but it hasn't mattered.

Until now. Suddenly, in December 1986, the party that had captured the hearts of a mere 11 per cent of voters in 1984 had done the unthinkable—it hit 30 per cent in the Gallup poll, behind the Liberals, but comfortably ahead of the collapsing Conservatives. Even more dramatic for a party that had never won a seat in Quebec, and had garnered just 9 per cent of the vote there in 1984—the NDP was suddenly appealing to 30 per cent of Quebeckers polled.

It was heady stuff for the NDP to be riding so high in public opinion—which, of course, is not the same as winning seats on election day—preparing for their first-ever national conference in Quebec, and enjoying the spectacle of Mulroney's Tories trying to fight off a case of terminal stupidity and John Turner struggling to convince Canadians he wasn't as lacklustre as he appeared.

Of course, success has its price. Abandoning moral victories also means compromising the moral tone. But on December 16, 1986, Broadbent did not even choke on his words when he welcomed as a "Christmas present" former Tory MP Robert Toupin. Toupin, a political roustabout, had been a Liberal, had won for the Tories in Terrebonne in 1984 after presenting himself as a fiscal conservative, and had subsequently left to sit as an independent. Finally he had decided to take a crack at democratic socialism. It made him the first New Democrat ever to represent a Quebec riding, but it was a cheap victory. In the old days, Broadbent might have shown better taste.

(Stephen Lewis discovered the perils of straying from ideological purity in Ontario in 1975. After the euphoria of his second-place victory disappeared, he was attacked from within for compromising principle to appeal to a broader base of support.)

Speaking at the Montreal convention on March 13, 1987, Broadbent told the exuberant 1,200 delegates that his recent success in the public opinion polls would not alter the party's commitment to its basic principles. "We want a fair deal for the many, not a special deal for the few. We have fought for it when we were at 9 per cent in the polls. We'll do it when we are at 60 per cent.

"We can aim higher. We can do more. We can dare to be bolder. We have a convenant with our founders and with the people of Canada, and we will not let them down," he roared.

Yet for all Broadbent's rhetoric, the convention had a decidedly less radical stamp than any previous gathering of the

socialist hordes. The convention had barely opened, for
example, when a delegate moved to nationalize the banks,
pretty standard stuff in the NDP lexicon of higher truths. But
that was quickly voted down by the delegates. As Robin Sears,
a former federal party secretary and principal secretary to
Ontario NDP leader Bob Rae, told a reporter, "Even people
who agreed with the thrust of the resolution realize the timing
is inappropriate."

Indeed. At 15 to 20 per cent in the polls, the party had
enjoyed the luxury of making promises they'd never have to
keep. But now, having graduated from the minors to what
Broadbent called the "major leagues" of Canadian politics, the
party didn't want to frighten off potential voters who might see
them as an option to the two main parties.

The party hierarchy carefully staged the resolutions sessions
so that the more radical ideas would be relegated to the rear.
Let's not hear talk of nationalizing the railways, the banks, or
cable television, or of pulling Canada out of NATO and NORAD,
or of supporting "the principles of world federalist government
and enforceable world law" and booting the dreaded multina-
tional corporations out of the country.

No, there was plenty of time for that after the election, the
same approach the socialists (oh, how they hate to be called
that—it's "democratic socialists," if you please) had railed
against the Liberals and Tories for using ever since their 1961
founding convention and in the CCF before that, right back to
the Depression-inspired Regina Manifesto. Anyway, party
officials rationalized, unlike the other two parties, the leader is
bound by formal policies and those policies are on record.
Why talk about them when the party is on a roll?

A compromise resolution on Quebec's place in Canada,
which just a few years ago would have sparked an all-out
ideological war, easily passed with Broadbent's open endorsement. The resolution recognized the "uniqueness" of Quebec.
It would give the province the right to opt out of future
constitutional changes that diminish provincial powers, with
full financial compensation, plus a modified constitutional veto
over language and culture.

In June, Broadbent was criticized by ideological purists
when he stayed conspicuously away from a bitter, violence-
plagued series of rotating walk-outs by the outside postal
workers. In July, campaigning for a by-election in St. John's,
Broadbent said many traditional NDP policies such as

"nationalization," long a sacred cow, may be outdated. He won that by-election and two others in a July 20 sweep.

But it was a long way from the resolution approved by the Quebec section of the party, which would have recognized the Quebec National Assembly as having exclusive right to legislate on linguistic questions. It also avoided other Quebec demands for entering the constitutional accord, such as more provincial authority over immigration and the appointment of Supreme Court judges. Nor did it touch the contentious issue of minority languages in schools, or what is called the "notwithstanding clause" in the Charter that allows provinces to pass some laws that override certain rights in the Charter.

The New Democrats had been high in the polls before— between elections—only to settle down to their traditional 19 or 20 per cent level on election day. But the Gallup taken between March 11 and 14 put the NDP at 34 per cent among decided respondents, just seven behind the Liberals and ten ahead of the Tories, the closest it had come to the leading party on the Gallup at any time since 1943.

Within months, the NDP had accomplished the unthinkable—it had moved into first place. A May 1987 Gallup poll gave the NDP 41 per cent. Newspapers were even writing long features on what kind of prime minister Broadbent would be.

But polls are not elections, and parliamentary seats are not won without money, hard work, and a party structure on the ground. At the next election, the NDP says it will spend $6 million, compared to $2.8 million in 1984. "You can't play in the big league with a little league budget," party official Terry Grier told the delegates in Montreal. But despite all the emphasis on Quebec, and record standings in the polls there, the party still has only about 4,000 party members in the entire province and no real campaign organization in any riding. And, for all the hype, less than 100 of the 1,200 delegates at Montreal were from the host province.

Still, Broadbent insists that times have changed for his party, especially in Quebec. "I say the growth is real, but as in all things in politics, it's not necessarily permanent. If we don't continue with the hard work that we've been doing, we won't necessarily stay where we are. And if the others gain some increased credibility, they might take some of the support back from us. There's no way of predicting that.

"But having said that, if I were making a guess, we are at a new plateau in our standing. . . . There's an increasing

acceptance of the New Democratic Party. . . ." Pointing out
that his party is seen to be concerned about job creation and a
more equitable distribution of society's benefits, he estimates
"with no great precision, that about 40 per cent of Canadians
could accept a social democratic approach."

A February poll conducted by Angus Reid Associates for
Southam News in January 1987 attempted to measure the
reasons behind the record-high level of NDP support. It
showed that 60 per cent of those asked felt the NDP would
improve the lot of "the poor, the elderly, and those in
economic trouble." Asked about "fairness and honesty" in
government, 45 per cent said it would improve, and 38 per
cent said unemployment would decrease.

That was the good news. On the other side, 42 per cent
predicted an increase in the deficit under an NDP government,
and 43 per cent felt their personal taxes would increase. Asked
when the NDP is likely to form a government, just 5 per cent
said it would be at the next election, but 36 per cent said it
could be done "within ten years." The greatest optimism was
in Quebec, where 51 per cent could see the party in Ottawa in
the next decade.

What accounts for the change? Hard work and the absence
of Trudeau and Lévesque, who, "at different times in their
lives," said Broadbent, "described themselves as social democrats and were seen by Quebeckers on economic and social
matters to be progressive." As long as they were there in
Quebec, Broadbent felt, "there was no room for us. . . . they
were already seen to be progressive on economic and social
matters."

At a weekend conference of the Centre for Investigative
Journalism in late March, René Lévesque said it was only
natural that the 300,000-odd *péquistes* who had abandoned the
Parti Québécois after the May 1980 referendum would move
toward the NDP. "I'm happy to see that. Many are disappointed
with [the Tories] in Ottawa. And they don't want to see the
Liberals back in power."

The next day, Mulroney's principal secretary, Bernard Roy,
told seven hundred delegates at a two-day convention of the
Conservative's Quebec wing that the next federal election
could be a three-way race. "The next election will be, by all
appearances, more difficult. The game will perhaps be a three-
way one instead of two, as it was in the past. We will have to
fight riding by riding. . . . We have known difficult mo-

ments. We can't ignore that there currently exists a certain unhappiness about our government."

This is not the first time, of course, that Tories have held up the spectre of the socialist uprising for their own ends, to frighten voters into coming to their senses. Former Ontario premier Bill Davis used to do it all the time, quite successfully, telling voters that unless they rushed out and voted for him, their entire society would soon be nationalized by the wild-eyed socialists. This tactic had the added advantage of shutting out the Liberals completely from the voting equation.

Broadbent, of course, recognizes the problem himself, which is why he's so busy rushing around speaking to non-socialist groups to argue that he does not have horns, despite his executive position in Socialist International. That was the theme, for example, of a speech to businessmen in late February in Terrebonne, the riding where Toupin had been elected a Tory only to embrace the NDP. He tried to allay fears that an NDP government would mean higher taxes and more bureaucracy, pointing out that an NDP government in Manitoba more than twenty years ago had lowered taxes for small- and medium-sized corporations.

At age fifty-one, after nineteen years in politics, the former political-science professor is a hot political property. A January Angus Reid poll put his public approval rating at 64 per cent, compared with 45 per cent for Turner and just 34 per cent for Mulroney. People like Broadbent personally. But, alas, they say, if only he were a Liberal he'd be prime minister. Well, he isn't a Liberal—although some party ideologues are wondering about that—and his chances of becoming prime minister are not great. But there is a chance, however remote, and that is something Canadians wouldn't even have dreamed of just three years ago.

As politicians go, Broadbent is considered to be an honest man. He also has an engaging personality, not nearly as intense as that of most of his fellow travellers, although he is not without a temper of his own. (He once tried to pick a fist fight with the author for a column describing how he'd lied to partisans in a speech in St. John's. His press secretary actually had to pull him by the arm to stop him from getting physical.)

Broadbent was born on March 21, 1936, in Oshawa, the Ontario city he now represents. Like most people there, his father worked for General Motors. A younger brother, David, still does.

Southam News journalist Ken MacQueen, who covers the NDP regularly, wrote recently of Broadbent that, "unlike previous leaders of the NDP and the Co-operative Commonwealth Federation, Broadbent's brand of socialism was not shaped by the Prairie dust bowl and the Depression. It came pouring through the filter of his own working-class ethics, the distilled political and economic theories restlessly gathered from all parts of the spectrum: from Machiavelli to Marx; from the anti-socialist novels of George Orwell to the works of one of his heroes, John Stuart Mill, who wrote extensively in the 19th century of the ethics of economics, politics and sexual equality."

Broadbent earned doctorates in political science from the University of Toronto and the London School of Economics. He began teaching at York University in 1965, and three years later was elected MP for Oshawa. In 1971, he married Lucille Allen, and also took an unsuccessful run at the party leadership, finishing a poor fourth behind winner David Lewis. In 1975, after Lewis stepped down, Broadbent won on the fourth ballot.

He frequently holidays in Quebec, as much to improve his stilted French as anything, visits his Oshawa riding about once a month for a day of constituency problems, and has consistently outperformed Turner in the Commons question period. But beyond Broadbent, his Commons caucus is weak. He has some able soldiers, Lorne Nystrom, Nelson Riis, Steven Langdon, and the competent but perennially sour Michael Morris Cassidy, but for the most part, the rest of his caucus seems either congenitally shrill or habitually uninterested.

When a group of his MPs heckled U.S. president Ronald Reagan in the Commons in April—led by radical homosexual-rights advocate Svend Robinson—Broadbent, who had rushed out of the Commons without comment to catch a plane to Rome, took time out from his Socialist International conference to telephone back and scold his rowdy subjects. When polls are high, image is everything. The party's house leader, Nelson Riis, conceded that some of the thirty caucus members were worried about the effect the heckling of their well-known guest would have on the party's standings with Canadians.

Broadbent attributes the rapid decline of the Tories to Mulroney personally and to the fact that many of his ministers "have not been nearly as competent as I expected." He said that the Tory collapse "ought not to have happened to the same degree given the economic upswing that Canada was going through—not all of Canada, I add right away—but certainly parts of Canada experienced an upswing and very specifically Ontario, and yet he's as unpopular there . . . . as almost anywhere else in the country.

"It's hardly original, but he [Mulroney] is a man who came to office with no deep sense of policy commitment about the kind of Canada that he really wanted to shape. I think to have this is very important for any politician, or you shouldn't be in politics. Whether you're on the left, right, or centre, you should have some conception of why you are entering the public domain, other than wanting to get to the top, other than wanting to get elected."

Broadbent said he was "trying not to personalize" the issue, but he compared Mulroney unfavourably in this regard with both Diefenbaker and Trudeau. "Trudeau clearly had a sense of what he wanted to do and was in public life for reasons other than simply getting to the top . . . there was a respect for the seriousness of the man . . . that here's a man in public life who had certain goals.

"Diefenbaker didn't have, I don't think, a coherent idea what he was for, but he was against something. Pretty clearly, he had an emotional against-the-Establishment grain in him, and he was a westerner. So it was always unfocused, imprecise, but none the less real populist instincts when he spoke out against the banks or Bay Street, or even in one or two remarkable speeches about American industry dominating our priorities. . . .

"A lot of Canadians across the political spectrum in different regions saw in Diefenbaker a kind of populist guy who was more likely to be on the side of the average person than he was on the side of the rich and powerful.

"Not only does [Mulroney] lack a set of morally defined goals, he's a guy who wants to be at the top, and he is more inclined to respect and want to be like the people who are at the top on Bay Street or run the iron-ore companies of this world, or are the President Reagans of this world. He identifies himself with those who already have the maximum amount of power, success, and wealth, whereas Diefenbaker was more likely to identify himself in his public role against those. . . ."

Broadbent said a "plus" for Mulroney is "a disposition to make friends. I have often said Trudeau would rather win an argument any day than win a friend and Mulroney would rather win a friend and is indifferent about the argument." He said Mulroney tried to smooth relations with the provinces, and did at first, "because in a sense he gave them everything they wanted . . . if you look at more recent meetings, you get not very far from the surface at all, open disagreement with him from premiers of his own party. That shouldn't surprise him, but I suspect he feels hurt because they, in the real world of the Canadian federalist state, have interests that conflict with his. . . ."

Broadbent said that Mulroney's "not very high regard for the truth" has led him to "make all kinds of fantastic promises that, contrary to what a lot of cynics say in politics, people do take seriously. You hear so much cynicism that people don't believe politicians. Well, they in fact do, and they hold them accountable.

"It was important particularly in Quebec because of the well-founded, historical antipathy to the Conservatives, where Quebeckers thought they would all be, in terms of social policy, dangerous right-wingers. Mulroney overstated his position. Instead of simply saying well, we are going to keep the social programs, he actually promised increases . . . so the pension thing really backfired.

"So there's his propensity to always want to please . . . and [he's] not deeply grounded in the view that you had to be as honest as you possibly could in politics . . . he always built up expectations he couldn't live up to and he did opposite things."

According to Broadbent, "When you have major responsibilities in the political system . . . people have to see you as having respect for the truth, which is different from always telling the truth. I think in some circumstances, you can make a moral argument for lying and people understand that. Especially in high-stakes matters of state . . . state security, things like that, sometimes it's going to be necessary." However, he concluded, "people have to sense you have a respect for the truth even if at times, in exercising your public responsibilities, you have to lie. I think that Mulroney doesn't convey the sense that he has a respect for the truth. He doesn't convey that."

Only eighteen men have been prime minister of Canada. John Turner is one of those. Not a bad accomplishment, although if he does not manage to come back from the political dead, his only real legacy will be that apart from (Conservative PM) Sir Charles Tupper in 1896, Turner's eighty days in office is the shortest term on record.

Like Tupper, who became prime minister after Mackenzie Bowell's incompetence left the Tories in disarray, Turner took over at the end of the Trudeau regime, inheriting a once-mighty Liberal party that was then in a shambles. Both men called quick elections. Both lost. Tupper to Laurier, Turner to Mulroney. Tupper, of course, didn't get another chance. Turner did. And with a healthy, consistent lead over the Tories in public-opinion polls, and most of his own internal leadership squabbles behind him, many are betting Turner will be back at 24 Sussex Drive before he's finished. Many still believe that much of the record NDP support represents Canadians parking there temporarily before ultimately opting for the more traditional choice between the Liberals and Tories. Given Canada's electoral history, it's difficult to discount that view.

For the Liberals the period of renewal began at a caucus meeting at the Guild Inn in Scarborough, a Toronto suburb, in February 1985. The period of depression from the crushing defeat had ended. The party was revamping its outmoded fund-raising and organizational charts—and trying to turn around its $2.75 million deficit—so it could rebuild itself and crawl back into the ring for the next fight.

Liberals poured out of the weekend gathering sounding more upbeat than they had since their September slaughter. Even so, with Gallup giving the Tories 53 per cent, compared to 25 for the Liberals and 21 for the NDP, they needed more than a pep rally. They needed help.

And they got it the next week. Within forty-eight hours of that meeting, Robert Coates resigned as defence minister after his foray into a sleazy strip bar in Germany while overseas on government business; then Solicitor General Elmer MacKay was in trouble for discussing the drug charges against New Brunswick premier Richard Hatfield in a private meeting with Hatfield while the investigation was still on. The first warts, which would soon grow to mountains on the surface of the Mulroney regime, were beginning to appear.

It made starting over a whole lot easier.

After that, the familiar white-thatched head and flashing blue eyes of Turner were everywhere, meeting small groups, and large groups; in public halls and private halls and private living rooms. There were media interviews and private get-togethers with party officials; meetings with students, farmers, pensioners, businessmen, women's groups, ethnic groups, artists, anybody who would listen. Turner began simply grinding it out, day after day, criss-crossing the country, absorbed in the long slow process of picking his wounded ego and shattered party off the political floor.

At the same time, he was working to get rid of his annoying staccato speaking-style, his habitual "ahem." Media consultants were called in to reshape the style, to make people want to listen to what he said rather than change the channel from embarrassment. He gave up patting bums and, for the most part, successfully controlled his old-school-jock habit of offering for humour what were often seen as sexist or boorish remarks, or both.

He took the blame for the defeat and admitted that the Liberals had made serious mistakes. In a speech in Saskatoon in June 1985, he said, "The Liberal party lost the confidence of Western Canada. There was some truth in the suggestion that this party was being run from Ontario and Quebec." It was hard to argue with that, since apart from Turner himself in Vancouver, Lloyd Axworthy in Winnipeg was the only admitted Liberal west of Ontario to be elected.

It was a lonely battle against formidable odds, but Turner set out on the journey in a single-minded quest to salvage his own and his party's reputation. Along the way, provincial Liberals, who had become almost extinct under Trudeau, began to emerge, winning more seats in the Atlantic provinces, even winning some eventually in the West, and forming provincial governments in Ontario, Quebec, and Prince Edward Island.

In the Commons a small group of young Liberal hotheads—Sheila Copps, Brian Tobin, John Nunziata, and Don Boudria—formed what became known as the "Rat Pack." They offended some with their loud accusations and rude interjections, but they certainly got under Mulroney's and the government's skin, and helped implant the notion that the government was bouncing around the parliamentary seas with a busted mast looking for another reef to hit.

But it was not all smooth sailing on the Good Ship Grit. On February 4, 1986, over a three-hour meal at Stornoway, Turner and Chrétien agreed to support Chrétien campaigner Jacques Corriveau for the vice-presidency of the party's Quebec wing and Francis Fox for the presidency. But hours later, Turner phoned Fox and persuaded him to withdraw, prompting the former Liberal heavyweight to tell *Maclean's*, "You don't put your nose in that sort of game. He's asking for trouble." Turner wanted his pick, Quebec City lawyer Paul Rothier, to run unopposed for the presidency. "We are not electing the Queen of Canada," said Lalonde. "It is not an issue of such paramount importance that the leader of the party should get involved."

The party rumblings soon became a full-fledged thunderstorm. Following weeks of infighting in the Quebec wing of the party, Chrétien retired after twenty-three years in the Commons. With the November leadership review for Turner looming, and Chrétien loyalists angered over what their man saw as a double-cross, the resignation of the popular Chrétien was a telling blow.

Mulroney, always ready to overstate any case, accused Quebec Liberals André Ouellet and Raymond Garneau of "plotting" to get rid of Chrétien. He said it was typical of a handful of Liberals who held a stranglehold over Quebec. "We had become the hostages of the Liberal party, these same people who plotted against Jean Chrétien, these are the same people who engineered the knifing of Chrétien three weeks ago—the Ouellets and Garneaus, that gang. Quebec belongs to no one, least of all the Liberals."

Liberal MP Doug Frith, chairman of the national caucus, called the comments "outrageous. They come from a man who publicly shook the hand of former Conservative leader Joe Clark, while knifing him in the back."

Later in the spring the Tories helped the Liberal cause again, albeit unwittingly, by getting embroiled in the tuna controversy, which forced fisheries minister John Fraser to resign and further undermined Mulroney's personal credibility with the public.

Despite internal and external threats to Turner's leadership and his lack of coherence on most of the major issues of the day, his Liberals continued their upward climb in the polls. Two years after his electoral defeat, having travelled more than 400,000 kilometres across the country, from St. John's to Victoria and back again several times, the party had climbed to 38 per cent in the polls, eight ahead of the Tories.

To complicate things for Turner, long-time Liberal backroom boy Senator Keith Davey had turned author, and his memoirs, appropriately called *The Rainmaker: A Passion for Politics*, were not kind to Turner, describing him as "a throwback to the 1950s." Davey openly argued that a Liberal could remain loyal and still vote against Turner's leadership at the November convention. As well, a party feud developed over proposals to bring Quebec into the constitution. Turner himself won praise in Quebec for a proposal that closely matched Quebec's own demands for entry. Some Liberals applauded, but others—notably senior Liberal NDP Donald Johnston—attacked him for abandoning the legacy of Trudeau.

In October, at the first Liberal caucus of the new parliamentary season, Senator Davey was called to account for publicly telling Liberals he thought it was not disloyal to vote for a review of Turner's leadership. In the meantime, Simon Dorval, president of Publi-Media in Montreal, was spearheading an anti-Turner fight for the convention. He and a group of disgruntled Liberals were calling delegates to the upcoming convention to urge them to vote for a leadership review and against Turner.

Chrétien insisted that he had nothing to do with any of this; but most of the disparate groups working against Turner were Chrétien supporters, and Chrétien's own stage-managed entrance at the convention itself belied his claims of sweet innocence. Ken Munro, president of the federal party in Alberta—what there was of it—and a prominent Chrétien supporter, called a news conference to say he was voting for a review and to urge other delegates to do likewise. As well, just before the convention, Marc Lalonde wrote to all 3,500 delegates listing a series of reasons why they should vote for a review. "One can deplore the fact that a leader's popularity plays such a large role in contemporary politics," he noted. "Deplore it if you will, but ignore it at your peril."

It all made great fodder for the media, but in the end what was seen as a ganging-up by the old Trudeau crowd actually helped Turner at the convention. Non-Liberals weren't the only ones who had come to hate the arrogance of the last days of the Trudeau regime, and the sight of Davey and Lalonde rushing to undercut Turner undoubtedly pushed many undecided delegates into the Turner camp.

When the vote finally came, at 1:38 P.M. on Sunday, November 30, at the Ottawa Congress Centre, Turner won a resounding 76.3 per cent. "I've been waiting a long time to say this, John," Doug Frith said after announcing the results, "but you're first in our hearts." It was a clear reference to comments made after Chrétien's failed 1984 leadership bid that he was first in their hearts, though second in the ballot. As far as the Liberal hierarchy was concerned, Turner was now in charge.

But exactly what he was in charge of was still not clear. The party was $5 million in debt. It had approved a series of conflicting resolutions at the convention—which, as Turner pointed out, weren't binding on the leader anyway. Turner had done a good job rebuilding from the grassroots of his party, but the public still had no clear idea what he stood for.

On the first day back in the Commons, the day after the convention, the problem surfaced with a public disagreement among his own MPs over controversial peace resolutions. The weekend votes against future cruise-missile testing and for declaring Canada a nuclear-free zone would violate Canada's NATO commitment, dissenting Liberals said.

People continued to wonder about Turner's commitment to issues, and his vagueness was frustrating to even some of his own loyalists. Toronto MP John Nunziata, for example, expressed astonishment that Turner, though an opponent of the death penalty, would not commit himself to abolishing it again if Parliament reinstated it. In addition, not all Liberals endorsed Turner's consistent opposition to Mulroney's major policy initiative, a free trade deal with the United States.

The disagreements were grist for the political mill in Ottawa and elsewhere, but there were signs that the public was paying little attention. A Gallup poll at the end of 1986 gave the Liberals 45 per cent among decided voters, compared to 30 for the Conservatives and 25 for the NDP. Still, many observers argued that, given Mulroney's dismal performance, Turner should be doing much better in the polls than he is.

"People haven't yet forgiven twenty years of Liberal power," Turner points out. "In certain parts of the country, that's still pronounced. In Western Canada, for example. They voted Mulroney for a new style, to get rid of the Liberals, and now they're bitterly disappointed, but they're not yet satisfied in their own minds that they want to go back.

"Also, I would think that it will still take me some time to live down the image of nineteen eighty-four. I can only re-establish a more positive image as months go by, and I think that's happening.

"In a period of renewal, we're reviewing policy as well as everything else. We haven't had a sharp enough image, we haven't had as sharp an image as we might have had, which we

will by election time. . . . But I don't buy the Norm Atkins
line that we should be at 60 [in the polls]. You know, we're as
high historically in parts of the country as we've ever been,
Quebec and Ontario for instance, we're close to 50 per cent. I
don't talk about polls, but if there were an election tomorrow,
there would be a majority government because of those
figures.

"It takes some time before people reverse their view when it
was so strongly expressed in such a massive way. People don't
like to admit that they may have made the wrong choice. We
still have time to turn that around."

Turner believes that the policy process should be "a period
of intellectual renewal . . . there are risks in having a
discussion, there are risks in moving away from an orthodoxy
which grew up over twenty years, particularly during the later
Trudeau years on a number of issues. . . . You will have
people who represent an older orthodoxy concerned as the
party breaks out of that mould into something new. That's the
risk we're willing to take."

On the party's financial problems, Turner comments, "Well,
1984 was not a vintage year. Eighty-five was not a vintage year,
either, when we were at the mid-20s in the polls. In eighty-six
we had this leadership thing hanging over us. . . . Since
then, it's been going fairly well." How well? He won't say,
other than, "We'll be in good shape by the end of the year."

Mulroney's first mistake, Turner believes, was making so
many electoral promises—by his count 338—that "it was
impossible to deliver. The rhetoric was excessive. That leads
inevitably to disillusionment." Another Tory problem has been
"the weather-vane factor. You know, the blowing with the
wind, the governing by polls. He had the most massive
majority in Canadian history and allowed the first two and one-
half years to escape without doing whatever might have been
on his agenda. He's now going to have more difficulty
because . . . he has less authority, less moral weight than he
would have had in the earlier days of his mandate."

Moreover, Mulroney's decision-making process "appears
cumbersome," a weakness resulting from "trying to impose a
presidential style on a ministerial system. . . .

"What's happened here is we've got a highly centralized
presidential style, (a) because I think it's part of the beast [he
chuckles] you know, and (b) because I think in a televised age
there is a leadership cult that tends to make our system

presidential. But then, you've got various layers now of decision making or advice or both. You've got the Lowell Murrays, the Norman Atkinses, and the Dalton Camps floating around up here. Then you've got Bernard Roy and Doucet and MacAdam and that level. Then you've got cabinet ministers. Then you've got chiefs of staff in each cabinet minister's office, many of them appointed directly by the PMO or at least approved by them. Then you've got the public service, Paul Tellier and all the deputy ministers. Now you've got Don Mazankowski and the deputy prime minister's office, which is kind of an operational centre.

"I mean, if Don is the chief operations officer of the government, you've got a new empire building up in there. But you've got a system there which I don't think decisions can move through and I don't think communications can move through.

"There's another phenomenon too . . . he [Mulroney] convinced people he was a let's-pretend Liberal. He moved into the classic traditional Liberal territory, much as the NDP is trying to do now. But now, with much of the momentum lost, the traditional constituency of the Conservative party is starting to reassert itself. So there are tensions there. You can see it in the capital punishment debate [which Turner says he wouldn't have reintroduced because it's too divisive], you can see it in the privatization game."

Asked about Mulroney's "trust factor," Turner was reluctant to make personal comments, but said, "It's major, it's major. Well, there's no doubt about it . . . it's partially tone, partially rhetoric, partially disaffection because of the excessive promises, partially an unconscious mixture of fact and fiction [he laughed], you know what I mean?" When asked if he believes it is unconscious on Mulroney's part, Turner shifted nervously in his chair and said, "I don't know. I don't know. You know what I'm saying there . . . you'd better talk to a psychologist about that, but it's a valid point."

CHAPTER FOURTEEN

BRIAN DIDN'T SAY NO
EITHER

The image remains fixed in the public mind. There is Brian Mulroney, confident, articulate, closing fast on the Liberals. Beside him, being watched by millions of Canadians coast to coast, sits John Turner, the prime minister, fidgeting, ill-at-ease, an old boxer who has lost many of his skills but still figures he can dance his way through one more championship bout, especially against an inexperienced contender. It is July 25, 1984, the mid-campaign television debate that would see Turner sink to the canvas, never fully to recover from one devastating punch from Mulroney on patronage.

Turner is trying to defend his ill-conceived agreement to hand out appointments to eighteen Liberal MPs to make good on a promise to outgoing prime minister Pierre Trudeau. Turner, desperately bobbing and weaving around the ring, foolishly decides to go toe-to-toe with Mulroney and raise the issue himself, having escaped earlier with just a glancing blow to the body. A year earlier, he reminds viewers, Mulroney had promised to dispense patronage jobs to every living, breathing Tory in Canada. And so he had. But whatever Mulroney had said couldn't match what the Liberals had actually done, and by raising the issue Turner reminded all Canadians just why it was they hated Liberals then. It was a gift from the gods for Mulroney. He would later say he couldn't believe his good fortune. At the time, looking appropriately shocked and appalled, and pointing his righteous finger directly at Turner, Mulroney asked the prime minister to apologize to the Canadian people "for having made these horrible appointments." Turner, his knees wobbly, said, "Well, I have told you and told the Canadian people, Mr. Mulroney, that I had no option." Mulroney then delivered the knockout punch. "You had an option, sir. You could have said, 'I am not going to do it. This is wrong for Canada. And I am not going to ask Canadians to pay the price.' You had an option, sir, to say no, and you chose to say yes, yes to the old attitudes and the old stories of the Liberal party." And so it was done. Bang! Whatever chance Turner had of winning the campaign ended with his limp, "I had no option, I . . . ," a pitiful display of weakness that, as far as most voters were concerned, put Turner down for the count.

If anything made Canadians sick to death of the Liberals, it was their blatant abuse of their power to reward their pals. Mulroney himself, in a June 29 interview with Selkirk News Service, said that a Tory government would dramatically cut partisan appointments. "What has happened is that the Liberals in the pork barrel have been so grotesque, their behaviour has been so odd, their abuse of the public trust has been so flagrant in their nominations that I think that it's now gone beyond the bounds of conventional politics.

"It now deserves a real jolt to get it back to some sensible behaviour and I plan to do that by cutting down dramatically on the attitudes to partisan appointments and restoring a semblance of decency and bipartisanship in order to regain public confidence in the process which has been just so badly abused by really quite a vulgar display of patronage at the trough."

Never mind that when Mulroney ran for the Tory leadership he constantly promised delegate meetings he would appoint Liberals and New Democrats to jobs, "when there isn't a living, breathing Tory left without a job in this country." That wasn't on national television. His attack on Turner's action was. Mulroney revealed even more of his character when he tried to explain that promise away by telling reporters, "I was talking to Tories then, and that's what they want to hear. Talking to the Canadian public during an election campaign is something else." Apparently.

A May 7, 1983, story by Montreal *Gazette* journalist Claude Arpin quoted Mulroney's promise, as he emerged from a closed-door meeting in the new Roussillon-Saguenay Hotel in Jonquière, to reward his friends once he was prime minister. The night before he had told forty Tories in a Ste-Foy hotel that, "Jacques Blanchard, Jean Sirois [two Quebec City lawyers long active in Tory circles]—what senators they'd make. And I can see at least five great candidates for the magistracy." On another occasion, Mulroney joked that he had promised fourteen senatorships in one day alone. At Jonquire, Arpin overheard a Mulroney organizer telling the local Tories, "Brian told us no later than last week, his pals go first. Lookit, Brian has never played coy about patronage; he's all for it. And you boys are in like Flynn."

A week before the TV debate, Mulroney let his true feelings slip when, chatting with reporters on the campaign plane about Liberal MP Bryce Mackasey's controversial appointment as ambassador to Portugal (which he later rescinded), Mulroney said, "Let's face it, there's no whore like an old whore. If I'd been in Bryce's position, I'd have been right in there with my nose in the public trough like the rest of them." When *Citizen* reporter Neil MacDonald broke from the cosy pack and acted like a journalist, writing a front-page story for the July 16 *Citizen* quoting Mulroney's vulgarities, Mulroney, rather than take his lumps, complained, "I got sand-bagged. It won't happen again." Mulroney said he was just kidding, and anyway he thought it was off the record. Two days later, in Sault Ste. Marie, campaign chief Norm Atkins talked Mulroney into apologizing. "I do not deny having made these remarks," he said. "I say simply they were made without any serious intent since they clearly do not represent either my attitudes or my position with respect to this important matter of public policy." Perhaps. But in his loving biography, L. Ian MacDonald reported that friends had heard Mulroney use the "no whore like an old whore" remark "hundreds of times in private." And in his July 24, 1985, column in the *Gazette*, MacDonald, writing about patronage said "Everyone in politics accepts it and every governing party exploits it. 'What this party wants,' the late Conservative Senator Allister Grosart used to say, 'is two feet right in the trough.' That line was often quoted privately by a friend and protégé of Grosart's named Brian Mulroney, during his first run for the Conservative leadership in 1976."

In any event, after his reluctant apology, the issue was dropped by the media (something that should have taught Mulroney something, but didn't) and he was able to regain the initiative after Turner's fatal error during the debate.

According to NDP leader Ed Broadbent, whose party was

riding historic highs in the polls early in 1987, the patronage issue has played a major role in the collapse of Mulroney's popularity. "He capitalized on that, very correctly in my view, in the election campaign when Trudeau saddled Turner and Turner accepted that whole batch of blatant patronage appointments. . . . Mr. Mulroney built up a lot of expectations that were very real to people that aren't so naive, that don't believe you're going to get rid of all partisanship in political decision-making. But he left the impression that there was one area that maybe he did believe in, that there would be real reform . . . he's completely betrayed that set of expectations.

"If he had said nothing about it and just carried on that banal and undesirable level of patronage we still have in our system, I don't think he would have become as unpopular as he has. . . ." But, as Broadbent points out, his high-sounding statements are continually at variance with his actions: "over Christmas, he made that speech about citizenship judges, that we have to clean up the system of appointments, and then the very next day there was the announcement of his old buddy [Jean Bazin] going into the Senate."

It's no surprise when his political opponents are critical, of course. But his friends are critical too. "The biggest hurtful issue has been patronage," said Bill Neville, president of Public Affairs International in Ottawa, former chief of staff during Joe Clark's 1979 government, and a widely respected senior Tory adviser. Neville's view is remarkably similar to Broadbent's. "Mulroney in effect changed the ground rules in mid-campaign when he put down Turner, and did it so effectively . . . that he set up new rules of conduct, but then [he] made the mistake of trying to go back and operate under the old [rules]. . . . He intended it at the time just to score political points, but it struck such a responsive chord [with] the electorate it raised genuine expectations."

During his nine months in office, Clark made about 150 partisan appointments, including 10 senators, but Tories remembered him for not doing more. When his government fell in December 1979, it had a list of 153 appointments going through the system. When a Tory MP complained to Clark about this, the defeated prime minister said, "I was saving them for Christmas presents."

Neville remembers the mood well. "Clark, of course, got burned because people in the party felt he didn't dispense enough patronage. That created some of the patronage atmosphere Brian inherited. . . . There is no question that a number of people in the party included that in their list of reasons why they were mad at Clark; and during the leadership campaign Mulroney certainly exploited that feeling."

While acknowledging that the government has not handled the patronage issue well, Neville argues that the media hasn't always been fair about it either. "The unfortunate thing is if you are a friend of the prime minister's, your public biography tends to stop there. There's the absurd notion that you have no other qualities beyond your friendship with Brian. To say, for example, that Jean Bazin, one of this country's leading lawyers, has no other qualities beyond having been a classmate of Brian's is nonsense, but that is what is being written. There is precious little effort to see if some of these people may not have other qualifications . . . which make them excellent appointments." Neville lists as his "most ridiculous" example, a reference to Montreal Canadiens president Ronald Corey, "who was kissed off in one story as being the man who supplies Mulroney with hockey tickets. Well, I'm sure he does that, but in addition to being president of the hockey team, Ronald Corey is one of . . . a new breed of aggressive young business leaders in Quebec who are helping turn that province around. He's a most impressive man, hardly the sort of person who can be reduced to somebody who supplies the prime minister with hockey tickets."

When the Trudeau regime was finally winding down in 1983, patronage appointments were going in the opposite direction. The Tories, sensing public unrest over Liberal abuses, constantly attacked the issue. In July, John Crosbie said that after twenty years in power the Liberals had turned the patronage system into a "brazen affrontery [sic]." In November 1983, veteran *Toronto Star* journalist Val Sears reported that the Liberals were handing out $60 million worth of advertising contracts, along with three thousand patronage jobs and that during a nine-year period under Trudeau they had appointed two hundred former Liberal candidates to high office, fifty-nine of them to judgeship. Sears also quoted a comment from Roch LaSalle (who ended up resigning under his own cloud in 1986) that "patronage is a fact of life at all political levels . . . and I don't intend to pass up our opportunity." Tory Perrin Beatty observed that dipping into the pork barrel to reward party members could adversely affect the quality of members on boards and commissions. "Too often . . . appointments are made with little attention to whether board members have had any experience in the industry involved or have ever served on a company board before." In December 1983, the Tories were outraged when Trudeau appointed his pal Jean Marchand to the $100,000 chairmanship of the Canadian Transport Commission. (Four years later, Mulroney gave the job to his pal, veteran Tory MP Erik Nielsen.) In February 1984, Tory Harvie Andre, who would become a Mulroney cabinet minister, said that a Tory government would gradually replace "every one" of the 3,300 Liberals on federal boards, commissions, and Crown corporations with "our people. We will be obviously appointing our people when they come for renewal."

On February 6, 1984, Mulroney told more than one thousand delighted Tories crammed into two ballrooms at the Lord Nelson Hotel in Halifax that he expected a cool welcome from the "Liberal-apponted" public service when the Tories won the election. "It is a fact of life that Liberal ideology and personnel are handsomely represented in all levels and in all areas in the government of Canada. . . . I think it would be ridiculous to think that 600,000 public servants, particularly at the top, would be waiting for us with open arms." He promised to replace them with Tories.

Four days later, speaking to three hundred Tories at an Ottawa-Carleton riding meeting, an area brimming with public servants, he was cheered again when he reversed his earlier position and praised the bureaucracy as "among the finest" in the world. He noted that it suffered from "poor productivity," but added that the Tories would not blame the public service. "The fault lies with their political masters." His plaudits for the public servants were off-the-cuff remarks. His criticisms were in the prepared text.

After wooing disaffected Tories by promising them patronage jobs during his successful 1983 leadership quest, Mulroney conveniently changed course and headed for the high road. He didn't fall off until after he got elected. In June 1984, on CTV's "Question Period," he righteously remarked: "The vulgarity of the Liberal patronage machine is such that we're all going to have to take a second look at our partisanship government . . . a determination to get away from it once and for all and that is going to require some dramatic moves from me to cut down on that."

During June 1984, his last month in office, Trudeau named people to 225 posts and, on July 10, after just eleven days as prime minister, Turner fulfilled his written pledge to appoint the disputed eighteen Liberals to various posts. Mulroney immediately attacked the move as "vulgar. Now there's the 'New Morality,'" he said, promising that if he ever made any patronage appointments as prime minister he would explain the criteria on which the selections were made. In August, before an audience in Kingston, Ontario, Mulroney challenged Turner to produce the written agreement he had made with Trudeau: "Canadians have the right to see the so-called letter of agreement and Canadians have the right to see the legal opinion on which Mr. Turner says he based his dubious action." On August 24, in Castlegar, B.C., he went a step further and promised to make the agreement public should he win the election. However, in November 1984, when the *Toronto Star* went through the federal Access to Information Act to try to see the material, it was turned down flat by the Privy Council Office on the grounds that the agreement was a confidential prime-ministerial document.

In his first press conference as prime minister, on September 29, Mulroney denied that he had ever poked fun at former agriculture minister Eugene Whelan or used Bryce Mackasey's name in vain during the campaign. Whelan had been named as ambassador to the U.N. Food and Agriculture Organization in Rome. Mackasey, of course, had been the object of Mulroney's derisive "no whore like an old whore" comment, and during the campaign Mulroney had regularly warmed up his Tory audience by telling them about a new lottery in which first place was a trip to Rome ". . . and Eugene Whelan won that."

In an effort to deflect criticisms of his partisan approach, Mulroney apointed two high-profile non-Tories to jobs during October:—former Ontario NDP leader Stephen Lewis was named as ambassador to the United Nations and former Commons Speaker Lloyd Francis was named ambassador to Portugal. Later on, Mulroney named union boss Dennis McDermott ambassador to Ireland. He has consistently used these examples to support his claim that his government "has appointed more nonpartisans than any government in our history." There is, of course, no way of knowing that. A request to Mulroney officials at the time for a partisan breakdown of his appointments compared to all other prime-ministerial appointments in Canada's history was dismissed as "frivolous and ridiculous."

The ballots were barely dry when Mulroney established a national network of advisers on potitical appointments to codify patronage. The eleven committees (one national group, plus one for each province) were known as PACs (provincial advisory committees) and the NAC (national advisory committee) by party insiders. All were staffed by high-ranking party members, MPs, and cabinet ministers. Mulroney friends and advisers Michel Cogger, Jean Bazin, Fernand Roberge, and Marc Dorion, along with Tory cabinet ministers Roch LaSalle and Marcel Masse formed the first Quebec PAC, for example. The entire patronage operation was directed by Peter White, a wealthy businessman from London, Ontario, who had befriended Mulroney at Laval University and backed Mulroney's leadership bid. White was appointments chief in the PMO from September 1984 until he returned to private business in April 1986. Despite the blue-chip partisanship of these committees, Mulroney insisted, when their existence became public in November, that it was a sign that the government was willing to talk with Canadians rather than make all these appointments in the legendary smoke-filled backrooms of politics. "They are consultative bodies that I consult with," he said, "and [I] consult with people, prior to making appointments." Ray Hnatyshyn, then Tory House leader, said that, despite their Tory exclusivity, the committees brought a broad approach to government appointments that was lacking under the Liberals.

In addition, Mulroney announced that MPs would soon be able to screen political appointments as promised during the election campaign, a promise he partially delivered on in September 1985 with what was called the public-sector ethics package. According to Liberal Don Boudria, "things got a little better after that, since we could review order-in-council appointments, but the process is seriously flawed because it only applies to some order-in-council appointments, and the way they're getting around it is hiring people on outside contracts." It doesn't apply to judicial appointments, for example, and Boudria argues that the Commons should have veto power (but doesn't) over the sixty-four senior appointments under the Speaker's jurisdiction. These include such things as commissioner of official languages, clerk of the Commons, and CRTC chairman.

In the meantime, the patronage machine kept perking right along. During the first four days of December, Mulroney offered rewards to seven prominent Tories. Huguette Pageau, widow of Rodrigue Pageau, a close friend of Mulroney's who had managed his 1983 leadership campaign, was named a citizenship-court judge, with a salary of between $41,220 and $48,490. Former Tory MP Ron Huntington was named chairman of the Canada Ports Corp. Richard Holden, a Montreal lawyer and longtime Quebec Tory who had backed Mulroney's 1976 and 1983 leadership bids, became a member and vice-chairman of the Restrictive Trade Practices Commission. Mulroney, in fact, had once lived with Holden and his family in Montreal, and in 1983 Holden joked with reporters that if Clark had given him the judgeship he wanted in 1979 he wouldn't have been able to help Mulroney defeat Clark in 1983. Another recipient was Irving Russell Gerstein, president of People's Jewellers of Toronto and a major Tory financial contributor. He was named a director of Canada Post Corp. (Keeping it in the family, his mother, Reva, had served on Joe Clark's transition team when he became prime minister in 1979.) Pierre Boutin, a wealthy Quebec City insurance broker and Conservative supporter, was named chairman of the board of trustees of the National Arts Center Corp., a part-time job. Earlier, Mulroney had named Helen Hunley, a former provincial Tory cabinet minister, as Alberta's lieutenant-governor. Former Tory MP Jean Pigott, who had handled patronage under the Clark regime, became head of the powerful National Capitol Commission, at a salary close to $100,000.

After all those years of watching Liberals enjoy the spoils of electoral victory, the Tories just couldn't wait to get even. Indeed, they moved so swiftly in February 1985 that William Hawkins, retired vice-president and general manager of Ford Motors' sales division in Oakville, and a longtime Tory activist, was approved by cabinet on February 8 as a member of Regional Industrial Expansion's Textile and Clothing Board before the Tories got around to telling him about his good fortune. Hawkins was among forty appointments and four reappointments listed in the order-in-council documents on February 11, bringing to seventy-one the number of appointments listed during the previous three weeks. When contacted by the Ottawa *Citizen*, he said he had no idea he had been appointed. "I guess they figure I won't have any conflict of interest when I'm not involved in that industry," he joked.

He said he had told party officials after the election that he was available to serve the party but had "heard nothing from anyone since then."

Another appointee in that corp was failed Regina Tory candidate Brian Keple, owner of Regina Cartage, a freight distribution company. Named as a director of the Canada Ports Corp. (which has a board member from each province, whether the province has a port or not), Keple would soon be getting his basic $3,000 director's fee plus $300 a day for sitting or travelling, plus all travel and living expenses. Keple said his experience in freight haulage allowed him to understand port problems, and "besides, sailing has always been my hobby and I've had a lifelong interest in the sea."

Among the reappointments to Canada Ports Corp., was Quebec business mogul Paul Desmarais, chairman and chief executive officer of Montreal's Power Corp., the man who Ian MacDonald called "Mulroney's mentor in the business world," his former boss, financial backer, and a frequent host to Mulroney at his Palm Beach home.

Also about this time, Camp Associates Advertising Ltd., headed by Ontario's Big Blue Machine engineer Norman Atkins, co-chairman of the 1984 PC campaign (who would become a senator two years later) was handed a $30 million federal tourism advertising account. And former Ontario attorney general Roy McMurtry (whose failed Ontario Tory leadership campaign had been run by Atkins) received as his sinecure the position of Canadian high commissioner to Great Britian.

On March 1, 1985, Richard Doyle, editor emeritus of the *Globe and Mail* (and former editor-in-chief) wrote in his editorial-page column that Mulroney should examine proposals for an elected Senate that could protect the French language and culture and offer "lighted harbors for special concerns in the West and Altantic Canada." He added that "in these recent days, the beached whales of Liberal fame have been using the forum of sober second thought to obstruct and harass an elected Parliament." Three weeks later, Mulroney appointed Doyle to the Senate.

In a case of reverse patronage in early March, Geraldine Copps, mother of controversial Hamilton East Liberal MP Sheila Copps, was bumped from her post as a citizenship-court judge for the Kitchener area after nine years on the job. In a case of punishing the mother for the daughter's perceived sins,

Secretary of State Walter McLean said to the *Kitchener-Waterloo Record,* "You check the record—what her daughter's had to say about the government." Copps was replaced by Lorna Van Mossell, a nurse and immigrant counsellor, whose husband, Bert, was a minister at Calvin Presbyterian Church in Kitchener and president of the Kitchener-Waterloo Council of Churches. McLean, who represents Waterloo for the Tories, is also a Presbyterian minister.

On March 19, the government named thirteen new directors for the Crown-owned Air Canada, all prominent Tories. Topping the list was former Newfoundland premier Frank Moores, then owner of Alta Nova, an Ottawa consulting firm purchased from two of transport minister Don Mazankowski's aides. Mazankowski was the man responsible for Air Canada. (Moores, a close adviser to Mulroney and, in the early 1980s, chief organizer for Mulroney of the dump-Clark movement, resigned his Air Canada post in September 1985, after the Montreal *Gazette* revealed in July that two lobbying companies owned by Moores were acting as consultants for Nordair and Wardair—both Air Canada rivals.) Joining Moores on the board were three Quebec appointees: David Angus of Montreal, head of the PC Canada Fund, the main party fundraising organization; Fernand Roberge, manager of Montreal's Ritz-Carlton Hotel, one of Mulroney's closest pals and the man who gave him a private suite for secret meetings before the 1983 leadership campaign; and Jacques Blanchard of Quebec City, a former Quebec vice-president of the party and chief Tory organizer for eastern Quebec in the 1984 campaign. Blanchard told reporters that he was proud to be a director, although he didn't know anything about running an airline. Another lucky Tory was former York mayor Gail Christie, a prominent Toronto politician who said in a television interview that she was qualified for the Air Canada board because she knew how to drive a car." At a time when one and a half million Canadians are out of work," thundered NDP critic Nelson Riis, "what kind of signal does it give to the people of Canada when [the prime minister] makes that appointment and the best qualification she can come up with is that she knows how to drive a bloody car?"

Piling on the rhetoric, Riis went on to speak of the "thirteen new Tory bagmen swilling at the public trough . . . pork-barrelling patronage hypocrisy . . . a stench of hypocrisy and broken promises . . . the same old Liberal approach. This is the kind of hypocrisy the people of Canada got sick of. They thought they made a change, but in fact they haven't." During the heated Commons exchange, Mulroney accused Riis of casting "a slur on one of the most outstanding women in Canada [Christie]" and shouted, "the people of Canada voted for a change and you may be certain that there will be changes. That you can be sure of."

Mulroney repeated his claim that "no prime minister has appointed non-party members to such high decision-making functions in such numbers," singling out Doyle, Lewis, Francis, and former CTV bureau chief Bruce Phillips, who was named communications chief of Canada's Washington embassy. (In 1987, the "non-partisan" Phillips was brought back as director of communications for Mulroney.) During his outburst, Mulroney did not mention that in addition to firing the entire Air Canada board (except for chairman Claude Taylor and president Pierre Jeanniot) and replacing them with Tories, a month earlier he had dismissed most members of the boards of VIA Rail and Petro-Canada, again replacing them largely by prominent Tories. The board of Canadian National Railways and Ports Canada would soon receive similar treatment. Among the new VIA Rail directors were: Robert Brunet, Quebec Conservative party president; Laura Sabia, a failed Toronto Conservative hopeful; Sandy LeBlanc, a New Brunswick organizer for Mulroney's leadership campaign; and Toronto lawyers and party activists Ian Outerbridge and John McElwain. The full-time chairman's job had been given earlier to Lawrence Hanigan, a star Conservative candidate in Montreal (and one of the few who lost). Hanigan, former head of the Montreal Transit Commission, had his salary increased by $20,000, to a maximum of $135,000 a year, at the same time as the Tories froze the salaries of VIA Rail workers. About that time, former Tory cabinet minister and Commons Speaker Marcel Lambert was given a ten-year term with the Canadian Transport Commission, a post that paid between $63,230 and $88,930 a year. When NDP leader Ed Broadbent complained about Lambert, Mulroney said that he was "appalled at the splenetic observations . . . he disparages a former Speaker of the House who served here for twenty-five years." Mulroney added that he had appointed "people with previous political backgrounds," again naming Lambert, Francis, and Lewis, "and I am proud of it." (Lambert had become so unpopular with his own constituents that he lost his own renomination bid in Edmonton west to a young, unknown accountant.)

On March 21, Liberal John Nunziata produced evidence obtained through Access to Information that almost all the 153 Ontario lawyers appointed since late December 1984 to process Canada Mortgage and Housing Corp. business were active members of the Conservative party. Another list from January 1985 showed that about 100 Ontario lawyers appointed by Ottawa to the Farm Credit Corp., the national farm-loan agency, were also predominantly Tories.

Public expectations were such that Kevin Ward of Port Hawkesbury, Nova Scotia, was picketing Tory Lawrence O'Neil's constituency office claiming that O'Neil had promised him a job in the offshore oil industry if he voted for him and the Tories won. By the end of March, Mulroney had appointed his friends and party loyalists to patronage jobs at a rate of one every three hours, firing almost as many people appointed by the former Liberal regime.

Things got so bad that the Liberal "Rat Pack" decided to start handing out "PAW" awards (for Patronage Award of the Week), and Don Boudria tallied over 1,200 partisan Tory appointments on the "Patronometer" he'd put on his office door. In response, Tory Ted Schellenberg said he would present his own "SOW" awards (Survivor of the Week) to the most deserving Liberal patronage appointee who still had a job. The first winner was CBC president Pierre Juneau, a former Liberal cabinet minister who, surprisingly, still has his job.

By this time, Jean Bazin, another of the Mulroney Laval University gang, had been appointed to the Petro-Canada board. Mulroney gave him an even bigger Christmas present in late 1986, however, elevating him to the Senate despite the fact that his law firm had acted for Swiss defence contractor Oerlikon in the controversial land flip in St. Jean, Quebec, that led to Mulroney's firing cabinet minister André Bissonnette. Bazin's estranged wife, Michele, was appointed to a seat on the Canada Council, at $220 for each sitting day, along with Jeanne Lougheed, wife of then Alberta premier Peter Lougheed. Michel Cogger, another charter member of the Laval crowd, was made a Queen's Counsel, but that was just a teaser leading up to his Senate appointment in May 1986. In addition, long-time personal friend and Laval chum Michael Meighen was named to the lucrative post of counsel to the Dechênes Commission on Nazi war criminals.

On April Fool's Day 1985, Walter McLean announced the appointment of two Toronto men to $46,000-a-year jobs as citizenship-court judges—Giovanni Rocca and Steven Walter. Rocca was described as a former teacher of citizenship classes in Ontario and Manitoba, but he was also a former full-time federal Tory organizer in Toronto and an unsuccessful Tory candidate against Davenport Liberal Charles Caccia. As for Walter, he was vice-president of the Canadian-Hungarian Federation and an active Tory promoter in the Hungarian community. In December 1986, Canadians discovered just how enthusiastic Walter was for the Tories when Al Roberts, an Indian immigrant, presented a signed statement to Nunziata saying that during his personal immigration interview, Walter had told him to vote Tory in the next election because voting Liberal would lead Canada "back to socialism and ultimately communism." Walter also called the Gandhi family a bunch of "communist bastards," and when Roberts said he was disappointed in the Conservatives and was leaning towards the Liberals "the judge totally lost his composure and cast [my] application aside with the comment 'I am disappointed in you.'"

This was a bit much even for the Tories, and at his final news conference of the year four days later, after Walter had resigned, Mulroney admitted that the naming of citizenship judges had been "a bit of a boondoggle," and that Secretary of State David Crombie would review the appointment process. He praised Walter as a "great Hungarian patriot," but agreed that it was "clearly . . . unacceptable" for him to press immigrants to vote Tory. Despite his government's problems, however, Mulroney said that his administration looked good compared to others—citing the "security and sex scandals" of Margaret Thatcher's British government, the student marches that have hurt French premier Jacques Chirac, and the Iranian arms scandal that has hit U.S. president Ronald Reagan. He also said that "any good politician should be sixty or ninety days ahead of the Gallup," predicting that better days were coming. "I think we're on our way," At the time, Thatcher, Chirac, and Reagan all were running higher than Mulroney in the polls despite their problems, and sixty days after Mulroney's prediction that "we're on our way," he hit 22 per cent in the polls, the lowest figure for a sitting government since Gallup began polling in 1942.

Meanwhile Crombie, who had acted swiftly in the Walter case, announced that new chief citizenship judge Elizabeth Willcock would conduct the review of the system. She's an expert. Given the job by the Tories in January 1985, she had been a former aide to Tory cabinet minister Jack Murta, research director for the Manitoba Conservative party, head of the national Conservative women's organization, and a defeated candidate for the national presidency of the party.

Things really heated up for the Tories on April 21 with news that Lawson Murray Ltd. of Toronto had been awarded a $234,000 Supply and Services contract, without bidding or competition, to advertise Bank of Canada bonds. The contract had been awarded just two weeks after Doug Robson, president of Michael Wilson's riding association, had completed his leave of absence from the firm to help establish the minister's office in the new government. In addition, the firm was partly owned by Douglas Lawson, Wilson's brother-in-law; and Wilson's sister, Wendy Lawson, was a company director. "It appears to us quite conclusively that the guidelines have been broken," John Turner told Mulroney moments before urging him to seek Wilson's resignation, to which Mulroney shot back, "No one has any lessons to learn [about] probity and integrity from the Liberal party." Perhaps not, but Turner did recall a Mulroney quote from a July 7, 1984, press conference, in which he said of the Liberals, "Brothers and brothers-in-law are appointed to positions all over the place. It's a real scandal to act with such scorn towards the people of Canada, towards the average Canadian." Now, in defending Wilson, Mulroney said that relatives of politicians were "people entitled to live their own lives in Canada. We respect their privacy and their competence and we plan and intend to continue." The issue dominated question period in the third week of April. At one point, Broadbent said, "Every Thursday, when the cabinet meets, the Liberal tide of patronage goes out and on Monday morning we read about decisions and the Tory tide of patronage comes in."

In the midst of the Commons uproar, Mulroney conceded that the Wilson matter "raises the question of appearance with which we must deal. I acknowledge that. . . ." But when asked about it by reporters shortly afterwards, he snapped, "For anyone to suggest that Wilson was directly or indirectly, intentionally or inadvertently, guilty of a conflict of interest or a breach of trust is to do him a grave disservice." When another reporter pointed out that Mulroney had himself suggested it by acknowledging that the issue "raises the question of appearance," Mulroney growled, "The perception you think is there. The perception that you are trying to create. . . . People are quite capable of discerning . . . they have long since decided that Wilson is incorruptible, that he's a man of unimpeachable integrity. And it's going to take a hell of a lot more than a bunch of discredited Grits saying that he's not, to change [Canadians'] view . . ."

At one point, when Turner was pressing for Wilson's resignation over what appeared to be a breach of cabinet conflict-of-interest guidelines, Mulroney said he agreed that ministers must avoid the appearance of conflicts and added that that was why Canadians had been "horrified" in the summer of 1984 when Turner kept his corporate directorships for a number of weeks after becoming prime minister. Turner immediately corrected Mulroney, pointing out that he had resigned all his directorships, as called for in the cabinet rules, on June 30, the day he was sworn in.

The next day, April 24, Sheila Copps rose in the Commons to accuse Mulroney of having breached his own rules because, unlike Turner, he hadn't resigned the last of his corporate directorships until November 30, 1984, about ten weeks after he became prime minister on September 17. Mulroney at first dismissed the charge, saying he'd resigned all his corporate directorships "long before that," but when Copps produced documents showing he had not resigned from the board of Labsea Inc., a St. John's-based holding company, he said he had meant to, and if he hadn't "it was inadvertent . . . [and] it would have been of no profit to me." Later that day, Mulroney's office released a terse written statement saying that Labsea (which also involved Frank Moores) has been "dormant, inoperative and inactive from its inception."

While the furor over Wilson's family activities was raging in Ottawa, news out of Halifax was that the directors of the International Centre for Ocean Development, a foreign-aid program announced by Pierre Trudeau at the 1982 Commonwealth Conference in Melbourne, had been bounced and replaced mainly by a group of Tories. ICOD was opened in 1983 with a start-up budget of $27 million to help poor countries develop their ocean resources, but the bulk of its resources were frozen when the Tories came to power. It had been chaired by Halifax lawyer Brian Flemming, a former legal associate of Mulroney's, a Liberal who had served as Trudeau's deputy principal secretary and had considerable experience in the law of the sea. The board included David Hopper, vice-chairman of the World Bank in Washington, Georges Leger, a diplomat and vice-president of Petro-Canada International, Dr. Verevat Hongskul of Thailand, president of the largest fisheries research institute in south-east Asia, and Wayne Hunte, a leading marine biologist from Barbados. All were fired from their unpaid jobs. The new chairman was Hanson Dowell, an adviser on sea law to the Nova Scotia government. Dowell admitted that his Conservative functions had got him the job (he was a national vice-president of the party and counsel and special adviser to regional economic development minister Elmer MacKay in the Clark government). Joining him on the board were Gastien Godin of Shippegan, New Brunswick, a Tory candidate in the 1979 election, and former Newfoundland Tory fisheries minister, Roy Cheeseman.

In the midst of this orgy of patronage, former Tory party president and long-time activist Dalton Camp, writing a column in the April 28 *Toronto Star*, advised readers that "this eternal media mumbling about patronage . . . ought to be heavily discounted" because every government does it. Apparently forgetting that Mulroney had promised to end the patronage system, Camp called media attacks a "cheap shot," and added that he had reached the "despairing conclusion" that the media did not understand the political system, did not care to understand it, and never would understand it. (Camp demonstrated his own understanding of patronage on August 25, 1986, when he accepted Mulroney's gift of a $120,000-a-year job as an adviser on long-term policy, considerably more than the *Star* was paying him to advise the prime minister. Liberal Don Boudria failed in a bid to have the appointment rescinded, after it was examined under the new rules allowing MPs to examine cabinet appointments but not cancel them. Boudria and others were especially angry because Camp had been named a civil servant, working for the Privy Council Office, which is supposed to be non-partisan, instead of more properly being hired onto the prime minister's personal political staff.)

Despite Camp's April 1985 dismissal of the patronage issue, a group of seven MPs—five Tories, one Liberal, and one New Democrat—holed up at the government lodge at Meech Lake outside of Ottawa in mid-June in a marathon session to hammer out a final report on parliamentary reform. The committee, headed by highly respected St. John's Tory Jim McGrath (who had been kept out of cabinet for not supporting Mulroney's leadership bid) was grappling with the task of preserving patronage as a political reality while finding a way to curb the obvious abuses. McGrath, who would later accept his own reward and become Newfoundland's lieutenant-governor, said at the time that patronage was by far "the most difficult thing to deal with in all of our discussions." Their report suggested that high-level appointments be subject to a parliamentary review process patterned after the congressional hearings in the United States. On October 23, a report tabled in the Commons from the Law Reform Commission of Canada concluded that boards and agencies particularly have been matters of "political prerogative" influenced significantly by partisan considerations. "Even the limited consultative mechanisms in the selection of judges, which are informal and themselves subject to continuous abuse and criticism, are absent in the process of agency appointments," the commission noted after a study of fifty agencies considered to have decision-making powers. It concluded that many excellent appointees currently occupy office "in spite of the system, not because of it."

Mulroney introduced his new guidelines on September 10, 1985, admitting that they were "long overdue and heaven knows this government has had cause to regret their absence." The guidelines imposed strict limitations on the hiring of family members and introduced a one-year "experimental" program of parliamentary scrutiny of some cabinet appointments. It also proposed a judicial-appointments review and the registration of lobbyists, another one of those sacred election-campaign promises Mulroney made but has yet to deliver on. The guidelines fell short of the McGrath committee recommendations, which would have given MPs a veto over some appointments, such as those to the Canadian Transport Commission, the CRTC, and the National Energy Board. McGrath argued that these shouldn't be the absolute prerogative of cabinet because they operate virtually independently of cabinet and wield immense influence over the lives of Canadians. Such appointments, he said, should require parliamentary confirmation. Mulroney, in a letter to all MPs, wrote, "we cannot look to the United States for a model, because their system is so different from ours." Turner called Mulroney a "shameless hypocrite" for waiting until over 1,200 Tories had already been given patronage jobs before announcing the guidelines. Even his justice minister John Crosbie, in the midst of a flap over the hiring of his two lawyer sons for government legal work, said, "I am not going to make a judgement [about Mulroney's guidelines] because I respect the rules . . . in another day and another context I wouldn't mind saying what I think, but due to my recent experience I have to be like Ivory soap, purer than pure."

Crosbie had earlier been called the Archie Bunker of Parliament for appointing the law firms his two sons worked for as legal agents for work from Crosbie's own department. Turner said, "It's all in the family," referring to the once-popular television show, and NDP critic Svend Robinson said, "Canadians have had their bellies full of this kind of nepotism and blatant pork-barrelling." Liberal Bob Kaplan said it was significant work for lawyers called to the bar only in 1983, adding that one of Crosbie's sons had failed two years in law school. A Crosbie aide said that the firm of Kendell and Crosbie had done $1,874 worth of work for the government on oil pollution and fisheries cases, but that Chesley Crosbie had done "little or no" work on the cases. He added that the firm of Chalker, Green and Rowe, which employed Michael Crosbie, had done $712 worth of government work. The next day, on June 5, 1985, after announcing that his two sons had quit as federal agents, an outraged Crosbie bellowed in a raucous Commons sessions that his sons had been victims of a "cowardly, despicable, dastardly" attack launched by "a cow-ardly, despicable, dastardly" MP (Kaplan). Crosbie's own department had made the appointments, but Crosbie admitted no wrongdoing, and said that his sons had asked to be relieved of the duties and "reluctantly, I have agreed. But I have agreed against my own better nature . . . because of your scurvy behaviour." Crosbie was so enraged at Kaplan (he pointed out that his son Chesley was a Rhodes Scholar), that when Speaker John Bosley ordered him to withdraw his charge of cowardice against Kaplan as unparliamentary, Crosbie did so, but added "I will deal with the honourable member outside . . . it is impossible to be in public life without having scum splattering you with mud." As Liberals heckled, Crosbie shouted across to Sheila Copps, "Quiet down, baby." Copps protested furiously, saying, "I am a member of Parliament, thirty-two years old, elected to represent the people of my area. I'm not his baby and I'm nobody's baby." (Copps later wrote her autobiography and called it *Nobody's Baby*.)

Also in June 1985, Liberal discovered that Marcia Clark, Joe Clark's sister-in-law, had been named a temporary member of the National Parole Board two days before the previous Christmas. That revelation came the day after Boudria and Nunziata had attacked Clark in the Commons over the appointment of Clark's brother, Peter, as lawyer for the Calgary Winter Olympics.

Not all Tory relatives were prospering, however. Charlottetown lawyer John McMillian, thirty-two, whose brothers Tom and Charles were a cabinet minister and a senior Mulroney adviser, respectively, complained in a June 7 article in the *Globe* that, given his connections, he should be doing better. He had been appointed a legal agent on March 15, 1985, two weeks after being admitted to the bar, but he said it hadn't brought in "a single cent" because other P.E.I. Tory lawyers had been given the good stuff, and "the work was all divvied up and I got what was left over. . . . I naively believed that because I was a good Conservative we would keep getting the government work. I mean, if I, who have a brother in the cabinet and another who is a senior policy adviser to the prime minister, can't keep at least the work we had before, well, there's something wrong."

Two days later, the Crosbie boys popped up again in a computer printout from Canada Mortgage and Housing Corp. showing that Michael had handled four cases for a total billing of $180, while Chesley had billed $425 for three cases. Crosbie, as the minister for Newfoundland, sits on the PAC committee and personally oversees all patronage appointments to the island province. One of those appointments was to Faith Good, fifty-three, the mother of Crosbie's chief of staff, who was named to the St. John's Port Corp. Her work credentials showed she was a hospital volunteer. The corporation oversees a busy seaport responsible for about $170 million worth of work each year.

Despite the growing criticism, friends of the government were still faring well. In May 1985, New Democrat Ray Skelly revealed that a prominent west-coast Tory had been chosen to administer a $5-million job-creation and -training program being run out of a building he owns. Thor Peterson, a millionaire businessman from Campbell River, B.C., would get $300 a day for fees and expenses and was under contract to work fifteen days a month on a program called MILAP (the Modified Industry and Labor Adjustment Program) aimed at giving job-retraining and -relocation assistance to people in forty coastal communities suffering the effects of a poor salmon fishery. Peterson was recommended by then fisheries minister John Fraser. He had acted as campaign manager for the Tories several times in Skelly's Comox-Powell River riding and had been a fund-raising chairman. To help him in his new task, Peterson hired two other prominent Tory workers, James Lornie and Stan Hagen, who would be paid $150 a day for their efforts. A spokesman for minister Flora MacDonald said that the men could earn $200,000 over the life of the contract. In addition, the committee operated out of an office Peterson owned in Campbell River, prompting Skelly to say it was "probably the grossest government pork-barrelling this House has seen to date, the pinnacle of patronage that even the Liberals didn't have the guts to try." The government explained that Peterson was renting his office to his own committee at "the commercial rate or below. Nothing extra is being garnered by virtue of this." Except of course, that he was collecting rent for an office that would otherwise be empty.

In July 1985, cabinet awarded a lucrative contract for the audit of Air Canada's books to the Thorne Riddel firm. Consumer and corporate affairs minister Michel Côté had been a partner there until the last election. In addition, Ernst and Whinney were given the contract to audit Petro-Canada. It had been the auditor for the Iron Ore Company of Canada when Mulroney was president.

Mulroney looked after yet another school chum, former Parti Québécois minister Denis de Belleval, who became president of Canada Ports Corp., and then unleashed another round of appointments, on August 9, 1985, to the boards of three major Crown corporations—Canadair Ltd., de Havilland Aircraft of Canada Ltd., and Eldorado Nuclear Ltd., all subsidiaries of the Canada Development Investment Corp. The twenty-six appointments, formally announced by Sinclair Stevens, included Gordon Slade (to Eldorado), a former chairman of the board of Falconbridge Copper and an unsuccessful Tory candidate in Nickel Belt riding; five people who had contributed $1,000 each to the party last year— Ronald Rarano (to Canadair), Daniel Williams, Camille Locrois, and John Fraser (to de Havilland), and Herb Pinder (to

Eldorado); Jeffrey Lyons, an influential Toronto Tory (to Eldorado); E. Lynn Hillingsworth, a long-time friend and business associate of then international trade minister James Kelleher (to Eldorado); and Micheline Bouchard, a Montreal-based engineer (to Canadair). Bouchard had previously been named to a blue-chip, seven-member Official Residences Council set up by Mulroney last December.

A week later, Montreal Canadiens president Ronald Corey was given a three-year, part-time job as chairman of the Montreal Port Corp., which pays $15,000 a year plus directors' fees and expenses. Corey, a close friend of Mulroney, would be helped out by two other Conservative loyalists—Montreal insurance executive Bernard Finestone, a losing Tory candidate in 1979, and insurance broker Andre Gingras, a $1,000 party contributor in 1984. In addition, Jock Osler, Clark's former press secretary, who had become a public relations man in Calgary, was given a three-year term as CBC director, at $250 a day plus expenses.

On August 23, Mulroney emerged from the second day of a cabinet meeting in Vancouver to say that it was "a matter of some indifference" to him who got jobs as long as they were competent and that "our regions are represented . . . we did suffer, and I think unfairly, but what else is new, since when has politics been fair? The fact of the matter is I'm standing here before you now as the prime minister of Canada who in eleven months has named more New Democrats, more Liberals, and more non-Conservatives to posts than Mr. Trudeau did in sixteen years, than any prime minister in Canada, and we received no credit for it whatsoever, none. That's because patronage got high priority (from the media) . . . I'm not apologizing for it. Nor am I complaining."

Broadbent said that Mulroney's plan to allow some parliamentary review but no power to veto appointments was a "half-assed" measure that had already been "considerably diluted" given the number of appointments already made. On September 4, 1985, the first anniversary of the election, the *Globe* quoted from the 1984 press conference that kicked off the Mulroney campaign in which Mulroney had called Liberal appointments "vulgar . . . the boys cutting up the cash . . . it will never, never happen again under a Conservative government." The *Globe* reported that the total number of order-in-council appointments to date was 2,730 (although many of those were routine government business orders rather than patronage appointments).

Ian Deans, then the NDP House leader, was incensed by it all. "Patronage has reached a point of obscenity," he said. "The government has lost control of the appointments process." (On March 11, 1986, Deans announced he wouldn't run again in his Hamilton Mountain seat because he could no longer stomach the Tory government. "I just don't think these people deserve to be in government . . . they just don't know or understand the necessity of forthrightness and being upfront with the Canadian people and to demonstrate an obvious integrity." On August 28, 1986, Deans quit his seat and accepted a government job as the $93,700-a-year chairman of the Public Service Staff Relations Board.)

On September 8, 1985, the Ottawa *Citizen* reported that a Toronto law firm had been awarded $200,000 worth of legal work shortly after Sam Wakim, one of Mulroney's closest friends, joined it earlier in the year. The Ottawa law firm of Gowling and Henderson had been doing specialized legal work for the Export Development Corp. since 1969, but the EDC had hired Wakim's Toronto firm, Weir and Foulds, in early July after receiving a directive from trade minister James Kelleher to consider hiring new outside law firms to augment the EDC's nine-member legal staff. Most of the EDC's work arises out of financing exports and insuring exporters against nonpayment on credit purchases and requires insurance and banking lawyers. When Wakim's firm was given the $200,000 worth of work, Gowling and Henderson lost about the same amount. Gilles Ross, vice-president of services at EDC, said that the corporation had been "extremely satisfied" with Gowling and Henderson. He also said that stringent conditions had been placed on Wakim's firm, including requirements for competitive pricing and availability of expertise. That expertise was bolstered when George Windsor, a veteran Gowling and Henderson lawyer, left the firm with another lawyer to join the new Ottawa office of Weir and Foulds.

Wakim, who had roomed with Mulroney at St. Francis Xavier University in the 1950s and been a Toronto MP during the short-lived Clark regime, had made an indirect approach through a third party to join Gowling and Henderson before going to Weir and Foulds and taking his EDC account with him. In 1984, Gowling and Henderson was called by then opposition leader Mulroney and asked to consider hiring another former Tory MP, William Jarvis. The firm's board, after a heated meeting, decided not to hire Jarvis because he wanted to work as a consultant-lobbyist, not a lawyer.

In the Commons, Turner told Mulroney, "I would suggest that we bring the whole issue before the committee on privileges and find out what Sam Wakim did to peddle his wares to a number of law firms in Toronto to see whether he could get the business and then invite two members of Gowling and Henderson to leave that law firm and join him with the new business." Outside the Commons, Liberal Bob Kaplan was asked how many firms Wakin had approached. He said, "I know of three."

Mulroney flatly denied any role in securing the work for his friend. "No, I played no role in business going to that very respectable firm." He said it is normal for lawyers to go out and seek business and accused Turner of having done that very thing when he left politics for private practice. "I won't offend any legal spirits if I say that it is widely known that [Turner] didn't join McMillan Binch to write trust deeds . . . all lawyers try to get business. What is wrong with that?" Turner angrily denied he had ever sought government business as a private lawyer and again called for a full airing of the Wakim affair, but Mulroney wouldn't budge. Wakim's name also came up later in the Oerlikon affair (via the records of secretay Shirley Walker during the 1986 Sinclair Stevens inquiry) as allegedly having tried to set up a meeting between Stevens and Oerlikon, the Swiss-based arms manufacturer, almost a year before that firm got a $600 million federal defence contract.

All this didn't seem to harm the close personal friendship between Wakim and Mulroney. In February 1987, Mulroney threw a surprise birthday party for Wakim at 24 Sussex Drive, making him one of the few lobbyists ever to enjoy a personal party at the prime minister's residence. But then, what are friends for?

In September 1985, Canadian Press reported from files obtained through the Access to Information Act that forty-six law firms or individuals lawyers had collected more than $500,000 each as special prosecutors or legal agents for the justice department during the previous fiscal year. That didn't leave much of the $12.2 million in legal business for anybody else. Many lawyers on the 1984–85 list had Liberal connections, having just finished up work given them by the previous Liberal regime. But the post-election list began coming up decidedly Tory.

In October, energy minister Pat Carney dismissed as a "sleazy suggestion" from NDP critic Lorne Nystrom that the Petro-Canada accounting contract went to Arthur Andersen and Co. because twenty of the firm's partners had each given $1,000 to the Tories (and $300 to the Liberals). According to Melvin Berg, a partner in the Toronto office, it was simply "an interesting coincidence" that so many similar amounts were given by so many partners.

A week later, Nystrom was at it again, revealing that Tories in P.E.I. had set up a system whereby Conservatives would get seven days' notice of public service job openings, but that the system had been abandoned as too hot to handle politically. Nystrom said that patronage chief Peter White had set up the system at a September 10 high-level meeeting and that it was abandoned on October 25 after word was leaked by angry insiders to outside critics. The idea was to weed Liberals out of the public service there, where the veterans' affairs department is located.

In October, former MP William Jarvis, who had not been hired after Mulroney's call on his behalf to Gowling and Henderson, was given two contracts from the Privy Council Office. The first, with a ceiling of $30,000 in fees, ran from September 17, 1984, to January 17, 1985. Jarvis said he was working with then deputy prime minister Erik Nielsen on conflict-of-interest guidelines. His other contract allowed for $1 in fees and $7,999 for expenses for a one-year term, starting in January 1985, to offer ongoing advice to Nielsen. "I always wanted to be a dollar-a-year man," said Jarvis, a former minister in the Clark government, "and now I am." Another former Tory minister, E. Davie Fulton, was hired by the Department of Indian Affairs and Northern Development to investigate a land claim by a Cree Indian band in Alberta. Fulton's $137,500 contract ran for six months, from March 15 to September 16. Mulroney, of course, had once worked as an aide to Fulton.

At the same time, it was learned that Media Canada Inc., a new Toronto-based advertising agency that handles all government advertising, had three contracts with Employment and Immigration worth $712,515, seven contracts with National

Health and Welfare worth $554,859 and one with Environment Canada for $2,337. The firm is owned by Roger Nantel, another Mulroney inner-circle pal, who directed communications for him in Quebec during the election, and by Peter Simpson, an Ontario Tory strategist. The company also receives a commission for government advertising contracts it places with other firms.

Decima Research Ltd., run by Tory pollster Allan Gregg, was on the receiving end of two modest contracts, one three-week stint from Consumer and Corporate Affairs for $34,500 in late 1984 and one for $50,000 from Employment and Immigration to poll public reaction to possible changes in unemployment insurance. Another Tory, former Northwest Territories leader George Braden, was given a four-month contract for $13,500 by the Department of Indian Affairs. Heward Grafftey, once the only Tory MP in Quebec, and Paul Curley, former national director of the party, also won small contracts.

In the two weeks between September 26 and October 10, 1985, cabinet made 145 appointments. Paul Creaghan, former New Brunswick justice minister, who resigned during a 1977 scandal over allegations that the Tories were collecting kickbacks from contractors who got government business, became a Court of Queen's Bench judge; Alfred Landry of Moncton, long-time president of the party there, also became a judge; Robert Campbell of St. Andrew's, who had handled communications for Premier Richard Hatfield, became a temporary member of the War Veterans Allowance Board; Fintan Aylward, senior partner in a major St. John's law firm, a long-time Tory and a former law partner of John Crosbie, was made a judge of the trial division, Newfoundland Supreme Court; Peter Georgakakos, a defeated Tory candidate in Quebec, was made chairman of the board of referees for UIC claims for the Quebec regional division; former Ontario Tory cabinet minister James Snow was named chairman of the newly created Civil Aviation Tribunal; Olive MacPhail, an aide to former Manitoba premier Sterling Lyon, also became an unemployment-insurance referee; Fred Dunbar, a Regina lawyer who lost as a provincial conservative candidate in 1975 became a UIC chairman, as did local Tory activist William Smit in Moose Jaw.

When Liberal Don Boudria complained that this was a bit much, deputy prime minister Erik Nielsen said that if he "were doing his job properly, instead of whining about appointments that are made, he would be making recommendations to the government with respect to those that he would like to see appointed."

The year changed, but the methods didn't. During the first week of 1986, Lorraine Duguay, a Montreal lawyer and former journalist, was appointed to a three-year term on the CBC board of directors. What the official release from communications minister Marcel Masse didn't mention was Duguay's political and personal connections. She was defeated by Liberal Jacques Guilbault in the Montreal riding of St. Jacques in 1984, despite the personal involvement of Mila Mulroney and Brian's mother, Irene. (In August 1984, Mulroney's mother visited Roman Catholic Auxiliary Bishop Andre Cimichella's palace on behalf of Duguay's campaign; Mila urged more women to join the political process during a $50-a-head fundraiser for Duguay in July 1984; and Mila's parents, the Pivnickis, accompanied Duguay to a meeting with a Hungarian social organization.)

On January 11, Mulroney named former justice minister E. Davie Fulton and former Ontario cabinet minister Bob Welch to three-year terms on the International Joint Commission. Three days later, he appointed Consiglio Di Nino, a senior Tory organizer in Metro Toronto, as chairman of Harbourfront. Di Nino, president of Cabot Trust, was to oversee a hundred-acre site stretching along Toronto's waterfront and containing more than a dozen condominium, commercial, and institutional developments. What was different about this appointment was that Toronto Liberals John Nunziata and Sergio Marchi both praised it. "It is significant that Mulroney named an ethnic person to the post because he has fared poorly so far in fulfilling his promise to appoint more ethnics to federal positions," said Nunziata.

In late January there was a brief kafuffle over the licence granted to a new Ottawa-based company to fish for clams near Mulgrave, off the Cape Breton coast. The story heated up briefly, but did not have a long shelf life even though several senior Tories admitted to lobbying fisheries minister Tom Siddon on behalf of one of the successful bidders, Mother Snow's Fine Foods Ltd. One of the losers, Kristan Seafoods International Inc. of Tampa, Florida, immediately filed a lawsuit disputing Mother Snow's licence. Among the principal shareholders of Mother Snow's (which was incorporated on November 7) are Ottawa businessmen Robert Van Eyk, Walter

Wainman, and Richard Logan (Logan, the controversial former chief of staff to ex-defence minister Robert Coates, now operates a local consulting company). Both Coates and revenue minister Elmer MacKay admitted lobbying Siddon on behalf of the firm but denied Liberal charges that the deal is outright patronage. Even Nova Scotia premier John Buchanan went to bat for Mother Snow's. Siddon admitted that he too had talked to Logan about giving Mother Snow's the licence, but said he hadn't known of Logan's interest in the firm. What's more, Siddon said he thought Logan was still working for Coates. (Logan had resigned, along with Coates and another aide, over their controversial visit to a West German strip club.) The opposition pointed out that it constituted a conflict of interest for the revenue minister to lobby on behalf of a principal shareholder (Dennis Snow of Halifax) who owed Revenue Canada several thousand dollars in outstanding court judgments. The opposition demanded MacKay's resignation, but didn't get it. Deputy prime minister Erik Nielsen promised "action" if it could be proved that MacKay had lobbied on the company's behalf. (Siddon had already admitted that that had happened, and MacKay himself had openly admitted that Logan had approached him to speak to Siddon about the licence.) Nielsen did not specify what "action" he might take. He took none.

Late that January, an official for then tourism minister Jack Murta said that a $20 million advertising blitz to lure U.S. tourists across the border would be unveiled soon. The campaign was the brainchild of Camp Associates, then owned by senior Tory strategist Norman Atkins, and the firm would earn about $4 million for devising it. The official said that Mulroney had personally approved the plan to brag about the cheap Canadian dollar. The theme is "Canada—A World Next Door."

Also in January, Mulroney's office released new salary schedules for high-level patronage appointees. There were increases of as much as $45,000 for those at the top end of the scale. The biggest salary range increase went to VIA Rail chairman Lawrence Hanigan, a Montreal friend of Mulroney, whose range increased to between $130,000 and $160,000 from its 1984 level of $97,000 to $114,260. Petro-Canada chairman Wilbert Hopper was eligible for a $300,000 cash payment from subsidiary or associated companies, and his salary range went up markedly to between $414,000 and

$435,000 a year. Petro-Can's president Edward Lakusta would have to get by with a range of between $397,000 and 414,260. Canadian National chairman J. Maurice Le Clair saw his range increase more than $45,000 to between $260,000 and $325,000. Air Canada president Pierre Jeanniot received an increase to between $200,000 and $250,000, and Bank of Canada governor Gerald Bouey's salary went up to between $120,000 and $150,000. CBC head Pierre Juneau, whose corporation imposed severe budget restraints on its staff last year, saw his salary increase to the same as Bouey's, up from between $97,090 and $114,260.

In the wake of Mulroney's appointments of labour leader Dennis McDermott as Canada's ambassador to Ireland, Jean-Paul Delisle, president of the Professional Association of Foreign Service Officers, the group representing Canada's diplomats, said that Mulroney had made more political diplomatic appointments in the past seventeen months than Pierre Trudeau had made in eleven years. In a letter to Mulroney dated January 29, 1986, Delisle wrote, "The apparently accelerated rate of such appointments calls into question your personal commitment, as well as that of your government, to the continuation of a professional career foreign service." The group said that Mulroney had made twelve political appointments since assuming power, while Trudeau had made eight between 1968 and 1984 and six between 1980 and 1984, three of which were revoked by Mulroney before the appointees got to their destinations. Mulroney's political appointments were: Roy McMurtry, high commissioner to Britain; J.G. Rowsome, counsellor in the Canadian high commission in London; Lucien Bouchard (whom Mulroney biographer L. Ian MacDonald described as the "only one who could see into Brian Mulroney's soul"), ambassador to France; Yoland Guerard, official with the Canadian cultural centre in Paris; Bruce Phillips, public-affairs counsellor in Washington; Stephen Lewis, United Nations ambassador; Pierre Lucas, consul general in Philadelphia; Joan Winsor, consul general in Los Angeles; Chris Pearson, deputy consul general in Dallas; Lloyd Francis, ambassador to Portugal; Douglas Roche, Canadian disarmament ambassador; and, of course, McDermott.

On March 9, the *Toronto Star* reported that Tories had been ordered hired as census commissioners in Ontario and Quebec even though many had failed miserably on the tests given to prospective candidates. They were hired on orders from supply and services minister Stewart McInnes, even though in some cases candidates scored in the 20s on the test (a passing grade is 60 per cent). Tony De Joseph, former Cochrane-Superior (Ontario) Conservative Riding Association president, admitted that he had nominated both himself and his wife as census commissioners. He later withdrew because of prior commitments, but his wife was ordered hired even though she failed her test and did not perform well in her interview. Census commissioners began their training on April 1 and were to work until mid-July. They were paid $5,500. Liberal Don Boudria's comment was: "This is flagrant abuse. It's not just that they're hiring Tories, they're hiring unqualified Tories. . . ."

Earlier that same week, youth minister Andrée Champagne had admitted under heavy Commons fire that she had signed a secret letter calling for taxpayers' money to be used to lure young people to the Conservative party, and MP Marcel Tremblay wrote a letter suggesting that untendered federal contracts should go to companies that support the Conservatives.

Asked about all this, Nipissing Tory MP Moe Mantha complained that his riding, a longtime Liberal stronghold, still has Liberals in all the key jobs. "This patronage thing is here to stay," said Mantha. "I'd be an idiot to put a New Democrat in something up here, but I can't get my people in here because the Liberals are all still here."

In March, Peter White left the PMO as chief patronage dispenser and was replaced by veteran party organizer Marjorie LeBreton. White's departure was quick and somewhat mysterious, although one insider said, "It certainly wasn't planned. He asked Mulroney to make some decisions to allow the thing to keep moving, but the Boss was worried about the political fall-out, so White just up and walked out."

In May, public works minister Roch LaSalle admitted to being puzzled that almost 90 per cent of federal contracts in Quebec were awarded without public tenders, but quickly added that things had been no different under the Liberals. "Why are we considered so wicked for doing something the Liberals did for thirty years?" Of 519 contracts awarded by LaSalle's ministry between September 1984 and May 1985, 86.5 per cent were awarded without public tenders. Contracts under $30,000 need not be tendered. Of the approximately 2,200 contracts in excess of that, 1,000 were let without tender. "When I saw the report Friday, I asked myself why there was such a difference" between Quebec's figures and those for other provinces, LaSalle said. (This was the same week during which Sinclair Stevens resigned as industry minister, Montreal Conservative MP Michel Gravel was charged with fifty counts of influence-peddling, and Montreal-area Tory Robert Toupin decided to cross the floor and sit as an independent—he later went to the NDP, giving that party its first-ever sitting member in Quebec.)

One reason why the Quebec numbers might have been different from those in other provinces is that Mulroney's Tories had instituted a system to control patronage from Ottawa, taking it away from local riding associations. As Montreal *Gazette* journalist Claude Arpin noted, after the election "they got rid of all the old-time Tories in the ridings." According to Arpin, the Tories who had been around for years, "knew how the system worked and would always say, 'Well, wait a minute, I have a friend here I promised a job.' They wanted to do patronage from the riding level, but the PMO said, 'No, no, that's too cumbersome. We know who gets what jobs and who deserves what. We're going to do it.'" In ridings like Longueuil on the south shore, "they kicked out four old-timers and had the riding association elect twenty-five people who knew nothing about politics, nothing about patronage. It looked democratic to have twenty-five people elected by the membership, but what in fact you're doing is you're putting in people who are neophytes, they don't even know that patronage exists. So that way, you have patronage being imposed on the riding from Ottawa and you have better control of things because you're not dictated to by the people at the riding level.

"The Liberals were just as bad. In 1984 they were sending cheques from Regional Economic Expansion, DRIE today, to bagmen in various ridings under the guise of a project being erected," said Arpin, "but that money was used to finance the elections of a number of ridings. I've never been able to prove this, but the Tories know about it and they're saving it for the next election campaign."

In July 1984, *Globe* reporter Graham Fraser went to Manicouagan to talk to these traditionally Liberal voters about their local Tory candidate, Brian Mulroney. "I'll never forget speaking to a hardware-store owner in a shopping centre in

Sept-Iles. I asked the guy how he was going to vote. He began by going on at some length about what a terrific MP [André] Maltais was and how he had always been a Liberal and he thought Maltais deserved to be in cabinet and he couldn't understand why Turner hadn't made him a minister.

"And then he said you've got to realize the importance in this riding of having a prime minister. How Diefenbaker put Prince Albert on the map. It would be like having an industry in the riding. And part way through this virtual speech on how important it would be to have a prime minister in the riding he said 'Now of course, I haven't seen the data from the west yet,' and it became clear that the guy was making an investment decision," said Fraser. ". . . Now he wasn't going to spend as much time looking at data before deciding whether to open another branch of the hardware store, but it was an investment decision, and certainly when the polling data showed Mulroney was going to win there's no question in my mind that that guy say it coming and he wanted to be on the winning side."

Clearly, many voters in Mulroney's riding saw it the same way—an investment decision, or, like the man said, like having an industry in the riding.

Well, much of that industry, that investment, came by way of patronage, and it didn't take long to start paying dividends, both in Mulroney's riding in particular and Quebec in general. In June 1986, Claude Arpin reported in the *Gazette* that airports at three small villages in Mulroney's riding were about to become equipped with multi-million-dollar instrument-landing systems that even airports with ten times the air traffic didn't have.

The airport in Baie-Comeau, Mulroney's home town, was slated for a $6.1 million facelift over three years. At the Pabos gravel-strip runway in the Gaspé, where planes are so infrequent that Statistics Canada doesn't bother to keep track of them, work would soon begin on the first stage of a $2.5 million renovation program. Transport Canada, in fact, planned to spend $43.6 million on small Quebec airports in 1985–86, and another $31.3 million for 1986–87, despite the fact that secondary runways aren't used as much as they were a decade ago. In Quebec, roughly 100 of the province's 155 airstrips are managed by municipalities. The *Gazette* contacted 50 and found an "airport development committee" at each one, "usually under the guidance of the local Progressive

Conservative MP." In Mulroney's riding alone, 7 small airports are slated for a total of $6.5 million in grants in 1986–87, and $12.7 million, or 40 per cent of Quebec's total allotment, the following year. Tiny Manicouagan villages like Chevery, Blanc Sablon, and Natashquan are receiving the costly ($1.2 million) Local/Distance Measuring Equipment (LOC/DME) instrument-landing systems. Statistics Canada estimates that air traffic at Chevery is about 2,000 aircraft movements a year. St. Catharines, Ontario, with 19,794 air movements in 1984, relies on a $150,000 non-directional beacon for its navigational aid. Forecast spending for the Baie-Comeau airport included $631,000 for a new plane taxiway, $720,000 for hangar renovations, $1,516,000 for new asphalt on existing taxiways, $450,000 to repave a road leading from the provincial highway to the airport, $721,000 for a new fence, $484,000 for runway irrigation, $641,000 for terminal expansion, $241,000 to lengthen the access road to the airport, $476,000 to lengthen a road from a nearby hotel to the airport, and $169,000 for a new computer and to trade in one truck and four other vehicles.

For those who want to visit Mulroney's riding by water, the Ottawa *Citizen* obtained documents in August 1986, showing that Mulroney's showcase $36.1 million port near Sept-Iles could be another giant white elephant, soon to be dubbed "the Mirabel" of Ports Canada. The new Pointe Noire facility won't result in more traffic because it depends on iron ore and that is declining. Government officials forecast total traffic to decrease from twenty million tonnes in 1983 to seventeen million in 1990. It was one of two Quebec ports approved by the Liberals in 1983. Jean-Luc Pepin, minister of transport at the time, told the *Citizen* it was not based on need. "Employment creation was the name of the game. It was done very much in that light." Mulroney was all too happy to keep the thing moving right along and even expand it. Under Tory rule, the original plan to close the nearby Sept-Iles facility when Pointe Noire opened was scrapped, and suddenly Sept-Iles' ancient docking facility was slated to be maintained and upgraded even though overall traffic in the area has been sinking, with 818 ships calling at the port in 1984 and only 700 in 1985. Overall, tonnage declined by one-half million tonnes between 1984 and 1985.

By September 1986, Mulroney had poured $195 million into his Manicouagan riding to build roads, ports, airports, and a prison. Visiting the small village of St. Augustine that month,

Mulroney told a cheering crowd, "You can be absolutely certain that, criticism or no criticism, Brian Mulroney as your MP and prime minister will do his damnedest to make sure you get these things." He had gone there to trot out a widow whose husband had died in 1985 after an accident with his three-wheeled all-terrain cycle. The injuries would not have been fatal had he been able to get to a hospital, but because of bad weather and no directional beacon or paved strip at the local airport, he couldn't be airlifted out until the next morning. He died in surgery. "I noticed that some people seem to think that it's funny that I would spend money on airports. I'll show you. I'll introduce you to some of the widows in this village." Experts point out that Mulroney's case is hardly iron-clad. Even large airports sometimes must close in heavy fog. Still, Karen Maurice, the widow, was brought to the school auditorium by Mulroney's brother, Gary. When Mulroney saw his brother come in with the woman, he told the locals, and more importantly the accompanying national media, "It wasn't so long ago that, at the fishing camp, young Jake Maurice used to catch the fish and I used to get my picture taken with him. Jake did all the work. And last year there was a tragic accident here, and I saw Karen coming in." Karen later broke into tears as she told reporters about her husband's death. However, the name of her husband, Brian's supposed fishing buddy, was André, not Jake.

None of Mulroney's lavish projects in his riding have raised as many hackles—or better symbolized his fall from grace—than the plan to construct a maximum-security prison at Port Cartier, a town of about 6,200 people 350 kilometers northeast of Quebec City. It is important to remember, as the prison story unfolds, that rather than accept responsibility, Mulroney has attempted to claim, despite compelling evidence to the contrary, that it was not his decision to build a prison where it is not needed and where it will cost taxpayers $41 million more than the planned Drummondville prison would have cost.

On a two-day swing through the region in June 1985, Mulroney personally announced the project, predicting that it would signal the beginning of the area's "long march back to prosperity." He said it would provide jobs for 700 people during the three-year construction period and create 260 permanent jobs and 200 additional spin-off jobs, welcome news for a town devastated in 1979 by ITT-Rayonier's closing of its pulp mill. Mulroney knew what it meant to these remote towns when their major industry closed, having personally closed the IOC plant at Schefferville. Like Schefferville's, Port Cartier's economy had collapsed with the mill. The population fell by half, and boarded-up apartments and empty store-fronts stood as stark reminders of former prosperity. The federal and provincial governments had enticed ITT-Rayonier to move into the little lumber town in 1972. Back then, the town had a civic debt of $1.5 million. By 1979, the debt was $235 million, a direct result of providing the infrastructure and support necessary to sustain a major industry and its employees. After the mill closed, 96 businesses went bankrupt, 1,350 residences were abandoned, and the town couldn't afford the $3.6 million a year necessary to service its debt. In making his announcement, Mulroney said, "This part of Canada has suffered too long from a lack of jobs." He set 1988 as the completion date (just in time for the next election), spoke of the "sophisticated modern electronic perimeter fencing," and displayed a "conceptual drawing . . . one impression of what the institution may eventually look like." Actually, it wasn't at all what the institution was to look like. The drawing he showed was of a different prison, because his hastily imposed deadline hadn't allowed time for new plans to be drawn.

Soon, however, Mulroney was claiming that the decision to build the prison in Port Cartier had not been his. He took the initial blows without flinching, and while local officials at first welcomed the news, experts in the prison system didn't. In March 1986, a coalition of thirteen groups involved in the prison field released a paper accusing Mulroney of using prisoners as political pawns and condemning them to a penal-colony exile. The paper said that the decision to build the 240-unit, $60 million prison had been based on political and economic motives, not a demonstrated penal need. According to Joshua Zambrowsky, executive director of the Canadian Criminal Justice Association, building a prison 900 kilometres from Montreal would make it virtually impossible for prisoners to maintain family ties and for the necessary training, rehabilitation, and medical support to be provided. Prohibitive travel and hotel costs would impose a "tremendous penalty" on prisoners' relatives (85 per cent of whom will be Montreal or Quebec City residents who are probably not at the top of the economic scale). Zambrowsky said the relocation would also increase the costs of lawyers, administrators, and suppliers.

On September 15, Mulroney flatly denied news reports that

he had directed the costly decision to build the prison in Port Cartier, rather than Drummondville, where the previous Liberal regime had planned to build it and where $1 million had already been spent on site preparation: Mulroney said reports that the change had been made on his orders "were full of inaccuracies." Asked to detail the errors, he could not, saying that would be done in a statement from Correctional Services later that day. Asked specifically if he had ordered the move he said angrily, "That's silly." When the departmental statement appeared, it said only that reports on the cost of the move were erroneous, and that the cost difference involved in building the prison in Mulroney's riding rather than Drummondville was $2.2 million less than the $18 million first reported. A month later, Auditor General Kenneth Dye revealed that the additional cost of the move will be $41 million.

On September 17, the *Globe* quoted a source who said that Mulroney had intervened in the decision. Mulroney retorted that "All of these matters are government decisions." The previous Liberal government, he added, had made a similar decision to build a new prison in Renous, N.B., instead of adding to an existing prison at Dorchester. "That was their decision. They didn't built it in Dorchester next to an existing prison. . . . It was the decision of another elected government to put a penitentiary in an area of Quebec [Port Cartier] with an unemployment rate in excess of 37 per cent. That was a decision made by a duly elected government. The fact is that federal installations do not, under the Constitution, all have to be built in the Golden Horseshoe" (a reference to the heavily populated, industrialized area that includes Toronto and the western end of Lake Ontario). Nobody, of course, had ever suggested the prison should go there.

When NDP leader Ed Broadbent attacked Mulroney for moving the prison, he shot back, "I didn't complain when I went down as prime minister of Canada and we arranged with General Motors to put $2 billion . . . in Broadbent's riding in Oshawa. He thought that was a good idea and so did I. There was $2 billion just flowing into, foreign investment, right into Broadbent's riding and he was just smiling as surely as if he had been the chairman of the policy committee of the Conservative party." Later, Nick Hall, a GM spokesman, said, "Well, it's confusing to us too," when asked about Mulroney's analogy. First, GM is already in Oshawa and was revamping its plant, not starting in a new location from scratch. And second, the $2 billion investment was all the company's own money. The federal government did not contribute a cent to the project.

On October 10, 1986, Liberal MP Jean Lapierre produced in the Commons confidential documents that, he said, showed conclusively that Mulroney "was directly and personally responsible for the decision to move the prison." (By this time, the $60 million total cost had jumped to $68 million.) Lapierre tabled confidential briefing notes prepared for Solicitor General James Kelleher that suggested the following response to questions about Mulroney's personal involvement: "Certainly, the Prime Minister as head of this government was involved in the decision to address the problem of regional disparity and the consideration of measures to address this serious problem." Public works minister Roch La Salle had been claiming that the choice of site was his alone. The briefing notes, which Kelleher confirmed were genuine, also contained a section suggesting he should say emphatically that "neither the Prime Minister nor any person on his staff intervened in this matter." But Kelleher had written in the margin, "Can't say this—can only say no record re Sol Gen."

Auditor General Kenneth Dye's report, released on October 21, said that Kelleher's department had neglected to tell the treasury board that there were no inmates to fill the new prison. Not only would it cost $11 million more than necessary to build the prison in Port Cartier (plus an extra $30 million over the next decade to operate it rather than at Drummondville, where most necessary services already exist), but also the government's own projections show that, even without the Port Cartier facility, there will be more than four hundred empty protective-custody cells by 1993, most of them in Eastern Canada. "The decision in 1985 to build the institution at Port Cartier cannot be justified on the basis of need," Dye said flatly. He said that the tight deadline had forced officials to circumvent normal bidding procedures on contracts and meant using blueprints prepared for a maximum-security prison being built at Donnacona, Quebec. The Port Cartier prison will therefore be maximum-security, even though such a facility is not needed. Dye also noted that the remote location ruled out a much-needed medium-security prison because the family visits afforded those kinds of inmates would be virtually impossible. He also noted that former Tory solicitor general Elmer MacKay had slipped the move past both the treasury board and Parliament by alluding to it only in a one-line reference tucked into an appendix to the otherwise detailed budget estimates used by MPs to monitor and debate government spending.

On October 24, Liberal Don Boudria told the Commons that the government had broken its own rules by allowing Simon Landry, an aide who assists Mulroney in constituency affairs, to sit on a planning board for the prison. Boudria pointed to the treasury board manual, which clearly states that members of such boards should not be representatives for individual MPs but must come from federal departments. The *Globe* reported on October 29 that the three architectural firms awarded a $4.2 million contract in 1985 to work on the prison had donated $16,947 to the Conservatives during that year, about $10,000 more than they had donated to the party a year earlier. Two days later, Port Cartier mayor Anthony Detroio told Southam News reporter Aileen McCabe, "I'm beginning to think it's not all that great having the prime minister as your MP. Maybe it's even a handicap." Detroio was worried that the fuss over the prison would make Mulroney wary of doing anything more for his Manicouagan constituency. "Now every time Brian Mulroney does anything here, he'll be watched with a magnifying glass." Detroio was grateful for the patronage that had come his way, and said that the $300,000-a-year grants in lieu of taxes from the prison might save the town from collapse. Without it, in his view, Port Cartier would have gone the way of Schefferville, Gagnon— and the Dodo bird. He admits it was "ridiculous" for Mulroney to build the prison there. "I didn't want a penitentiary. I wanted something else," he said, but added that he had been in no position to be fussy when he approached Mulroney for help in 1984. "I was willing to accept [the prison] because it was all I could get. I needed something and I needed it fast."

By December, the opposition was demanding a full-scale inquiry into the prison controversy, particularly when treasury board president Robert de Cotret had to cancel an engineering contract at the site because an investigation determined that it violated Mulroney's conflict-of-interest guidelines. The $600,000 contract with Bechtel Quebec Ltée. was ended, de Cotret said, because a Bechtel engineer, Robert McCulloch, the project manager for the prison, had been working on an exchange program at the federal correctional-services department when Bechtel was awarded the contract.

Still Mulroney refused to budge. The decision to build the prison had been fair for the region and "good for Canada," and any suggestion to the contrary was "purely insipid."

In early December 1986, career diplomat Ian Clark, who had served as Canada's permanent delegate to UNESCO in Paris since July 1983, received an overseas telephone call from a friend. It seems Canadian Press was reporting that he would be replaced by long-time Montreal mayor Jean Drapeau. Nobody had told Ian Clark, but three weeks later external affairs minister Joe Clark made it official. The ailing Drapeau, another long-time Mulroney friend, would get the $90,000-a-year posting, despite the fact that he had not run for re-election, after thirty years as mayor, because of health problems. Drapeau walks with a cane after suffering a stroke and a broken hip in 1982 and a fractured vertebra in 1985. Critics wondered aloud if he could handle a demanding overseas posting. After all, he had said when he announced his retirement that "the question I asked myself serveral times was whether I could continue. I found that I did not have the inner conviction that I would be able to complete another term."

Drapeau's family and friends dismissed these criticisms in a published interview in September, though Drapeau himself had said that some days even simple tasks like looking up a word in the dictionary or searching through a file gave him trouble. "I always have to be careful I don't drop the book or the file on the floor or it will take me half an hour just to pick them up," he said.

The Professional Association of Foreign Service Officers again complained about the partisan appointments of "amateur diplomats" and questioned Drapeau's physical ability to handle the job. But the most intriguing aspect of the appointment was the revelation by a senior external affairs official that the deal had been struck before Drapeau announced he was not seeking re-election as mayor.

About the same time, Clement Richard, another former Mulroney classmate at Laval, became the fourth former Parti Québécois partisan to get a federal appointment. Richard, long-time PQ culture minister, joined former PQ finance minister Yves Duhaime, former PQ public service minister Denis de Belleval, and pro-independent activist leader Lucien Bouchard on the federal gravy train. At the same time, three Tory women were named to the senate: Ethel Cochrane of Newfoundland, Eileen Rossiter of P.E.I., and Mira Spivak of Manitoba.

Mulroney's old school ties made news again on December 15 when *Maclean's* magazine unearthed a memo, from those presented as evidence in the Sinclair Stevens inquiry, showing that the Chase Manhattan Bank of New York had been instructed in March 1986 to find work for St. Francis Xavier alumnus Bob Shea. Shea, a member of a large family from Boston, had had three brothers at the university at the same time as Mulroney, and Mulroney still frequently visits the family. The instructions came under the terms of a proposed contract with the Canadian government. In a letter of April 29, 1986, to Nova Scotia premier John Buchanan about a thermal-energy proposal, Stevens, then industry minister, had written, "I had discussed with Bob Shea his participation in the project. Mr. Shea is quite enthusiastic with respect to involving himself." The proposed contract with the bank which was never awarded because Ottawa was unable to reach agreement with the province, would have involved consulting work on two projects in Cape Breton. The memo instructed the bank to find work for "Mr. Shay [*sic*] of Boston (a friend of the prime minister)." Shea, incidentally, was a board member of Government Consultants International, an Ottawa lobby firm headed by Frank Moores. In the Commons, Liberal Bob Kaplan called the move "blatant cronyism," but Mulroney insisted that he and his ministers had behaved "with dignity at all times. We followed the rules, the procedures, at all times." He said that the federal employee whose name appeared at the bottom of the memo [assistant deputy industry minister John McLure] had denied ever signing the document. "What kind of proof is that?" said Mulroney. *Maclean's* quoted McLure as saying that he had not been pressured to recommend Shea and that the reference in the memo to Shea's friendship with Mulroney was poor drafting. He added that he would never have signed "something like this" and had never seen the memo. However, he did concede that the matter of Shea's employment "kind of came up" once in a conversation with Shea.

There were no denials of any kind on December 29, when Mulroney elevated yet another close friend to high office. This time the beneficiary was Laval University buddy Jean Bazin, a long-time Conservative organizer in Quebec, a key player in Mulroney's leadership contests, and (with Norm Atkins) co-chairman of the Tory campaign in 1984. Norm Atkins, of course, had been named to the Senate on July 2. Opposition critics asked Mulroney to delay Bazin's appointment pending the outcome of an RCMP investigation into the Oerlikon affair. Bazin, president-elect of the Canadian Bar Association and a senior partner in the Montreal firm retained by Oerlikon, had refused to discuss with reporters his role in the awarding of the $1 billion contract to Oerlikon, saying that lawyer-client confidentiality prevented him from speaking. Mulroney refused to delay the swearing-in, and in February Bazin brought to thirty-one the number of Tories in the Red Chamber, well behind the sixty-seven Liberals, but closing fast.

By this time, even Quebec Tories were getting fed up with the patronage-infested, scandal-ridden image of Mulroney's government. On February 8, 1987, following an admission by Mulroney to his Quebec caucus that the government has a "serious perceived morality problem," the caucus recommended a flurry of reforms, including a ban on corporate political donations. Several Quebec Tories had tried that at a Conservative convention in Montreal the previous March, but the party hierarchy had blocked the move. The registration of lobbyists was also recommended. Mulroney had promised such a requirement several times both during and after the campaign, along with strict limits on campaign donations.

On January 30, 1987, Brian Boyd, interim assistant deputy minister of supply and services, sent a memo to the heads of procurement sections in his department outlining a new "contract reporting" system set up at the request of the minister, Monique Vézina. The memo said that the change would "provide material suitable for press releases and for notification to members of Parliament." The MPs Vézina had in mind, of course, were all Tories. The system requires public servants to inform officials in her department before awarding contracts worth over $25,000 in six eastern-Quebec ridings. Vézina's chief of staff, Robert Letendre, told the *Globe* that the idea is to allow the Tory MPs to be able to announce federal contracts awarded in their ridings more often. The other ridings affected are Gaspé, Matapédia-Matane, Kamouraska-Rivière-du-Loup, and Bonaventure-Iles-de-la-Madelaine.

Regions in other provinces were affected too, but the reporting thresholds were higher, ranging from $100,000 to $400,000.

In January, when Mulroney's old buddy Brian Gallery, head of the 500 Club, the party's most prestigious fund-raising group, went on a short holiday, wouldn't you know it, his fellow CNR directors elected him acting chairman of the giant Crown corporation. Mulroney had named Gallery to the board in June.

In February, the foreign-service officers were upset again at the appointment of Mulroney family friend Pierrette Lucas as consul general in Boston. It was, they said, the sixteenth political appointment to the Canadian Foreign Service, matching Pierre Trudeau's record for his entire regime. "No other Government since Confederation has made as many political appointments to the foreign service," PAFSO said in a news release. What's more, Lucas was the only Head of Post to be given a similar assignment in the wake of the closing of austerity reasons of seven Canadian posts in December. (She had been consul general in Philadelphia since 1985, but her position was declared redundant.) The other people in similar posts, all of whom had put in an average of twenty years in the public service, were either recalled to Ottawa or reassigned to more junior positions. "It is unfair and damaging to the high professional standards of the Canadian foreign service for these officers to be shunted aside to make room for persons whose main claim to appointment is political affiliation or friendship with those holding political power."

In April 1987, Ottawa's weekly tabloid, the *Sunday Herald,* itemized $358,000 worth of government contracts received by Mulroney's longtime friend Roger Nantel since 1984. Subsequent stories gave details of other contracts for his firms, Nantel and Associates of Montreal and Synchrocom Communications of Toronto. The federal contracts were discovered during routine research projects by the Ottawa firm of Access Information Consultants.

The awards included $54,626 from the Department of Regional Industrial Expansion to define the department's policies for communication with the public. Among other things, Nantel was to be paid for interviewing ministers Sinclair Stevens, Tom McMillan, and André Bissonnette, along with Ian Anderson, then director of communications in the PMO. The firm got another $50,000 from DRIE for a "special study on Minister's office," one part of which was to include an "autopsy of Domtar incident [India] as model of typical communications breakdown." That tragedy was hardly "typical" of anything. The firm got yet another $50,000 contract from DRIE to develop a communications plan for the Province of Quebec, and $25,000 from consumer minister Michel Côté to develop a communications strategy for the government's controversial patent-drug bill.

For organizing the public relations for DRIE during Export Month in Quebec, (October 1985), the firm was paid $24,600. Another $50,000 for planning and executing a government communications strategy at the regional level in Montreal was also forthcoming.

Every government department, of course, has a large, multi-million-dollar communications bureaucracy of its own. But even that provided fodder for Nantel's firm when Consumer and Corporate Affairs paid him $48,000 to prepare a report on that ministry's communications section.

He also picked up $10,000 for advising Côté "on an appropriate strategy for implementing the communications aspects of the government's policy on metric conversion," plus $41,000 in "profesional fees" from Côté and $5,000 to write a speech on language and culture for then communications minister Marcel Masse, who, of course, already had speech writers on staff.

Let us end this chapter where Brian Mulroney began his elected career, in the Nova Scotia riding of Central Nova. In 1983, of course, Elmer MacKay had stepped aside to allow Mulroney to get his first Commons seat in a safe Tory riding. In 1984, when Mulroney moved over to Manicouagan, MacKay slipped back to his old seat and won easily. He was subsequently elevated to Mulroney's cabinet, where he served as solicitor general before moving over to Revenue.

The people of Central Nova, who had voted for Mulroney in the by-election and been told he'd never forget them, had nevertheless been feeling forgotten. Their former member hadn't set foot inside the old riding since becoming prime minister. Earlier this year, he decided to send money instead. On February 25, 1987, the *Globe* reported that the federal government had awarded what treasury board and justice department officials called an "exceptional" $1 million grant to build a Nova Scotia courthouse in the riding. There are no federal programs for this kind of expenditure, and it had never been done elsewhere, despite several requests for federal help to construct court facilities.

MacKay called the unusual award "appropriate . . . judicious . . . admirable." Ron Marks, a member of the board which oversees administration of new courthouses, said that the negotiations had begun more than two years ago and that MacKay was an important part of those discussions.

CHAPTER FIFTEEN

MAN IN THE MIDDLE

It hit the national press gallery like a bomb. On November 5, 1986, *Toronto Sun* reporter Derik Hodgson wrote that two female reporters had complained that they were asked out on dates by Michel Gratton, then Mulroney's press secretary, when they attempted to arrange interviews with the prime minister.

To the public, it offered a smidgen of titillation, a whiff of sex on the Hill, and another example of Mulroney's ability to surround himself with people who are capable of loutish behaviour. But to people in the news business, particularly the press gallery, it was the hottest topic in town, the endless subject of debate, pro and con for weeks.

It brought out both the best and the worst in the media. It showed that some people, very few, are prepared to stand up against heavy intimidation, not only from the PMO but from their peers as well. And it underscored the media penchant for internal bickering, linguistic paranoia, blatant sexism, and rampant self-interest and, alas, its terrible tendency to circle the wagons under fire. For a trade that makes its living exposing the warts of the world, the media recoils in horror at those who expose its own warts.

There were as many journalists offended at Hodgson for writing about it, and at the women for complaining as there were at Gratton for being rude and unprofessional.

Some of the most senior and influential journalists in Ottawa dismissed the story out of hand—"a chicken-shit story," said *Globe* columnist Jeffrey Simpson. "A cheap shot." The CBC's popular superstar Mike Duffy even offered to intervene on

Gratton's behalf with the *Toronto Sun* to see if he could do something about it before it was published. The French-speaking reporters saw it as another Anglo attack against one of their own—Gratton, a popular former press-gallery president, had been a well-known Francophone journalist before going to Mulroney's office. Canadian Press, the national news-gathering agency, which barely misses a word that is spoken in Ottawa, refused to report the incident for several days, even though the issue was raised in the Commons and more than one of their female employees was involved. Other large newspapers—like the *Toronto Star*, the country's biggest paper—also ignored it until it became impossible to do so. Deputy prime Minister Don Mazankowski's press aide, Tom Van Dusen, a former journalist himself, called the story an example of "blind passionate hatred for the PMO."

The problem was, the story hit too close to home; it crossed the Rubicon, the unspoken, unwritten line that is drawn between the political—where all is fair in love and war—and the personal—where love is, well, personal. It made people uneasy. A story like that always does, because it might be about the guy you play squash with—some journalists have regular tournaments with cabinet ministers and other politicos—or the guy you're lunching with in the National Press Club tomorrow, or who came over to your house for dinner last week.

As much as anything else, that is what made it a good story.

The details were simple enough. CBC radio reporter Judy Morrison, married, a one-time press-gallery president who had known Gratton for years, phoned him to set up an interview with the prime minister. Rather than talk about that, Gratton said, How about a date? When Morrison brushed off the request and went back to business, Gratton asked again. He asked a third time, too, telling Morrison that if anything ever happened between her and her husband, he'd be around. Another reporter, a much younger woman, was also asked for a date under similar circumstances. She told her boss, CP bureau chief Gord Grant, about it later, but when the story broke, Grant refused to send it out, dismissing it as "of internal interest only."

Gratton admitted that he'd asked the women for dates but said he was just kidding. He is, after all, a gregarious chap. However, he wasn't sitting in a darkened corner of the press club on his personal time; he was acting as a gatekeeper between the reporters and the prime minister. Even if he was kidding—a dubious claim—he put the women on the spot. Morrison said it wasn't sexual harassment, she didn't believe Gratton was trying to trade favours for an interview—although she also said he promised an interview if she went out with him—but both women thought it was hurtful and tacky.

Gratton threatened Hodgson with a suit if he printed it. The next week, after he'd hired a lawyer, he apologized publicly.

The night before the story ran, Gratton was in the press club with Duffy having a few drinks, moaning about it. Hodgson had run the story by him and Gratton was justifiably worried that it might harm his career. Indeed, it may have. When he was fired several months later, the only real victim in what was to have been a PMO shake-up, he was in the press club blaming Hodgson and promising to get even.

Later in the evening, Don MacDonald of the Halifax *Chronicle-Herald*, a close friend of Hodgson, wandered in for a drink and sat down with Duffy and Gratton. They were still talking about the story and Duffy told MacDonald he was worried Hodgson was being set up. Then he pulled out a series of business cards, began looking through them, and pulled one out of the pack belonging to Tom MacMillan, general manager of the *Sun*. Duffy offered to phone MacMillan about the story and see if anything could be done. Gratton, to his credit, declined the offer. When the author wrote a column later about this, Duffy flatly denied he'd done it. "That isn't true to begin with. I really have no interest in getting involved in this one way or the other. I think it's all very unfortunate. See you later pal." And he hung up abruptly. MacDonald, on the other hand, swears it's true. "It happened. I was there. I was appalled that he'd try something like that."

The day after Hodgson's story hit, CP reporter Kathryn Young went to Grant, her boss, and said that Gratton had made sexual advances to her both in a taxi cab and in her apartment two years earlier, after they'd shared a ride home from the press club. "I was a junior reporter at the time. . . . I wanted the whole thing to go away." She was prompted to speak out after hearing some Conservative MPS and fellow reporters laughing when New Democrat MP Margaret Mitchell raised the matter in the Commons. She said she was tired of the "good-old-boy" attitude of her colleagues and the government.

Press-gallery president Leslie Shepherd said that other women had complained about Gratton, but that no others had ever come forward publicly. Little wonder. Both Young and Morrison were subjected to incredible criticism from reporters.

A CP reporter had written stories about the issue—which had by now been picked up by some radio and TV stations, but was completely boycotted by the Quebec media—but the wire service still wouldn't tell their client newspapers what was happening and let them judge, as they normally do, whether it was a story or not. Finally, on the third day, Mitchell accused Gratton of "unprofessional, sexist conduct" and called for an investigation. Even CP couldn't ignore that, and the story moved late on the Friday afternoon, still getting good play in Saturday papers.

While this was going on, the press-gallery executive was having a fit. Morrison had been upset enough about the incident to complain to her producer at the time, and when it became public, CBC English radio chief Michael Enright fired off a letter to the PMO demanding an apology. Leslie Shepherd felt that the gallery had to take action, so she phoned seven of the ten executive members and got their approval to send a letter of protest to Mulroney's chief of staff, Bernard Roy. Shepherd, who was leaving for England in two days, was in a hurry to arrange a meeting between the executive, Roy, and Mulroney's senior aide Fred Doucet.

She sent the letter, but when Quebec columnist Michel Vastel, then with La Presse, found out about it, he submitted his resignation as treasurer, claiming it was a deliberate snub by Shepherd of French-speaking executive members. Of the ten members, three were French. Both Vastel and director Gilbert Dupuis were not reached, but vice-president Patrick Crampont was. "To me it [Shepherd's snub] was deliberate," Vastel said. "She deliberately avoided the opinion of minority members, and I deliberately use the word deliberate."

If this seems odd to you, it's only because you haven't worked in Ottawa, where the French-English division rivals the Grand Canyon, and where the French minority in particular see every story, every action in the context of their cultural bias. It would not have hurt Shepherd to call, but she was in a hurry, had a majority anyway, and got sloppy with Vastel's well-known hypersensitivity on this score.

The gallery executive met with Doucet and Roy and emerged from the meeting to announce that both sides had agreed not to comment. When Hodgson, who was also on the executive at the time (as was Kathryn Young), was interviewed on CBC radio about the affair, gallery vice-president Patrick Crampont called him up to tell him to stop talking to the media. On November 11, six days after the original story, Gratton apologized in writing to both Morrison and Young.

Globe columnist George Bain, who often comments on current press-gallery practices from his vantage point in Nova Scotia, wrote as far as he could tell, Gratton had not done "anything more reprehensible than be his somewhat macho self."

"Perhaps that's just the trouble," wrote respected Southam columnist Don McGillivray. "Macho conduct that once was greeted with a wink and a shrug—at least by men—is no longer as acceptable, especially by women."

Morrison says that when she first came to the Hill in 1973 for Newsradio, there were stations that wouldn't use her reports because "I was a woman, and women just didn't report serious news then. They'd take my reports, 'rewrite' them word for word, and have a male newsreader read them." That has changed, but not everything else has. The gallery is still predominantly a male bastion—263 to 55. In Canada's centennial year, the gallery had 122 men and just 4 women members. By 1977 it was 177 to 30; in 1980, 196 to 41. "If you look at the newsrooms today and the journalism schools they are dominated by women," said Morrison. "But that sure isn't reflected in this place. It's still pretty much a male sanctuary."

The gallery has had only two women presidents—Morrison in 1984 and Shepherd in 1986—but neither was actually elected; both stepped up from vice-president when the president quit. Ironically, in Morrison's case, she got to be president when Gratton left to work for Mulroney.

Brian Mulroney had a golden opportunity to get good press. And for a while, he did. After all—forgetting about the brief regime of John Turner, which everybody does—Mulroney followed Pierre Trudeau, a man whose disdain for the media equalled his disdain for the general public. And in both cases, the feelings were mutual.

But Mulroney, a mediaphile who just can't get enough of reading about himself or watching himself on TV, has never been able to adjust to the press gallery, where everybody does not applaud his every word and deed. Montreal *Gazette* journalist Claude Arpin, who has covered Mulroney for a decade, says that when Mulroney was closing down Schefferville in 1983, "even then, he talked about the Ottawa press gallery, how, should he go on to win the leadership he'd have trouble with them. He knew they wouldn't be subservient. He knew then. It's all part of his psyche of how far back you go with him. He knew the English media in Ottawa were, well, from Toronto, and he didn't know them. They didn't know him. But he did all right at first, until they did get to know him."

"It was the same with the Canadian people," Arpin believes. "It took them a while to catch on. We wrote it. We reported that he said he'd give every Tory a job, every friend of his would get a promotion somewhere, and they didn't believe us. Now they do."

During his successful leadership bid and the subsequent election, Mulroney worked hard at expanding his already extensive network of reporters whom he phoned on a regular basis. He also tried to get journalists onside by promises of favours. One of his most common was to offer them a swim in the pool at 24 Sussex Drive after he had won the election. "He was promising everybody a swim in the pool," said Southam's Peter Maser. "He offered me a swim, then a week later he said to me, 'Not only will you have a swim, but you'll have a towel there with your fucking name on it.'" In 1984, when Mulroney and a small group of journalists were sitting around one night in the Auberge du Gouverneur in Sherbrooke, the question of the pool came up again and Mulroney offered them all what he called a "Manicouagan Fuck-You Call." As Maser explains, "You go for a swim in the pool, you get out, you get on the phone to anybody in the country, the person you hate most, and you say, 'I've just been for a swim in the prime minister's pool, so fuck you.' Then you hang up. He promised a lot of people that, but I don't think any of us ever got invited to the pool."

Steward MacLeod sees Mulroney as a throwback to the pre-Trudeau days. "Trudeau insulted us, told us off constantly. It took guts to stand up at a Trudeau press conference and ask a question because if it didn't challenge him intellectually, he thought it was stupid and he would say so. Nobody likes to be put down in front of a TV audience. So while Trudeau intimidated us, Mulroney was a throwback . . . to the old-time, swaggering politico . . . there was something like ten press conferences in a row where Mulroney would trot out all his job-creation statistics. There's a hell of a difference in being used as a Trudeau studio audience . . . for put-down purposes [and being] used as a launching pad for all that hyperbole. Even though we didn't like Trudeau, and he didn't like us, there was respect. . . . Mulroney tried to get everybody to like him and in the process he not only failed at that, he didn't earn much respect."

Mulroney loves to be praised, but he can't handle criticism and refuses to grant interviews to journalists he doesn't like. On the other hand, those he does like not only get interviews, they are called from time to time, fed stories by Mulroney officials, and generally praised as responsible and fair in their coverage. Favourites such as George Bain and Dougas Fisher, for example, have no problems getting direct access. And even when interviews are granted to a particular news organization, Mulroney stipulates in advance which reporters from that organization are acceptable to him and which reporters aren't acceptable.

It is not hard to tell when Mulroney dislikes a journalist. In St. John's, Newfoundland, at a scrum following a cabinet session there, Canadian Press reporter Tim Naumetz asked Mulroney a policy question but, rather than answer, Mulroney just glared at him, turned around, and walked away, ending the scrum on the spot. During the 1984 election, a herd of journalists had Mulroney surrounded and the Star's Bob Hepburn, who was leaning right against Mulroney in the crush, asked him to react to a major policy announcement from John Turner. "He just looked straight ahead and said nothing. So I asked him again. Still nothing. It was quite bizarre. For about thirty seconds everybody was standing there waiting for his answer, saying nothing, until finally when it became obvious he wasn't going to answer, somebody else threw another question at him," said Hepburn.

On CBC's "Media File," Mike Duffy has said that the Liberals were "very clever" about their media relationships. "The prime minister pretended he didn't watch the news or read or listen to the news on radio and his staff were always courteous and polite and rarely ever engaged in any kind of debate with journalists about their kinds of coverage. The Conservatives have a quite different approach. They feel that if their point of view is not represented the way they think it should be they have no hesitation to call, to confront the journalist directly and make their complaints known. . . . part of the reason [this approach] is resented by the press gallery is the result of the fact they hired journalists to become their press agents. Someone that you covered the campaign trail with. . . . who is suddenly on the other side of the fence and who adopts a very partisan line does their own credibility some harm and strains relations with members of the media. . . ."

Graham Fraser of the *Globe and Mail* says that Mulroney got a better shake with the media on the 1984 election campaign than John Turner did because of "an ecology that favoured him over Turner. Once Mulroney decided he was going to run in Manicouagan every major news organization had to assign a bilingual reporter to the plane, if not all the time, at least when Mulroney was in Quebec. At that point, most of the bilingual reporters had worked in Montreal . . . they knew Mulroney personally; or, if they didn't, they felt at least some sense of being able to identify with an English Montrealer who was doing pretty well."

Fraser says the media, like most Canadians, felt it was time the Liberals lost. As well, Turner had come back to a press corps he didn't know any more: "To the extent that the press corps knew Turner at all, they knew him as someone Allan Fotheringham wrote about having lunch at Winston's and waiting to be crowded prime minister. . . . But a substantial number of reporters who went to Manicouagan with Mulroney had spent some time with him, had drinks with him or had known him from the Cliche Commission. That inevitably created a more favourable climate of reporting . . . more favourable than Mulroney himself ever got or has ever got from the Ottawa press gallery, because with virtually no exceptions, there are few people in Ottawa who go back with Mulroney at all, who have a personal relationship with him. If anything, they saw him as an outsider. . . ."

Mulroney got off to a bad start with the press gallery when he and some of his ministers, notably Joe Clark, ordered bureaucrats never to talk to the media. Mulroney himself refused to hold news conferences, despite formal pleas from the press-gallery executive. Clark ordered his staff not to socialize with journalists even though Mulroney had attacked the Liberals during the campaign for their "secrecy, stealth, and stonewalling."

· Of course, while journalists complain about secrecy, they play the game themselves. During the campaign, for example, when Ottawa *Citizen* reporter Neil MacDonald reported Mulroney's "no whore like an old whore" quip from the plane, many journalists were furious—not with Mulroney, but with MacDonald, for quoting from what many of them unhappily considered an off-the-record conversation. The fact is, journalists never consider anything off the record unless it is explicitly agreed in advance. But, like anybody else, there's a certain amount of guilt if reporters find themselves sucked in the way they did with Mulroney's hyperbole. There is also considerable jealousy in the press gallery, a tendency when one reporter writes or broadcasts a good story, for many reporters to dump on it rather than congratulate the reporter. In April 1987, for example, when the *Globe's* Stevie Cameron wrote about Mulroney's fifty pairs of Guccis and other excessive spending habits, the dominant view was to dismiss the story as "cheap and sensational," although reporters know that this sort of story has far more impact on ordinary Canadians than long, thoughtful analysis pieces about the national debt or constitutional change.

In November 1984, Clark told a group of Alberta businessmen that "a very powerful élite" of journalists and academics and public servants were out to thwart the Tories. Even Mulroney recognized how paranoid and silly the speech was and gave Clark a dressing down. A few days later, Mulroney released a new set of guidelines for public servants in their dealings with the media, cancelling some of the previous gag orders but imposing a new one that ordered public servants to speak to journalists only on the record. That way, of course, public servants would not dare criticize government actions for fear of being fired once their names and quotes were published.

Whenever Mulroney travelled, he had videotaped newscasts and transcripts of newspaper stories dispatched to him on a daily basis. He couldn't bear to overlook anything written about him, and he couldn't stop getting angry when the reviews were bad. For a man who consistently personalized his attacks on his political opponents, Mulroney just as consistently complained about "mean-spirited . . . personal attacks" on him by the media. In a June 1985 interview, he said, "It is sad to realize that we have become subjected to all kinds of possible attacks, all kinds of personal criticisms, aimed at a family life that has now become open to the public."

Meanwhile "friendly" journalists were rewarded with interviews. Columnist Douglas Fisher, for example, had Mulroney on his show on Ottawa's CJOH-TV twice during a four-month period in 1985 when most organizations couldn't get in the door. In one of those interviews, Fisher began by apologizing to Mulroney for having cricitized him when he first arrived in Ottawa and added, "Well, that's where you turned out to be so bloody good. . . . I didn't think anybody could come in and do as well there." Mulroney was unable to deny the greatness Fisher had bestowed upon him.

In a September 1985 interview with Global TV, Mulroney said, "I personally enjoy the company of many members of the media." No doubt he included his three interviewers—Peter C. Newman, Peter Trueman, and Douglas Small—whose annual get-togethers with Mulroney on the lawn at 24 Sussex Drive are embarrassingly syrupy. At one of those sessions, former Global news boss Roy Heard joined his staff and the prime minister for coffee and cookies after the interview. "Mulroney was just raving about the media," said Heard, "quoting verbatim from columns which had been written months earlier criticizing him. It bothered him that much. I couldn't believe it. For a guy who's so absolutely taken by the media, he doesn't understand how it works."

In early 1986, Mulroney's officials announced what was to be a new communications strategy—getting their man out of Ottawa and away from the "hostile media" they claimed reported only scandals and ignored the government's "positive" achievements. On his first trip under the new strategy, in Halifax on February 2, Mulroney was met by about 150 angry demonstrators, from his old Central Nova riding, who accused him of lying to them when he said he would never forget them for electing him.

The other problem was that when local media learned of the strategy, they resented the implication that they were viewed by Ottawa as no-account hicks who, unlike the National Press Gallery, could be conned. As a result, many of those interviews backfired, and the new strategy was quickly abandoned.

In 1987, after a furious series of scandals, the Tories jumped all over the media when a few reporters, caught up in the rush for the latest twist in the Tory decline, went too far. Mulroney and his aides were constantly telephoning senior personnel at media organizations complaining about their coverage, and when mistakes were made, the pressure began to have some impact. At Canadian Press, for example, PMO pressure resulted in a new policy whereby stories critical of the government had to be cleared through the Toronto head office first instead of by senior personnel in Ottawa before being sent across the country. Even then, the *Globe and Mail* became upset with CP's aggressive—and, for the most part, solid—news gathering and wrote complaining that CP was breaking too many news stories. According to the *Globe*, CP should have been content to cover committee meetings and question period, and leave investigative journalism to others—presumably the *Globe*.

Stories of PMO pressure against many organizations, including the *Toronto Sun*, the *Toronto Star*, the CBC, and the Montreal *Gazette*, were circulating the gallery in early 1987, while cabinet ministers and Tory MPs launched a series of speeches in which complaints of unfair media coverage became standard fare. At the same time, Mulroney's crony Pat MacAdam began sending out regular "good news" batches to various reporters, in which he collected all the "positive" stories about Mulroney—or "negative" ones about the Liberals and the NDP—and mailed them to press-gallery members. Also about that time, Mulroney's Tories hit 22 per cent in the Gallup poll, the all-time low for a sitting government, which suggests that the press gallery was not alone in its general lack of enthusiasm for Mulroney's performance.

Underlining the Tory attack on the media was the charge that the press gallery acts as a "pack," as a cohesive unit that somehow decides as a group what approach it will take and then goes out to prove the correctness of its decision. Since the media generally is held in the same disregard as politicians, it is not difficult to convince people that this pack mentality exists. Indeed, to some extent, it does exist, although not in any formal, organized way.

If, for example, a cabinet minister resigns, then all the journalists in Ottawa would have that resignation as the main story—not because they met as a group and decided that that was the story, but simply because it's news. That's the nature of the beast, particularly during elections when political parties stage-manage the "news" by feeding reporters a daily Gaines-burger—usually in a setting that is good for TV pictures, and in plenty of time for the evening news—leaving little but the managed event to report. What's more, if a reporter from, say, the *Toronto Sun* decided to ignore the "event," while his competitor with the *Toronto Star* did report it, the *Sun* reporter would have some explaining to do to his editors.

While journalists decry secrecy in government, and most other places, they are not above some gag rules of their own. In late 1986, for example, the National Press Club bulletin reminded members that things said in the club can not be reported. "Some conversations have been repeated, with no authority from others involved. Let's have it known now that the Executive will not, repeat not, tolerate such abuses." A similar note from a government agency would be a front-page story and subject to violent attack by most of the gallery's daily columnists.

The French-English split in the gallery also affects the way stories are, or are not, reported. When both Mulroney and Erik Nielsen, for example, suggested that English reporters were being "racist" for criticizing former environment minister Suzanne Blais-Grenier, the Quebec media jumped all over the story—as Mulroney and Nielsen knew they would—accepting the groundless criticism as true, and ignoring the fact that the same English media hadn't exactly been kind to such ministers as Bob Coates, Elmer MacKay, and John Fraser.

Veteran Quebec TV journalist Michel Guenard says the French-speaking reporters focus on Quebec by definition, since that's their market, and that they have "a tendency to represent the cultural bias of the tribe. It's in your blood . . . all minorities operate on the premise of black-mailing the majority. It's fundamental, and the Quebec reporters on the Hill are reflecting that reality."

When Sinclair Stevens, who is unilingual English, was industry minister, the Quebec media constantly hammered him, assuming that someone who wouldn't learn the language was anti-French. Stevens really took a beating when Mulroney sent him to Montreal to announce the closure of an east-end oil refinery, a move that had become a major story in Quebec.

Despite the constant carping from the Tories that the press gallery as a group has been unfair to them, some journalists argue that they've received better coverage than they deserve.

According to Ottawa *Citizen* columnist Roy McGregor, "You can't rule out stupidity with these people. For the first while, when they kept messing everything up, everybody was looking for a reason and they were getting off lightly. But after a while, it became clear that these [PMO] people are stupid, plain and simple."

"You look at a guy like Fred Doucet and figure he's smart because he has a Ph.D. Well, look at the way he acts, the advice he gives and it soon becomes clear he's not smart. The same with [Bill] Fox. I've known Fox a long time as a journalist and he's got some good qualities. But I don't think he's as smart as I am, and I wouldn't want to be in the position of a senior adviser for a prime minister," (Fox, who in spite of his ability to be charming had alienated a lot of his old journalist friends by using bully-boy tactics, left the PMO suddenly in late April 1987, after an argument with the newly appointed chief of staff Derek Burney over who controlled access to the prime minister.)

An Angus Reid poll in March conducted for Southam News showed that 65 per cent of respondents across the country felt that the news coverage of Mulroney's government troubles had been fair, as compared to 22 per cent who said it was unfair, roughly the same percentage who were still backing the Tory government in other opinion polls.

Senator Lowell Murray agrees that "something has to be done" about the relationship between the government and the parliamentary press gallery. "It has to be put on a more professional footing. I don't know just what the problem is, but it sure as hell is a mutually venomous attitude, almost as bad— if not worse—than it was in the worst of the Trudeau years.

"Sure, you have to allow for some professional tension which is always going to exist between the two . . . but, oh God, the relationship seems absolutely poisonous. . . . I don't know how it can be done, but one way is to take the political and strategical and tactical role away from the press office and leave them to deal with the very factual, above-the-fray kind of relationship . . . the current relationship is sadly lacking. Dief's went sour too, Trudeau's went sour very quickly, Pearson's didn't. Somehow, he managed to keep some kind of professional relationship, and Clark did, in his way. He got a bad rap for a while, all that stuff about his luggage getting lost, then there was some guilt feeling on the part of the gallery to make up for this over time. But the relationship was not terrible between Clark and the gallery at the worst of times, not as bad as it is now."

One of the things Mulroney did to improve that relationship was to invite the press gallery members and their families to an outdoor barbeque at 24 Sussex Drive in July. Most journalists accepted the invitation and had a good time. That was followed by a flurry of stories about how Mulroney was making a comeback even though there was no evidence in the opinion polls to show that.

When Gratton was fired early in 1987 and Fox was kicked upstairs as a senior adviser to Mulroney—leaving the PMO altogether a few months later—public servant Marc Lortie was named press secretary and former Ottawa CTV star Bruce Phillips was brought in from Washington, where he'd been Ambassador Allan Gotlieb's chief flack, to be director of communications. Lortie's appointment was generally applauded in the gallery, but Phillips gave an early indication it was going to be business as usual when news of his appointment was leaked by the PMO to a few friendly reporters and the news release was delivered about 10:00 P.M. to the press gallery, long after everyone had gone home.

What it meant was that, instead of starting all over and generating goodwill, the PMO had forced most gallery reporters to come back to work late at night, after they'd seen the announcement on CBC or heard it on Radio Canada. That resulted in more negative coverage than a professionally managed announcement would have brought them. Not surprisingly, as well, many of the Quebec journalists concentrated on the fact that Phillips is the first official in Mulroney's press operation to speak no French. Quebec journalists also remember Phillips' outspoken attacks against the "French power" in the Trudeau regime when he aired his views in regular CTV editorial commentaries.

Phillips also didn't win many friends in the press gallery with his handling of the aftermath of the infamous Slapshot Summit when Sondra Gotlieb whacked her social secretary in the face at a high-society dinner. Rather than be straightforward about it, Phillips offered only a terse statement and became openly hostile with reporters who pressed for details.

Shortly after Phillips had arrived and Fox had quit unexpectedly, Southam's Don McGillivray's column on Mulroney's media problems carried a picture of Mulroney with the mustachioed Fox hunkering down right beside the prime minister's right ear. McGillivray wrote that for all the short-comings of Fox, Gratton, and others who had either left the PMO or been shuffled to other jobs "the tragedy is that the PMO cleanup probably won't work. The problem isn't the heavy in the moustache [Fox] in the old photos. It's the man in the middle."

CHAPTER SIXTEEN

COLLAPSING HALOS

Bob Coates was the first casualty. Not everyone was surprised. In the five months he had held the prestigious defence portfolio, the tough-minded right-winger had seemed slightly out of synch and had been dogged by rumors about high living abroad (all unproven) and stories about the dissatisfaction of military leaders with his inflexible approach, particularly his single-minded drive for spiffy new uniforms, which he hoped would make the three military branches distinctive again.

It was such a minor thing on the surface. On February 12, 1985, the Ottawa *Citizen* published a report that, on November 29, 1984, Coates and two aides—his chief of staff, Rick Logan, and his press secretary, Geoff Matthews—had made a late-night visit to a sleazy strip bar not far from the Canadian base in Lahr, West Germany. The minister was on the first leg of a twelve-day NATO tour of West Germany, Turkey, Belgium, and Great Britain. Inside the bar—called Tiffany's—the strippers alternately serve drinks, chat up the customers, and periodically interrupt the steady stream of hardcore skin flicks by waltzing onto the stage themselves and slipping into something really comfortable.

The *Citizen* said that Coates had sat drinking at the bar and talking to Micki O'Neil, a long-legged pink-and-brown-haired German divorcée. The mother of two teenagers, the woman claimed to be thirty-eight and would not divulge her real name. The story said that while Coates had talked to O'Neil—before she did her "Fantasy in White" number to a Julio Iglesias record—Logan and Matthews had gone off to a different part of the club with two other women.

Coates and his party had left Ottawa on the damp, overcast

evening of November 27 aboard a Canadian Armed Forces
twin-engined Challenger jet. The first leg of the journey was a
two-hour flight to Goose Bay, Labrador, where the aircraft
refuelled and the party spent the night. Next day, at 10:30
A.M., the Challenger took off for Lahr, a town of about 48,000
in the picturesque Black Forest area of Bavaria, where about
fourteen thousand Canadian service personnel are stationed.
Coates and his party landed at 7:00 P.M. local time and were
met by Major-General David Wightman, commander of the
Canadian forces in Europe. After introductions, the visitors
and some senior officers and their wives were guests at an
informal dinner hosted by Wightman. The gathering broke up
about midnight, and Coates, Logan, and Matthews left the
base in Wightman's car in search of a nightcap. At $20 a
cocktail, the local servicemen don't frequent Tiffany's, but
O'Neil, who expressed shock at the whole incident later,
remembered Coates as "very charming, very polite. They all
were."

Typically, there would be a variety of stories about what
happened next. Coates insisted that he had resigned. Mulroney said that he had learned of the incident on January 22
when Privy Council clerk Gordon Osbaldeston brought allegations of a possible security breach to him. Mulroney said he
had received a series of reports that confirmed there was no
security breach. When Coates quit, Mulroney said that the
minister (a veteran of twenty-eight years in the Commons) had
offered his resignation as a "man of honour" who felt parlimen-
tary tradition required it. A close friend of the minister
reported that Coates felt that he had done nothing wrong, but
decided to resign "the second he saw the *Citizen* story. He
didn't want to embarrass the government, and he wanted to do
what was right." Two months later, Mulroney altered his
version and said he had advised Coates that "his resignation
would be appropriate."

In any event, Coates was gone. Mulroney said his choice of a
bar was "an error in judgement," but that a comeback was
possible; "all doors" remained open to Coates for the future.

Coates, a former national party president, had long been a
leading member of a right-wing rump of the party that didn't
like either Robert Stanfield or Joe Clark, both of whom are
"pink" Tories. He had little time for lefties, whether in his
party or not. Shortly before Coates resigned, Mulroney felt
moved to give him a public slap on the wrist for saying that it

was "only right and proper" that Canada's peace movement had attracted little interest. Coates had also joked about the arrest of sixteen peace protesters in Halifax. Mulroney agreed at a news conference that it "was not the most felicitous remark."

However, many observers were stunned that Coates would resign over what appeared to be a tacky but petty interlude. Liberal MP Robert Kaplan, a former solicitor general, said, "In itself, from what we know, going into a bar in West Germany might have been more moderately dealt with by the prime minister."

This seemed particularly cogent because during the same week, another veteran Nova Scotia, solicitor general Elmer MacKay, was being attacked for what seemed a far more serious breach of his mandate—a private meeting in an Ottawa hotel with New Brunswick premier Richard Hatfield to discuss the RCMP investigation of the celebrated marijuana incident, while the investigation was underway and before charges of possession were laid against Hatfield. MacKay didn't resign even though his indiscretion, on the surface, seemed more serious.

NDP leader Ed Broadbent also seemed perplexed. He compared Coates and MacKay and said that Mulroney had "showed a considerable vacillation and lack of firmness—and perhaps depth—in judgment when he accepts the resignation of one man who, according to all the evidence, committed at best a misdemeanour, and on the other hand, [supports] a man who completely abrogates his responsibility as solicitor general. . . . It shows very bad judgment, and because of the bad judgment, Mr. Mulroney has contributed to his own mess this week."

MacKay had met with Hatfield in the Château Laurier just twelve days after marijuana was found in Hatfield's luggage during the royal visit. Hatfield would eventually be acquitted in the incident, but not without considerable political embarrassment for him and the federal Tories. Mulroney's only response to repeated opposition demands for answers, and for MacKay's resignation, was that RCMP commissioner Robert Simmonds (who reported to MacKay) had concluded that neither MacKay nor any other federal official had tried to interfere in Hatfield's case. Hatfield accused the RCMP of leaking information and deliberately trying to hurt him because they did not like his lifestyle.

* * *

On Tuesday, September 17, 1985, CBC TV'S "Fifth Estate" program reported that fisheries minister John Fraser had personally overruled his own department's inspection service and released nearly a million cans of tuna that had been classified as "unfit for human consumption." The tuna had been packed at the Star-Kist plant in St. Andrews-by-the-Sea on the picturesque south shore of New Brunswick.

The plant employed four hundred people and produced 40 per cent of the canned tuna sold in Canada, but random samplings by inspectors had not measured up to Canada's exacting standards. Months earlier, the Department of National Defence had bought $100,000 worth and sent it back after the mess-hall cooks complained. In fact, that was the second lot that DND had sent back, not the first. The problem was undetected until Fred Ennis of News-radio reported that DND had returned some tuna. Even then the story didn't get picked up immediately. CTV's Robert Hurst got onto it, interviewed Fraser—who admitted on tape that he'd overruled his own inspectors—and did interviews at the plant in New Brunswick. But CTV, smarting over the recent loss of a major lawsuit, wouldn't run the story, so it remained essentially under wraps until the "Fifth Estate" program in September.

A major question quickly became who knew, and when? Mulroney claimed he knew nothing about it until it aired on the CBC. Under opposition questioning, he later conceded that two of his senior staffers—Pat MacAdam and Ian Anderson— had known about it in July, but that nobody had told him. Local Tory MP Fred McCain told Canadian Press that he had raised the matter in caucus because he was worried about the possible loss of jobs in his riding's major industry; but he quickly recanted after MacAdam called him to "remind" him that he must have been mistaken.

The opposition did not believe Mulroney's claims of innocence, particularly when he and Fraser publicly disagreed over who had ordered the tainted tuna removed from supermarket shelves after the problem became public. Fraser said the order was his, but Mulroney also claimed the credit. Most people believed Fraser, but the minister's days were numbered the moment he contradicted the boss in public and, before the week ended, he was gone.

The department was so concerned with the political potential of Fraser's decision that it had prepared a "press line" with seven questions and answers on Star-Kist tuna. The document was dated June 24, 1985. Beginning in early January 1985, a former departmental employee had discussed the problem several times with then deputy minister Art May. Fraser himself had been cautioned about the political ramifications in February, well before he decided to release the detained canned tuna in March 1985. One official told him it would "blow you out of the water politically. You can blow $1 billion on the banks, but if you start fooling around with food, that's when the public gets up in arms."

Fraser didn't listen. He was too busy trying to satisfy Richard Hatfield, who was pressuring him to release the tuna to avoid risking the four hundred jobs. Company officials in New Brunswick and the United States, notably Pennsylvania Senator John Heinz, were also pressuring Fraser. Five Consecutive MPs confirm privately that McCain had raised the issue not only in the Maritime caucus but in full caucus. "Mulroney was there. It was discussed. Fred would be pretty damn derelict in his duties if he wasn't worried about the biggest employer in his own riding." Another regional MP said, "Those bastards really put the heat on Fred when he spoke out. Bad enough they pressured him into eating his words, they started telling people he was old and a bit senile. It's a dirty business."

In early May, when Fraser was at the Fisheries Council meeting in Montreal, he was warned again by departmental officials of the political perils involved in his decision. "He just shrugged it off," said one official who was there. Before leaving on a European trip, Fraser told his deputy minister to order other officials to stop bugging him about it.

Mulroney claimed that the PMO hadn't heard about it until July, but a former departmental official says that MacAdam, for one, knew in "late February or early March, certainly before Fraser allowed the stuff to be marketed. . . . Pat [MacAdam] later had a lapse of memory on that. He said he didn't know before it was released. He did. It was discussed several times. "When one departmental official at an early stage asked if Mulroney knew what was going on, MacAdam said, "The boss knows, I assure you."

As for Fraser, he wasn't as innocent as he claimed either. He went secretly to Halifax before releasing the tuna and met with some departmental officials and inspectors in a laboratory. "There were at least a dozen people there," said one of those who witnessed the experiment. "They opened about twenty numbered, unlabelled cans, the one-litre, institutional size. When he got to a Star-Kist can, although he didn't know what it was at the time because the labels had been removed, he smelled it and said, 'No thanks.' It didn't look that bad. It just stank. And of course, 99 per cent of people the first thing they do when they open a can of any fish is smell it. If it doesn't smell right they don't risk it. Fraser knew that, but he succumbed to pressure from Hatfield and the industry."

At a September 19 news conference, a beleaguered Mulroney snapped, "It is pretty damned obvious" that the rancid tuna should never have been shipped to supermarket shelves. "I was not the first to know," he said, but added that it had been ordered off the shelves "as soon as I found out."

The Research and Productivity Council, a New Brunswick Crown corporation, revealed that it had tested fifty-seven different lots of the rejected tuna and that fifty-one lots had been recommended by the council for release. However, the council reported, Fraser had ordered the release of all the tuna to the market before the test results were issued.

During the first day of the dispute in the Commons, Mulroney defended Fraser's decision, and the minister refused opposition demands to have the tuna removed, saying that there was no health hazard. But fears mounted, and supermarkets actually began pulling the product off the shelves themselves. The next day Fraser announced: "I have today asked my colleague, the minister of national health and welfare [Jake Epp] to invoke the power of the Food and Drug Act and to effect the seizure of the disputed product." Fraser told reporters, "I have not considered resigning and I've not been asked to resign."

At his Friday morning news conference, Mulroney claimed it had been his decision to remove the tuna from supermarket shelves, but in question period shortly afterwards, Fraser claimed he had made the decision. Neither Mulroney nor any of his officials had told Fraser about the prime minister's claim, so he blithely blurted out the truth and ended up getting fired for it. Fraser also told the Commons that the issue had been "in the prime minister's office in detailed form a couple of weeks ago," a version at serious odds with Mulroney's claim that he knew nothing about it until the CBC show.

Fraser has always discreetly refused to discuss details in public, but at a private gathering in his parliamentary suite on

March 8, 1987, when a delegation of unemployed Star-Kist employees from St. Andrews were in Ottawa seeking federal help, Fraser unloaded. At an off-the-record meeting, Fraser said he had believed the issue was "dying out" by the end of the first week, but that Mulroney's comments at the Friday news conference had "revived the whole thing again." Fraser complained that he hadn't been informed about Mulroney's version before he told his story to the Commons that day. At that point, Fraser's aide Eric Alexander said, "Well, maybe there wasn't time. The news conference was held just before question period." Fraser, suddenly angry and red-faced, snapped, "Of course there was time. If they had wanted me to know they could have told me."

Fraser admitted to being "furious" at what Mulroney had done. He "stewed about it over the weekend" and met with the prime minister early on Monday. He said that Mulroney gave him a "lecture" about being a "good and loyal soldier, and, if I offered my resignation, he clearly indicated I would get back in cabinet down the road. When I left for home that day, I left with the impression that after things died down, I would get back in cabinet." But when time went by and nothing was happening for him, he felt that Mulroney had "misled" him. "I was very bitter about that. I felt betrayed." Asked how he could still deal with Mulroney after being "shafted" that way, Fraser, who had long since become the Commons first-ever elected Speaker, said, "I was very angry about it at the time and I remain angry now. But we're still cordial in our relationship."

On September 23, 1985, Mulroney's office released a terse, three-sentence announcement reporting that Fraser had resigned and Mulroney had accepted the resignation with "considerable regrets." An official close to the Mulroney-Fraser meeting said, "Fraser was ordered to resign. He was summoned to appear and the resignation was all typed when he arrived. Mulroney was furious. He lecturered Fraser. Yelled at him for contradicting him in public. And finally, after Fraser tried to answer back, Mulroney shouted, 'No questions. Sign the fucking thing,' and threw the resignation at him."

The issue in the Commons quickly centred on Mulroney's personal integrity. Windsor New Democrat Howard McCurdy asked, "Does the prime minister remember Richard Nixon?" Liberal Brian Tobin produced correspondence showing that

McCain had been corresponding with Fraser about the tainted tuna as early as September 25, 1984. "I'm telling the absolute and total truth," shouted Mulroney in the Commons, challenging anyone who thought he could prove differently to put his seat on the line against Mulroney's seat and calling the allegations against him "cheap . . . without any basis . . . totally unfounded. . . ."

A week later, the public learned that eight New Brunswick Tory MPs had toured the Star-Kist plant one week before the release of the tuna, had spoken with union officials about the inspector problem, and had promised to "raise the matter in the highest councils of the government." Liberal leader John Turner, saying "Now that's not a coincidence," asked if Mulroney "still expects Canadians to believe" that the matter had not been raised in caucus or with him directly.

Mulroney stuck to his story, but the public wasn't buying. On October 8, Mulroney tossed out the first baseball from his front-row seat on the home-plate side of the third-base dugout to open the first ever American League baseball play-off in Canada. The Toronto Blue Jays beat Kansas City 6 to 1, but in the fifth inning, when Mulroney left his seat to join the local radio commentators in the Jay's broadcast booth, he was greeted by thousands of fans chanting, "Tuna, tuna, tuna."

On November 20, Mulroney switched Tom Siddon from minister of state for science and technology to Fisheries. (Erik Nielsen had been handling the job on an interim basis.) In a year-end CBC interview, Mulroney expressed the view that he had come out of the tuna scandal with his integrity "completely intact." He had opened the year with a 53 per cent rating in the Gallup, compared to 25 for the Liberals. By the end of 1985, the two were tied at 38.5 per cent of decided voters.

Even then, Mulroney just couldn't leave it alone. In March, when he flew to Washington for his annual summit with U.S. president Ronald Reagan, he told a *New York Times* interviewer that, "When it [the tuna scandal] was brought to my attention, bang! Immediately the minister's resignation was secured." In fact, Fraser had not resigned until six days after Mulroney claimed he had first learned of it. But his latest version might have gone undetected, since it was of no news interest to the *Times* reporter, had not Mulroney's officials released transcripts of the interview to Ottawa reporters to show that their man was so important that the *Times* would spend an hour interviewing him.

The transcripts, which were released both in the Ottawa press gallery and in a hotel press room for the reporters who accompanied Mulroney to Washington, were quickly retrieved by PMO officials, but it was too late. Several reporters already had copies of the unabridged version and, when Mulroney returned to the Commons, Liberal John Nunziata shouted, "He's a liar," as Mulroney brushed aside questions. Outside the House, Nunziata said that the Tory "mandate was dissipated because of the dishonesty of the prime minister and the public perception that not only is the prime minister dishonest, but the government's dishonest.

"The prime minister is a compulsive liar," he said. "He once again got caught in his own lies . . . he's a bloody liar."

Meanwhile, the Star-Kist plant closed its doors, and the people of St. Andrews found themselves out of work. In July, a study of the issue by University of Guelph food-science professor Alex Morrison criticized federal inspectors for rejecting some tuna that should have been released, but blasted the plant, citing "insufficient vigilance concerning general sanitation." He recommended that Star-Kist be allowed to export eighteen million stored tins that it had kept off the market by government order. Siddon, the new fisheries minister, recommended it be used for pet food.

The Tories consistently argued that the tuna affair was a minor problem. They claimed great success on the "big" issues, such as the economy and world affairs, and attacked the media and the opposition for concentrating on the "minor" issues. In September 26, campaigning in Shawinigan for a by-election, Mulroney listed what he described as his government's achievements and said, "I'm not speaking to you about a tin of tuna. I'm discussing serious things."

By December 1986, federal inspectors had worked their way through half of Star-Kist Canada's twenty-two million cans of disputed tuna, and had rejected two-thirds of what they sniffed and tasted. General manager Gerry Clay threatened court action, saying that food technicians at H.J. Heinz, the American parent company, had tested the product and found nothing wrong with it. In March, Siddon said that about 90 per cent of the tuna was failing to meet minimum standards after being tested for the second time and urged the company either to reopen the plant or to tell the community what it intended to do about the factory and its 440 laid-off workers. In response, the company issued a news release saying, "our difficulties with the government centre around subjective and unscientific inspection practices and not quality standards." They said the plant couldn't re-open because federal inspectors would continue to use the same methods that had resulted in the shutdown. Siddon replied that Ottawa wouldn't bend its rules to accommodate the company, but a month later, he did in fact bend, agreeing on chemical testing for the tuna that should allow the plant to re-open in the fall and export 90 per cent of previously rejected fish. Clay announced that it would take the company four months to complete about $200,000 in modifications and that about half the workers would be rehired initially. The tuna that passed the chemical test would be shipped to West Germany, Belgium, and Israel.

Two days after the Fraser resignation, when Mulroney was under heavy pressure to defend his own integrity, yet another shoe dropped—his autocratic Quebec lieutenant Marcel Masse resigned after learning he was being investigated by the RCMP for alleged election-spending irregularities. Once again, Mulroney claimed he knew nothing about it, but national PC party director Jerry Lampert said publicly that he had told "senior PMO people" two months before that Masse was being investigated. He had also written to Masse on June 14 to tell him of the investigation by Elections Canada.

None of that cut it with Mulroney. He offered to resign if any MP could prove he had lied, and said that Lampert might "have communicated this information . . . to someone, to a senior person, but not to a senior person in my office." Mulroney ordered an "urgent" investigation into the dispute by party president Peter Elzinga.

In a 1987 interview, Senator Finlay MacDonald said, "There's no denying what appears to be an accident-proneness of this government. When I think back on the things that anger me, why isn't someone there . . . to tie things together?" According to MacDonald, Mulroney had been at caucus that morning, had left for a luncheon, and had returned just before 2:00 P.M. when he was told that Masse planned to quit at 3:00 P.M. "I'll tell you what should have happened. Between the caucus and Brian Mulroney returning to his office, Eric Nielsen or Bernard Roy should have had Marcel Masse in a cage somewhere. As soon as Brian came back, they should have said, 'Marcel is in there, speak to him, stop this madness.' But nosiree, Brian was confronted with this fait accompli."

MacDonald said that Masse should simply have issued a statement of the facts, saying he was innocent of any wrong-doing, but offer to resign if any irregularities were proven. "So what's he do? He quits. He causes total chaos in his department for three months. He causes banner headlines saying 'Second Minister Quits in Two Days.' Surely the PM must have somebody he can trust, somebody with enough judgment to make sure a minister doesn't do something absolutely idiotic. There are still people today who say what an honourable thing Masse did. It was the stupidest goddamn thing I ever heard of. It sparked all that Black September stuff and set an image we're still with today."

At a news conference at the end of that dreadful week, Mulroney said, "You've got cheap and unproven allegations that have been vigorously rejected by the Prime Minister of Canada and have not been sustained by a shred of evidence. Allegations is all they are, allegations with no evidence . . . and I answered honestly each one." Repeating his now-familiar refrain, Mulroney said, "I am telling the absolute and total truth."

Liberal leader John Turner offered the obvious retort. "Somebody is lying there—either Lampert or the officials in the prime minister's office." Well, Elzinga's "investigation" determined that nobody had lied. Lampert apologized (and quit four months later), Masse was acquitted and returned to cabinet in December, Mulroney declared, "I came out unsul-lied," and the Tories settled back to live happily ever after.

The problem with politics is that "ever after" isn't necessari-ly a very long time. Environment minister Suzanne Blais-Grenier made sure of that. As if the Tories needed any more from the controversial minister, veteran Southam News jour-nalist Chris Young revealed that in two trips in the spring, Blais-Grenier had spent $64,000, much of it zipping around the continent in chauffeur-driven limousines and going on a trip, even though the conference she was going for had been cancelled.

In what became known as "April in Paris," she, her husband, and two aides spent $17,000 (they also went to Stockholm), about $4,000 of that on chauffeur-driven limos. During four days in Stockholm, Blais-Grenier ran up a limo bill of $1,430.35. Health minister Jake Epp, who was in the same city at the same time, charged $113.19 for his transportation. Blais-Grenier's hotel was $385 a night, plus $120 for a harbour cruise and dinner. In June and July, she took along several staff members on a fifteen-day tour of France, Finland, and the Soviet Union. That time she spent $46,947.

Blais-Grenier had been controversial from the outset. She refused to meet with many of her senior bureaucrats for several months after her September 17 appointment. Her serious lack of knowledge of her department showed when she approved Michael Wilson's elimination of several important research programs and the virtual dismantling of a branch of the Canadian Wildlife Service, for a "saving" of $46 million. Environmentalists were outraged, but Blais-Grenier dismissed their concerns, refused to meet Ken Brynaert, executive vice-president of the Canadian Wildlife Federation, for months, then demanded an apology from him for criticizing her in the media.

Eventually she caved in to pressure, and reinstated some of the projects, but Mulroney was so anxious to keep her out of sight that she was not allowed to attend the March Shamrock Summit with Reagan in Quebec City, even though acid rain was one of the major topics on the agenda. A week later, when some toxic PCBs were spilled on the Trans-Canada Highway in northern Ontario, she brusquely told reporters she wouldn't talk to them about it until she had put on some lipstick. When she did speak, she said that the dangers of PCBs had been "overly dramatized" and were "unduly alarming the population." In June, she made the remarkable statement that she was considering allowing mining and logging in Canada's national parks. Mulroney was forced to calm outraged environmentalists by publicly rejecting the notion.

Her poor record made it particularly nasty when, in a first-anniversary interview on the Radio-Canada public affairs show "Le Point," Mulroney suggested that Blais-Grenier was the victim of anti-French feeling in the media. When her lack of success with environmental issues was mentioned, Mulroney waved his hand dismissively and said (in French) that, "notwithstanding the opinion of Anglophones" his minister had made "historic" achievements. (This seemed a little extravagant, given that he had moved her out of her environmental portfolio by that time.) *Globe and Mail* journalist Graham Fraser wrote that "it was one of the most gratuitous ethnic slurs since Daniel Johnson told Quebecers that 'except for the English and the Jews,' the Union Nationale had won a majority of the popular vote in 1966."

A month later, deputy prime minister Erik Nielsen repeated Mulroney's accusation of racism when the Southam column on Blais-Grenier's expenses became the subject of a Commons controversy. Having read the column, said Nielsen, "I ask myself . . . whether or not the motivation wasn't to arouse some kind of racism. . . ." Nielsen, to his credit, later apologized. Mulroney didn't. When asked to by Liberal leader John Turner, Mulroney said he had nothing to apologize for because during the last election a Liberal candidate had accused him of being the "leader of a party of Orangemen." He said he found that accusation "deplorable" (and the opposition agreed that it was), but that hardly excused him for hurling racist barbs himself.

On New Year's Eve, in a twenty-word statement from the PMO, Mulroney accepted Blais-Grenier's resignation from cabinet as junior transport minister. The day before, she had publicly criticized the government's decision to allow Ultramar Canada Inc. to buy the eastern Canadian assets of Gulf Canada, including Gulf's east-end Montreal refinery, for $120 million. She said she was resigning "in order to not call into question the principle of cabinet solidarity." Liberal Marcel Prud'homme said aloud what everybody was thinking: "most likely she was convinced that she was going to be dropped, so she decided to beat those who wanted to get rid of her by a week or two."

In the midst of his "Black September" Mulroney did manage to introduce tougher rules designed to prevent conflicts of interest and promised a "new day of trust and confidence" in government. Tied up with a bright blue ribbon and tabled in the Commons on September 9, 1985, the package banned the hiring of a minister's immediate family members, broadened and clarified the rules about what jobs could be taken by departing government officials, and promised legislation to register lobbyists and list their clients. It also set the stage for a limited review of cabinet appointments. In an open letter to MPs and Senators, Mulroney wrote, "It is a great principle of public administration—I could even say an 'imperative'—that to function effectively the government and the public service of a democracy must have the trust and the confidence of the public they serve."

That "trust and confidence," already badly shaken by Tory failings, took it on the chin again, literally, early in 1986 when Mulroney's annual summit with Reagan was rocked by the widely publicized social faux pas of Sondra Gotlieb, wife of

Canada's ambassador to Washington Allan Gotlieb, when she slapped the face of her social secretary, Connie Connor, at a top-drawer black-tie dinner at the ambassador's residence. The main accomplishment of the meeting—Reagan's admission that acid rain is a problem—got lost in the publicity surrounding the slap.

In a two-page article in the *Washington Post,* entitled, "A Big Chill for Canada?" reporter Lois Romano wrote, "Many guests were genuinely shocked by the insensitivity and arrogance Sondra Gotlieb's behavior implied," adding that some Washington luminaries were now having second thoughts about attending Canadian Embassy functions. And so, when Mulroney flew back to his troubles in Ottawa, he was upset at much more than just another in a series of embarrassments. (He clearly made a big impression on a Senate committee, however. After the meeting, Rhode Island Democratic Senator Claiborne Pell emerged to tell the media: "We're very lucky to have Muldoon as Prime Minister.")

A perhaps more enduring embarrassment also flowed from that meeting. Lobbyist Michael Deaver, a former Reagan confidant, was accused of five charges of lying to investigators about his lobbying activities, one of which included lobbying on Canada's behalf—at the behest of Mulroney's old pal Fred Doucet—on acid rain. Deaver was accused of breaking the U.S. conflict-of-interest law forbidding senior staffers from lobbying anyone at the White House for a year after leaving it. He was accused of taking part in at least six meetings on acid rain with the White House during the restraining period, as part of his $105,000 contract with the Tory government.

Deaver, deputy White House chief of staff for five years, claimed at one point that he did not even know what acid rain was. This prompted Liberal George Baker to say, "If he doesn't know what acid rain is, what does he actually do for his $105,000?" That question was also on the minds of congressional investigators, but the Canadian Embassy refused five times to co-operate with the investigation. At last Ambassador Gotlieb wrote a letter confirming that the first discussion of a contract with Deaver had occurred on May 16, 1985, six days after Deaver had left the White House. Gotlieb's account contradicted published reports in which unidentified Canadian diplomats were quoted as saying that informal discussions had taken place during preparations for the March 1985 Shamrock Summit in Quebec City. Three days later, Gotlieb acknowledged in another letter that Doucet, a deadly serious man, had made "a lighthearted conversational remark" to Deaver during the preparatory meetings that Canada could use his "talents."

The grand jury charged that Deaver had been active in pushing a proposal—later accepted by Reagan and Mulroney—to appoint two acid rain envoys (Bill Davis for Canada and Drew Lewis for the United States) to study the problem and report back. The investigation found that Deaver had allegedly perjured himself in claiming he did not recall having lunch with Gotlieb in January 1985, at which time Deaver told Gotlieb he had discussed the envoy idea with Secretary of State George Shultz and that Shultz had not objected.

In late March 1987 Deaver pleaded not guilty to charges of lying to a congressional subcommittee and a grand jury. One of the five perjury counts was laid on the basis of information supplied by Gotlieb, who gave written answers to questions posed by the U.S. independent counsel. This unusual procedure was designed to protect Gotlieb's diplomatic immunity, which he would have had to waive in order to testify personally before the U.S. grand jury. (There was still a real possibility that Gotlieb would be subpoenaed to testify in the affair, since the written statements would not likely be admissable as evidence.)

As for Mulroney, he said on March 19, 1987, that allegations of wrongdoing by Deaver on behalf of Canada were "scurrilous" and that there would be no parliamentary inquiry into the matter.

It was not so easy to dismiss allegations of conflict-of-interest published against industry minister Sinclair Stevens in April and May of 1986, although Mulroney at first tried to slough off the stories as "unfounded speculation in newspapers."

In early April, the *Globe* raised questions about the relationship between Stevens and the Hanil Bank Canada, a South Korean bank with ties to the Hyundai Motor Co. The report said that a company controlled by Stevens had borrowed $3.6 million from the bank in 1983 before the Tory victory and Stevens's appointment as industry minister. Since then, Hyundai had agreed to set up two plants in Canada, one in Stevens' riding north of Toronto, the other in Bromont, Quebec. The latter plant was awarded $55 million in aid from the Department of Regional Industrial Expansion.

Later that month, Mulroney angrily rejected opposition calls for Stevens's resignation after it was learned that the minister's wife, Noreen, had negotiated a $2.6 million loan for his company from Anton Czapka, co-founder of and now consultant for Magna International Inc., a giant auto-parts manufacturer with extensive government dealings. Mulroney accused the opposition of "McCarthyism and slander." The loan, with one year's free interest worth more than $300,000, had been negotiated by Mrs. Stevens, as vice-president of Stevens's firm Cardiff Investments Ltd., to refinance the money-strapped company. Stevens himself owned the firm through a blind trust.

Noreen Stevens, a lawyer, had been referred to Czapka by Frank Stronach, Magna's mercurial chairman, who had been appointed by Stevens to the board of directors of Canada Development Investment Corp., the holding company for Crown corporations. The story broke on the eve of Mulroney's departure for the Tokyo summit. Stevens claimed he knew nothing about the loan his wife had negotiated; and Erik Nielsen, obeying the order to stonewall the opposition in Mulroney's absence, said he had checked with the deputy registrar general and was assured there was no violation of conflict-of-interest guidelines by Stevens.

Liberal leader John Turner, who was in Vancouver at the time, upset some of his colleagues by refusing to return to Ottawa to lead the fight in the Commons. He did, however, send Stevens a letter asking him to step down until an investigation was completed to remove the "cloud of suspicion." "The facts, however," Turner added, "speak louder than anything: the loan was made; you have benefited from it; and the company with which the lender has had close dealings has benefited from you in your ministerial role."

Day after day, the issue dominated the question period, with Nielsen, not Stevens, deflecting the questions. On May 5, Stevens broke his week-long silence and defended himself over new conflict-of-interest charges, this time involving an unasked-for $300-million break he had given to Hyundai when he overlooked the company's contractural obligation to buy Canadian goods worth half the annual value of its automotive sales in Canada. "I don't feel making good deals, especially in the province of Quebec, is any reason why this minister or any other minister should step down," Stevens said.

The issue became so heated that, on May 7, opposition MPs attempted physically to block Stevens's departure from a parliamentary committee meeting. At one point, Liberal Sheila Copps jumped over a chair to get at Stevens. "We want some answers now, Stevens," she shouted angrily. She had to be restrained by another Liberal, Marcel Prud'homme. As Stevens was being escorted from the building by his aides, another cabinet minister, André Bissonnette, who would have his problems in 1987, bumped against Liberal John Nunziata, clenched his fist at him, and tried to shove him out of the way. "Take your paws off me," shouted Nunziata. He later accused Bissonnette of assaulting him.

Nielsen continued to insist in the Commons—on direct orders from Mulroney—that Stevens had done nothing wrong. But new revelations were being reported almost daily. On May 9, the *Toronto Star* reported that Stevens's wife and former campaign manager had approached three major Toronto investment dealers about putting $5 million into the minister's troubled company. The firms were later hired by Stevens to help the government sell off several Crown corporations. Nielsen also dismissed that story, which quoted Brascan president Trevor Eyton. Eyton (a Stevens appointee to the board of the Canada Development Corp.) confirmed that he had held two meetings, one with York Centre and the other with the brokerage firms, to discuss Noreen Stevens's proposal: ". . . we took a fast look at York Centre and its affiliated companies with a view to see whether or not it could be publicly or privately financed, and in our judgment it was difficult. There was value there, but the size was just too small." According to the *Star* report, Dominion Securities Pitfield Ltd., Burns Fry Ltd., and Gordon Capital Corp. had also turned down the investment chance.

As Liberal Robert Kaplan said, "When a minister's wife starts hustling around to raise private money from them, how can they not believe that there's some connection between the way in which they perform in relation to the wife and how they're going to make out in relation to the government?" NDP leader Ed Broadbent saw it as further confirmation that Noreen Stevens had been commercially active with companies that were doing business with her husband's department. "The blind trust is anything but blind. It's open for the whole world to see, not only the minister."

Stevens, who held a controlling interest in York Centre Corp. but had placed it in a blind trust in 1984, accused the media and opposition of conspiring to discredit him. Finally, after denying any wrongdoing for two straight weeks, Stevens resigned on May 12, the fifth minister to quit, after writing a letter to Mulroney asking him to appoint an "impartial person" to investigate the whole affair. From Seoul, South Korea, where he was at the time, Mulroney predicted that Stevens would eventually return to cabinet completely cleared of conflict charges against him.

At the Seoul press conference, Mulroney had read a brief statement, then stormed away, refusing to answer reporters' questions. Stevens himself, near tears as he beat a hasty retreat from Parliament Hill, denounced the "lynch-mob" mentality directed against him and his wife. "The accusations are totally unfounded," he said, and an inquiry "is still so unnecessary," a tip-off that it was Mulroney's idea to hold a public inquiry, not Stevens's.

Only two days after Stevens resigned, Quebec backbench Tory MP Robert Toupin added to the government's problems when he announced his decision to leave the Conservative caucus to sit as an independent. He later joined the NDP. In addition, Quebec MP Michel Gravel was charged with fifty counts of influence peddling and abuse of public trust. Court documents allege that the east-end Montreal MP had obtained several thousand dollars in cash or benefits from government contractors. His preliminary hearing is set for October 1987.

Mulroney returned from his sixteen-day tour to find things in an even worse shambles than they had been when he left. He refused to comment on Toupin's defection or Gravel's criminal case, but named William Parker, chief justice of the trial division of the Supreme Court of Ontario, to head a formal commission of inquiry into the Stevens affair. "The only thing certain about public life is that it will be filled with uncertainties and challenges," Mulroney said. "My job is to deal with that as best I can."

Senator Finlay MacDonald says he thinks that the rules on blind trusts and conflicts of interest are "on the wrong track . . . all that should be expected [of cabinet ministers], if you're going to attract your best and brightest . . . is that he declares publicly what he owns, everything he owns. They know when to declare an interest, when not to vote. You don't have to legislate morality. He knows where he stands. The British don't get into this nonsense. It certainly limits your attractiveness for candidates, I can tell you that."

The inquiry itself created a sensation—day after day of front-page news stories and lead items on broadcast news. Shirley Walker, a longtime employee and officer of the Stevens companies who had resigned her directorships in 1984 to become Stevens's special ministerial assistant in Toronto, testified that she had continued to act on behalf of companies in the minister's blind trust. Senior ministerial staff are prohibited from such action under the conflict code. Walker also admitted that she had removed a bundle of financial documents from a vault in downtown Toronto two weeks before the inquiry opened and had placed in the vault a plastic bag containing sixteen notebooks in which personal and company activities were recorded. The diaries were discovered at York Centre's offices by commission staff seven days after the inquiry began, and the disclosures contradicted Walker's testimony of the previous week that she had not conducted business dealings for Stevens after she became his special ministerial assistant.

In July, Mulroney said he could no longer wait for Stevens to be cleared before filling his portfolio, so he handed it to Michel Côté, former consumer and corporate affairs minister. "In light of the present circumstances, clearly the ministry would have to be filled and we will look at his situation when the inquiry has been completed."

In November, cabinet agreed to pay up to $350,000 of taxpayers' money "to assist in the payment" of Stevens's legal bills. His lawyer, John Sopinka, had already been paid $250,000 of that amount, (at a rate of $175 an hour), since the inquiry began on July 14. The government was also paying more than $10,000 towards Shirley Walker's legal bill and $150 an hour to Toronto lawyer Ian Binnie for representing the government's interest at the inquiry.

In late November, Stevens testified at the inquiry that the accusations were "pure McCarthyism," based on "the lumping together of unrelated facts. It's a disgrace that this type of thing has gone on in our country." He flatly denied any breach of conflict-of-interest guidelines when his wife had obtained a $2.6 million loan from Anton Czapka. (According to Czapka, he didn't know that Noreen Stevens was related to Sinc when he gave her the money.)

The most bizarre testimony came from Noreen Stevens, who said that her husband had never helped her manage the family firms after being named to cabinet, but that he had joined her in a complex plan to market a "Christ coin" to commemorate the two-thousandth birthday of Jesus. "This type of conceptualization is our hobby," she said. "A lot of people talk about weather. We talk about concepts." The plan was to involve the Vatican in marketing the coins. Investors would avoid tax by buying (for $400) a gold coin redeemable at a fixed rate ($1,350) in the year 2000, after which it could be sold to collectors for more than the fixed rate. In December 1985 she had asked her husband to call G. Emmett Cardinal Carter, the Roman Catholic archbishop of Toronto, to approach the Vatican for help in marketing the coins. She said there was no conflict of interest in her husband's involvement because "the business would be a hobby." In any event, the Chase Manhattan Bank had rejected the idea, and the Vatican had said the proposal would violate its agreements with the Italian government.

In February 1987, commission counsel David Scott presented an eight-hundred-page final argument that accused Stevens of being in conflict on at least eleven occasions. Lawyers for Stevens and his wife slammed Scott's conclusions and argued that since media allegations had prompted the $3 million inquiry, in future anyone making allegations that proved to be unfounded should pay all or part of the cost of the investigation. After hearing the final arguments, Parker went off to determine his conclusions, a process that would take several months.

Besides the obvious casualties—Stevens and Mulroney—the whole episode also wounded Erik Nielsen. A former fighter pilot with a reputation for destroying Liberal cabinet ministers while he was in opposition, Nielsen lost face for his lead role in stonewalling legitimate opposition questions about the Stevens affair. A year later, after being dropped from cabinet, Nielsen resigned his seat and later was named head of the Canadian Transport Commission.

Nielsen, nicknamed "Velcro Lips" because of his penchant for secrecy, endured a mini-scandal of his own in February 1986, when *Toronto Star* reporter David Vienneau picked up on the transcript of an interview Nielsen had given to Peter Stursberg in 1973 for his book *Diefenbaker: Leadership Lost 1962-67*. As an opposition MP in 1966, Nielsen said, he had regularly taken advantage of a temporary mix-up in wiring to eavesdrop on Liberal caucus meetings in Room 308 of Parliament's West Block.

On July 27, 1984, in a major campaign speech in Quebec City, Mulroney had listed among a series of Liberal "abuses of power," the "electronic surveillance of MPs." However, he didn't seem especially offended when he learned his own deputy prime minister had made a habit of listening to the private Liberal caucus meetings.

It was another essentially minor matter that through government mishandling got blown up into a major media affair. Rather than apologize on the day the story appeared—after all, electronic eavesdropping was not illegal in the 1960s—Mulroney defended Nielsen's actions. He insisted that his deputy was "not the initiator" of the eavesdropping and that he had done nothing illegal or improper.

"Somebody walks past an open window, apparently, and hears himself and his family savaged and his reputation being attacked. I suppose you have to not be human not to listen," said Mulroney. Broadbent replied, "It's human to listen when you stumble upon it. It becomes spying to repeat it without informing the people that you're listening to."

With his government already under attack for tainted tuna, bankrupt banks, and ministerial resignations, Mulroney chose to stay out of the Commons the next day, a Friday, leaving Nielsen to defend his own actions. This prompted the opposition parties to storm out of the Commons, paralysing Parliament for the day, and drawing even more attention to the affair. Finally, after a weekend of heavy media attention, Nielsen came into the Commons on Monday and apologized. Had he done so four days earlier the matter would have ended much more quietly.

One of the more mysterious links in the Mulroney network is that between former Newfoundland premier Frank Moores, Austrian-born multi-millionaire Walter Wolf, and two charter members of Mulroney's old boys' club, Michel Cogger and Fred Doucet. Like weeds, the names keep popping up either individually or in connection with the names of other Mulroney confidants. There is no scandal in the traditional sense. No cabinet ministers have fallen, no criminal matters have been suggested. But it continues to attract interest as a potential source of embarrassment to the Mulroney regime.

In June 1985, Frank Moores emerged from the shadows long enough to spark a brief row in the Commons. It was learned that Ulf Snarby, a Nova Scotia fisherman, had paid $2,000 to Government Consultants International (a firm owned by Moores and Fred Doucet's brother, Gerald) to arrange a meeting with then fisheries minister John Fraser. He also paid a retainer of $500 a month to the firm for a year on a trial basis. Mulroney was visibly upset in the Commons when Liberal Robert Kaplan asked if he thought "selling instant access" was proper. "If the member keeps this up, you're going to give McCarthyism a bad name [sic]," Mulroney snapped, adding that there was "no evidence of impropriety . . . and there is no evidence because none exists." He did not deny the story.

In August 1985, Ottawa had agreed to pay $362,761 to a Wolf company, Wolf Sub-Ocean Ltd. of St. John's, to help finance a joint project with another Newfoundland firm, COSEL Ltd., to develop an underwater vehicle for offshore mineral exploration. Liberal Sheila Copps accused Mulroney of settling political debts with taxpayers' money. "I think Mr. Mulroney is paying off his friends," she said. Broadbent said, "There is a great abuse of responsibility over public funds here." Science and technology minister Thomas Siddon said that no formal contract or tender was involved in the funding for the project, because it was part of a regional-development agreement between Ottawa and Newfoundland and the two firms were the only ones in Atlantic Canada capable of meeting Ottawa's needs. But Newfoundland premier Brian Peckford issued a statement saying that five other Newfoundland firms had applied for funds to develop the undersea vehicle.

At the same time, a $61,225 Transport Canada contract to develop Coast Guard communications in Quebec was awarded to Raymond Doucet, a director of the Quebec-based firm of Doucet et Associés Conseils (Québec) Ltée.

Meanwhile, in March 1985, Mulroney had made Moores a director of Air Canada. Moores by this time had taken over Alta Nova Associates Inc. While he was an Air Canada director, he was also a consultant for Nordair Inc. and Wardair Ltd., the Crown-owned airline's competitors in the skies, as well as a consultant for British Aerospace PLC and Messerschmitt-Bolkow-Blohm (MBB) GmbH of Munich. Both firms were part of the Airbus Industrie consortium, which was interested in selling the wide-bodied A-320 passenger aircraft to Air Canada to replace its aging fleet of thirty-five Boeing 727s. MBB was also one of the potential buyers of the aircraft assets of the Canada Development Investment Corp., principally Montreal's Canadair Ltd. and Toronto's de Havilland.

In July 1985, Moores said that he saw nothing wrong at all in serving as a director of Air Canada and acting as a consultant to two of the airline's competitors. He maintained that because other people in his consulting firms were handling the Nordair and Wardair accounts, there was no conflict. Moores added that he supported then St. John's Tory MP Jim McGrath's private member's bill to regulate lobbyists by requiring them to disclose the names of all the firms and individuals they represent.

In September, Canadian Press reporter Bob Fife was snooping around about the Moores connection to the Airbus deal when an Air Canada public relations man tipped off Moores that Fife had been asking questions. "He called me up and asked if I wanted a story," said Fife. "I said of course, so he asked me to come over to his office right away. When I got there he threw his resignation from the Air Canada board on the desk. 'Does that meet with your approval?' he asked. 'I wrote it myself.'"

Moores told Fife to write the story and then leave copies of the release in the press gallery afterwards. Then he added the kicker, "I guess there's no need to mention Airbus now is there?" Fife said, "I couldn't believe it. He figured if he gave me the one story I'd forget about the other one. It doesn't work that way."

Immediately afterwards, Moores resigned from the board of directors of Air Canada, saying he was fed up with "continuing harrassment" from the media and opposition MPs. He said he hoped the media would stop "hounding" him now that he had no official link with the government. "Unfortunately, certain forces seemed determined, by using innuendo, or slanting the facts, or both, to hurt Air Canada and/or the government and/ or myself because of my Air Canada directorship," he said.

Moores didn't seem to be hurting too badly. The next week he announced a blue-ribbon list of board members to his firm Government Consultants International, including former Liberal cabinet minister Jean Marchand, a past chairman of Imperial Oil Ltd., Jack Armstrong, and a Quebec City lawyer, Gary Ouellet, a close friend and long-time Mulroney supporter, who became the company's new chief executive officer and vice-chairman. Moores also apppointed George Hulme, a Calgary-based energy consultant and past vice-president of TransCanada PipeLines Ltd. and announced that he had quit as a paid consultant for the two Air Canada competitors to avoid the appearance of conflict.

Moores was in the middle of another controversy in the fall of 1985 while lobbying for Gulf and Western Industries, Inc. of

New York in its attempts to persuade Ottawa to approve its indirect acquisition of Prentice-Hall Canada Inc., a Toronto-based book publisher. During the protracted controversy over that issue, which acted as a rallying point for economic nationalists until the sale was approved, the Moores-Mulroney tie-in was a constant source of irritation for those opposing the sale and of political embarrassment for those favouring it.

In December, consumer and corporate affairs minister Michel Côté agreed to introduce the long-promised legislation to govern lobbyists like Moores, but active lobbying against it by the lobbyists convinced the Tories to back off and write a discussion paper to give the whole question yet another airing before bringing in legislation. (In the United Stated, registration of lobbyists has been required since 1946, and hired lobbyists must disclose who they were working for and how much money they spend trying to sway the policy makers.)

Just after Christmas 1985, federally owned Petro-Canada hired Moore's firm, GCI, for what was called a "private arrangement" to provide information and advice, primarily on energy issues in Atlantic Canada. Three weeks later, the Montreal *Gazette* reported that Gerry Doucet, a partner in the Moores firm, also owned a law firm whose clients included potential Petro-Canada competitors. Edmond Chaisson, a senior lawyer with Doucet and Associates of Halifax, confirmed that energy issues are a "specialty area" for the firm and that they have "very significant interests other than Petro-Canada." GCI's contract had been criticized because last July privy council clerk Paul Tellier had instructed all federal corporations and agencies not to hire consulting firms that act as "paid intermediaries" with the government. As Liberal MP Don Boudria said, "It seems there is one set of rules for Frank Moores and another set for everyone else." Indeed it does.

Back in January 1983 during the bitter leadership battle between Mulroney and Joe Clark, veteran Tory guru Dalton Camp said on CTV's "Question Period" (on January 20) that, "The evidence seems pretty clear that it [the anti-Clark campaign] was lavishly financed by person or persons unknown. I have a good idea where some of that money came from, and some of it came from offshore." A year later, Camp identified Wolf as one of those helping to finance the anti-Clark campaign. A Canadian citizen, although not officially resident in the country, Wolf had admitted to spending about $25,000 in the campaign. (Others set Wolf's contribution to the dump-

Clark campaign at $250,000.) Wolf says he paid retainer's fees for several months to Mulroney aide Michel Cogger, now a senator, and to Frank Moores, who spearheaded the dump-Clark movement for Mulroney. They were retained to work against Clark, not as directors of a Wolf company.

Doucet gets into the picture through Wolf's ties to East Coast Energy Ltd., a relationship that has led to lawsuits and even accusations that Mulroney himself interfered in the legal process on behalf of Doucet to get the matter settled. Hoping to raise $8.2 million, East Coast Energy, with Doucet as chief executive officer, made a public offering in November 1982 of convertible preferred shares. The next month, Wolf invested $500,000 in the company. Among other investors attracted by Doucet's offer were Brian Mulroney, who invested $15,000, and Michael Meighen, who put in $7,500.

Although Cogger claimed to have severed all ties with Wolf by September 1983, when he went on Mulroney's payroll as chief counsel, in June 1984, he was still listed as Wolf's nominee on the board of directors of a Montreal firm, Voyageurs Marine Construction Co. Ltd. Meighen was also listed as a director of one of Wolf's largest companies in 1984, along with several other prominent Tories from various provinces.

Wolf says that he paid Frank Moores roughly $12,000 over the twelve months leading up to the June 1983 Conservative leadership convention to be a director of Wolf Sub-Ocean Ltd. of St. John's. He approved of the political activity of Cogger and Moores because Clark's leadership "was embarrassing. . . ." However, Moores says, "I never received one nickel from him [Wolf]."

Wolf claims he is just a casual acquaintance of Mulroney's. Nevertheless, at the 1976 leadership convention, he sat with Cogger, then Mulroney's campaign manager. He was also at the 1983 leadership convention when Mulroney won. In a 1984 interview, Meighen said that Wolf "knew Brian back in the early seventies when they were both around Montreal." In the late sixties and early seventies, Meighen was Wolf's lawyer, but Cogger took over in 1974 when Meighen became national president of the Conservative party.

Cogger introduced Wolf to Moores in 1978 when Moores was still Newfoundland premier. By May 1980, when Wolf Sub-Ocean Ltd. was formed, Moores had quit politics, and Wolf invited both Moores and a former provincial Tory cabinet minister (now a senator), C. William Doody, to become directors of the firm. Moores says he was never asked to attend a single meeting and that he resigned after eighteen months. Wolf says Moores didn't resign until after the 1983 leadership convention.

In May 1984, Mulroney, by then opposition leader, was still registered as a minor shareholder in East Coast Energy, the company formed by Fred Doucet and his brother, Gerald, a former Nova Scotia Tory education minister. The company was linked to an offshore natural gas project that generated considerable political controversy in Mulroney's Nova Scotia riding in 1983, but neither Mulroney nor his aides at the time disclosed the business relationship he had with the company (he held 333 preferred shares). East Coast had a small share in the Venture natural gas field off Sable Island and was part of a consortium that wanted to build a pipeline to the mainland. Opponents of the project tried to enlist Mulroney's help but complained that he was uncooperative.

In April 1985, a $200,000 suit against Wolf, arising out of the stock transaction in Doucet's firm, was filed in the Supreme Court of Ontario by McLeod Young Weir Ltd. Cogger, then Mulroney's chief counsel, was named as co-defendant but the action against him was dismissed. The writ gave the address for service as 161 Laurier Avenue, Ottawa, the Progressive Conservative party's national headquarters. In February 1987, the Supreme Court of Ontario ordered Wolf to repay a bitterly disputed $198,000 loan made by McLeod Young Weir on June 28, 1983, to Cogger on Wolf's behalf. Cogger and Wolf had claimed that the money was not a loan, but an advance on shares in the ill-fated firm. However, Wolf was ordered to pay $234,000, including interest, and to cover the firm's court costs.

Wolf also took legal action against Fred Doucet for misrepresentation. According to Wolf, Doucet had said the shares would be listed on the Toronto Stock Exchange by March 31, 1983. They weren't, and are now worthless. Doucet denies giving that assurance and is defending the action vigorously. The legal dispute has not reached the trial stage as yet.

East Coast Energy went bankrupt in 1985, but early in 1987 the $300,000 Wolf-Doucet lawsuit sparked a political uproar in the Commons when it was learned that Mulroney had become personally involved. Wolf claims that Mulroney called Cogger and "gave him shit" over the Wolf suit after Doucet "went to the prime minister [to] complain that I [Wolf] took legal action against him."

Wolf made the accusation in sworn statements at the examination-for-discovery stage of the civil suit against Doucet. The statements are included in court records filed in connection with the suit. Cogger does not deny that he spoke with Mulroney about the case, among other things, in a call to the prime minister from Paris in October 1985. He denies that Mulroney tried to influence the suit. "During this conversation, no threats of any kind were made against anyone," Cogger said in a prepared release.

Hamilton Liberal Sheila Copps said that Wolf described the threat to her during a private conversation in May 1986, after she had raised questions in the Commons about the lawsuit. Under pressure from the opposition, Deputy Prime Minister Don Mazankowski blurted out, "If there was any such conversation [between Mulroney and Cogger] it was a private matter." He later accused the opposition of muckraking. Copps's comment was, "When the prime minister uses his influence in whatever way possible to convince someone to drop a lawsuit, then it is an improper use of his position as prime minister and shows very bad judgment. I couldn't believe [Mazankowski] would try to defend it as a private matter."

For his part, speaking in Laval, Quebec, a few days later, Mulroney dismissed it all as "rumours and fabrications." But Mulroney did not deny that he had raised the question of an out-of-court settlement in the case. Wolf was sticking to his story despite Mulroney's dismissal of it as "unfounded rumour." Wolf's lawyer, Michael Eisen, said that his client's recollection of the incident was "not in accordance" with Cogger's version, that Wolf was "very upset" about Mulroney's intervention, that he clearly understood what he was telling the court under oath, and that "as far as I am concerned [Wolf] was telling the truth."

After all his trouble in 1986, Mulroney came back from the Christmas holidays tanned and relaxed and ready for a fresh start. It didn't take long to shatter that dream.

Erik Nielsen finally resigned his Commons seat on January 19, 1987, after twenty-nine years as an MP. He would soon be chairing the Canadian Transport Commission. The announcement was made in a one-paragraph note read by Speaker John

Fraser. When Nielsen arrived back in Whitehorse, a reporter from the local paper was waiting for him at the airport, but true to form, Nielsen brushed right by him without a word. The reporter went back to his office, telephoned Nielsen's constituency office and explained to an aide that it was a big local story and he needed a few quotes from Nielsen about his plans. A few minutes later the phone rang, the reporter said hello, and a voice said, "This is Erik Nielsen, I have no comment." Then Nielsen hung up.

Two days earlier Mulroney had suffered a major blow when the Montreal *Gazette* reported a questionable $3 million real-estate flip connected to a huge defence contract in the Montreal-area riding of junior transport minister André Bissonnette. Mulroney fired Bissonnette the day before the session resumed and also ordered the RCMP to launch an immediate investigation.

During the debate that followed Bissonnette's firing, Liberal John Nunziata said that the Mulroney government had "lost its moral right to govern," and NDP leader Ed Broadbent asked, "When is integrity going to become the rule of public business for this government instead of the exception?"

Speculators had made close to $2.2 million in ten days early in 1986 by buying and re-selling some vacant farmland, three months before Ottawa awarded a $1 billion contract to Swiss-based Oerlikon Aerospace Inc. Oerlikon planned to build a plant on the site to develop a low-level air-defence system.

Mulroney was praised for at least acting quickly, rather than letting the scandal drag on. But according to Senator Lowell Murray, Mulroney's federal-provincial relations minister, the government had come close to doing the same thing again.

"The Saturday when this broke, I was out there [24 Sussex Drive] to see the prime minister about Quebec," said Murray. "There were a couple of other ministers and we were delayed seeing him, left cooling our heels for quite a while. People from External Affairs were sitting around wanting to brief him on the George Bush visit. He [Mulroney] came in and saw the ministers alone and told us what was developing, and what seemed to be developing was there was this flip, flip, flip. Some people had speculated and made a lot of dough. It wasn't public money, but still, one of them was close to Bissonnette.

"But even having met Bissonnette, this was late Saturday afternoon, Mulroney and the rest of us were talking about this in terms of, well, Bissonnette has got to go into the House on

Monday and simply say, 'Look, I know this looks bad, but I'm not involved. I'm pained that this has happened. I want an investigation by a parliamentary committee.'

"That was Saturday," said Murray. "He [Mulroney] had spent some time talking to Bissonnette. On Sunday morning we had a caucus. At noon Sunday, some of us saw the PM and it was just at that time, during that morning—somebody had finally pounded it out of Bissonnette, or gotten it somewhere else—they got additional information and the PM had to say 'I want your resignation.'

"It's interesting though how close we came to having carried this thing into the House, to having our friend Bissonnette go into the House and say 'I'm fine,' and everybody saying we have to accept his word for that, and go along until God knows what else spilled out and we really got hammered again," said Murray.

As it was, things were rough for the Tories again. "This Bissonnette thing made me sick," said Senator Finlay Mac-Donald. "It's just something he [Mulroney] did not need."

The more that came out, the less he needed it. It was bad enough that Bissonnette himself was implicated, but some of Mulroney's good old boys were also involved to varying degrees. The law firm of newly appointed Senator Jean Bazin had done legal work for Oerlikon, and Bazin had become a director of Oerlikon's land-purchasing subsidiary after the contract was awarded. Another Mulroney crony, Roger Nantel, was doing public-relations work for Oerlikon as well.

Oerlikon immediately accused St. Jean's Conservative riding president Normand Ouellette of receiving $970,000 from the company without its knowledge in the $2.9 million land transaction. Oerlikon sent a letter to Ouellette (who had managed Bissonnette's 1984 election campaign) demanding $1,036,013.10, representing the $970,000 plus 12 per cent interest since June 1986. Both Ouellette and Bissonnette denied that the riding asociation had received such a sum from the deal.

On January 20, the opposition turned their guns on Bazin, demanding that his Senate swearing-in ceremony be delayed until his role in the affair was resolved. Mulroney flatly refused. A letter outlining alleged irregularities in the land deal had been sent to Bazin's law firm of Byers Casgrain in August 1986. The opposition charged that Bazin had known for months that the deal was dodgy but had only told Mulroney, his longtime friend, because *Gazette* reporter Claude Arpin was closing in on the story.

In the Commons, Mulroney suggested that criminal charges would result from the RCMP investigation. "Information that was imparted to me and what I'd seen indicates to me that there were transactions that appeared to be odious and completely unacceptable, at variance with the kind of conduct that Canadians expect and are entitled to receive," he said.

The same week, Canadian Press reported that Ouellette, a close friend and business partner of the millionaire Bissonnette, was the manager of the former minister's blind trust and a partner in at least two firms owned by Bissonnette. CP also reported that Bazin had lobbied for Oerlikon before it got the defence contract in June. Mulroney countered that Bazin, president-elect of the Canadian Bar Association, was not a lobbyist, only "a distinguished attorney" who may from time to time "represent people here or elsewhere."

The same day, Radio Canada reported that Bazin had become a director of Oerlikon Aerospace Inc. On April 29, 1986. Bazin had mentioned becoming a director of an Oerlikon subsidiary in August 1985, but had not revealed that he was a director of the parent company except to say in a statement that he had links with it. The CBC French-language network obtained documents showing that Bazin and John Lemieux, a partner in his law firm, had been appointed directors on the same day, thirteen days after Oerlikon won the defence contract and about six weeks before the company signed the purchase agreement for the disputed property. Mulroney defended Bazin, saying it was he who had told the PMO about it, but opposition critics declared that he had told the PMO only after learning that the newspaper was about to publish its story.

On January 21, 1987, U.S. vice-president George Bush spent the morning and lunch time meeting with Mulroney in what was to have been a small public-relations triumph for the beleaguered prime minister. But the Bush visit, which would normally have generated considerable media attention, got buried by the ongoing Bissonnette-Oerlikon saga, particularly after the Liberals revealed that three former government employees—who had sat on the technical-evaluation team that awarded the contract to Oerlikon—had gone to work for the company shortly after the contract was awarded. In the Commons, associate defence minister Paul Dick inadvertently gave the opposition something to laugh about when he replied that the three men had not joined Oerlikon "until after the contract was signed." Another tie-in with Mulroney was that Peter Ohrt, the prime minister's former executive assistant, had also been hired by Oerlikon as project manager.

On January 23, Candadian Press reported that Mulroney had evidence that Bissonnette and his wife had profited personally from the land deal. The Montreal *Gazette* also reported that Bissonnette's wife, Anita Laflamme, had received money from the transaction through a numbered company, 2416-2653 Quebec Inc., which she had incorporated May 5, 1986. That company's business address was the Bissonnette family home. The accusations have never been proven and no charges have been laid.

On January 26, 1987, the *Globe and Mail* reported that Lette and Associates, an internationally known Montreal law firm, had been replaced after its lawyers told Oerlikon that the land it planned to buy had tripled in price over an eleven-day period. The firm was replaced by Bazin's firm, Byers Casgrain. In another development, former St. Jean mayor Ronald Beauregard told the *Toronto Star* that Bissonnette had pressured him to agree to rezone the land in question. Beauregard described a rapid-fire sequence of secret meetings and arm-twisting sessions that culminated in city council's approval of rezoning to allow an arms manufacturing plant.

For a time, it appeared as if the flood of revelations would never end. On January 27, CP reported that at least one of the companies bidding for the defence contract eventually won by Oerlikon had been interviewed by Bissonnette himself as part of the tendering process. Then defence minister Perrin Beatty found himself defending retired Brigadier-General Bin Peart, a former chief of defence staff, who had been hired by Oerlikon for a job described as "interfacing" with government.

On February 16, the RCMP made public two search warrants alleging that Bissonnette and three other men had conspired to defraud Oerlikon of $968,857.60. The warrants allege that Bissonnette, Ouellette, André Roy, Bissonnette's executive assistant, and notary Bernard Tanguay conspired to defraud Oerlikon "through deceit, lies and other harmful means" between September 1985 and June 30, 1986. The documents charge that the four men led Oerlikon to spend $2.98 million for land in St. Jean, a price "artifically and fraudulently inflated by $968,857.36." Again, there have been no charges laid.

When Bissonnette returned to Parliament Hill on February 17, his first appearance on the Hill since the affair broke, he accused reporters of slandering him. "Let the RCMP do their job," he said. In a speech to the Canadian Bar Association's midwinter meeting on February 23, Bazin defended his silence in the Oerlikon affair, saying that as a lawyer it was his duty "to let the rule of law take its course." In late March, Bissonnette announced that he wasn't finished with politics yet. "Everything is unfolding as it should," he said. "You can be sure of one thing, I'll be in the next election, and with joy." Recent polls showed that the Tories, with fifty-eight of Quebec's seventy-five seats in 1984, were now running a poor third behind the Liberals and NDP with barely 20 per cent of popular support.

In affidavits filed in Session Court in St. Jean, Bernard Roy, Mulroney's principal secretary, told police investigators that Bissonnette and his wife had sought and received cash payments from the land sale. Roy also said that some money had "found its way to the blind trust set up by the minister Bissonnette when he entered cabinet."

On February 3, 1987, Jean Bazin was sworn in to the Senate. In a brief statement, Bazin touched on the Oerlikon affair. "I have been a lawyer for twenty-two years and I intend to continue for at least twenty-two more. The legal profession is never easy and certain cases represent greater challenges. In this affair, my firm and myself have always tried to act as lawyers within the mandates that were given to us. This raises two fundamental questions, such as the solicitor-client privilege and all it implies, as well as the fact that I am prohibited from publicly commenting on a case pending before a court, particularly when it is under investigation. Moreover, the code of ethics of my profession states very clearly that: 'The advocate must not, directly or indirectly, in any manner whatsoever, publicly comment on a case pending before a court which he or one of his associates has under-taken.'

"If there be some that prefer innuendoes and lies as opposed to what the duty of a lawyer should be, so be it.

"I think the time has now come to join my new colleagues."

Many thought he should have waited until the Oerlikon affair was resolved. (On August 20, 1987, the Quebec Justice Department formally charged Bissonnette with six charges of fraud, bribery and conspiracy.)

* * *

In its January 19, 1987, issue, *Maclean's* magazine reported that Roch LaSalle, minister without portfolio and veteran Quebec MP, had hired Frank Majeau as a special assistant without a security check. Information from court documents and police in Montreal, Ottawa, and Toronto showed that in 1983, while Majeau was operating a nude-dancer booking agency in Toronto, a business partner in the venture, Réal Simard, had killed one man and critically wounded another. A second business partner, Richard Clement, is being sought in connection with the crime, as a result of Simard's testimony that Clement took part in the shootings. The victims were drug couriers who had once used Majeau's Toronto apartment as s drop-off point for cocaine. Majeau, a sometime roommate of both Simard and Clement, was fined $1,000 and sentenced to two years' probation in 1983 for assault.

LaSalle fired Majeau after the magazine began to question his background. RCMP officials in Ottawa were puzzled because they had never been asked to conduct a routine check on Majeau. Majeau had worked on Parliament Hill for almost six months without a security clearance.

Two weeks later, LaSalle was forced to fire another political aide because of a hidden criminal record. Gilles Ferland, a special assistant in LaSalle's riding office in Joliette, had pleaded guilty in 1984 to charges of attempted fraud and mischief after he falsely claimed that his $5,000 car had been stolen in an attempt to defraud the insurance company. The former journalist was sentenced to two years' probation and ordered to make a contribution to a local charity. LaSalle denied any knowledge of Ferland's record, although he had known him for seventeen years. LaSalle continued to deny any knowledge of Majeau's convictions as well, although he had known the man for twenty-five years and, before he entered politics, had sold cigarettes to Majeau's restaurant.

On February 8, it was learned that the RCMP was conducting a criminal investigation into an influence-peddling case in which one Tory advance man had already been convicted. Pierre Blouin, who had died in January of a heart attack, had pleaded guilty the summer before of trying to use his influence with the Tory government to help businessmen in Drummondville, Quebec, get a $1 million building rental contract for federal offices. The RCMP suspected that others were involved.

Blouin, a Montreal businessman who had travelled with Mulroney's official party during the campaign, had tried to get $70,000 from André Hamel, owner of Hama Inc., which had previously held the rental contract. Hamel is a prominent Liberal. Blouin had also tried to make a deal with Richard Dionne, one of the owners of Les Immeubles Brodilaf, a real-estate investment group that included several well-known Conservatives. The Brodilaf group eventually got the contract, but only after the first bidding process had been cancelled by the headquarters of the federal public works department. LaSalle was minister at the time.

On February 8 Liberal MP Jean Lapierre said he had evidence that two senior cabinet ministers and PMO officials may have been involved in awarding the $1 million rental contract to the Tory sympathizers over the Liberal competitor. A letter dated March 25, 1986, from Tory MP Jean-Guy Guilbeault of Drummond was sent to LaSalle, communications minister Flora MacDonald (she was employment minister at the time), Bernard Roy, Mulroney's principal secretary, Pierre-Claude Nolin, a former Mulroney aide who has since been named chief Quebec organizer for the Tories, and Camille Guilbault and Benoît Roberge, also Mulroney aides.

When the contract was awarded, Nolin was chief of staff to LaSalle in public works. Lapierre said that the letter sought immediate support for steering the contract to the Brodilaf group, even though Hama Inc. had held the contract and the public works department had recommended that the firm retain it.

The next day, Bernard Roy protested his innocence in a two-hour interview with the Ottawa *Citizen*, saying he had become involved in the case "against my will. . . . I did not, either directly or indirectly, involve myself in any way in the decision-making process which culminated with the award of that contract." In a raucous Commons session, Mulroney accused the opposition of being "right down in the gutter with the rats and garbage," accusing Lapierre of behaving "in such a scurrilous manner as to make Joe McCarthy look like a choirboy. . . . If they think I am going to roll over and play dead for a bunch of hacks, they have it wrong."

Mulroney's rhetoric aside, it was soon revealed that the Tory-linked Brodilaf group that had won the contract had submitted a slightly higher bid than the losing Hama Inc. Public works minister Stewart McInnes had tried to defend the award in the Commons by claiming that the winning firm had been the lowest bidder, but his chief of staff Ron Lefebvre later conceded that the losing proposal was $65,000 cheaper. Several of Brodilaf's principals had helped finance the 1984 election of Jean-Guy Guilbeault, the Tory who had written to the PMO and various cabinet ministers pushing Brodilaf's bid.

Finally, on February 11, McInnes admitted for the first time that Brodilaf had attempted to use political influence in the deal. "Yes, that's right. There's no doubt about it," McInnes said when asked whether Guilbeault had tried to intervene with the public works department on Brodilaf's behalf. However, he said he did not think there had been any "undue" influence and that he did not know how Guilbeault could have gained privileged access to confidential documents in the department that might have helped him swing the contract for the Tory firm. (A Guilbeault aide claimed that her man never wrote the letter in question, but that she knew who did, and was considering taking legal action.) Later, McInnes admitted that his department had quietly changed its criteria for awarding rental contracts without telling all of the bidders.

Throughout this controversy, LaSalle managed to keep a low profile, but on February 12, CBC-TV reported that he had been the guest of honour at a party that businessmen paid $5,000 each to attend in the hope of getting government contracts. "I will be reflecting on my future," was LaSalle's comment after the story broke. The Montreal party, in July 1985, held when LaSalle was public works minister, had been attended by thirty businessmen who paid the host a $5,000 entry fee. It was held at the home of Tory MP Michel Gravel. Gravel was later charged on fifty counts of corruption, including ten counts of bribery, offences alleged to have occurred between December 1984 and February 1986. CBC got onto the story after some of the businessmen complained that they had paid but had not received any government contracts. They also said they had been warned by LaSalle's chief of staff, and by André Bissonnette, never to mention LaSalle's name in connection with the matter.

LaSalle said he had not been told that people were paying to see him and that he had "never received a cent." In an interview with Southam News in Joliette, LaSalle said, "I'm not guilty. I'm a victim." In the Commons, Mulroney admitted that he had known about the party a year earlier and had acted "immediately" by turning the relevant information over to the RCMP.

On February 19, a "physically and spiritually exhausted" LaSalle finally handed his resignation to Mulroney—the second Quebec minister in five weeks to leave cabinet and the seventh to resign or be fired since Mulroney took office.

After he left, LaSalle became the centre of yet another controversy. In April, news broke that he had renegotiated a twenty-year lease in Hull, Quebec, for a building used by the environment department. Though the rental agreement had not expired, LaSalle had reopened it and negotiated a lease at double the rent. The old lease, at $1.6 million a year, had eight years to go. The new twenty-five-year lease, with Jean-Paul Tessier of Les Entreprises Duroc Inc., was for $3.1 million annually in rent. LaSalle said he had renegotiated the lease because the building was getting old and lacked air conditioning. The terms of the new lease would save the government the cost of renovations and of "having to move all those public servants into a new building." Until 1985 Tessier had been Bernard Roy's lawyer, and he described himself as a long-time friend of Roy. The government said that Roy had had nothing to do with renegotiating the lease. Opposition critics charged political influence and a "multi-million-dollar boondoggle," but the Tories stuck to their argument that it was a good deal for the taxpayers.

Once again, the RCMP were called in to investigate the deal, which the opposition parties say will needlessly cost taxpayers $15 million, but which the government says will ultimately save taxpayers money.

The most recent bonanza of damaging revelations prompted Liberal John Turner to say, "This government is just piling scandal upon scandal." He called the Tories corrupt and incompetent, and said the "coincidence" that the scandals involved senior Tories and friends of the prime minister "indicates a style of government that ought to be challenged with a public inquiry."

He's not likely to get his wish. At least, not until the next election.

THE YELLOW BRICK
ROAD

The yellow brick road must have looked particulary enchant-ing to Brian Mulroney as he skipped his way across Canada in search of his own shimmering city of Oz on the banks of the Ottawa River in 1984.

Surrounded by his adoring Munchkins, cheered endlessly by the crowds, and finally handed the biggest majority in Canadian history, our hero could have been forgiven for believing the road really did lead to the magic city.

For reasons now clearly on public record, however, it didn't quite work out that way. He and his pals were so busy creating potholes, and running off to their nearest bank with some of the bricks, that the golden road to wisdom and power soon fell into a state of dilapidation.

The key question is: Has he allowed the golden road to deteriorate beyond repair?

In politics, only a fool would pretend to have the definitive answer to such a question. It looks bleak, yes, but in early 1986 the polls had Britian's Margaret Thatcher out the door, and in June of 1987 she won another majority. In late 1979, Pierre Trudeau, a spent force, announced he was quitting as Liberal leader, only to change his mind, come back and clobber Joe Clark in the 1980 election. Who is to say that the man has managed to bring his party down from 54 per cent to 24 per cent in the polls in two years can't change the trend just as dramatically in the other direction?

Still, even his most sycophantic supporters would admit that, as he approaches the three-quarter mark in his term,

Mulroney won't find electoral salvation simply by begging forgiveness for his political sins.

For any chance of recovery, Mulroney needs more than hope. He needs a plan. Even that can't guarantee recovery in time for the next election; but, without a drastic shift in both personnel and policies, Mulroney has precious little chance of hanging around for the second term.

His major immediate problem is what may be politely called the "trust factor," or how he grapples with his image as "Lyin' Brian."

During the 1983 leadership contest, Mulroney's convention manager, John Thompson, wrote an internal memo saying: "People are scared of your candidacy because . . . they don't trust you . . . every voter is looking for these traits in political leaders: 50 per cent trust, 25 per cent competence, 10 per cent dynamism and 15 per cent sociability. They don't trust you because of [your] slickness, smoothness, pat answers, feeling that there is no substance, plastic image. . . ."

After Mulroney's first year in office, a Southam News poll showed that Canadians thought he was a nice guy but wouldn't buy a used car from him. Of five characteristics, he rated lowest on trustworthiness, scoring just 2.8 out of a possible 5 points. He got 3.48 for personality, 3.43 for attractiveness, 3.14 for competence, and 2.87 for decisiveness.

Veteran Tory adviser Bill Neville concedes that "the blarney factor is part of him. You couldn't eliminate that from Brian. But the thing is, there's a lot more besides that . . . the country hasn't seen much of this guy in a personal sense."

In late February 1987, Senator Norman Atkins, the soft-spoken but ruthless chief mechanic of Ontario's legendary Big Blue Machine, orchestrated the beginnings of Mulroney's new strategy, convincing former premiers Peter Lougheed and Bill Davis to telephone the prime minister and urge him to clean out his senior office personnel.

In 1984, Atkins and other Ontario-based officials had tried to wrest control of the operation from Mulroney's personal Quebec-based mafia and had failed. But now, with Mulroney at 22 per cent in the polls—the lowest showing for a government since Gallup began its political polling during the last war—Atkins saw his chance.

That same week, CBC-TV correspondent David Halton reported that Atkins had taken a hit list into a private meeting with Mulroney. Atkins later denied have a specific list—

although he did tell Halton that he had asked Mulroney to initiate a "top-to-bottom clean-out."

Within weeks of that meeting, Mulroney personnel began what turned into a major exodus. By June, Lee Richardson, Bill Fox, Michel Gratton, Ian Anderson, Bill Pristanski, and Charles McMillan had gone elsewhere, and Fred Doucet was pried out of his PMO office, put in charge of summit planning, and ensconced in an office in Vanier, about three miles from his old seat of power.

The only survivors were former schoolmates Pat MacAdam and Bernard Roy, although even Roy's hold over internal office affairs was weakened by the appointment in March of career diplomat Derek Burney as chief of staff. Burney, a former Canadian ambassador to Korea, immediately tried to impose a semblance of order on the operation, closing the revolving door into Mulroney's office, where his most trusted aides used to freely wander in and out at will.

To replace the mercurial Fox and Gratton, Mulroney appointed former CTV correspondent Bruce Phillips as director of communications and Marc Lortie, a career foreign service officer, as press secretary.

"What we had was amateurs running a very complex process which ought to be studied first," comments veteran *Toronto Star* journalist Val Sears. "Those without experience take the view that the fact they are there will change politics and make it easier to govern in the way they want to govern. Mulroney, for example, said things will improve simply because we're there. It simply isn't so. There ought to be a school for prime ministers so the can learn how to govern. Instead, they learn at public expense."

In Bill Neville's view, it's "understandable" for a leader to surround himself with friends, but "what you don't want is ten clones of yourself, people whose background and mind-set are identical. The good advisers are your best critics."

Neville sees Mulroney as having "a first-level emotional response to things." He needs level-headed advisers "to cool him out. . . . He doesn't need someone to say, 'Right on, let's get 'em,' he needs somebody to say, 'Wait a minute' . . . sometimes his senior people egg him on. That's not constructive at all."

The rest of the "comeback policy" quickly emerged. Mulroney would avoid the National Press Gallery, where he tended to mispeak himself with embarrassing regularity; he would act in a more statesmanlike manner in the Commons, particularly during question period where he tended to react badly to opposition goading.

The "new" civil Mulroney emerged during his passionate appeal on June 22 in the Commons against a backbench Tory drive to reinstate the death penalty. Calling it "repugnant" for a civilized society, Mulroney likely influenced some fence-sitters on the issue as the motion to approve the death penalty in principle lost eight days later 148 to 127, ending a highly charged, four-and-one-half month debate and satisfying Mulroney's 1984 campaign promise to hold a free vote on the controversial question.

In addition, he would hope for happy headlines following a series of big-ticket policy announcements, primarily the constitution, tax reform, and free trade. Tory strategists also felt that their man would gain political brownie points by appearing as a world statesman at the highly theatrical Commonwealth and Francophone summits he will host this fall, and the Economic summit in Toronto in 1988, featuring the world's seven largest industrial economies.

Another critical part of the strategy is the hope by Tories that John Turner would continue to falter, as he did over his party's internal divisions on the June constitutional agreement. In addition, the Tories have begun a concerted ideological attack on the NDP, referring to them constantly as the "socialist party." In early June, Tory party president Bill Jarvis, a former cabinet minister, began a campaign to rasie $560,000 for a special fund to fight the NDP. In a four-page fund-raising letter, Jarvis warned potential Tory contributors about the NDP desire to set up a "Soviet-style" government and use its contacts with other socialist organizations to form a "one-world totalitarian state" as part of its "radical-left agenda."

Some of Mulroney's problems were simply organizational. He tried to transfer what he knew about running the Iron Ore Company into running government. In essence, Erik Nielsen became chief operating officer. "It tended to fail mainly because of the managerial style of Erik," Senator Finlay MacDonald has commented. In the senator's view Nielsen was too secretive, so that everybody else ended up "working in a vacuum."

When Nielsen was bounced, Don Mazankowski, his successor in the job, set up a high-powered committee of aides and cabinet ministers to sift through the mountain of work. But it wasn't long before he was being treated for stress and began showing flares of temper in response to routine questions in the Commons.

According to Tom Van Dusen, Mazankowski's press secretary, the internal-reporting system has improved considerably, but it hasn't affected the government's public image yet. "You have to factor in all sorts of things—bad management, leadership, bad luck . . . it's not irrevocable . . . all it takes is just one score of some kind and you could get those polls climbing again, something like the Falkland Islands, although we don't want to play the Argentinian role."

Van Dusen says that, "because of his [Mulroney's] credibility factor, people do believe the worst. We're at the point where it's hard to convince people on anything . . . a lot of the mistakes date back to the brand-new government. It's not brand new anymore, but it set the tone. In this business, no excuse is permitted. You have to get it right or you're gone."

Comparisons between Mulroney and Diefenbaker are inevitable. Diefenbaker, too, campaigned well but governed poorly. He captured the Liberal fortress in Quebec, then quickly lost it. He held the record number of seats (208) until Mulroney passed him in 1984. And he squandered his massive 1958 majority, allowing the dispirited Liberals to recapture power by 1963—a historical precedent that could serve either as a goad to Tories to try to stop it from happening again, or as a bleak reminder that history does indeed repeat itself.

As Mulroney enters the home stretch of his first—and possibly last—term, the outcome remains uncertain. But the fact that failure is even considered a possibility is a tell-tale sign that the rot may be terminal.

AFTERWORD

During a good chunk of 1987, people were talking as if the Tories would be history the minute voters got another crack at them. But, as often happens in politics, things changed. During the fall and into early 1988, the Tory comeback strategy actually seemed to be working.

When Canada and the United States reached a tentative free trade deal in October and Mulroney and Ronald Reagan both initialled it on January 2, 1988, public opinion polls showed that support was gradually growing for both the deal and the Tories.

It wasn't without the odd embarrassment, of course. In January, forty tonnes of promotional pamphlets praising the free trade deal and Mulroney, having become outdated by the time the deal was signed, were literally flushed down the toilet after being fed through shredders and turned into toilet paper and paper towels.

Still, things were looking better for the Tories, partly because John Turner continued to have problems of his own. Veteran Montreal MP Donald Johnston quit the Liberal caucus to sit as an independent Liberal after months of public disagreement over Turner's support for the Meech Lake constitutional accord and his opposition to free trade.

During a taped interview January 13 with CTV's Pamela Wallin, Turner endured further public humiliation when he was asked about rumours being spread by his own party critics that he had a drinking problem. "Ya, I like a good party and I've enjoyed myself over the years," he replied, having been forewarned of the question by Wallin, "but I have never allowed any pleasure or distraction to interfere with doing the job. . . . I mean, I keep my eye on the ball."

Shortly afterwards, Quebec's premier Robert Bourassa gave him something else to keep his eye on when, to the chagrin of many federal Liberals who cried foul, he introduced Mulroney at a Montreal luncheon as a "great artisan of national unity" and a man of "courage, determination, and insight."

Worse, Paul Martin, Jr., a man who would be Liberal leader, openly criticized Turner's oft-repeated promise to rip up the free trade deal should he become prime minister again.

Even the NDP was suffering. While Ed Broadbent was still enjoying immense personal popularity, he was desperately trying to juggle the conflicting interests of his party hardliners with the pressure from less strident socialists to modify some long-held policies in order to appeal to a broader spectrum of the electorate.

This was particularly difficult for a party that claims allegiance to ideological purity and disdain for the political pragmatism of the two older parties. It manifested itself publicly when, in conjunction with NDP successes in public opinion polls, a host of seemingly sacrosanct policies came under active review, particularly the party's sacred oath that a socialist Canada would opt out of the NATO alliance.

Not all the NDP fighting was ideological, or public. Dennis Young, the party's federal secretary from 1984, left his job early in 1988 after being quietly squeezed out in an internal power struggle with, among others, former party president and now Hamilton Mountain MP Marion Dewar.

There was a brief reminder of past Tory sins December 3, when Chief Justice William Parker of the Ontario Supreme Court released a 461-page report into conflict allegations against former cabinet minister Sinclair Stevens, finding him guilty of fourteen different conflicts of interest. Stevens, unbowed, said he was innocent, and shortly after began an appeal of Parker's findings in federal court. Mulroney, who had stonewalled shamelessly when the controversy began in May 1986, now said he accepted the Parker verdict and agreed "that the very high standards Canadians have a right to expect from ministers of the Crown were not observed in this case."

For the most part during this period, however, Mulroney and his minions were managing to maintain a reasonably high standard of public behaviour. Mulroney strayed a bit during a year-end CBC-TV interview when he praised Israeli soldiers for showing great "restraint" at a time when they were using live ammunition against rock-throwing Palestinian youths in the occupied territories. Even the Americans, Israel's strongest defenders, were criticizing their friends at the time.

Still, compared to past performances, Mulroney clearly was coming back from the dead. What's more, his ministers were staying out of trouble, and with free trade, Meech Lake, child care, and tax reform all being successfully pushed to the forefront, the Tories finally were giving the impression of a government in control of its own agenda. As a result, they hit the 30 per cent mark in January public opinion polls, still trailing their opponents, but clearly gaining momentum on the way back to the magic kingdom of public favour.

At last, the bloom was back on the rose. But not for long. A severe frost was just around the corner.

The first chill arrived January 28 when the Supreme Court of Canada struck down the federal abortion law by a 5–2 ruling, leaving the federal government to reassemble the pieces of a medical and moral puzzle that no politician wants to touch.

On the one side, the pro-abortionists were hailing the ruling as a victory for women and freedom, so-called reproductive rights, and demanding federal action to guarantee equal access to abortions across the country. On the other side, anti-abortionists, appalled at the prospects of unrestricted abortions (they were already hitting about 70,000 a year in Canada), were applauding British Columbia's Bill Vander Zalm's decision to cut off funding for abortions except where the mother's health was in danger.

Either way, it was an issue that would not go away. After two weeks of fence-sitting, justice minister Ray Hnatyshyn announced that abortion law would be given "an urgent priority," though he left both the timing and the specific approach up in the air. He wanted a breathing space, an understandable desire when one is faced with the task of finding a workable compromise between two irreconcilable and well-organized forces.

In the meantime, another political storm cloud descended upon the Tories when they decided to ignore the grumbling of their own backbenchers and go ahead with debate on Bill C-72, a much tougher Official Languages Act. It proved embarrassing, and perhaps costly, when the government was forced to retreat temporarily in the wake of a well-directed verbal assault by a group of tough-minded, right-wing backbenchers who felt the bill went too far in imposing mandatory bilingualism on the federal public service and discriminated against unilingual, mainly English-speaking Canadians.

The bill was seen by Mulroney and his champions as a way to shore up flagging Tory support in Quebec. The party's Quebec caucus was wildly enthusiastic about it to the point where Charlevoix MP Charles Hamelin even threatened to work for the separatist Parti Quebecois if the bill was scuttled. But opposition within the party was widespread among Tories from all other parts of the country. The party brass gambled that the disgruntled MPs would complain in private but play their usual public role as lemmings marching off to the sea. It was a serious miscalculation.

The critics, of course, were instantly labelled "dinosaurs" and worse by opposition parties and the media, a sad fact of life in Ottawa for those refusing to worship automatically at the altar of bilingualism. Many of those same Tories had supported the original Official Languages Act in 1969, an irony that did not go unnoticed when Deputy Prime Minister Don Mazankowski, who had then publicly attacked the act, had harsh words for his colleagues who opposed the revised act.

The opposing forces argued it would institutionalize bilingualism for about 85 per cent of the federal civil service, as well as for all judges and heads of all federal tribunals. Mazankowski and others denied this, even though a secret justice department review of the act, not to mention the act itself, made it clear that that's exactly what Bill C-72 would do. Both opposition parties, keeping their eyes trained east across the Ottawa River to Quebec, unequivocally endorsed the bill.

For all that, however, Mulroney still seemed to have momentum on his side. He had climbed steadily back in the polls from the dark days of the low 20s to the 30 per cent mark. Everybody was talking a quick election, and Mulroney, buoyed by this apparent return from the political grave, confidently embarked on a series of election-style jaunts around the country.

And then it happened. Trouble returned with a vengeance.

On January 22, journalist Michel Vastel published a leaked November 1985 letter in the Montreal newspaper *Le Devoir* that again plunged energy minister Marcel Masse into a prolonged controversy about his election spending habits, setting the stage for another rapid-fire round of Tory scandals.

Masse had resigned from cabinet in September 1985 when the RCMP began an investigation into complaints he had violated the Canada Elections Act. He was returned by Mulroney after Joseph Gorman, then elections commissioner, had "cleared" him.

But the 1985 Gorman letter to Masse, leaked to Vastel, accused the minister of having "participated in an infraction" of the law. Gorman did not prosecute because it was not in "the public interest," although three of Masse's campaign workers and Lavelin Inc., his former firm, were charged, pleaded guilty, and paid fines.

Masse claimed he had barely read the Gorman letter before stuffing it into a desk drawer next to a spare shirt. A few days later, however, his Montreal lawyer Jean Guilbeault, contradicted him, saying Masse had telephoned him the day he had received the letter and had read it to him.

Once again, the question arose over just how much Mulroney knew and when. He claimed he knew nothing of the letter, but his communications director Bruce Phillips told the *Toronto Sun* that the PMO had known Masse had violated the elections act, although he had no knowledge of whether Mulroney had been told.

The opposition stepped up demands for Masse's resignation after a *Globe and Mail* report on February 1. RCMP investigator Corporal Andre Gauthier had claimed in a sworn affidavit that Masse had personally requested that Lavalin reimburse one of his campaign workers for $780.21 in election expenses. (Only official agents can authorize such expenses.)

When Gorman testified before a Commons committee, he said he hadn't prosecuted because the amount of money was small and Masse had won by a landslide. Later, Masse told the committee that he was innocent but the RCMP had misread the act.

It really began to reek of old times on February 2 when the PMO released a terse, late-night, three-sentence announcement that supply and services minister Michel Côté had been fired for failing to report a personal loan as required under cabinet guidelines.

In a flash, Côté became the eighth minister to either be booted out unceremoniously or leave under a cloud, reminding Canadians again just why the Tories had spent such a long time at the bottom of the public opinion polls.

Whatever brownie points Mulroney had won by moving

quickly—although he acted only after learning a journalist was on to the story—he forfeited the next day when neither he nor Côté would lift the veil of mystery surrounding the precise details of the affair. But by then, journalists had already discovered that Côté, an accountant, had not reported $246,000 in personal loans from his friend Rene Laberge, a prominent Quebec City contractor who was described by Mazankowski as Côté's "godfather."

Mazankowski subsequently released an analysis of government business with Laberge showing that three companies he controlled had received $2,460,356 since April 1981, with a dramatic increase since the Tories took power in 1984. Mazankowski said it showed a possible appearance of conflict of interest, but no evidence of improper gains.

While the Tories were still reeling over this, federal officials refused to reveal whether Mulroney himself had registered personal loans worth $324,000 from the PC Canada Fund to refurbish his two official residences. The opposition immediately accused him of violating his own guidelines.

Mazankowski told the Commons the loan was "not a loan in the traditional sense" but was an "advance" from a sort of "petty cash." But associate deputy registrar Jean-Pierre Kingsley, who administers the rules, told Canadian Press an advance would be considered a liability and therefore fall under the rules.

Two days later, Mulroney broke a four-day personal silence on the week of scandals, angrily denying he had broken his own rules, calling the charges "a falsehood fabricated by the Liberals and others." The next day, a Monday, Kingsley mysteriously released a statement contradicting himself, saying now that Mulroney's loan did not constitute a conflict and that such loans "do not require to be reported under the code." His aides denied opposition charges that pressure had been put on Kingsley to release his unsolicited statement.

In the meantime, lawyers for another fallen minister, André Bissonnette, failed to have breach-of-trust charges dropped. The trial, with its subsequent daily headlines, began in Quebec Superior Court the same week that Côté was dumped. Later that month, a jury acquitted Bissonnette of fraud, conspiracy, and breach-of-trust in the Oerlikon affair.

The Tories were also enduring political heat after the *Montreal Gazette* reported they had sold about 24,280 hectares of land (expropriated by the previous Liberal regime for Mirabel Airport) for just over 30 per cent of its market value. Many of the bargains went to prominent Tories. Francios Romeo, a Tory organizer, bought three houses on a 178-hectare farm for $148,000 and sold it all to a Montreal developer for $400,000 just twenty-four hours after the deal was registered.

Former minister Roch LaSalle, boasting about the deal, said he had faced systematic opposition to his plan from civil servants, so, "I went to see Brian Mulroney and in thirty minutes I convinced him to get those fuddy-duddies off my back so I could deal with this problem in my own way."

On February 11, finance minister Michael Wilson introduced a self-congratulatory, stand-pat budget, which featured a penny-a-litre hike in the excise tax on gasoline and little else. More a review of the Tory economic record, one of the few areas where they can legitimately boast, it contained an extra $100 million in the refundable child-tax credit for low-income families but offered nothing else besides a promise (for the third consecutive year) to get the deficit below $30 billion.

Even without large tax hikes in their budget, bad luck seemed to be clinging to the Tories. Sharing the headlines with Wilson's budget, alas, was the latest Gallup poll showing the scandal-ridden government had slithered back down to 27 per cent, while the Liberals were up sharply to 41 per cent (from 36), with the NDP holding firm at 31.

Kitchener Tory MP John Reimer told his local riding association meeting that "[Mulroney] has already told us: 'I carried a lot of you [MPs] the last time around; this time you'd better be prepared to carry me.'"

It promises to be a heavy load.

INDEX

ABOUT THE AUTHOR

CLAIRE HOY is a well-known journalist and political commentator. Born in Ontario in 1940, he graduated from Ryerson Journalism School in 1964. Since then, he has written for a number of southern Ontario and Toronto newspapers, including the *Toronto Telegram*, *Toronto Star* and *Toronto Sun*. During his tenure at the *Star*, he was Queen's Park Bureau Chief (1970–72) and Atlantic Bureau Chief (1972–73). Currently with the *Sun*, he has been Queen's Park Bureau Chief (1975–84) and is now the Ottawa daily columnist. Claire Hoy is the author of *Bill Davis*.

SEAL BOOKS

Offers you a list of outstanding fiction, non-fiction, and classics of Canadian literature in paperback by Canadian authors, available at all good bookstores throughout Canada.

SIX BY

W. O. MITCHELL

His first book, WHO HAS SEEN THE WIND, is a Canadian classic. A work of brilliance, sheer beauty, and rare perception, this tells of a child's search for "the ultimate meaning of the cycle of life."

In JAKE AND THE KID Mitchell shows his special skill in capturing the peculiar individuality of his characters. This is the story of a hired man and a ten-year-old boy and their homely, whimsical adventures.

THE VANISHING POINT presents the complex dilemma of native peoples and the well-meaning whites who try to help them. Much of the power of this novel lies in the rendering of the Indian characters, authentic and strong.

Remarkable for its descriptive beauty, humour, and original characterization, THE KITE is written with vitality and affection, and will warm the reader's heart in its presentation of time and old age.

What begins as a dream of boyhood in HOW I SPENT MY SUMMER HOLIDAYS ends in a nightmare of corruption and insanity. Most somber of Mitchell's novels, this is a haunting, powerful tale of lost innocence.

With rollicking humour and spellbinding narrative, SINCE DAISY CREEK grips the reader with the tale of a man terribly wounded by a violent confrontation with an enraged grizzly. A darkly comic odyssey of a stubborn man's struggle to survive, to laugh, and to love again—a journey of the heart that probes both the raw passions and the sweet magic of living.

 Available in Seal paperbacks at all good bookstores throughout Canada.

CANADA'S GREATEST STORYTELLER

FARLEY MOWAT
Chronicler of man against the elements

Bestselling author, Farley Mowat, portrays true-life adventure and survival with unique passion. His courageous stories of remote lands, people, and animals have been read in over twenty languages in more than forty countries. And now, the most cherished of his stories can all be read in paperback.

The Mark of Canadian Bestsellers

SEAL BOOKS PRESENTS
THE CANADIAN MEDICAL LIBRARY

℞

HEART ATTACKS, HYPERTENSION, AND HEART DRUGS
by Dr. Gabriel Khan

Dr. Khan is a renowned cardiologist, and this is his common-sense guide to a healthy heart. In addition to looking at risk factors and the importance of fitness and a sensible diet, Dr. Khan provides a thorough review of the newest in heart drugs such as beta-blockers.

SURVIVING BREAST CANCER
by Carole Spearin McCauley

Ms. McCauley, once a science writer for the National Institute of Health, has assembled the latest facts about breast cancer in an effort to suppress the widespread fear spawned from ignorance. Readers will find comprehensive information about the necessity and advisability of mastectomies, as well as many personal anecdotes and case histories.

OLD ENOUGH TO FEEL BETTER
by Dr. Michael Gordon

Dr. Gordon is a renowned authority on geriatric medicine and here he offers a practical and medically sound source book which will help the reader meet the challenges of aging. This invaluable book will show you how to take an active part in enjoying good health and increased vitality in the golden years. Such matters as choosing the right doctor; coping with the psychological problems of aging; the best combination of work, recreation, and exercise; and such common complaints as weakness, insomnia, pain, and dizziness are all reviewed in this compassionate and reassuring guide.